Negotiating World Order

Negotiating World Order

The Artisanship and Architecture of Global Diplomacy

Edited by
Alan K. Henrikson

With Essays by

Gamani Corea
Alan K. Henrikson
Max M. Kampelman
T. T. B. Koh
Leonard H. Marks
Jean Mayer
Joseph S. Nye, Jr.

Alejandro Orfila
Gardner Patterson
John Roberts
Nathaniel Samuels
Gerard C. Smith
Leonard Unger
Brian Urquhart

 *SR Scholarly Resources Inc.*
Wilmington, Delaware

The paper used in this publication meets the minimum requirements of the American National Standard for permanence of paper for printed library materials, Z39.48, 1984.

Scholarly Resources Inc.
104 Greenhill Avenue
Wilmington, Delaware 19805-1897

Library of Congress Cataloging-in-Publication Data

Negotiating world order.

Includes bibliographies and index.
1. International organization.   2. Diplomatic
negotiations in international disputes.   3. International relations.   I. Henrikson, Alan K.
II. Corea, Gamani.
JX1954.N43   1986   341.2   86–6544
ISBN 0-8420-2239-2

Contents

Preface   vii
Acknowledgments   ix
Introduction   xi
Contributors   xxv

NATURAL AND TECHNOLOGICAL BASES OF WORLD ORDER

International Agreements in the Food and Health Fields   3
  By Jean Mayer

The Diplomacy of Acid Rain: The North American Experience
in Global Perspective   19
  By John Roberts

Negotiating a New World Order for the Sea   33
  By T. T. B. Koh

International Communications and World Order   47
  By Leonard H. Marks

COOPERATIVE AND STRATEGIC BASES OF WORLD ORDER

The United Nations, Collective Security, and International
Peacekeeping   59
  By Brian Urquhart

The Great Illusion: "Star Wars" and World Order   69
  By Gerard C. Smith

The Diplomacy of Nuclear Nonproliferation   79
    By Joseph S. Nye, Jr.

The Lessons of the Madrid CSCE Conference   95
    By Max M. Kampelman

REGIONAL BASES OF WORLD ORDER

The North Atlantic Alliance as a Form of World Order   111
    By Alan K. Henrikson

The Organization of American States and International Order
in the Western Hemisphere   137
    By Alejandro Orfila

The International Role of the Association of Southeast
Asian Nations   149
    By Leonard Unger

ECONOMIC BASES OF WORLD ORDER

Creating a Framework to Strengthen and Stabilize International
Commodity Markets   167
    By Gamani Corea

The GATT and the Negotiation of International
Trade Rules   181
    By Gardner Patterson

Dealing with the International Debt Issue   199
    By Nathaniel Samuels

STRUCTURES AND PROCESSES OF WORLD ORDER

The Global Foundations for a Diplomacy of Consensus   217
    By Alan K. Henrikson

Index   245

Preface

Negotiating World Order: The Artisanship and Architecture of Global Diplomacy is a celebration, a culmination, and a challenge.

The volume is a celebration of the fiftieth anniversary of the founding of the Fletcher School of Law and Diplomacy, the senior graduate school of international relations in the United States and an institution that has served as a model for higher education and professional training in its field the world over. Its own graduates, now numbering more than 3,500 men and women, currently reside and work in responsible positions in more than a hundred countries in virtually every part of the globe.

The book is a culmination of the Fletcher School's efforts to reveal the merit of its distinctive approach to international affairs education. Against the narrowing tendencies of geographic "area" studies and disciplinary overspecialization, the school has insisted upon taking a global view and upon integrating disciplines—particularly international law, diplomatic history, political science, and international business and economics. Moreover, as this volume demonstrates, it has emphasized the value of marrying the theoretical insights of the academic expert with the experience of the practitioner.

The book is a challenge because it is only one step, an intermediate one, on the road to improving understanding of the increasingly complex realities of our global situation. A wide range of subjects is covered in the volume, which we hope will prove useful to advanced undergraduate and graduate students in international relations and also to interested members of the general public and to professionals involved in international diplomacy. Besides illustrating what can be done toward the negotiating of world order in the fourteen specific subject areas discussed, it indicates further work that is necessary, in those areas and in others.

Negotiating World Order emerges from a project under the thoughtful and able leadership of Professor Alan K. Henrikson. Based on a series of public lectures and discussion sessions which took place during the academic year 1983–84, the project involved faculty, students, and staff of the Fletcher School, as well as many alumni and alumnae who sponsored their own, related seminar on the theme of negotiating world order. The contributors to this book have honed their opinions in exchanges with faculty, students, and guest experts at these meetings. They have helped provide direction for scholarly research and public effort by the Fletcher School during its next half century, and through its work, it is hoped, the future of international education everywhere.

Theodore L. Eliot, Jr.
The Fletcher School of Law and Diplomacy
Tufts University

Acknowledgments

The Negotiating World Order Project, which made *Negotiating World Order* possible, owes its achievement to many persons, but in particular to the scholar-statesmen who have contributed as coauthors of this book. In the process of editorial preparation of the chapter texts, which were developed in light of advancing scholarship and changing international circumstances from their original lectures, they have proved excellent literary colleagues. It has been an honor to work with all of them.

Within the Fletcher School itself, I would like to thank, for specific acts of assistance to the project, my faculty colleague Benjamin J. Cohen, who has been an intellectual partner in it from the beginning, and also Philip G. Alston, Robert S. Dohner, John D. Field, Leo Gross, Andrew C. Hess, Robert F. Meagher, Robert L. Pfaltzgraff, John P. Roche, Alfred P. Rubin, Hewson A. Ryan, and Robert L. West. A number of these persons also served on the Negotiating World Order Project faculty steering committee, which gave valued collegial support. Without the institutional backing and personal participation of Theodore L. Eliot, Jr., who served as Fletcher School dean from 1979 to 1985, and the assistance of his staff, particularly Eugenia C. Dyess, this cooperative undertaking on the occasion of the fiftieth anniversary of the school's founding would not have been organizationally possible. The enthusiastic involvement of Sol Gittleman and Jean Mayer, provost and president, respectively, of Tufts University, is also greatly appreciated.

It is with special gratitude that I acknowledge the willing help given me by a number of remarkable Fletcher School students: Paula A. Tavrow, who organized discussion sessions and served as research assistant for the project; Cathy S. Mysel, who prepared transcripts of the formal addresses; and, for a variety of valuable research and editorial contributions, Andrea Cogliano, Anne C. Frenette, Timothy H. Hiebert, Sunaina Lowe, and Abiodun E. Williams. Amy S. Finkelstein and Jonathan W. Kott independently conducted discussion sessions. The task of word-processing successive versions of many of the chapter texts was performed masterfully by Rhonda M. Vitanye. Karin W. McMaster assisted with the typing of manuscripts and in countless other ways.

The costs of the Negotiating World Order Project were mostly covered by gifts from private individuals—Joseph W. Bartlett, Leo L. Beranek, Martin Horwitz, and Josephine L. Murray—whose generous financial assistance at the outset was essential. Certain of the Negotiating World Order addresses and related social events were made possible through joint sponsorship with other lecture series at the Fletcher School: namely, the Charles Francis Adams Lectures, the William L. Clayton Lecture, the Maurice S. Segal Lecture, and the John M. Olin Distinguished Lectures in International Business.

A group of Boston area alumni and alumnae, led by Douglas Henderson and Josephine W. Shane, contributed spiritually and intellectually to the project by shaping the Fletcher Alumni/ae 50th Reunion Symposium around the negotiating world order theme. The speakers on that occasion, besides several already mentioned, were Terry L. Deibel, Judith T. Kildow, Robert H. Legvold, Philip Morrison, John Edwin Mroz, John P. Scanlan, Paula Stern, Seth P. Tillman, Malcolm Toon, and David Williamson. Other featured Negotiating World Order speakers during the fiftieth anniversary year were Daniel Deudney, René Dumont, William G. Miller, Laura Reanda, Crocker Snow, Jr., and Philip C. Habib. The articulated expertise and experience of these persons enriched everyone who heard them.

Finally, I would like to acknowledge a most pleasurable and fruitful collaboration with Philip G. Johnson, managing editor, and Ann M. Aydelotte, project editor, at Scholarly Resources, Inc.

Introduction

The field of international relations has long been divided between two traditional modes of thinking. One is that of the "world order" builder—the international architect—who envisions global structures and grand designs, and everything fitting into them. From this intellectual perspective, the meaning of international relations consists, at a basic level, in the logical symmetry and symbolic unity of their patterns. Such structures may be conservative and historical, as in the balance-of-power concept, or progressive and utopian, as in the idea of world government.[1] The other traditional style of internationalist thought is that of the "negotiator"—the diplomatic artisan.[2] From the point of view of the professional diplomat or other regular participant in international affairs, often the most important value to be preserved is the actual process, or give and take, of diplomacy itself. The blueprint may be of less significance to him than the task of building.

The distinction I have drawn is not simply the conventional contrast between the theorist and the practitioner, for a person can be highly theoretical in studying the processes of diplomacy and very practical in designing global structures.[3] Nor is it merely the difference between taking a broad view and being a specialist, for generalism, too, can be developed as a specialty, and specialized knowledge need not always be applied narrowly.[4] Neither distinction is, in many cases, a very profound one. The separation between the world-order advocate and the protagonist of negotiation can be deeper, reflecting different basic traits of mind. There are persons who characteristically demand of themselves in their thinking, about the world as about other subjects, clarity, coherence, and comprehensiveness. There are other persons, perhaps less systematic but sometimes even more analytical, who are more

---

[1]Contrast, for example, Henry A. Kissinger, *A World Restored: Europe After Napoleon—The Politics of Conservatism in a Revolutionary Age* (New York: Universal Library, 1964), and Richard A. Falk, *A Study of Future Worlds* (New York: Free Press, 1975).

[2]See, for example, Elmer Plischke, ed., *Modern Diplomacy: The Art and the Artisans* (Washington, DC: American Enterprise Institute for Public Policy Research, 1979).

[3]Contrast Howard Raiffa, *The Art and Science of Negotiation* (Cambridge, MA: Harvard University Press, 1982), and Edward S. Mason and Robert E. Asher, *The World Bank Since Bretton Woods* (Washington, DC: Brookings Institution, 1973).

[4]Examples, respectively, are Immanuel Wallerstein, *The Modern World-System: Capitalist Agriculture and the Origins of the European World-Economy in the Sixteenth Century* (New York: Academic Press, 1974), and John Von Neumann and Oskar Morgenstern, *Theory of Games and Economic Behavior* (Princeton, NJ: Princeton University Press, 1944).

keenly conscious of the frequent ambiguity, inconsistency, and singularity of human affairs.

One may detect in the difference between these two styles of thinking, the order-oriented and the negotiation-oriented, even different attitudes toward the dimension of time. World-order thinking tends to be static—fixed on a past, present, or future ideal state of affairs. The negotiating mode of thought tends toward the dynamic—geared to motion, to development, which though progressive is always, at any given moment, incomplete and therefore imperfect. Similarly, different basic conceptions of space may be manifest. A world-order thinker, often being "visual," perceives international territorial and other problems with clarity, as if from some vantage point *outside*. The negotiator, relatively more "tactile," senses the international flow of events directly, if only partially and somewhat amorphously, as from *within*. Walter Lippmann, having in mind the chaotic condition of current international affairs as well as other phenomena, grasped the essence of this distinction in his seminal study, *Public Opinion* (1922). "A 'clear' thinker," he wrote, developing a theme of the French philosopher Henri Bergson, "is always a good visualizer," but for that same reason he is "external and insensitive." The same is sometimes true of doctrinaire proponents of world order. By contrast, Lippmann pointed out, nonclarifying, nonsystematizing thinkers may have better insight: "For the people who have intuition, which is probably another name for musical or muscular perception, often appreciate the quality of an event and the inwardness of an act far better than the visualizer. They have more understanding when the crucial element is a desire that is never crudely overt, and appears on the surface only in a veiled gesture, or in a rhythm of speech." The "intermediate and internal," he therefore concluded, is often "badly caricatured" by the visualizer.[5] In the present context, the focus of the former, visualizing outlook, idealistic but also at times impossibly perfectionist, is on the international *solution*, which permanently and completely resolves issues. The object of the latter, intuitive approach, more realistic but often insufficiently bold, is the diplomatic *settlement*, which only temporarily and partially adjusts them.[6] In international politics, unlike geometry, the order which is possible may never be more than a "settled state," always precarious and requiring diplomatic maintenance. It is not, however, the only kind of international order that is imaginable, and in fact historically has been imagined.

In the study of international history, as in the history of international relations itself, the intellectual realms of world order and negotiation seldom have been well joined. Global planners, notably during the early days of the League of Nations and, later, of the United Nations, have projected elaborate

---

[5]Walter Lippmann, *Public Opinion* (New York: Free Press, 1965), p. 104. An analogous distinction, applied in detail to diplomacy, is drawn in Alan K. Henrikson, "The Geographical 'Mental Maps' of American Foreign Policy Makers," *International Political Science Review/Revue Internationale de Science Politique* 1, no. 4 (October 1980): 495–530.

[6]For the solution-settlement distinction, see Bertrand de Jouvenel, *The Pure Theory of Politics* (New Haven, CT: Yale University Press, 1963), pp. 189, 204–12.

schemes of international law and organization ("blueprints for peace") that were never realized and, perhaps, given their excessive lucidity and complexity, could not have been.[7] As a result of the disillusionment of these architectonic thinkers by the breakdown of international order during the interwar period and the Cold War, the continuators of this tradition, such as Richard Falk and Samuel S. Kim, increasingly have emphasized that just world ordering is "an outcome of the play of social forces rather than a consequence of abstract modeling of new forms of world order." Nonetheless, the highly normative, value-oriented global strategies contemplated by adherents of "world order studies," which are aimed at creating an "alternative," or poststatist, world political system, would appear to be equally unrealistic.[8]

There are, at the same time, thousands of transaction-minded internationalist thinkers—not only career diplomats but also international bankers, multinational businessmen, corporate lawyers, commodity traders, and others involved in international negotiation—whose experience, knowledge, and reflections are not having the broader impact on the world system that they should have. Unlike academic or research-institute world-order designers, these more engaged persons naturally tend to concentrate on what is negotiable, i.e., immediately and fully attainable. In the ordinary course of their daily international activity and even in emergency situations abroad calling for special deliberations and actions, they tend to take the existing framework of international affairs, in both its institutional aspects and its basic systematic nature, as a given. They accept, as frequently they must in order to function effectively, the weakness of most international organizations and the dominance of the nation-state and the strength of international market forces. As a result, most international transactions today, including the bulk of official diplomatic traffic between countries, takes place within very narrow conceptual limits.

In 1983, scholars at the Fletcher School of Law and Diplomacy recognized a need to connect the vision of the architects of international order with the craft and skill, as well as the insights and wisdom, of some of the master craftsmen in the international field. The school, whose name fortuitously combines the normative and the procedural aspects of international relations, seemed an appropriate sponsor and location for such a project. In planning the undertaking, entitled the Negotiating World Order Project, a specific focus was chosen. The emphasis was to be on the *negotiation* of international order in each of the subject areas to be considered, not merely

---

[7]For example, Grenville Clark and Louis B. Sohn, *World Peace Through World Law* (Cambridge, MA: Harvard University Press, 1960); Elisabeth Mann Borgese, ed., *A Constitution for the World* (Santa Barbara, CA: Center for the Study of Democratic Institutions, 1965); and Clarence K. Streit, *Union Now: A Proposal for a Federal Union of the Democracies of the North Atlantic* (New York: Harper and Brothers, 1939).

[8]Richard Falk and Samuel S. Kim, *An Approach to World Order Studies and the World System*, World Order Models Project, Working Paper No. 2 (New York: Institute for World Order, 1982), p. 2.

on the ideological and institutional contents of the resulting international arrangements themselves. Of special interest was the handling of international problems which, because of the large number of countries or other parties involved and the high degree of international interdependence and related technical complexity associated with them, seemed to require *multilateral* diplomatic action.

The particular topics chosen for detailed examination were to be those which met two further criteria: 1) there had to be, in the given field in question, a serious challenge to existing international arrangements, owing either to a changing ideological climate or to shifting economic and political circumstances; and 2) there had to appear to be at least some possibility of establishing, through bilateral and especially multilateral diplomacy, an improved norm-setting and rule-making system, or regime, in the field. Useful lessons could be learned, it was believed, from previous diplomatic experiences in the creation of international regimes. Hence historical reflections, including recollection of personal experiences, were invited. So, too, were assessments of current trends and projections into the future, as well as, of course, policy recommendations.

A question held centrally in mind from the outset of the project was whether world-order negotiation, or multilateral regime creation, differs in essential respects from other kinds of international diplomacy—for instance, postwar peace conferences aimed at one-time territorial and political settlements, economic summit meetings or other high-level gatherings of political leaders, and ordinary sessions of multilateral bodies such as the United Nations. The hypothesis of the Negotiating World Order Project, to be tested in this volume, was that international negotiations aimed at creating, maintaining, or reconstructing an international order are in some ways sui generis.

What, exactly, are the meanings of the various concepts the contributors to *Negotiating World Order* were asked to consider? World order, the master concept, is highly problematical. In the early planning sessions of the project, in fact, another term was used: "world peace." Adapting an old Roman motto, *si vis pacem para bellum* (if you wish for peace, prepare for war), a possible theme was stated: *si vis pacem para pacem* (if you wish for peace, prepare for peace).[9] "Peace," however, proved a difficult word to define. While there is a sense of the term in which it is the summum bonum of values (as in "the peace of God, which passeth all understanding," Phil. 4:7), it is so transcendent and comprehensive as not to provide a very clear focus for policy. Some realist writers in fact have denied that peace actually is the objective that governments pursue, or even should pursue; instead, government leaders should work to preserve the "national interest," which in certain circumstances

---

[9]"Si Vis Pacem Para Pacem" was printed on the green leather box encasing the foot-long gold pen given to U.S. Secretary of State Frank B. Kellogg in Le Havre. It was used by him and others in Paris on August 27, 1928, to sign the Kellogg-Briand antiwar pact.

can require the resort to war.[10] As a result of these and other considerations, the term "order," certainly an essential and large element in peace but also a word that can integrally be related to the national interest, emerged.[11]

Order, it was recognized, also is a multivocal term. It, too, is rich in historical connotations, negative as well as positive. To an older generation, it stirs memories of the talk about a "new order" in the 1930s; to the extent that this new order actually was imposed by Nazi Germany, it threatened the survival of Western civilization. Today some find discussions of a "new international order" in various fields equally alarming in their suggestion of authoritarianism and repression. There is a sense, however, in which international order, understood as the minimum standard of stability that is vital to the maintenance of any society, must be judged of benefit to humanity in almost any circumstances, especially in a nuclear age.

The truth is that order has been an objective of American foreign policy during most of the twentieth century, and it has been viewed, for the most part, in a positive light.[12] Especially since the Second World War, the United States has been the principal defender of order in the world and has regarded its contribution to itself and others in this respect as perhaps its greatest historical service. It is the declining ability of the United States today to perform that traditional function, in fact, that has caused the problem of world order again to be so widely discussed.[13] America's role as the upholder of international order had come to be taken, by much of the world and even many Americans themselves, as a given. The question now being raised is whether it will be possible for states to maintain international stability in many fields at one time, when there is no single organizing power, no central sun around which the planets, and their respective moons, can still revolve.

Without ignoring the historical encrustations of the concept or the inherent complexity of the idea as applied in different settings, one nonetheless should be able to identify the central meaning of order. For the common

---

[10]Walter Lippmann, *U.S. Foreign Policy: Shield of the Republic* (Boston: Little, Brown, 1943), pp. 50–54; Hans J. Morgenthau, *Politics Among Nations: The Struggle for Power and Peace*, 3rd ed. (New York: Alfred A. Knopf, 1963), pp. 95–96; Arnold Wolfers, *Discord and Collaboration: Essays on International Politics* (Baltimore: Johns Hopkins Press, 1962), pp. 67–80.

[11]The 1983 Catholic bishops' letter, *The Challenge of Peace*, interestingly defines peace as "the fruit of order." National Conference of Catholic Bishops, *The Challenge of Peace: God's Promise and Our Response—A Pastoral Letter on War and Peace*, Publication No. 863 (Washington, DC: United States Catholic Conference, 1983). p. 73.

[12]Lloyd C. Gardner, *A Covenant with Power: America and World Order From Wilson to Reagan* (New York: Oxford University Press, 1984). For a review essay, see Alan K. Henrikson, "Ordering the World," *Reviews in American History* 12, no. 4 (December 1984): 606–11.

[13]Symptomatic is Henry Kissinger's emphasis on the need for a "structure of peace . . . a new international order that would reduce lingering enmities, strengthen friendships, and give new hope to emerging nations." Henry A. Kissinger, *White House Years* (Boston: Little, Brown, 1979), p. 1476. For a reflective analysis, see Stanley Hoffmann, *Primacy or World Order: American Foreign Policy Since the Cold War* (New York: McGraw-Hill, 1978).

reference of participants in the Negotiating World Order Project, a basic working definition was stipulated. World order, according to this standard, was understood simply to be a regular arrangement or pattern—a constellation— of relationships among nations that serves as a foundation for confident expectations about the future. The essence of order is thus the psychological anticipation of regularity, not merely the fact of regularity itself. In this sense, order, as an alternative to fear of anarchy, surely may be acknowledged to be a "good thing."

As Rudolf Arnheim rightly has pointed out in *The Dynamics of Architectural Form*, "order must be understood as indispensable to the functioning of any organized system, whether its function be physical or mental. Just as neither an engine nor an orchestra nor a sports team can perform without the integrated cooperation of all its parts, so a work of art or architecture cannot fulfill its function and transmit its message unless it presents an ordered pattern."[14] In short, the maintenance of order is necessary for a thing to be completely itself, to perform at its very highest level, to realize the fullest potential of its nature. Order does not, it should be clear, preclude freedom. Indeed, order is the necessary basis of freedom and, in a sense, permission for the exercise of it.[15]

There are, of course, substantive differences in kind and quality among ordered systems, including international systems. Some international arrangements, such as the United Nations family of organizations, are relatively "open," to new members, new functions, and new ideologies. Others, such as the Organization of Petroleum Exporting Countries and other cartels, are in comparative terms "closed." Much depends, in assessing the character and merits of any international regime, on the principles on which the order is based. Order, though a necessary virtue, is rarely a sufficient one in itself. Among the additional criteria by which international arrangements have been, and should be, judged are universality, harmony, and equity, as well as uniformity, efficiency, and stability. It should be recognized that trade-offs between these values, or mutually exclusive choices, are sometimes necessary.

For analytical purposes, and for convenience of reference during Negotiating World Order Project discussions, a set of terms was chosen for examining world-ordering international arrangements on four different levels.[16] A world order, in any field, thus has the following component strata: 1) *principles*,

---

[14]Rudolf Arnheim, *The Dynamics of Architectural Form* (Berkeley: University of California Press, 1977). p. 162.

[15]For an interesting discussion of the idea of order and its relation to freedom in the realm of art, see E. H. Gombrich, *The Sense of Order: A Study in the Psychology of Decorative Art* (Ithaca, NY: Cornell University Press, 1979), p. 3. In *Doctor Faustus*, Thomas Mann has his central character, the composer Adrian Leverkühn, describe the "strictness" of music (the "moralism of her form") as "an excuse" for the ravishing fluidity of her sound. Thomas Mann, *Doctor Faustus: The Life of the German Composer Adrian Leverkükn as Told by a Friend*, trans. H. T. Lowe-Porter (New York: Modern Library, 1966), p. 69.

[16]The terms are adapted from Stephen D. Krasner, ed., *International Regimes* (Ithaca, NY: Cornell University Press, 1983).

that is, values, truths, or doctrines, more or less integrated into ideological systems (as in liberal capitalism or Marxism-Leninism), that embody overarching philosophical beliefs about what is acceptable and possible in world affairs; 2) *norms*, that is, explicit standards of international behavior (the preamble of the United Nations Charter, North Atlantic Council declarations, Economic Summit communiqués, etc.) that articulate general rights and obligations; 3) *rules*, which are more specific prescriptions and prohibitions requiring or forbidding the performance of specific actions and sometimes stipulating benefits to be gained or penalties to be suffered (e.g., the binding articles of the UN Charter, the North Atlantic Treaty, the General Agreement on Tariffs and Trade, or the Anti-Ballistic Missile Treaty); and 4) *procedures*, or the institutional practices and diplomatic methods used in making and implementing collective decisions within international organizations and other multilateral groupings (e.g., the veto prerogative of permanent members of the UN Security Council, the weighted voting system of the International Monetary Fund, or the method of consensus employed in the UN Conference on the Law of the Sea).

In negotiating world-ordering regimes, all four of these components can be important, and the interplay between them is worth carefully examining. It is not uncommon for explicit concessions in the realm of principles and norms to be compensated for by technical agreements concerning operational rules and procedures, which may enable a party to regain much of what it has given away on the policy level. Often the best test of the relative strength of the parties in an international regime, in fact, is the precise arrangement and balance of its dispute-settlement mechanism. In the early stages of a new international order such critical disputes usually are hypothetical only: it is nonetheless there, in this quasi-judicial setting, that the practical value of guarantees accorded to minority interests and also general policy commitments ultimately may be determined. As a result, the decisional system of a regime in formation may receive what appears to an outsider to be an inordinate amount of attention. In broad North-South negotiations especially, long-term issues of organizational control and conflict resolution can be crucial.[17] The rich, developed countries of the North, though outnumbered, may seek to safeguard their positions by such devices as weighted voting and tightly restrictive definitions of terms. The developing countries of the South, lacking in financial power and sometimes also in technical expertise, nonetheless may be able to secure their futures through insistence upon ultimate respect for majority rule.

Given the tensions that exist within international orders, why are they desirable? Basically, the answer is that they enable a higher level of international understanding, cooperation, and comity than would otherwise be

---

[17]See Robert L. Rothstein, "Regime-Creation by a Coalition of the Weak: Lessons from the NIEO and the Integrated Program for Commodities," *International Studies Quarterly* 28, no. 3 (September 1984): 307–28, at p. 308.

possible. "Such regimes are important," as Robert O. Keohane has comprehensively stated,

> not because they constitute centralized quasi-governments, but because they can facilitate agreements, and decentralized enforcement of agreements, among governments. They enhance the likelihood of cooperation by reducing the costs of making transactions that are consistent with the principles of the regime. They create the conditions for orderly multilateral negotiations, legitimate and delegitimate different types of state action, and facilitate linkages among issues within regimes and between regimes. They increase the symmetry and improve the quality of the information that governments receive. By clustering issues together in the same forums over a long period of time, they help to bring governments into continuing interaction with one another, reducing incentives to cheat and enhancing the value of reputation. By establishing legitimate standards of behavior for states to follow and by providing ways to monitor compliance, they create the basis for decentralized enforcement founded on the principle of reciprocity.[18]

This description of the processes of international regimes brings us to a consideration of the other titular concept of the Negotiating World Order Project: namely, negotiation. Seemingly a much less problematical notion than world order, it is in fact a somewhat difficult and uncertain idea too—not at all simple. The briefest possible definition of negotiation is offered by Roger Fisher and William Ury: "It is back-and-forth communication designed to reach an agreement when you and the other side have some interests that are shared and others that are opposed."[19] The key elements to be noted, besides the essential ingredient of communication itself, are the facts that the communication is *explicit*, that it is *reciprocal*, that it takes place *directly* between the parties, that the process of it is *designed*, that its intended objective is *an agreement*, and that the interests represented in it are *in competition*, a complex relationship which is a mixture of cooperation and conflict and neither purely one nor purely the other.

Negotiation is not mere conversation, nor is negotiation on the international level mere conversation between persons of different nationalities, or even between professional diplomats. In diplomacy, negotiation can be used as a technical term, denoting the stage of a formally constituted bargaining process, usually following a period of noncommittal exploratory talks, during which authorized delegates, instructed and operating within mutually agreed terms of reference, attempt through reasoned dialogue to draft a binding

---

[18]Robert O. Keohane, *Beyond Hegemony: Cooperation and Discord in the World Political Economy* (Princeton, NJ: Princeton University Press, 1984), pp. 244–45.

[19]Roger Fisher and William Ury, with Bruce Patton, ed., *Getting to YES: Negotiating Agreement Without Giving In* (Boston: Houghton Mifflin, 1981). p. xi. For a systemic treatment of negotiation, see Raiffa, *Art and Science of Negotiation*, and Fred Charles Iklé, *How Nations Negotiate* (New York: Harper and Row, 1964).

international agreement, to be initialed or signed and referred to their respective governments for ratification. Multilateral negotiations, such as major international conferences, involve further complications, including decisions about the number and the status of the parties (the shape of the table) and the identity, role, and powers of the chairman, not to mention myriad logistical considerations. International negotiation thus has characteristics, deriving from the traditions of diplomacy, that distinguish it from other kinds of meaningful interchange within and between societies.[20]

The fundamental distinguishing characteristic of international negotiation is the fact that the delegates at international conferences or to international organizations normally are representatives of sovereign states. Despite the discrepancies in their power, these sovereign entities are, in principle, equal to one another. A certain egalitarianism as a result is built into the diplomatic process, as it is inherent in the structure of the interstate system underlying it.[21] The only way to achieve international agreements, therefore, is to negotiate them, that is, to engage in a more or less voluntary dialogue among free and equal partners. A negotiated international regime is characterized by a sharing of responsibility and decision making.[22]

Negotiation, of course, is not the only imaginable way to achieve world order. Historically, it is actually a relatively recent innovation, coinciding with the rise of the Italian city-states, the great powers of continental Europe, and the European and extra-European world powers, such as the United States.[23] There are two other models of world ordering well worth considering, in order to sharpen our idea of what negotiation implies. The first of these alternative ordering concepts, derived from the examples of the Roman Empire and the Roman Catholic Church, is that of establishing international regimes

---

[20]On diplomatic tradition, see François de Callières, *On the Manner of Negotiating with Princes*, trans. A. F. Whyte (Notre Dame, IN: University of Notre Dame, 1963); and two studies by Harold Nicolson, *The Evolution of Diplomacy* (New York: Collier Books, 1962) and *Diplomacy*, 3rd ed. (New York: Oxford University Press, 1964).

[21]From the time of the Congress of Vienna (1814–15), a distinction has existed between the "great powers" (Austria, France, Great Britain, Prussia, and Russia, and, nominally, Spain) and smaller countries. This two-tiered stratification was perpetuated in the next century in the structure of the League of Nations and the United Nations, each divided into a council and an assembly, but it is becoming politically less tenable today. Many diplomatists, including former Israeli Foreign Minister Abba Eban, have lamented the new egalitarianism: "The absurdity of the UN voting system is aggravated by the most grotesque inequalities of power between states having equal votes. China, Russia and the United States equal Fiji, Papua and the Maldive islands. The knowledge of this anomaly has deprived the voting process in the General Assembly of all solemnity and restraint." Abba Eban, *The New Diplomacy: International Affairs in the Modern Age* (New York: Random House, 1983), p. 280.

[22]This use of the term, "negotiated," is borrowed from Benjamin J. Cohen, *Organizing the World's Money: The Political Economy of International Monetary Relations* (New York: Basic Books, 1977), p. 9.

[23]Although diplomacy was practiced in Greece and Rome, the foundations of the modern diplomatic system were established during the Renaissance. See Nicolson, *Evolution of Diplomacy*, chap. 2, "The Italian System"; and Garrett Mattingly, *Renaissance Diplomacy* (Boston: Houghton Mifflin, 1955).

through the exercise of supranational authority. In our own time, elements of supranationality, as it may briefly be termed, can be perceived in the operations of the European Economic Community, the International Monetary Fund, and certain other autonomous, powerful international institutions. Granted limited sovereignty by their members over certain functional areas, these organizations are centralized, unified authorities.[24] Their specific decisions are accepted because their powers previously have been generally accepted. They are, to use the words strictly, better called collective organizations than international ones. The second type of nonnegotiated international regime, whose characteristics only recently have been carefully distinguished by scholars, is what may be termed, without negative historical or ideological connotations, hegemonic order.[25] The modern archetype of a hegemonic international regime is the Pax Britannica maintained by Great Britain in the nineteenth century. The Pax Americana upheld by the United States in the years following the Second World War was comparably extensive. In essence, a hegemonic order is an imposed order. Its imposition may be tolerated, however, because of the benefits received from the primacy of the leader. The accepted leadership of the United States within the North Atlantic Alliance is a case in point. The "unilateral internationalism" of the Reagan administration perhaps is another expression of the postwar American hegemonic tradition. The leader in any hierarchically structured international order has responsibilities for system maintenance that must be discharged in order to warrant exercise of that leadership.

An implication of the foregoing description of supranational and hegemonic regimes is that in neither is genuine negotiation, between truly free and equal partners, possible. In the first case, this is because the right to negotiate previously has been ceded to a higher authority; in the second, it is because that privilege has been either deferentially waived or imperiously disregarded, owing to the dominant influence of a leader. In the analyses of particular subjects presented in the following chapters, this exclusion-by-definition of negotiation may not appear empirically justified. Negotiation may be, in reality, a widely pervasive phenomenon, characterizing discussions even within international regimes that are supranational and hegemonical. A tendency toward negotiation in these relatively authoritarian contexts may presage a breakdown of the collective and hierarchical ideals of these systems.

---

[24]The distinguishing features of supranationality, as identified by Raymond Aron, are three: renunciation of the principle of unanimity (or veto right); direct relations between the higher authority and citizens or enterprises of the various member nations; and the existence of agreements between the authority and foreign states. Raymond Aron, *Peace and War: A Theory of International Relations*, trans. Richard Howard and Annette Baker Fox (New York: Frederick A. Praeger, 1966), p. 744.

[25]Compare Hoffmann, *Primacy or World Order*, p. 13. For further development of "hegemony" as an analytical concept, see Keohane, *Beyond Hegemony*, where it is defined (p. 32), largely in economic terms, as a fourfold "preponderance of material resources"—raw materials, capital, markets, and industrial capacity.

That is to say, a new international consensus today may be emerging in which negotiation, rather than imposition in its overt or subtle forms, increasingly is the preferred norm for international rule creating, decision making, and dispute settling.

It should be mentioned, for completeness of theoretical exposition, that there is still a further manner in which international order can be imagined to come about: automatically. More than just a residual category, the assumption that the world system basically is self-equilibrating and needs no interference exerts a strong and widespread influence. To some extent, this assumption derives from a centuries-old philosophical tradition according to which there is a "natural order," in the legal, economic, and political spheres as well as in the physical universe. The norms of this order may be understood in two senses: either as abstract, ideal standards for the measurement and assessment of lapses in the conduct of man, or as regularities to which human behavior actually conforms—if not in the short run, then at least in the long run. The familiar prejudices that "justice will prevail," that "market forces will predominate," and that "power imbalances will be rectified" all illustrate these preconceptions about the automaticity of the world's mechanics.

With these conceptions of world order and world ordering in mind, one can construct a simple matrix exhibiting them (see Figure 1). Across the top may be placed the different "structures" of world order: first, what may be

Figure 1. World Order

Structures

Processes	International	Supranational	Hegemonic
Negotiated			
Imposed			
Automatic			

termed for this special purpose *international* order, in which responsibility is more or less freely shared by autonomous and equal nations; second, *supranational* order, in which responsibility is established and exercised more collectively; and, third, *hegemonic* order, in which a single, dominant leader has the primary responsibility. Down the side, one can display the several world-ordering "processes"—that is, the means by which order in the world comes about, or is believed to come about. The first of these, *negotiated* ordering, means the reasoned give and take of organized diplomacy, public and private, conducted in various nonauthoritarian settings. The second is *imposed* ordering, or the method, now widely discredited but nonetheless occasionally appreciated, of forcing a solution or settlement upon unwilling, if sometimes grateful, recipients. The third process is *automatic* ordering, a wholly spontaneous, nondirected means of international stabilization and rectification. The particular focus of most of the contributors to *Negotiating World Order* is the extreme upper left corner of this scheme, that is, "negotiated, international" order. The reader of this book, if so inclined, will be able to fill in many of the remaining squares with evidence from the many, varied experiences of world-order building discussed.

The chapters of *Negotiating World Order* fall into four major sections. Each group is defined by the general character of the factors on which order in the several fields seems most heavily or most distinctively to depend. Thus, within the first section on "Natural and Technological Bases of World Order," there are chapters by Jean Mayer, a distinguished nutritionist, on international agreements in the food and health fields; by John Roberts, a former Canadian environment minister, on the North American acid rain problem; by Tommy Koh, the president of the Third United Nations Conference on the Law of the Sea, on the newly negotiated international regime for the world's oceans; and by Leonard H. Marks, former chairman of the U.S. delegation to the World Administrative Radio Conference, on world ordering in the international telecommunications field.

In each of the above cases, it will be seen, it was in significant part the nature of the physical world itself and, inseparable from that, man's scientific understanding of it and technological ability to manage it which determined the success or failure of attempts at international negotiation. The scope of international order as well as its structure are, in fundamental ways, dictated by the sheer facts of earthly existence—the land's finite if flexible capacity to produce food, the broad sweep and uncontrollability of wind flows, the fixed and uneven width of the continental shelf and irregularity of the seabed, and the location of the geostationary orbit for satellites above the equator. These realities, revealing the earth's character as a self-contained biosphere with a scarcity of certain resources, have caused thinkers to envision a "global commons," whose assets, in the view of some disadvantaged nations, should be recognized legally as the common heritage of mankind. It was a natural scientist, Massachusetts Institute of Technology physicist Philip Morrison, who reminded us during one of the project discussions of the intimate relationship between "positive law" and "natural law." Human beings have tended to regard the physical world as merely a "natural background" for their economic, social, and political activities. Professor Morrison urged much closer and more specific, responsive attention to "what the world says to us, creatures on the earth, about the tasks of a global commons and how we can deal with it."[26] In specific ways, the chapters in this section are efforts to address this issue.

The next group of chapters is headed, "Cooperative and Strategic Bases of World Order." The four contributors are: Brian Urquhart, longtime under secretary-general of the United Nations, assessing the current state of collective security and international peacekeeping; Gerard C. Smith, a former director of the U.S. Arms Control and Disarmament Agency, examining the likely impact of the Strategic Defense Initiative strategy and program, on the Soviet-American arms control regime; Joseph S. Nye, Jr., a Harvard University political scientist and a former senior U.S. State Department official, discussing the continuing diplomatic effort to prevent the proliferation of nuclear weapons; and Max M. Kampelman, former chairman of the U.S. delegation to the Madrid Conference on Security and Cooperation in Europe and currently the chief U.S. arms control negotiator, on the politics and diplomacy of human rights. All of these presentations emphasize the critical importance of upholding, through persistent international action as well as by means of public verbal commitment, the agreed norms and rules of international political order—specifically, the United Nations Charter, the 1972 Anti-Ballistic Missile Treaty, the 1968 Non-Proliferation Treaty, and the 1975 Helsinki Final Act of the Conference on Security and Cooperation in Europe. Moreover, all of these chapters, centering (as most of them inevitably do) on the Soviet-American strategic relationship, analyze the complex connection between the possession of military power and the preservation of world order. The "rules" of strategic interchange, even though more akin to the contingent precepts of game theory than to the universal principles of political philosophy or international law, nonetheless can be used to reinforce international order. They are its buttresses if not its pillars, indispensable if not essential to it.

The third part of the book, more geographical in focus, gathers three reflections on the theme of "Regional Bases of World Order." My own chapter, written from the perspective of a diplomatic historian, considers the role of international negotiation within and through the North Atlantic Treaty Organization. Alejandro Orfila, recently secretary-general of the Organization of American States, discusses the institutional evolution of the OAS and also its current diplomatic capabilities, in face of such disturbances to the Western Hemisphere as the Falklands/Malvinas conflict, the Grenada incident, and the

---

[26]Panel on "Global Commons," 50th Reunion Alumni/ae Symposium, Fletcher School of Law and Diplomacy, Medford, Massachusetts, May 19, 1984.

Central American struggle. Leonard Unger, former U.S. Ambassador to Laos, Thailand, and Taiwan, recounts the events leading to the formation of the Association of Southeast Asian Nations. Each of these three organizations is analyzed both in its regional setting and in its wider international context. Owing in part to the relative weakening of the two superpowers and a decline in the influence of the UN Security Council, the regional route to world order may be gaining in international attractiveness. These chapters provide a basis for judging the wider utility of the novel forms devised by the Atlantic, Pan-American, and Southeast Asian communities.

Finally, the last three chapters concern the "Economic Bases of World Order." Specifically, the interrelated problems of commodities, trade, and finance are treated. Gamani Corea, who has served as secretary-general of the United Nations Conference on Trade and Development, discusses UNCTAD's efforts to establish an "Integrated Program for Commodities" to strengthen and stabilize international markets for Third World agricultural and mineral exports. Gardner Patterson, an economist who has been deputy director-general of the General Agreement on Tariffs and Trade, describes the GATT system and the current challenge to it of protectionism. Nathaniel Samuels, an investment banker who has served as U.S. under secretary of state for economic affairs, confronts the liquidity problems of Mexico, Argentina, Brazil, and other large international debtors and considers what the banking community and, in particular, the International Monetary Fund can do to alleviate their difficulties.

A shared concern throughout all fourteen chapters is the problem of negotiation: whether it should be bilateral or multilateral, whether it should treat issues comprehensively or deal with them on a case-by-case basis, and whether it should be conducted within established international institutions or attempted within new diplomatic frameworks. By focusing on these and other institutional-procedural questions, as well as on systemic-substantive ones, the authors of *Negotiating World Order* have sought to bridge the gulf between the craft of the diplomat and the designs of the global planner. To the extent that this common purpose has been fulfilled, and the gap between diplomatic artisanship and globalist architecture spanned, a new measure of unity will have been brought to the study of international relations.

Contributors

GAMANI COREA, an economist and diplomat from Sri Lanka, was secretary-general of the United Nations Conference on Trade and Development (UNCTAD) in Geneva from 1974 to 1984. Before that he was Sri Lanka's ambassador to the European Economic Community and the Benelux countries (1973–74). From 1970 to 1973 he served as deputy governor of the Central Bank of Ceylon and, from 1965 to 1970, as permanent secretary of the Ministry of Planning and Economic Affairs of the government of Ceylon. His special international assignments include service as secretary-general of the UN Conference on the Least Developed Countries (1981), chairman of the UN Committee on Development Planning (1972–1974), independent chairman of the UN Cocoa Conference (1972), chairman of the Expert Group on Development and Environment (1971), and chairman of the first and second UNCTAD Expert Groups on International Monetary Issues (1965, 1969). He studied at the University of Ceylon and at Corpus Christi College, Cambridge (M.A., economics), and Nuffield College, Oxford (D.Phil., economics).

ALAN K. HENRIKSON, chairman and director of the Negotiating World Order Project, teaches American and European diplomatic history at the Fletcher School of Law and Diplomacy, Tufts University. He is an associate of the Center for International Affairs at Harvard University and has been a member of the University Consortium for Research on North America. He has taught at Wellesley College and, during 1978–79, was a Fellow at the Woodrow Wilson International Center for Scholars at the Smithsonian Institution. His writings include studies of the Atlantic Alliance, U.S.-Canadian relations, the U.S.-Latin American security relationship, the diplomacy of détente, and political geography and foreign policy. A native of Iowa, where he served as research assistant to the governor, he received A.B., A.M., and Ph.D. degrees in history from Harvard and B.A. and M.A. degrees from Oxford University (Balliol College), where he studied philosophy-politics-and-economics as a Rhodes Scholar.

MAX M. KAMPELMAN, a lawyer, diplomat, and educator, currently serves as ambassador and head of the U.S. delegation in Geneva to the negotiations with the Soviet Union on nuclear and space arms. Until his retirement in 1985, he was a partner in the Washington law firm of Fried, Frank, Harris, Shriver, & Kampelman. In 1984 he was cochairman of the U.S. delegation observing the elections in El Salvador. From 1980 to 1983 he was ambassador and chairman of the U.S. delegation to the Madrid follow-up meeting of the Conference on Security and Cooperation in Europe. He has been a senior adviser to the U.S. delegation to the United Nations (1966–67) and, from 1949 to 1955, was legislative counsel to Senator Hubert H. Humphrey. Long active in many organizations, he has served as chairman of Freedom House, vice-chairman of the Coalition for a Democratic Majority, and chairman of the board of trustees of the Woodrow Wilson International Center for Scholars. He was born in New York City and received his B.A. and J.D. degrees from New York University. He subsequently earned a M.A. and Ph.D. from the University of Minnesota, where he taught political science (1946–1948).

TOMMY THONG BEE KOH was president of the Third UN Conference on the Law of the Sea (UNCLOS III) since its tenth session, from 1981 to 1982, and also chaired the Singapore delegation to the conference. Currently he is ambassador of the Republic of Singapore to the United States. Prior to that, he served as Singapore's ambassador and permanent representative to the United Nations, high commissioner to Canada, and ambassador to Mexico. Long active in the deliberations of the UN General Assembly, he was chosen a vice-president of its thirty-fourth session. He represented Singapore at UNCTAD V, at the sixth summit meeting of Non-Aligned Nations, and at the meetings of foreign ministers of the nonaligned countries in New Delhi in 1981 and Lima in 1975. From 1971 to 1974 he was dean of the law faculty of the University of Singapore. He received an LL.B. from the University of Singapore and an LL.M. from Harvard University, where he studied as the recipient of a Fulbright award. He also holds a postgraduate diploma from Cambridge University.

LEONARD H. MARKS was ambassador and head of the U.S. delegation to the World Administrative Radio Conference on shortwave broadcasting, held under the auspices of the International Telecommunication Union in Geneva in 1984. A lawyer with broad experience in public service in the international communications field, he also has been chairman of the U.S. Advisory Committee on International Educational and Cultural Affairs (1974–1978), chairman of the International Plenipotentiary Conference on Communications Satellites (1968–69), director of the United States Information Agency (1965–1968), and a director of the Communications Satellite Corporation (1963–1965). A native of Pittsburgh, he received B.A. and LL.B. degrees from the University of Pittsburgh, and he is currently a partner in the Washington law firm of Cohn & Marks. He is active in the work of the World Press Freedom Committee and International Rescue Committee, and he recently has served as chairman of the Foreign Policy Association.

JEAN MAYER, president of Tufts University and an internationally known nutritionist, served as chairman of the White House Conference on Food,

Nutrition, and Health (1969), chairman of the Nutrition Division of the White House Conference on Aging (1971), general coordinator of the U.S. Senate National Nutrition Policy Study (1974), and vice-chairman and acting chairman of the Presidential Commission on World Hunger (1978–1980). He also has been an adviser to a number of international agencies, including the Food and Agriculture Organization, the World Health Organization, and UNICEF. A native of France, he was educated at the University of Paris and at Yale University, where he received a Ph.D. in physiological chemistry; he also has a Dr. ès Sc. in physiology from the Sorbonne. His previous academic appointments include positions at Yale, George Washington University Medical School, and Harvard University, where he served as a professor of nutrition, lecturer in the history of public health, and member of the Center for Population Studies.

JOSEPH S. NYE, JR., a professor of government at Harvard University, served as U.S. deputy under secretary of state for security assistance, science, and technology (1977–1979) and chaired the National Security Council Group on Nonproliferation, which formulated the Carter administration's policy regarding that subject. Currently he serves as the director of the Center for Science and International Affairs at the John F. Kennedy School of Government at Harvard, where he is also a principal co-investigator in the Kennedy School's Avoiding Nuclear War Project. He has written works dealing with the nuclear nonproliferation problem, U.S.-Soviet relations, and energy and security, as well as on various aspects of international organization. He received an A.B. in public affairs from Princeton University and a B.A. in philosophy-politics-and-economics from Oxford University, where he studied as a Rhodes Scholar. His doctorate, in political science, is from Harvard.

ALEJANDRO ORFILA, an Argentine diplomat and business executive, was secretary-general of the Organization of American States (OAS) from 1975 to 1984. Previously he served as ambassador of the Republic of Argentina to the United States (1973–1975), after working for a number of years in private international financial and economic consulting. He was Argentina's ambassador to Japan (1960–1962). His earlier official positions include minister plenipotentiary in the Argentine embassy in Washington (1958–1960), director of information for the OAS (1953–1958), and secretary of the Argentine embassy in Washington (1951–52). He also has represented Argentina in consular posts in New Orleans, San Francisco, and Warsaw. During 1946–47 he was secretary of the Argentine embassy in Moscow. Born in Mendoza, Argentina, he studied law at the University of Buenos Aires. He also attended Stanford University and Tulane University, where he studied political science and foreign trade, respectively.

GARDNER PATTERSON was deputy director-general for trade policy of the General Agreement on Tariffs and Trade (GATT), Geneva, from 1973 to 1981. Before that he was assistant director-general of the GATT. Between 1949 and 1969 he taught economics at Princeton University where he served, in addition, as director of the International Finance Section (1949–1958) and director of the Woodrow Wilson School of Public and International Affairs (1958–1964). In 1961 he headed the U.S. Economic Survey Mission to Tunisia and served earlier as economic adviser in Turkey and Israel. Between 1946 and 1948 he was U.S. member of the Greek Currency Committee, Bank of Greece, in Athens. During World War II he served in the U.S. Navy in economic intelligence in the Balkans and western Europe. Before that, he worked as a U.S. Treasury representative in Africa and the Near East and also as a junior economist for the War Production Board in Washington. He received his formal education at the University of Michigan, from which he earned A.B. and A.M. degrees, and at Harvard University, from which he earned the Ph.D. in economics.

JOHN ROBERTS was minister of the environment in the Canadian government from 1980 to 1983, when he became minister for employment and immigration (1983–84). He also has held the positions of minister for science and technology (1980–1982) and secretary of state (1976–1979). First elected to the House of Commons as a member of the Liberal Party in 1968, he served as chairman of the Committee on the Official Languages Act and chairman of the Subcommittee on Peacekeeping and the United Nations. In 1973 he was named program secretary to Prime Minister Pierre Elliott Trudeau. Before entering politics, he was a lecturer at the University of Toronto and a foreign service officer with the Department of External Affairs, posted in France. He is a graduate of the University of Toronto and has studied at the École Nationale d'Administration in Paris and at Oxford University, from which he received a doctorate. Currently he is a professor of politics at Concordia University in Montreal.

NATHANIEL SAMUELS currently is a managing director of Shearson Lehman Brothers, Inc. Formerly, he was the managing partner of Kuhn, Loeb & Co. From 1969 to 1972 he served as under secretary of state for economic affairs, in which capacity he served also as U.S. alternate governor of the International Monetary Fund, the International Bank for Reconstruction and Development, the Inter-American Development Bank, and the Asian Development Bank. He was, in addition, a director of the Overseas Private Investment Corporation (1971–72). His earlier government service includes assignments in Paris as special adviser and then director of the Division of Industrial Resources of the U.S. Mutual Security Agency in Europe, and in London as secretary of the Coal Committee of the Combined Production and Resources Board. During World War II he served in Europe in the U.S. Army at Supreme Headquarters (SHAEF). A graduate of Harvard University, from which he received the S.B. degree, he subsequently studied law privately and became a member of the Illinois bar.

GERARD C. SMITH was the director of the U.S. Arms Control and Disarmament Agency (1969–1973) and chief delegate to the SALT I negotiations, which he described in his book *Doubletalk*. From 1977 to 1981 he served as ambassador-at-large and special U.S. representative for nonproliferation matters, as well as U.S. representative to the International Atomic Energy Agency (IAEA) in Vienna. He began his public service as an assistant to the Atomic Energy Commission (1950–1954). In 1954 he became special assistant for atomic energy affairs to Secretary of State John Foster Dulles, in which capacity he contributed to the IAEA treaty negotiations, the first Atoms for Peace conference, and talks with the Soviet Union regarding the diversion of nuclear materials for weaponry. From 1957 to 1961 he served as assistant secretary of state and director of the Policy Planning Staff, when he originated the Washington-Moscow "hot line" concept. He was educated at Yale College and Yale Law School and has served in the U.S. Navy. Currently he is president of the Consultants International Group, Inc., and chairman of the board of the Arms Control Association. He is a recipient of the Presidential Medal of Freedom (1981) and the Einstein Peace Prize (1982).

LEONARD UNGER, a professor of diplomacy at the Fletcher School of Law and Diplomacy, served as U.S. ambassador to the Republic of China (Taiwan) from 1974 until normalization of relations with the People's Republic of China in 1979. He also has served as ambassador to Thailand (1967–1973) and Laos (1962–1964). From 1965 to 1967 he was deputy assistant secretary of state for East Asian and Pacific Affairs. Educated at Harvard University, from which he received an A.B. in geography, he joined the Office of the Geographer of the State Department in 1941. At the end of the war, he served on the U.S. delegation to the Council of Foreign Ministers and at the Paris Conference of 1946 negotiating postwar peace treaties with Italy and the Balkan countries. After serving as U.S. political adviser in Trieste and then at the NATO Command in Naples, he was a member of the special mission that in 1954 went to London to negotiate the Trieste settlement. At the Fletcher School, he has organized and chaired a series of conferences dealing with the Association of Southeast Asian Nations and a number of its individual member countries: Thailand, Indonesia, Malaysia, and Singapore.

BRIAN URQUHART was under secretary-general for special political affairs of the United Nations from 1974 to 1986. Affiliated with that organization since its establishment in 1945, he has served it in a wide variety of capacities, as personal assistant to Secretary-General Trygve Lie, secretary of the Collective Measures Committee, member of the office of Under Secretary-General Ralph Bunche, executive secretary of the first and second UN International Conferences on the Peaceful Uses of Atomic Energy, deputy executive secretary of the preparatory commission of the International Atomic Energy Agency, assistant to the secretary-general's special representative in the Congo, UN representative in Katanga, and assistant secretary-general from 1972 to

1974. Much of his work has related to the peacekeeping operations of the United Nations. During World War II he served in the British Army in infantry and airborne units in North Africa, Sicily, and northern Europe. He was educated at Christ Church, Oxford, and is the author of the biographical study, *Hammarskjöld*.

NATURAL AND TECHNOLOGICAL BASES OF WORLD ORDER

International Agreements in the Food and Health Fields

JEAN MAYER

Workable international agreements must have two components: first, a human commitment to fill a need and, second, the empirical information on which to act. In many instances the commitment antedated the information, and the effective conclusion of international agreements in most cases did not take place until we had the scientific understanding and the technological means with which to act.

In addition, if we are going to talk about international agreements, we must have bona fide nations to conclude them. Here in the United States, we consider ourselves to be a young nation, scarcely more than two hundred years old. Americans tend to assume that the concept of nationality, and of the nation-state, is a very old one. Actually, the Constitution of the United States is one of the oldest constitutions still being applied, while the concept of nationality is a very young one. It derived much of its meaning from the French Revolution and the change in the concept of citizenship that took place at the end of the eighteenth century. It is important to realize that, before the American Revolution, there were at most three sizable modern nation-based states in the sense we now understand the word "nation": France, England, and Spain, and the last of these was a relatively more recent nation. Italy, Germany, and Russia—most of the countries we today think of as well-established nations—were not really unified. The enormous majority of the countries in the United Nations did not yet even exist.

This fact is relevant to the present theme of negotiating world order, because one of the major problems we face right now, in the nutrition and health field as well as in some other areas, is that we frequently find ourselves negotiating unsuccessfully with countries that are totally artificial creations, with no national existence in the modern sense of the term. We keep on

3

dealing with them—Lebanon, for instance—as though they are divided, unstable nations instead of artificial assemblages of tribal societies that may not want to live together. This misunderstanding conceals a basic problem. International agreements, particularly when they deal with technical problems such as those of food and health, require the solidity of established nations.

Large-scale work in food and health (with the reservation that it was not international at all in the modern sense of the term) is fairly ancient. This legacy should be recalled, for it suggests a possible alternative way of organizing ourselves to deal with technical problems that are wide in scope. The Roman Empire, to cite the greatest case, was an enormous assemblage that had very large-scale organizations germane to what we think of now as international food and health. The city of Rome itself had water coming from fourteen aqueducts, many of them bringing water from as far away as some Alpine areas that are not in Italy at present. Its food supply was clearly international, with enormous amounts of food and grain arriving daily at the port of Ostia from the Middle East, Egypt, and Libya, as well as from Tunisia and Sicily. The people who dealt with the administration of the water and food supplies of Rome (and we have a great many of their writings, such as Sextus Julius Frontinus's *De aquis urbis Romae* on the water system) were, in effect, large-scale international administrators. The organization of health care itself also was extensive. A very elaborate medical organization followed the Roman legions, and regional and local administration of health care was established in conquered territories.[1] By "conquered territories" we should not have the image, when dealing with the Roman Empire, of an occupied, exploited series of territories. After all, within one hundred years of Caesar's conquest of Gaul, Galba, a Gaul, became emperor of Rome. In many ways, the organization of the Roman Empire—a scheme of central authority and decentralized administration—is the perennial model that people unconsciously have had in mind about what the organization of order in the world might be.

The model of Rome continued to exert an influence with the advent of the Church as the dominant social organizing feature of Europe. While perpetuating Rome's attempt at universal organization, the Church destroyed much of the intellectual basis on which solid health administration would have to be built. The Latin Church Father Tertullian considered that the Gospel made investigation into health unnecessary, saying, "He who has washed in the blood of the lamb need never wash again"—not a strong public health prescription. Pope Innocent III later pronounced it a blasphemy to consult earthly physicians instead of praying to Saint Gregory of Tours. At the same time, Christianity brought about a much greater concern for one's neighbor than had existed previously: what I have called a human commitment to fill a need. Hospitals were created by the Church for the poor. The first charity

---

[1]John Scarborough, *Roman Medicine* (Ithaca, NY: Cornell University Press, 1969), pp. 66–93.

hospital in Rome, for example, was organized in the fourth century by a Christian lady, Fabiola. However, much of the previous work in medicine, by important figures such as Galen, was lost during the Dark Ages.

I may say that the same decline took place in the East, as a result of the Turko-Mongol invasions of the eleventh century and afterward. The most sophisticated medical system outside the Christian realm had been in the capitals of Arabia. The great hospital in Baghdad had basically the same division in services as a modern hospital, with out-patient, in-patient, and social services for out patients and the same sort of divisions into wards (surgical, medical, ophthalmological, and so on) as still exists today. We are in many ways the children of the rediscoverers of the organization of the great Baghdad hospital in our modern system. All this was destroyed by the conquests of the East, as it had been in the West, by the advent of Christianity.[2]

At the same time, the widespread movement of peoples, pilgrims, Crusaders, and others dictated some organizations that we now would consider to be international. This embryo of modern international organization in public health was very largely created, again through the Church, by the establishment of hospital orders such as the Order of St. John, the Order of St. Lazarus (which particularly concentrated on lepers), and what survived as the various orders of Malta to this day. In an organization which was very extensive, there were thousands of leprosaria; there were large numbers of hospitals in cities such as Paris, Strasbourg, London, and Santiago de Compostela in northwest Spain. Again, as in Roman times, some sort of transnational or transregional awareness of this activity existed, which probably made people feel better. The medical care given was itself often ineffective, because of the lack of understanding of the nature of the diseases being treated and because of the primitive views then prevailing about infection and contagion.

The truly modern era in international health dates back to two very different events. The first was the International Sanitary Conference in Paris, which opened in July 1851, for the purpose of dealing with international epidemics, and the second was the Battle of Solferino in June 1859, which was the key encounter in the war for Italian independence. The Sanitary Conference had been spurred by the successive epidemics of cholera that had hit western Europe during the previous twenty years. The meeting was called specifically to reach agreement among the twelve nations represented on minimum quarantine requirements in the new era of unprecedented world trade. Solferino, a confrontation mainly between the French army allied with the Piedmontese and an Austrian army composed of many nationalities, had been an extraordinarily bloody conflict with 40,000 dead on the battlefield. Two months later, the number of deaths had doubled from fever, disease, and neglect among the wounded. After Solferino, following three days of nursing the wounded and the dying, the traveling Swiss banker Henri Dunant,

---

[2]For background, see Manfred Ullmann, *Islamic Medicine* (Edinburgh: Edinburgh University Press, 1978).

the founder of the Red Cross, set out on his lifelong mission to mitigate the physical sufferings of war and to fight against war itself.[3]

Each of these initiatives had a practical and immediate motivation: the control of epidemics of infectious diseases and the lessening of casualties from battle, respectively. Of the two efforts, that of Dunant, who conducted a campaign of personal advocacy and private diplomacy, was the more immediately successful. In his *Un Souvenir de Solférino*, published in Geneva in 1862, Dunant called for the organization in peacetime of relief societies with the purpose of caring for the wounded in war. Already a good deal of experience had been gained in this field, and surgical practice was improving. When the heroine of the earlier Crimean War, Florence Nightingale, objected that such an organization was already in place in England, Dunant saw his road clearly: "What I want is a general mobilization of all the charities of the world! I want an organization which will be confined neither to England nor to any other country, but which will automatically go into action in every conflict—anywhere."[4] In February 1863, the Geneva Public Welfare Society appointed a committee, including Dunant, to examine the question of attaching a voluntary medical corps to armies in the field. An unofficial international conference called by the committee in October 1863 voted to recommend the creation in all countries of voluntary committees for the relief of the wounded and requested the early convening of an official diplomatic congress to consent to the legal "neutralization" in wartime of the wounded, together with the medical personnel and hospital facilities involved in their treatment. On the invitation of the Swiss Federal Council, an international conference was held in the town hall of Geneva in August 1864. In addition to the principal European powers, the United States, the only non-European country, was represented. The outcome was a convention for "the Amelioration of the Conditions of the Wounded in Armies in the Field"—the first Geneva Convention.[5] By 1867 this convention was ratified by all the great powers, with the exception of the United States, which signed fifteen years later thanks in large part to the advocacy of Clara Barton, who had worked with the wounded during the American Civil War.[6] Since then, almost all the world's governments have become signatories either to the original convention or to the several revised conventions.

The first International Sanitary Conference had a very different history. Its purpose, it appeared, was fairly well defined: to reach agreement on minimum quarantine requirements and thus, in the words of the president of

---

[3]Martin Gumpert, *Dunant: The Story of the Red Cross* (New York: Oxford University Press, 1938). See also Pierre Boissier, *Histoire du Comité international de la Croix-Rouge, de Solférino à Tsoushima* (Paris: Librairie Plon, 1963).

[4]Quoted in James Avery Joyce, *Red Cross International and the Strategy of Peace* (New York: Oceana Publications, 1959), p. 21.

[5]For the text of this document, dated August 22, 1864, see ibid., app. A.

[6]Clara Barton, *The Red Cross in Peace and War* (Washington, DC: American Historical Press, 1899).

the conference, to "render important services to the trade and shipping of the Mediterranean, while at the same time safeguarding the public health."[7] Twelve nations were represented, each by two delegates, one a diplomat and one a physician. The product of their labors, almost six months later, was an international sanitary convention with an elaborate set of specific regulations annexed to it. A draft was signed by all the delegates, but this did not commit their governments. Four months later, only five powers had signed the convention. It actually came into force between France and Sardinia when they exchanged instruments of ratification in May 1852. Portugal also later adhered to the convention but eventually withdrew, as did Sardinia. Thus the convention became completely inoperative.

The reasons for the failure of this first international sanitary collaboration may have been partly procedural. After lengthy discussion, it had been agreed that voting would be by individual delegates rather than by the powers represented, with the result that the voting could represent a difference in outlook between administrators and physicians, rather than the unified view of national governments. However, the principal reason for the ultimate ineffectiveness of this and later conferences is clear from the address of the French minister of agriculture and trade at the close of the first conference. He congratulated the participants on their discretion and wisdom in divorcing themselves from all questions of politics—and also all questions of science! In point of fact, neither the diplomats nor the physicians had any idea of the nature or mode of the propagation of cholera, bubonic plague, or yellow fever, the three diseases that the conference was trying to regulate.

By 1903, when the eleventh International Sanitary Conference opened in Paris, there was for the first time a body of scientifically accepted facts about the mode of transmission of these three diseases. For that reason, the conference marked a turning point. It remained to convert the new knowledge into public health measures. The French delegates proposed the establishment of an international health office. Their proposal was readily accepted, with the proviso that the organization not in any way interfere with the national administration of health. At the same time, it was accepted that such a body should have the right to communicate directly with national health administrations. Four years later in December 1907, representatives of twelve nations, including the United States, signed the Rome Agreement for the creation in Paris of the new Office International d'Hygiène Publique (OIHP). Its constitution stipulated that the governing committee of delegates be "technical representatives" of their countries. However, while most of the first members of the Permanent Committee were medically qualified, a number were diplomats.

---

[7]Quoted in *The First Ten Years of the World Health Organization* (Geneva: World Health Organization, 1958), p. 6. The following account of the International Sanitary Conferences is based largely on Part I (chaps. 1 and 2) of this book.

The original membership of the OIHP, whose main purpose was to disseminate to member states information about communicable diseases, reflected the historical evolution of the previous International Sanitary Conferences. Camille Barrère of France, who presided over the inaugural meeting of the Permanent Committee, celebrated the OIHP as the creation of "the marriage of diplomacy and medicine" and as the fruit of "long and persistent European cooperation."[8] The eventual adherence to the Rome Agreement of almost sixty countries, not all of which were sovereign states, gave the OIHP a somewhat more worldwide character.

By the time of the First World War, the OIHP had initiated studies on a wide range of subjects. (Deratting ships to confine the plague was its first major technical problem.) Besides investigating a variety of diseases, it also had started to work in the fields of food hygiene, hygiene of schools and workshops, and construction and management of field hospitals. Biological standardization was another OIHP initiative. The Permanent Committee had called the attention of governments to the need for international agreement on standards for serums and vaccines. The logic of public health increasingly pointed toward international intervention in national health administration. The Permanent Committee, for instance, had warned that central health authorities should not leave to local governments the sole responsibility for the control of drinking water and effluents, and it had urged compulsory notification of cases of tuberculosis, the addition of antityphoid inoculation to traditional measures against typhoid fever, and obligatory notification with surveillance, or isolation, of instances of leprosy.

At the first postwar session of OIHP, President Rocco Santoliquido proposed ideas for the future, which were still considered innovative many decades later, and which since have become a cornerstone of international health work.[9] The chief guarantee of international security from disease, he asserted, lay in the standard of public health of each nation. The concept of quarantine, of erecting barriers, was a superstition. Rather, the emphasis should be on the creation of indigenous public health services and the spread of public education appropriate to the areas and conditions within each nation. The proper objective was to circumscribe or eliminate the endemic foci of communicable diseases. Such action would be impossible without having consolidated nation-states capable of taking action internally that can make international action effective.

The OIHP itself was not destined to pursue this course. Professor Santoliquido resigned from the Permanent Committee to become technical adviser

---

[8]Quoted in ibid., p. 18.

[9]On international health issues during the interwar period, besides chap. 2 of *First Ten Years of the World Health Organization*, see Norman Howard-Jones, *International Public Health Between the Two World Wars—The Organizational Problems* (Geneva: World Health Organization, 1978), and Frank G. Boudreau, "International Health Work," in Harriet Eager Davis, ed., *Pioneers in World Order: An American Appraisal of the League of Nations* (New York: Columbia University Press, 1944), pp. 192–207.

to a new federative Ligue des Sociétés de la Croix-Rouge, a kind of parliament of the national Red Cross organizations. This body was formed at the instigation of a remarkable American, Henry Pomeroy Davison, who, as chairman of the War Council of the American Red Cross, had come to see the Red Cross not merely as a convenience for the wartime wounded but as a mechanism for the worldwide coordination of governmental and voluntary efforts to improve public health in peacetime. Davison's dream never materialized, in part because of the organization in 1919 of an intergovernmental institution, the League of Nations.

Spurred by two general motives, the League of Nations ultimately resolved to set up its own permanent health organization and to place the OIHP, with some modification of its statutes, under its authority. The first motive was the growing desire for formal international coordination, the belief that it was desirable that the new League be the central body through which international activities of every sort be coordinated. Article 24 of the League Covenant was explicit about this point. The second motive was the sense of moral urgency and outright fear generated by the breakdown of sanitary conditions in many war-ravaged countries, particularly Poland and Russia. In 1919, nearly 250,000 cases of typhus were reported in Poland; the number reached more than 1.6 million in Soviet Russia. The concern was that typhus, and cholera as well, might spread across Europe. The great influenza epidemic of 1918–19, it was believed, had killed some 15 million people. The OIHP, with its small staff and budget, did not seem capable of coping with postwar health problems on this scale.

A Provisional Health Committee, including delegates from France, Great Britain, Italy, and Japan (the four permanent members of the Council of the League), together with representatives of the International Labor Organization (ILO) and the League of Red Cross Societies, plus members of the OIHP Permanent Committee, was established in 1921 and immediately ran into complications. Earlier, the United States had refused its consent to the incorporation of any international organization of which it was a member into the League of Nations. To get around this veto, the members of OIHP were asked to join the Provisional Committee on the strength of their technical qualifications rather than their nationality. Whatever the merits of appointing a standing committee of health experts in their personal capacity, the arrangement did not survive the establishment of the League's Health Organization in its definitive form. (It is worth noting, however, that a similar principle was later embodied in the constitution of the executive board of the World Health Organization.)

Perhaps the outstanding example of the leadership of the League of Nations Health Organization was its work in the new field of nutrition. We often forget how very recent is most of our knowledge of the effects of foods in the body. The major vitamins were not identified until the 1920s and 1930s. Understanding of the role of trace minerals is still partial. The Health Organization made the decision to enter the field in 1934, and in 1936 its Technical

Commission published *The Physiological Bases of Nutrition*, a report that defined the first international standard of food requirements. It attracted more attention than any other report issued by the organization, and it still is considered a document of historic importance.

These standards had a very practical genesis. The world food problem was first brought before the League in 1925 by Yugoslavia, which proposed that the Health Section of the secretariat should examine and report on all aspects of food for health. The Health Section responded by sending two of its officers, Dr. W. R. Aykroyd and Dr. Etienne Burnet, to a number of countries to investigate the prevailing state of nutrition. Their report, issued in 1935, was the first synoptic account of the extent of hunger and malnutrition throughout the world. By that time, the world economic crisis was acute. Agriculture had collapsed. It is generally forgotten that in that period economists considered agricultural overproduction a major cause of economic depression. In a world ravaged by hunger and threatened by starvation even in its most industrialized and prosperous areas, the only remedies seemed to be tariff barriers and measures to restrict production in order to raise prices. Aykroyd and Burnet were members of a small group of international economists, nutritionists, and physiologists which included Ludwik Rajckman, E. J. Bigwood, Sir Edward Mellanby, F. L. McDougall, Hazel Stiebeling, John Boyd Orr, and my father, André Mayer. At the International Labor Conference of 1935 they appealed for the "marriage of health and agriculture." The pioneer French surveys, organized by Mayer and carried out in the early 1930s, linked minimum salary, employment, nutrition, and health, paralleling surveys done by Orr in Scotland and by Stiebeling in the United States. Together, these surveys led to a recognition that maldistribution of income and goods and the collapse of buying power had brought about agricultural surpluses, rather than vice versa.

At the World Monetary and Economic Conference in London in 1933, S. M. Bruce, later Viscount Bruce of Melbourne, influenced by McDougall's account of the Aykroyd-Burnet surveys, had warned that an economic system that restricted the production of food and other necessities of life required by the majority of mankind could not endure. Bruce and Lord de la Warr, later chairman of the United Kingdom's Freedom from Hunger campaign, subsequently introduced the subject before the Assembly of the League. It was this debate that generated the international committee of physiologists that produced the report on the physiological bases of nutrition. The League then appointed the Mixed Committee on the Problem of Nutrition, composed of world leaders in nutrition, agriculture, and trade, to make recommendations on every aspect of the food problem, including production, transport, and trade. As a conference was being organized to consider the committee's recommendations, the outbreak of war in 1939 put an end to the effort and to the League of Nations itself.

The focus shifted thereafter to the United States. During the 1930s, Franklin D. Roosevelt had argued that there were so many people "ill-fed, ill-clothed, and ill-housed" that, if the nation purposefully set out to supply their needs, there would be work for every man and woman willing to work. In January 1941 he voiced a commitment, later also embodied in the Atlantic Charter and the Declaration of the United Nations, to the principle of "freedom from want." In 1942, Mayer and McDougall approached Mrs. Roosevelt and, through her, President Roosevelt, with the view of implementing that pledge with the creation of an international organization devoted to food and agriculture. The president was impressed by the arguments of these two veterans of Geneva, and he agreed to call a preliminary conference, really the first meeting of the United Nations, in Hot Springs, Virginia, in May 1943. A decision was taken there to elaborate a constitution for a Food and Agriculture Organization (FAO). Mayer took a leading part in this work and, at the first meeting of the FAO Conference in Quebec City in October 1945, was elected chairman of the executive committee of the FAO. He represented that organization at the United Nations on the Coordination Committee of the United Nations Agencies (the "seven wise men") and at the councils of UNRRA and UNICEF.[10]

UNRRA, the United Nations Relief and Rehabilitation Administration, was created in 1943 as a temporary organization to deal with the gigantic emergency situation following World War II.[11] At the first session of UNRRA's council, it was decided that health work would be one of its fundamental responsibilities. Accordingly, in 1945 it took over the OIHP's traditional duties with respect to international sanitary conventions. The work of its Health Division in combating epidemics, administering sanitary agreements, providing essential medical supplies, and aiding governments of some fifteen countries in rebuilding and improving their health services provided the essential link between international health activities before the Second World War and those after it. It ended in 1947, however.

Under Orr, the first director-general of FAO, that organization, initially situated in Washington, continued the postwar relief effort on a more permanent basis. Its first action was to form the International Emergency Food Council (IEFC), an agency with powers to cope with the immediate short-term food chaos caused by the devastation in Europe and Asia. Concerted action was urgently needed. Despite pressure from a number of Western governments, particularly the United States and Great Britain, which feared interference with their own national food supply arrangements, Orr succeeded in calling a meeting of the major food importing and exporting countries in May 1946. It was decided that immediate action was required, and the IEFC, staffed and financed by FAO, distributed exportable food in accordance with

---

[10]Ruth B. Russell, assisted by Jeannette E. Muther, *A History of the United Nations Charter: The Role of the United States, 1940–1945* (Washington, DC: Brookings Institution, 1958), pp. 65–70; Gove Hambidge, *The Story of the FAO* (New York: D. Van Nostrand, 1955); Ralph W. Phillips, *FAO—Its Organization of Work and United States Participation* (Washington, DC: U.S. Department of Agriculture, 1969).

[11]Russell, *History of the United Nations Charter*, pp. 60–61, 70–71; George Woodbridge, *UNRRA: The History of the United Nations Relief and Rehabilitation Administration*, 3 vols. (New York: Columbia University Press, 1950).

individual countries' needs, taking measures to prevent sudden price fluctuations.

Even in 1946, Orr was acutely aware of the world's longer term food problems as well, problems that are still on our agenda today. He knew that there must be an exponential increase in food production to meet the needs of an exploding world population, especially in the underdeveloped food-deficit countries that had to devise an economic, educational, and industrial infrastructure to support a modern agricultural system. Orr therefore proposed to create a World Food Board with the funds and authority to buy and hold in reserve surplus food and other agricultural products for release after a bad harvest in any area.

His proposals were submitted at the FAO conference in Copenhagen in 1946. People acknowledged that the proposals were entirely justified but considered that the world was not yet ready for such bold, centralizing measures. The participating governments agreed to set up a commission, and six months later, when it reported, Orr's proposals were dead. In essence, Britain and the United States were not prepared to surrender either money or authority to a world organization over which they did not have full control. Instead, the commissioners recommended a Food Council with the power to advise on world food problems but not to solve them.

This is not to say that FAO, today headquartered in Rome, is an ineffective organization. It makes a contribution in a very broad field of activities, including nutrition, on a budget that is smaller than the agricultural budget of many medium-sized countries. It has been accused of carrying a large bureaucratic overhead, but it is doubtful that the overhead would expand greatly if FAO's budget were, appropriately, multiplied by a factor of ten. It retains much of its original potential.

The World Health Organization (WHO), the lineal successor to the OIHP and the League of Nations Health Organization, came into being in June 1946 at the International Health Conference in New York, the first international conference held under the formal auspices of the new United Nations Organization.[12] All fifty-one members of the United Nations sent delegations, and thirteen nonmember states were represented. The results were a constitution for WHO, a protocol for the termination of the 1907 Rome Agreement with provision for the duties and functions of the OIHP to be performed by WHO, and an arrangement for setting up an interim commission to prepare for the first regular World Health Assembly. The proposed constitution really sees WHO as doing more than just dealing with diseases, but it tries to use WHO as well as a vehicle for universal peace.[13] Indeed, WHO

---

[12]For the establishment of WHO, see *First Ten Years of the World Health Organization*, Part II.

[13]For the text of the WHO constitution, signed on July 22, 1946, see ibid., Annex 1. One of the "principles" of the preamble declares: "The health of all peoples is fundamental to the attainment of peace and security and is dependent upon the fullest co-operation of individuals and States."

has been given functions that governments normally do not allow international organizations, such as corresponding directly with technical organizations within states and receiving direct reports from them on disease conditions. It is a rare instance of an activity that is more than supranational but which is, as well, intranational.

A recurrent theme in every discussion of international action is non-interference in the internal affairs of states. Thus, while WHO is empowered to act as the directing and coordinating authority in international health work, its assistance depends upon the acceptance by, or request of, the national governments concerned. The World Health Assembly can adopt by resolution regulations relating to a broad range of specified technical subjects, and these regulations can come into force after a stated period unless member states actively reject them, or accept them with express reservations. However, a proposal that delegates should have full powers to sign international conventions on behalf of their governments was dropped. It was replaced by a clause authorizing Assembly adoption by a two-thirds majority vote, with the proviso that the conventions could come into force only when and if member governments acted in accordance with their particular constitutional processes. In the U.S. case, this preserved the prerogatives of the Senate in advising and consenting to treaties. Perhaps one of the most potentially useful innovations in international legislation is the clause in Chapter XVI that authorizes WHO to consult and cooperate with nongovernmental international organizations and, subject to government consent, with national organizations, both public and private. Thus the League of Red Cross Societies was brought into official relation with WHO.

This emphasis on collaboration is evident in all of WHO's activities. Through WHO, members of the public health and medical professions in UN-member nations exchange knowledge and experience. Regional health organizations, like the Pan American Health Organization (PAHO), also are linked integrally to WHO.[14] WHO works closely with other UN agencies; for example, with FAO in its programs of food production and conservation and also nutrition. In addition, it works with ILO on industrial health, with the United Nations Children's Fund (UNICEF) on maternal and child health, and with the United Nations Research Institute for Social Development in its health-related investigations.

International commitment has now put in place a network of organizations that, consistent with our current knowledge, provide a base for the achievement of the first two statements of principle of the constitution of the World Health Organization: "Health is a state of complete physical, mental and social well-being and not merely the absence of disease or infirmity. The enjoyment of the highest attainable standard of health is one of the fundamental

---

[14]The Pan American Health Organization can be traced back through several name changes to 1902, making it "the first international health bureau with its own secretariat." Ibid., p. 31.

rights of every human being without distinction of race, religion, political belief, economic or social condition."[15]

Whether this high and distant goal can be achieved solely through multilateral action is an open question. Multilateral aid has the advantage that it has no, or relatively few, strings attached. That also can be a disadvantage, however. The achievement of health, in the definition above, is clearly dependent on a wide range of factors, some of which can only effectively be treated within individual countries. International agencies are understandably reluctant to pressure national governments to accept decisions that may involve intervention within their domestic societies. Bilateral aid, by contrast, can be given unabashedly with strings tied to it. The United States, for example, is in a very much better position than the United Nations to offer conditional help. It can stipulate that a recipient nation agree to institute agrarian reform or adopt a progressive income tax, thereby making it more certain that aid intended to benefit all citizens does so. There is room for a judicious balance between multilateral and bilateral aid. In addition, compulsory reporting agreements are clearly essential in health matters. Owing to the speed of jet travel, cholera seen in Hong Kong today can appear in New York tomorrow. Some other reporting, on crop conditions and yields, for example, also ought to be international. Some special projects, however, can be carried out better on a bilateral basis. A good example is the cooperative arrangement made by the Fletcher School of Law and Diplomacy and the School of Veterinary Medicine at Tufts University, working with the U.S. Agency for International Development, with the government of Niger for the improvement of livestock management in that country.

These events and developments demonstrate that the will to achieve effective international collaboration in public health, broadly defined, in most cases preceded by many years the scientific knowledge needed to take effective action. The great era of discoveries in medical bacteriology at the end of the nineteenth century at last provided the necessary foundation. The activities of the OIHP in the years just before the First World War were to a great extent focused on the control of those communicable diseases whose mode of transmission finally had been identified. The twenty years between the two wars saw no less fundamental discoveries concerning noncommunicable diseases, in particular the great nutritional deficiency diseases. Once again, basic scientific knowledge made possible more effective measures in international health. During the Second World War, the use of penicillin and DDT completely transformed the outlook for control of some communicable diseases, such as scarlet fever and malaria. The development of streptomycin promised the containment of the centuries-old problem of tuberculosis. Owing to the discovery of the Salk and Sabin polio vaccines, the threat of infantile paralysis has been eliminated virtually from industrial countries. When the necessary

---

[15]Ibid., Annex 1.

scientific information and technical solutions are available, international organizations like WHO, and the governments that belong to them, can act efficiently and quickly.

Where we go from here is difficult to predict. Remembering that health as defined by WHO comprises not merely physical but also mental and social well-being, it is worth noting that no condition is more essential to the preservation of health than the absence of war and of the threat of war. In the area of international action for peace, we are in a situation analogous perhaps to that of the delegates to the first International Sanitary Conferences. We do not really know ourselves as individuals or as societies. The social sciences are in about the same state of evolution as was medicine during the last century. As at Solferino, we have no organization, no agreements, no methodology. Groups like International Physicians for the Prevention of Nuclear War, an organization born in Boston largely under the influence of Dr. Bernard Lown of Harvard's Medical School and School of Public Health, are beginning to deal with the problem of nuclear war by focusing on its medical consequences. It is necessary to impose a greater fear of the effects of war, because we are not yet equipped by psychiatry to see the problem of war itself as a medical problem, a problem of national and international mental health. As an incident like the Soviet-American confrontation over the shooting down of Korean Air Lines Flight 007 in September 1983 tragically illustrates, there are paranoias on both sides. The price of such madness is high. If we are to progress toward world health in the full sense of the term, we are going to have to address the problem of the Cold War with far greater understanding. In terms of international psychiatry, episodes like that of the Korean airliner are being dealt with in about the same way as people in 1860 dealt with great epidemics.

One other factor is crucial throughout the history of international action in health. That is the role of individuals: men and women of vision and determination who initiate what then becomes a collective endeavor. Dunant, Nightingale, Aykroyd and Burnet, McDougall, Bruce, Orr, and Mayer are just a few examples. Unfortunately, the success of these individual efforts at mass mobilization often depends on the occurrence of some sort of disaster—a war, a famine, or an epidemic—to exploit. Without the motivating personal experience of seeing such disasters, the individuals themselves would not necessarily have attempted to exert any leadership or have had the will to sustain it.

I have tried, as my own personal crusade for the past fifteen years, to get an international agreement on nations' renouncing starvation as an instrument of war and of peacetime oppression.[16] This, too, stems from personal

---

[16]Jean Mayer, "Time to Ban the Use of Starvation as a Weapon of War," *Christian Science Monitor*, December 24, 1984. In two Additional Protocols (1977) to the Geneva Conventions, nearly a hundred governments adopted by consensus measures permitting the relief of civilian populations during armed conflicts and declared the starvation of civilians "as a method

experience. I have had the sad privilege of seeing famines on three continents: in Europe, during World War II and at the liberation of the concentration camps; once in India; and several times in Africa, particularly during the 1967–1970 Biafran war. Starvation has been used as an instrument of policy many times: against the South during the American Civil War, against France by the Prussians in 1870, against the Central Powers by the Allies during the First World War, against the city of Leningrad by the Germans during World War II, and against the Viet Cong by the United States during the Vietnamese conflict. In the situation in Nigeria, where I was present as an observer, starvation was being used as a weapon of terror by the Nigerians and as a weapon of propaganda by the Biafrans. At no time did I see any shortage of food in the Biafran army, which was nonetheless eventually defeated. The persons who are most vulnerable in a plight like that, as the present situation in Ethiopia illustrates, are not combatants but children, pregnant and nursing women, and the elderly—those who die first in a famine. The weaponry of starvation is worse than indiscriminate, like bacteriological warfare; it discriminates against those who, by any standard, least deserve it.

In addition to advocating, with limited success, the outlawing of military and political starvation, I have proposed positive measures to deal with famines and thus foster the world's health.[17] There should be an early-warning system comparable to the procedures already set in place, and administered by WHO, for monitoring and controlling the spread of infectious diseases. It should have three elements: 1) a meteorological component, enabling WHO and other international organizations to have sufficient access to satellite data in order to monitor the weather and changes in the color of vegetation; 2) an economic and agricultural component, permitting surveillance of crop prices and stocks and a current listing of the whereabouts of grain-carrying ships for possible diversion to famine sites; and 3) a health component, allowing the collection of data on the growth rate and health of poor children, a sensitive indicator of approaching large-scale trouble. The public health dimension of famine relief is important for political and diplomatic, as well as medical, reasons. Governments, such as the central government of Nigeria or perhaps Ethiopia today, tend to be more responsive to pressures for humanitarian intervention from outside when it is suggested that the spread of famine is accompanied by contagious diseases. Once national governments recognize that such outside assistance is in their interest, they can be extremely helpful. The more internally consolidated the nations are, the more effective is this help, and the more reliable any agreements they make.

---

of combat" prohibited. For the texts, see United Nations, *Diplomatic Conference on Reaffirmation and Development of International Humanitarian Law Applicable in Armed Conflict: Protocols I and III to the Geneva Conventions* (A/32/144), August 15, 1977, Annexes I and II. The United States (like the Soviet Union) signed the protocols on December 12, 1977. Neither yet has ratified them.

[17]Jean Mayer, "A Five-Point Plan for Action," *Newsweek* 104, no. 23 (November 26, 1984): 58.

We will not have more effective international agreements in the fields of food and health until we truly desire a solution, we know exactly what we are confronting, and we know precisely with whom we are negotiating. I think it is encouraging to see that greater knowledge does tend to induce not only a heightened sense of responsibility but also very often much more satisfactory action. One can hope that the progress that was made in international health, which then spread to food and agriculture, may at some point spread to other fields of international endeavor.

FOR FURTHER READING

On the history and activities of the International Committee of the Red Cross, see Pierre Boissier, *Histoire du Comité international de la Croix-Rouge, de Solférino à Tsoushima*, cited in the footnotes; André Durand, *From Sarajevo to Hiroshima: History of the International Committee of the Red Cross* (Geneva: Henry Dunant Institute, 1984); Georges Willemin and Roger Heacock, *International Organization and the Evolution of World Society: The International Committee of the Red Cross* (The Hague: Martinus Nijhoff, 1984); and David P. Forsythe, *Humanitarian Politics: The International Committee of the Red Cross* (Baltimore: Johns Hopkins University Press, 1977). On the Nigerian civil war and the role of the Red Cross, see Suzanne Cronje, *The World and Nigeria: The Diplomatic History of the Biafran War, 1967–1970* (London: Sidgwick and Jackson, 1972); and Thierry Hentsch, *Face au blocus: La Croix-Rouge Internationale dans le Nigéria en guerre, 1967–1970* (Geneva: Institut Universitaire de Hautes Etudes Internationales, 1973).

Accounts of UNRRA, FAO, and WHO, respectively, may be found in the following works, mentioned in the footnotes: George Woodbridge, *UNRRA: The History of the United Nations Relief and Rehabilitation Administration*; Gove Hambidge, *The Story of the FAO*; and *The First Ten Years of the World Health Organization*.

On the interrelated subjects of agriculture, nutrition, and disaster relief, see *Agriculture: Toward 2000* (Rome: Food and Agriculture Organization, 1981); Lester R. Brown, with Erik P. Eckholm, *By Bread Alone* (New York: Praeger, 1974); Raymond F. Hopkins and Donald J. Puchala, *Global Food Interdependence: Challenge to American Foreign Policy* (New York: Columbia University Press, 1980); Jean Mayer, *Human Nutrition: Its Physiological, Medical and Social Aspects* (Springfield, IL: Charles C. Thomas, 1972); Jean Mayer, "Coping with Famine," *Foreign Affairs* 53, no. 1 (October 1974): 98–120; Jean Mayer and Johanna Dwyer, *Food and Nutrition Policy in a Changing World* (New York: Oxford University Press, 1979); Swedish Nutrition Foundation, *Famine: A Symposium Dealing with Nutrition and Relief Operations in Times of Disaster* (Stockholm: Almquist and Wiksell, 1971); and J. R. K. Robson, ed., *Famine: Its Causes, Effects and Management* (New York: Gordon and Breach, 1981).

The Diplomacy of Acid Rain:
The North American Experience in
Global Perspective

JOHN ROBERTS

My perspective on the problem of acid rain is that of a working politician, who struggled actively for three years to reach an agreement for joint action by Canada and the United States to resolve a common problem. After I had accepted, as minister of the environment of the Canadian government, the invitation to deliver this lecture at the Fletcher School of Law and Diplomacy, Prime Minister Pierre Trudeau relieved me of my post and transferred me to other political responsibilities. Therefore, I now speak privately rather than officially on this subject, a matter of deep and continuing concern to me. I shall offer some personal reflections based on my three years, from early 1980 to mid-1983, as the official of the Canadian government charged with the exciting but frustrating task of concluding an agreement on acid rain with our American neighbors. That agreement still eludes us. I do believe, nonetheless, that the diplomacy of acid rain, in light of the difficulty that issue has posed for relations in general between our two countries, merits careful analysis, even though it is not a success story I have to tell.

Acid rain is a harbinger of what may be a host of international environmental issues, complex in their substance and not well adapted to resolution through existing diplomatic and political mechanisms. I hope to show why these international environmental problems have seemed so intractable. I am skeptical, however, of my ability to do more than hint at how changes of structure or approach might make these questions more easily managed by Canada and the United States, and by the international community at large.

Let us begin with a description of the evolution of environmental policy in Canada, for two reasons. First, the divergence of approach in basic environmental policy between Canada and the United States is the source and explanation of some of the tensions that have developed between our governments concerning the acid rain issue. Second, changes in the approach to environmental problems, at least in Canada, reflect an understanding that these environmental challenges are far more complex than had originally been believed, as well as an understanding that this complexity, and consequent difficulty of taking responsive action, must be resolved partly at the international level.

It is extraordinary how quickly our thinking about the environment has developed. The Canadian Department of Environmental Affairs, Environment Canada, was established in 1971. It was one of the responses to the worldwide outburst of concern represented, and also stimulated, by Rachel Carson's *Silent Spring*, which drew attention to the pervasive, poisonous effects of pesticides on organic life.[1] It also reflected a more specific, traditionally Canadian concern about protecting our country's vast, invaluable resources of fresh water. Since the 1909 Boundary Waters Treaty between Canada and the United States, our government has maintained a practical interest in the many aquatic aspects of the North American environment. The Canadian identification with the evolving environmental field was highlighted internationally when, in 1972, my countryman Maurice F. Strong served as secretary-general of the pioneering United Nations Conference on the Human Environment held in Stockholm. From that time forward, environmental thinking in Canada evolved rapidly. The development of our environmental policy in the years since then occurred in three distinct stages, or generations.

The first-generation policy concentrated on the direct and obvious effects of pollution. Our focus was on the most visible sources of pollution that we could see, and sometimes even smell, such as the effluent from a pulp and paper mill, the smoke from a coal-fired generating plant, and the open garbage dump. We took an essentially regulatory and control approach to try to abate, after the fact, these gross sources of pollution. Our approach was reactive and defensive—"find out what the polluters are doing and tell them to stop"— and the major instrument of the action we took was regulation. Government played a policeman's role in bringing polluting malefactors to heel. A whole array of regulatory measures, ranging from control of phosphorous levels in detergents to lead in gasoline, was promulgated. Better regulation of present generators of pollution was complemented by government action to clean up the hazardous legacy of the past. The Love Canal in the United States, across the border from us in Buffalo, is perhaps the most dramatic example of the unintended and unimagined consequences of these past acts. Canada faced similar, if less grave, hazardous-waste situations. Here, too, our action was essentially retroactive, a belated response to existing conditions.

The second generation of Canadian policy led to environmental planning to prevent pollution, not simply to combat it. As the 1970s wore on, our

---

[1]Rachel Carson, *Silent Spring* (London: Hamish Hamilton, 1963).

knowledge and understanding began to become more sophisticated. We realized that we had to anticipate and prevent, not just clean up—at greater cost—after the fact. We had to collect vast amounts of data about the physical environment and understand its basic processes. With this knowledge, we could start to incorporate into our projects environmentally acceptable technology at the less expensive design stage and, by environmental assessment, to plan projects in an environmentally acceptable manner in advance of construction. This advance planning is particularly relevant in Canada to large energy projects, such as offshore drilling, gas and oil pipelines, and hydroelectric dams. The importance of energy production to our economy and the sensitivity of our physical environment to damage from energy development made such careful planning essential.

During this same period, we began to grapple seriously with toxic substances, those by-products of the Chemical Revolution that have transformed our lives since the end of World War II. The small percentage of these substances that cause us such concern today, like PCBs, dioxins, and mirex, tends to be widely dispersed, very persistent in the environment, and long term in effect on the physical environment and human health. We have to discard the concept of "safe" levels of pollution where these substances are concerned. We understand their workings very inadequately. We have to deal with a balance of evidence and to control instead according to the concept of "acceptable levels of risk."

The instrument for pursuing the objective of pollution prevention was institutionalized environmental assessment and review. In Canada, major development projects were, and are, assessed for environmental consequences before they proceed. The fragility of our northern environment makes this doubly necessary. A concern for the ecological consequences of development leads inevitably also to a concern for the social and economic consequences of industrial growth.

This has brought us to a third generation of environmental policy, one which we are as yet only beginning to understand conceptually and apply practically, of seeing environmental policy as the long-term planning of the prudent use of resources. This concept is based on the growing knowledge that man's existence on earth depends increasingly on his ability to learn to live in harmony with his environment. The idea is captured by Lester Brown's famous statement, paraphrasing a UN report: "We have not inherited the earth from our fathers; we are borrowing it from our children."[2] It reflects a shift from an image of ourselves as a consuming society to a view of ourselves as a conserver society, and from this altered viewpoint flows the realization that pollution and the environmental degradation that results from it are a mismanagement of the resources of the future.

---

[2]Lester R. Brown, *Building a Sustainable Society* (New York: W. W. Norton, 1981), p. 359.

There are still some people who seem to think that the choice to be made is between the "luxury" of a cleaner environment and the hard necessity of employment and income generation deriving from economic activity. In the shorter term, and for a specific industry or plant or town, this definition of the problem may be valid. At least in my country, which is so heavily dependent on a natural resource base, and particularly renewable natural resources such as timber, that alleged choice is a false one. The Canadian government's policy framework paper, *Economic Development for Canada in the 1980s*, recognizes that "the maintenance of the quality of our water, our air and our soil is essential to our long-term development and the quality of life to which that development must contribute."[3]

In short, environmental policy in Canada is increasingly seen as an adjunct to, and as essential to, proper economic planning. One of the most difficult administrative challenges we have faced in my country is how to translate these longer term environmental considerations into present-day decisions. In both government and business, our planning perspective tends to be short range. Without an institutionalized system for calculating longer term environmental consequences, short-term development gain is likely to cause substantial long-term environmental pain.

Obviously, these three stages, or generations, of environmental policy that I have described have not been mutually exclusive, but overlapping and cumulative. They have led, albeit somewhat imperfectly, to a mixture of programs of pollution control, resource management, and conservation policies designed to meet our overriding objective of sustainable long-term benefit to the country.

What does all this imply for environmental relations between Canada and the United States? I hope I have not left the impression that I believe we in Canada have found all of the answers in environmental policy, and that if the rest of North America and all of the world accepted them as the true faith all would be well. On the contrary, what I have described is a ragged evolution in my country's thinking about environmental policy. It is an evolution that I believe has been taking place, more or less rapidly and intelligently, in the minds of forward-looking people in the United States and in most of the industrialized world. It is reflected in such thoughtful works as *Global 2000*, commissioned by President Jimmy Carter, and the *World Conservation Strategy*, produced by the International Union for Conservation of Nature and Natural Resources in cooperation with the United Nations.[4]

---

[3]Government of Canada, *Economic Development for Canada in the 1980s* (Ottawa: Government of Canada, 1981), p. 17.

[4]U.S. Council on Environmental Quality and Department of State, *The Global 2000 Report to the President: Entering the Twenty-first Century*, Gerald O. Barney, study director, 3 vols. (Washington, DC: U.S. Government Printing Office, 1980); International Union for Conservation of Nature and Natural Resources, *World Conservation Strategy: Living Resource Conservation for Sustainable Development* (Gland, Switzerland: International Union for Conservation of Nature and Natural Resources, 1980).

Nevertheless, it is clearly fair to say that the evolution I have described taking place in Canada has not been embraced by the present U.S. administration. Rather than regarding economic and environmental interests as properly complementary to each other, the United States seems to view them as contradictory. Rather than seeing environmental policies as planning instruments, officials in Washington seem to look upon them as regulatory control and often economically harmful. Whereas in Canada we have a tendency to establish overall objectives to be attained and leave open to the private sector or regional governments the choice of means to achieve them, the United States has tended to focus on the process of legal and regulatory restrictions. In short, while the U.S. government has been viewing the environmental challenge with first-generation eyes, the Canadian government has been trying to attain broader third-generation objectives. It is hardly surprising that there is a tension between the two countries regarding environmental problems.

The matter of acid rain is for Canadians without doubt the single most important irritant in the relations between our two countries. It is not an issue reflecting political partisanship. The concern with acid rain is felt as strongly and expressed as vigorously whichever political party happens to hold government power.

Acid rain is caused by the emission into the atmosphere of sulphur dioxide and also nitrous oxides. These substances, often transported hundreds of miles, fall to the earth as dry depositions or as rain or snow, to an intensity that can reach the acidic level of vinegar. The cumulative effect of this deposition, or the sudden shock of its entry into lakes in the spring runoff, can damage water systems in sensitive areas to such a degree that they can no longer sustain fish life. Lakes so affected—and there are thousands of them in Canada and the Adirondacks—are clear, and beautiful, and dead.

Canadian concern over this phenomenon is not simply a result of the agitation of environmental fringe activists. Acid rain poses a threat to the basic economic resources of my country. The sports fisheries in eastern Canada amount to a billion-dollar industry. It is in danger. The salmon fishery in the Atlantic provinces is beginning to show the impact of acid rain on spawning streams. They are in jeopardy. Canada's forest industry is the largest single element of our economy; one Canadian in ten is directly or indirectly employed by it. It, too, is at risk. There are increasingly strong fears that acid deposition is retarding the regenerative powers of the forest floor. There also is reason to be concerned about the impact of acid deposition on human health, especially for those who suffer from respiratory diseases, and on the quality of drinking water through the acidic leaching of toxic substances into water supplies. People's homes and offices are themselves affected. Erosion and decay of buildings from acid rain costs hundreds of millions of dollars each year to repair. Major Canadian interests are, thus, threatened by this phenomenon. It is not surprising that all governments and all political parties in Canada are united in calling for international action to combat this problem.

It is a problem outside the powers of Canadian action alone to control. Over half the acid fallout in Canada comes from U.S. sources, mainly thermal power plants. It falls on geographically sensitive areas with little capacity to recover from the damage. It constitutes about two-thirds to three-quarters of our environmental problem. Canada, in turn, exports acid deposition, mainly from smelters, to the United States. About 15 to 25 percent of the acidity falling on the sensitive Adirondacks in the eastern United States is from Canada. Acid rain is inescapably a joint problem for our countries, made so by territorial proximity and the prevailing path of weather systems. Neither of our two countries can alone provide a remedy. The impact of the problem is particularly great in Canada, however, because the acidic fallout attacks the heartland of the country and its key resource bases. This is not true to nearly the same degree in the United States.

There is a deep ambivalence in the Canadian character concerning the United States, as those who are students of Canadian international relations are aware. Canadians, on the whole, are people whose ancestors, or who themselves, decided for reasons good or bad not to become Americans. At times throughout the country's history they have been skeptical, even fearful, of the purposes of the United States. However, they share so much in attitude, in culture, and in neighborly economic interest that Canadian-American ties of respect, affection, and friendship are very strong. Most Canadians believe that Americans would not knowingly or willingly cause Canada harm. They believe, therefore, that the inaction by the U.S. government in the face of our common acid rain problems must flow from ignorance or inattention, and not from design. If they should come to believe that lack of cooperative action with us is calculated and deliberate, then the potential for a serious disruption of Canadian-American relations is very grave.

Why has this acid rain problem been such a thorny and difficult issue for our two countries to resolve? The answer to this question lies partially in the divergence in our general philosophical approaches to environmental matters. Even more important is the fact that acid rain brings to the international level a complex environmental issue of a kind for which no satisfactory mechanisms of resolution have been found, even at the national level. Acid rain is in this respect a new type of environmental problem. There are at least two salient characteristics to the problems posed by acid rain: 1) they require risk assessment and management based on insufficient scientific knowledge, and 2) they are characterized by an interjurisdictional transfer of costs.

Complex issues like acid rain puzzle scientists. Enough evidence is available to suggest that there may be a serious and intensifying problem for society if nothing is done. More knowledge could be helpful, but the time necessary to do the desired research may delay action so long that the worsening situation becomes irretrievable. So, one must assess the risks, both of action and of inaction. Determining what level of risk is acceptable and what is not necessitates social, economic, and environmental trade-offs: in other words, political decision. Such assessment involves estimates of risk probability and magnitude as well as a measure of the public's willingness to accept such risk. The degree of possible gain must also be estimated. How much is society willing to pay for how much approximate surety? How does society precisely quantify the benefits in terms of reduction of risk and damage in order to stack them up against the costs?

Acid rain exemplifies this dilemma. There is clear damage to aquatic systems and buildings and growing evidence of adverse effects on soil and forest growth. However, transformations in the atmosphere, variable wind patterns, and the great distances that separate the sources of emission from the areas of impact make the correlation of cause and effect difficult. All this points to the importance of scientific comprehension but also to the need to take action now.

The point I again stress is that environmental policy has become enormously more complex in the last decade. The difficulty of forecasting the effect of industrial changes on the environment makes rational political decision making much more difficult. The inevitable uncertainty of scientific knowledge provides a ready and credible rationale for the failure to decide anything at all. When there is weakness of political will, it is easy to claim that no regulatory action should be taken until irrefutable, definitive information is available. Too often those seeking remedial action for environmental problems are faced by a "Catch-22" response: action should be delayed until the base of scientific knowledge is complete; without some action at the outset, such a base of scientific knowledge may be impossible to build.

That certainly has been the reaction by the U.S. government to Canadian pleas for action on acid rain, action continually deferred on the ground that more research is needed but not very urgently. It also was the reaction of Sweden's neighbors to the concerns expressed by that country a decade ago about the increasing acidity in its lakes. Now its neighbors are prepared to admit that indeed there was cause for concern, but half of Sweden's lakes are already dead. The time for saving them is past. We do not intend to let that happen to Canada.

This difficulty of political decision making, when a lack of scientific knowledge provides an excuse for procrastination, is greatly compounded by the transferability of the social costs of inaction from one jurisdiction to another; e.g., from the industrial Middle West to the Northeast, or from the United States to Canada. When the costs, pollution, are found in one jurisdiction and the benefits, employment, in another, the proper management of an environmental problem is difficult to achieve. To attempt to apply cost-benefit approaches to interjurisdictional disputes is problematic in any case. It would be hard to agree, for example, that Canada should put up with being the recipient of U.S. pollution on the grounds that it would cost Canada less to clean it up than it would cost to have the United States stop creating it, just as one could not accept that a neighbor would be justified in dumping his garbage in your backyard because you might have an easier time than he of disposing of it. Political decisionmakers do make assessments of costs and benefits, but the main problem inhibiting political action in such international areas as the handling of acid rain is the disjunction between the power to act and the ability to be the beneficiary of that action.

In the 1960s, the sight of environmental problems was immediate. Cause and effect were, or were thought to be, closely linked geographically. If a lake or water system was clogged by eutrophications, the sewers and effluent that caused that condition were palpable. The sources could be identified. If parks and forests were blighted by smoke or exhaust from factories and tail pipes, the remedies were sought in the locale. The costs could be assessed, and the benefits for action were anticipated, close to home.

In environmental questions, failure to act generally constitutes a shift of costs from the private sector to the social sector. Where impacts are felt far from pollution sources, failure to act shifts costs from one jurisdiction to another, domestically from region to region or internationally from country to country. When the costs of remedial action are high and the jurisdictions are nation-states, the inertia of inaction takes on a rock-like immobility, unless the affected economic interests of the states concerned are approximately equal. One partner, usually the poorer and more vulnerable one, suffers more. This has been Canada's experience with acid rain.

What is remarkable about the acid rain issue is not just that it has been a continuing cause of friction between our two countries. It is that the instruments of diplomacy, between two nations of such long-standing friendship and mutual interest, have been so utterly useless in resolving it.

Faced with the imperative need for action, the government of Canada examined the possible use of legal processes to support Canada's interests, either at the international level or by intervention in the U.S. courts. However, court processes are agonizingly slow. The connection of cause and effect is often general rather than precise, so it is difficult to prove responsibility. Our legal advisers were not even certain that the Canadian government would be given standing before the courts of the United States. Property owners, or other individuals who were damaged by upwind polluters, would have a cause of action, but would the government have a right to initiate action on their behalf? Moreover, our diplomatic advisers feared that if we opted for legal redress we would in practice have to forego the possibility of redress through negotiation. Those who choose to go to court may find that their adversaries argue that the use of other channels must await the court's determination.

The Canadian government therefore decided that, while it might assist in practical ways any private individuals or provincial governments who launched court actions, it itself would seek to resolve acid rain problems with the United States through the instruments of diplomacy. The approach we followed was modeled on the earlier successful negotiation between our two countries for resolving our transboundary water problems.

The keystone to that approach was the 1909 Boundary Waters Treaty. That treaty set forth orderly procedures for our two countries to deal with each other regarding boundary waters and, by extension, other transboundary environmental issues. It established a framework of principles to bring about rational management of the waters flowing across or along the boundary. The acceptance by each country that it would not disregard the interests of the other in matters of water levels and flows constituted a distinct limitation on each country's right to do as it wished with an important segment of the continent's waterways. In effect, the treaty amounted to a voluntary limitation on sovereignty.[5]

While focused primarily on water flow, the treaty also contained a brief but very strong reference to water quality. Article IV reads in part: "It is further agreed that the waters herein defined as boundary waters and waters flowing across the boundary shall not be polluted on either side to the injury of health or property of the other."[6] That is a very comprehensive statement. I draw to your attention its similarity with Principle 21 adopted in Stockholm in 1972 by the first United Nations Conference on the Human Environment. That principle reads as follows:

> States have, in accordance with the Charter of the United Nations and the principles of international law, the sovereign right to exploit their own resources pursuant to their own environmental policies, and the responsibility to ensure that activities within their jurisdiction or control do not cause damage to the environment of other States or of areas beyond the limits of national jurisdiction.[7]

In addition to establishing some basic procedures and principles, the Boundary Waters Treaty created the International Joint Commission (IJC). Made up of six appointees (three from each country), the commission is the only permanent public institution working in the field of Canadian-U.S. environmental relations. The IJC would have little unique to offer to the better management of the Canadian-U.S. relationship if, within it, business were to be conducted along national lines, with an automatic division between the Canadian and U.S. commissioners. On only two or three occasions since it first began to function in 1912 has the commission divided along national lines. It almost always has acted in a spirit of collegial objectivity, its decisions and recommendations based on the jointly established facts of each case, in an atmosphere one or two steps removed from competing national political and diplomatic interests. The same concept of independent objectivity has historically applied also to the commission's technical advisory boards, even though these are made up of well-qualified technical officials drawn from agencies of each federal government, and sometimes state and provincial governments as well. Board members also are expected to operate on a

---

[5]The text of the Boundary Waters Treaty may be found in John E. Carroll, *Environmental Diplomacy: An Examination and a Prospectus of Canadian-U.S. Transboundary Environmental Relations* (Ann Arbor: University of Michigan Press, 1983), app. I.

[6]Ibid., p. 316.

[7]United Nations, *Report of the United Nations Conference on the Human Environment*, Stockholm, June 5–16, 1972 (A/CONF.48/14/Rev.1), 1973, p. 5.

collegial basis and to give their best professional advice to the commission, not simply to relay their respective employers' views.

The IJC plays three basic roles. It can be asked: 1) to approve applications for raising the level of waters flowing across the boundary; 2) to inquire into and report upon any matter arising between the two countries, not necessarily confined to boundary waters; and 3) to arbitrate between the parties. This third power, arbitration (Article X), has never been invoked. Our two goverments, both of which must consent to arbitration, have never asked the commission to play this role. It is a role, however, whose time may have come. We should think of realizing the potential of this unique mechanism by building on the commission's credibility and enhancing its capability to assist in the handling of thorny bilateral environmental issues. Its ability to play this role depends simply on our two countries' political will to activate a power that so far has lain dormant.

Approving applications for raising water levels has the commission operating in a quasi-judicial fashion. For example, when an entity in one country wishes to build a dam and, in the process, to flood a portion of the other country's territory, an application must be made to the commission. The commission appoints a Canadian-U.S. technical board to study the matter. This board, in turn, makes recommendations to the commission, which usually after public hearings issues or does not issue an order of approval for the project and sets out conditions as appropriate. The St. Lawrence Seaway, for example, is covered by such a commission Order of Approval. Normally, the commission appoints a control board to monitor the activity for compliance and to keep it technically informed.

The second IJC role, inquiring into and reporting upon various matters, is probably where the commission has made its greatest mark. While such references can be submitted by either government singly, they are almost invariably submitted jointly. The commission's method for dealing with these references is essentially the same as that for applications, except that the final product is a report to the two governments of a purely advisory nature, rather than an order carrying legal force. I have touched on the role of the IJC in some detail because I wish to suggest that this type of institution offers the best hope of evolving into the kind of management system we need for handling international environmental questions, not merely between the United States and Canada but between neighboring countries in other parts of the world as well.

The negotiation of the Great Lakes Water Quality Agreement of 1972, renegotiated and updated in 1978,[8] followed an approach similar to that of the Boundary Waters Treaty. The 1972 agreement specifically recognizes the general obligation of both parties not to pollute one another. It goes on, in effect, to define that obligation by establishing specific water quality objectives. However, this de facto definition is dynamic rather than static. The

---

[8]Carroll, *Environmental Diplomacy*, app. 2.

objectives are meant to be reviewed as further scientific data are produced. Indeed, the 1978 version of the agreement made some significant changes in, and additions to, the 1972 objectives. It even added a provision addressing deposition of pollutants from the air, a mark of our growing understanding of air as a medium of transport for pollutants whose primary impact is felt on the ground or in the water.

Two points are especially significant about the negotiations leading to, and occurring under, the Great Lakes Water Quality Agreement. First, the agreement proceeded even though it was recognized that the requisite knowledge for pollution control strategies was insufficient. Rather than holding action back until knowledge was complete, however, our two governments decided to act in stages, undertaking what could reasonably be done in the first stage, while further research was undertaken leading to agreements of more precision in the subsequent stages. Second, the agreement did not seek to impose the mechanisms or processes of actual pollution control. Instead, it established the general and specific objectives to be reached and left to each country the task of determining how best to achieve those objectives.

It is understandable that Canada believed that this same approach, developed in relation to water pollution, could be followed in relation to airborne pollution. Indeed, we succeeded in signing a memorandum of intent with the Carter administration to do exactly that in the summer of 1980.[9] The negotiation of that commitment was one of my first responsibilities when I became Canada's minister of the environment earlier that year. We were very hopeful of further, practical results. In the event our hopes proved fruitless. The following years of discussion with the Reagan administration are a record of extraordinary effort but continuing frustration. We seem as far today from fulfilling the undertakings of 1980 as we were when they were made, yet it would be wrong to ascribe these delays simply to changes in the personalities of one administration by another. By the same token, having a new set of leaders in Washington or in Ottawa will not automatically result in an agreement.

There are fundamental factors behind our failure to create a regulation scheme for acid rain that have little to do with who is in political power. If one asks why the approach we used was successful with the Great Lakes and not for acid rain, a large part of the explanation appears to me to be that the heavy concentration of American population around the Great Lakes made it clear to all that the benefits of remedial action upon water quality would be equally substantial for the United States. The mutuality of benefit for action on acid rain, a more diffuse problem, is not established so clearly.

Given the inadequacy of legal remedies and the frustration of the diplomatic remedy, the Canadian government decided in 1981 to turn to the political arena in an attempt to provoke action on acid rain. We launched an information and communications campaign that, so far as I know, is unprecedented in Canadian relations with the United States. It had many elements,

---

[9]Ibid., app. 4.

including vigorous representations to Congress by our officials, efforts to interest the U.S. media, communications by provincial governments to the governors of those states that were involved, use of Canadian lobby groups who proceeded to establish offices in Washington, liaison with similar environmental interest groups in the United States, and distribution of information brochures and films aimed directly at U.S. citizens. In short, we used every device we could think of to bring home to Americans the nature and the consequences of acid rain.

Despite the inevitable annoyance we caused, we have had some success. Several years ago, Congress and the Reagan administration were talking of gutting the amended 1970 Clean Air Act; now they are talking about strengthening it, especially in relation to acid rain. Our success, while welcome, should nevertheless cause us concern. We have been successful by persuading many Americans that acid rain is their domestic problem, not by causing them to recognize that it is a common international problem. We calculated that Americans would not act "to do Canada a favor," or fulfill an international obligation. American governments are designed to respond to how U.S. citizens define their own interests. It was because we were able honestly to convince Americans that important interests of theirs were at stake that political institutions in the United States became more sensitive to the problem.

Unfortunately, our success has been confined to the arena of public opinion, rather than to that of the decisionmakers in Washington. The political pressures that we helped to generate in the United States have not been sufficiently strong or sufficiently focused to cause the Reagan administration to act. There is, moreover, still the paradox that what support we have obtained is mainly for domestic action, rather than for international action, the plane on which the problem of acid rain can be most clearly seen and effectively mitigated.

We very much need the international spirit of the Boundary Waters Treaty and of the two Great Lakes Water Quality Agreements. It is this that must permeate U.S. and Canadian actions on an international air quality agreement. The sense of environmental responsibility and concern for the neighbor's yard as well as one's own must be kept clearly before us if our two countries are to have a healthy physical environment and are to ensure the continued benefits possible from our natural resources. We cannot sit by idly as our most basic assets, our soils and our waters, are degraded by assault from the air.

Further defining the role which the IJC could play in monitoring and regulating that which we in North America do unto others is, in my view, one practical and positive solution to our problem. It may in fact be the most promising avenue for progress.

The IJC could also provide a model for other countries, particularly the industrialized nations of the Organization for Economic Cooperation and Development (OECD), which will face inevitably similar challenges as the technical complexities of our technological society increase in the future.

How will environmental management be shared? How will responsibility be divided? How will the costs be assessed? Can sovereignty be internationalized sufficiently to permit such cooperation? This is surely the theme of the fourth generation of environmental policy. It is a subject that must be addressed as swiftly as possible and at the highest level.

It is encouraging to see worldwide attention focused increasingly on this issue. The International Conference of Ministers on Acid Rain, which took place in Ottawa in March 1984, is a welcome step in recognizing the inherent transboundary implications of this new environmental challenge.[10] Meetings of this kind, however, mark only tentative advances toward confronting issues that go to the very heart of international economic and environmental responsibility. The difficulties of managing economic development with imperfect scientific knowledge of the long-term consequences of that development require fundamental solutions and institutional mechanisms that are genuinely international in scope to carry them out.

FOR FURTHER READING

On the politics of the Canadian-American acid rain problem, see especially John E. Carroll, *Environmental Diplomacy: An Examination and a Prospectus of Canadian-U.S. Transboundary Environmental Relations*, cited in the footnotes; John E. Carroll, *Acid Rain: An Issue in Canadian-American Relations* (Washington, DC: National Planning Association, 1982); and John E. Carroll, ed., *Pollution Across Borders: Acid Rain–Acid Diplomacy*, the proceedings of a 1984 conference at the University of New Hampshire. The problem is briefly discussed in John Roberts, *Agenda for Canada: Towards a New Liberalism* (Toronto: Lester and Orpen Dennys, 1985). On the economic and legal, as well as political, aspects of the issue, see Gregory Wetstone, Armin Rosencranz, and Sarah Foster, *Acid Rain in Europe and North America* (Washington, DC: Environmental Law Institute, 1983); Anthony Scott, "Transfrontier Pollution: Are New Institutions Necessary?" in *Economics of Transfrontier Pollution* (Paris: Organization for Economic Cooperation and Development, 1976), pp. 177–218; Jeffrey Maclure, "North American Acid Rain and International Law," *The Fletcher Forum: A Journal of Studies in International Affairs* 7, no. 1 (Winter 1983): 121–54; and Alfred P. Rubin, "Pollution by Analogy: The Trail Smelter Arbitration," *Oregon Law Review* 50, no. 259 (Spring 1971): 259–98.

---

[10]The Final Communiqué (March 21, 1984) of the International Conference of Ministers on Acid Rain committed the ten participating countries—Austria, Canada, Denmark, Federal Republic of Germany, Finland, France, the Netherlands, Norway, Sweden, and Switzerland—to undertake to reduce national annual sulphur emissions by at least 30 percent as soon as possible, and at the latest by 1993. The parties also agreed to urge that other signatories to the 1979 Geneva Convention on Long-Range Transboundary Air Pollution of the United Nations Economic Commission for Europe (ECE) take similar action. This was an attempt to encourage the United States, which had signed the 1979 convention, to reconsider its refusal to join Canada in a commitment to reduce North American sulphur dioxide emissions. For the text of the 1979 ECE Convention, see Carroll, *Environmental Diplomacy*, app. 3.

On the 1909 Boundary Waters Treaty and the International Joint Commission, see Maxwell Cohen, *The Regime of Boundary Waters—The Canadian-United States Experience* (Leiden: A. W. Sijthoff, 1977); William R. Willoughby, *The Joint Organizations of Canada and the United States* (Toronto: University of Toronto Press, 1979); and Robert Spencer, John Kirton, and Kim Nossal, eds., *The International Joint Commission: Seventy Years On* (Toronto: Centre for International Studies, University of Toronto, 1981). On Canadian-American relations in general, see Charles F. Doran, *Forgotten Partnership: U.S.-Canadian Relations Today* (Baltimore: Johns Hopkins University Press, 1984).

International environmental relations are treated comprehensively in two works by Lynton K. Caldwell, *In Defense of Earth: International Protection of the Biosphere* (Bloomington: Indiana University Press, 1972) and *International Environmental Policy: Emergence and Dimensions* (Durham: Duke University Press, 1984). See also David A. Kay and Eugene B. Skolnikoff, *World Eco-crisis: International Organizations in Response* (Madison: University of Wisconsin Press, 1972), and Jan Schneider, *World Public Order of the Environment: Towards an International Ecological Law and Organization* (Toronto: University of Toronto Press, 1979).

On the scientific problem and the physical consequences of acid raid, see Gene E. Likens et al., "Acid Rain," *Scientific American* 241, no. 4 (October 1979): 43–51, and two studies by Ross Howard and Michael Perley: *Acid Rain: The North American Forecast* (Toronto: Anansi, 1980) and *Acid Rain: The Devastating Impact on North America* (New York: McGraw Hill, 1982).

Negotiating a New World Order for the Sea

T. T. B. KOH

The UN Convention on the Law of the Sea of 1982 took almost nine years to negotiate. The opposition of the present U.S. government notwithstanding, the treaty represents one of the major achievements of the United Nations during the past decade. For the last two years of the Third UN Conference on the Law of the Sea, I was privileged to serve as its president. In what follows, I shall attempt to tell the remarkable story of negotiating a new world order for a realm that encompasses more than two-thirds of the surface of the earth.

I shall divide this lecture into five parts. First, I shall trace briefly the evolution of the traditional law of the sea. Second, I shall discuss the different forces that eroded and then finally brought about the collapse of the old legal order, leading to the eventual convening of the Third UN Conference in December 1973. Third, I shall give selected examples of the subjects and issues that were negotiated at the conference. In doing so, I shall discuss the nature of the competing interests that had to be reconciled and the mutual accommodations that had to be made in order to reach a successful result. Fourth, I shall discuss some of the more interesting, perhaps even unique, features of the negotiating process that we used. Finally, I shall answer the question: What is the long-range significance of the new legal order governing the uses and resources of the world's oceans, as embodied in the 1982 UN Convention?

First, we need to place our subject in its historical context. From the end of the fifteenth century to the beginning of the nineteenth, the law concerning the uses and resources of the sea was unsettled. There were two contending schools of thought. The first, Mare Clausum (Closed Sea), held that the sea and its resources were capable of being subject to appropriation and dominion. The second school of thought, called Mare Liberum (Free Sea), was brilliantly expounded by Hugo Grotius in the legal opinion he wrote for the Dutch East India Company. He argued that things which cannot be seized or enclosed cannot become property. According to Grotius, on the high seas no one can claim dominion or exclusive fisheries rights or an exclusive right of navigation.

In the course of the eighteenth century, the Grotian view came gradually to predominate over the opposing view. Coastal states were permitted to claim a narrow belt of the sea off their shores for the purpose of fishing, as well as for protecting their neutrality. Beyond that belt, the sea and its resources were *res communis*, no one's property, and subject to the freedom of the sea.

By the beginning of the nineteenth century, following the end of the Napoleonic Wars and the Congress of Vienna, the three-mile territorial sea became almost universally accepted. Great Britain, which emerged from the Napoleonic Wars as the world's greatest power, became the champion of the Mare Liberum idea. It was logical for it to adopt such a position. "In manufacture, in merchant marine, in foreign trade, in international finance, we had no rival," as the British diplomat and historian Lord Strang has explained. "As we came, by deliberate act of policy, to adopt the practice of free trade and to apply the principle of 'all seas freely open for all,' we moved towards the *Pax Britannica*, using the Royal Navy to keep the seas open for the common benefit, to suppress piracy and the slave trade, and to prepare and publish charts of every ocean."[1]

This British-dominated maritime legal order prevailed for over a hundred years. New forces, however, began to challenge it, as well as British supremacy. An American scholar, Sayre A. Swarztrauber, has suggested that the old legal order began its decline in 1930.[2] In that year, the Hague Codification Conference was held under the auspices of the League of Nations. The objective of that conference was to codify the international law regarding the territorial sea. Forty-eight states attended the Hague conference; of these, only ten favored a three-mile territorial sea, provided that a contiguous zone was added. (A contiguous zone enables a state to exercise the control necessary to prevent and to punish infringements of its customs, fiscal, immigration, or sanitary laws and regulations within its territory or territorial sea.) Six states favored a six-mile territorial sea, and six others wanted a six-mile territorial sea together with a contiguous zone. Because the views expressed were so divergent, no formal vote was taken on any of the proposals. A possible compromise consisting of a three-mile territorial sea and a nine-mile contiguous zone was quashed by strong British opposition. The 1930 conference, therefore, ended in failure. Swarztrauber has argued that, by allowing the conference to fail, "the great maritime powers ended their oligarchical maintenance of the maxim Mare Liberum. The Conference suggested to all

---

[1]Lord William Strang, *Britain in World Affairs: The Fluctuation in Power and Influence from Henry VIII to Elizabeth II* (New York: Frederick A. Praeger, 1961), pp. 99–100.

[2]Sayre A. Swarztrauber, *The Three-Mile Limit of Territorial Seas* (Annapolis: Naval Institute Press, 1972).

that the great powers were no longer committed to the enforcement of the three-mile limit."[3]

Ironically, the United States struck a second blow to the traditional law of the sea following the Second World War. In 1945, President Harry S. Truman issued two famous proclamations relating to the sea. In the first, the United States asserted its jurisdiction and control over the natural resources of the subsoil and seabed of the continental shelf contiguous to the U.S. coast. The term "continental shelf" defined generally that portion of the seabed extending from land to the point where the waters reached a depth of 600 feet, or 200 meters isobath.[4] In the second proclamation, the United States declared that it "regards it as proper to establish conservation zones in those areas of the high seas contiguous to the coast of the United States wherein fishing activities have been or in future may be developed and maintained on a substantial scale."[5] The proclamation provided that the conservation zones would be established and maintained through direct agreement with those states whose subjects traditionally had fished the areas in question.

These unilateral actions of the United States were immediately emulated and exceeded by its regional neighbors. Mexico issued a similar proclamation one month after the United States did. A year later, Argentina not only claimed sovereignty over its own continental shelf but also to the water column above the shelf. Between 1946 and 1957, ten other states claimed sovereignty over their continental shelves and the superjacent waters. Between 1947 and 1955, five Latin American states declared 200-mile limits for exclusive fishing rights.

It was in these circumstances of a rapidly eroding legal order that the United Nations held its First Conference on the Law of the Sea in 1958. That international gathering succeeded in adopting four conventions: the Convention on the Territorial Sea and the Contiguous Zone, the Convention on Fishing and Conservation of the Living Resources of the High Seas, the Convention on the High Seas, and the Convention on the Continental Shelf. The First UN Conference failed, however, to arrive at agreed limits on the territorial sea and on the coastal states' exclusive fishing rights. In the Convention on the Continental Shelf, the rights of the coastal states were to extend "to a depth of 200 metres or, beyond that limit, to where the depth of the superjacent waters admits the exploitation of the natural resources."[6] The second of these two criteria, the exploitability criterion, was imprecise and soon gave rise to

---

[3]Ibid., p. 140.

[4]Proclamation No. 2667, "Policy of the United States with Respect to the Natural Resources of the Subsoil and Sea Bed of the Continental Shelf," September 28, 1945, 10 *Federal Register* 12303; also printed in S. Houston Lay, Robin Churchill, Myron Nordquist, K. R. Simmonds, and Jane Welch, comps. and eds., *New Directions in the Law of the Sea, Documents*, 11 vols. (Dobbs Ferry, NY: Oceana Publications, 1973–1981), 1:106–09.

[5]Proclamation No. 2668, "Policy of the United States with Respect to Coastal Fisheries in Certain Areas of the High Seas," September 28, 1945, 10 *Federal Register* 12304; also printed in Lay et al., *New Directions*, 1:95–98.

[6]Convention on the Continental Shelf, done at Geneva, April 29, 1958, in Lay et al., *New Directions*, 3:101–05.

trouble. In 1960, the United Nations held its Second Conference on the Law of the Sea in order to find agreement on the limits of the territorial sea and the fishing zone. This gathering also failed.

During the decade of the 1960s, the British, Dutch, and French colonial empires, in decline for many years, largely disintegrated. The former colonies of the European states in Asia, Africa, and the Caribbean acceded to independence, joined the United Nations, and became new members of the international community. Most of these newly independent countries had not participated in the 1958 and 1960 UN Conferences on the Law of the Sea and therefore took no proprietary interest in them. They also felt dissatisfied with the traditional law that they regarded as the product of European experience. Therefore, they wanted an opportunity to remold the international law of the sea to reflect their aspirations and interests.

In the fall of 1967, the then permanent representative of Malta to the United Nations, Dr. Arvid Pardo, drew the attention of the world to the immense resources of the seabed and ocean floor, beyond the limits of national jurisdiction. He proposed that the seabed and ocean floor should be used exclusively for peaceful purposes and that the area and its resources should be considered the common heritage of mankind. He argued that neither the freedom of the sea nor claims of sovereignty then being asserted by coastal states could ban the specter of pollution, exhaustion of marine life, and international political strife.[7] Dr. Pardo and others further urged that a constitution or charter be adopted that would deal with ocean space as an organic and ecological whole. This was a revolutionary concept, one that conditioned subsequent international discussion of the law of the sea problem. Unlike lawyers, who tend to favor dealing with issues in manageable packages, statesmen such as Dr. Pardo, influenced by scientists' discoveries of the interrelatedness of oceanographic matters, persuasively advocated a more unified treatment. The focus of this new vision and approach was the seabed. As a result, the United Nations established the Seabed Committee to examine the question and to elaborate a legal regime for the exploration and exploitation of the resources of the ocean floor area.

At about the same time, the Soviet Union approached the United States and other countries in order to discuss the idea of recognizing a twelve-mile territorial sea, provided that a high-seas corridor was preserved in international straits. In 1968 and 1969, the United States started determining the views of its NATO partners, the Soviet Union, and other countries about the desirability of conceding twelve miles as the maximum permissible breadth of the territorial sea in return for free navigation of warships and overflight of military aircraft—the right of innocent passage—in and over straits used for international navigation.

---

[7]For a statement of his views, see Arvid Pardo, "Who Will Control the Seabed?" *Foreign Affairs* 47, no. 1 (October 1968): 123–37.

By 1970, it was clear to all that the old maritime legal order had collapsed. Support for the convening of the Third UN Conference on the Law of the Sea seemed logical and timely. Such a meeting was needed to resolve the unfinished business of the First and Second UN Conferences: namely, the limit of the territorial sea, the limit of the fishing zone, and the replacement of the exploitability criterion by a more precise continental-shelf definition. It was necessary to replace the chaos created by the unilateral and conflicting claims of coastal states. The great maritime powers, especially the two super-powers, felt the need for a new internationally agreed regime for the passage of ships and aircraft through straits. The newly independent countries of the Third World wanted a new conference in which they could participate. Such a conference would be a model for the New International Economic Order in which they were greatly interested. In addition, the world community would have to agree on rules, as well as institutions, for the exploitation of the mineral resources in the seabed and ocean floor beyond the limits of national jurisdiction. Finally, there was the pollution issue. The historic 1972 Stock-holm Conference on the Human Environment and a series of accidents involv-ing oil tankers had raised the world's consciousness regarding the threat to the marine environment. There was a consequent desire to adopt new rules to protect and preserve it.

The agenda of the Third UN Conference on the Law of the Sea (UNCLOS III)—which gathered initially in New York and then moved to Caracas, alternated between Geneva and New York, and concluded at Montego Bay in Jamaica—consisted of some twenty-five subjects and issues. Although it is impossible for me to discuss all of these questions, I wish to elaborate on a number of especially significant examples and to explain what were the competing interests and how those competing interests were reconciled.

First of all, the maximum breadth of the territorial sea and the regime of passage through straits used for international navigation were related sub-jects. At the 1930 Hague Conference, as well as at the 1958 and 1960 conferences, the international community was unable to agree on the maxi-mum breadth of the territorial sea. By the time UNCLOS III convened in December 1973, only a minority of states, 27 out of 111 coastal states, claimed a three-mile territorial sea. Nearly a majority, 52 out of these 111 states, claimed a territorial sea of twelve miles. The great powers could not accept twelve miles as the maximum permissible breadth of the territorial sea, how-ever, unless it was also agreed that there would be a special regime for passage through and over straits used in international navigation. This was because there are 116 straits in the world whose breadths are between six and twenty-four miles. With the extension of the territorial sea from three to twelve miles, the waters in these straits would become territorial waters, and the high-seas corridor would be lost.

The United States and the Soviet Union are, of course, global powers with allies and interests in areas far from their own shores. They require the use of the seas and the air space above them for the purpose of projecting their conventional military power. Freedom of navigation for their navies and of overflight for their military aircraft is a strategic imperative. The straits constitute choke points in the world's communications system, and the question of passage through them is critical. Each superpower also keeps part of its stockpile of ballistic missiles in submarines at sea. It is considered important by each superpower for its adversary not to know the precise location of its nuclear-armed submarines because this works as a deterrent against either of them launching a first strike against the other. As long as each superpower retains a second-strike capability, safe at sea, this acts as a deterrent against the temptation of launching a sneak attack. Because secrecy and mobility of their respective submarine fleets are critical, the two superpowers have demanded free and submerged passage for their submarines through straits.

The negotiators of the UN Convention sought to reconcile the competing interests of coastal states and of the great maritime powers. The outcome, embodied in the 1982 convention, recognizes twelve miles as the maximum permissible breadth of the territorial sea (Article 3) and, at the same time, prescribes a special regime, called "transit passage," for ships and aircraft through and over straits used for international navigation (Articles 37 to 44).[8] The text uses the words "freedom of navigation and overflight" to describe the nature of transit passage. Significantly, these are words normally used in connection with the high seas, where the great maritime powers have always enjoyed freedom of movement.

A second issue is fisheries. There were at least four competing interests that the conference had to reconcile. First, there was mankind's general interest in the conservation as well as the optimum use of fish resources, for many countries and peoples the cheapest source of animal protein. The second interest was that of the coastal states, some seventy-six in all. In many countries, there are numerous communities that depend solely or mainly on fishing for their livelihood. Many of the coastal states, which for certain purposes operated as a group at UNCLOS III, complained that the traditional law was unfair to them. The developing coastal countries felt unable to compete with the technologically more advanced countries in catching the fish stocks lying off their own coasts. Because, under traditional law, fish stocks beyond the narrow belt of the territorial sea constitute a common property, many of the world's fish stocks have become dangerously depleted owing to overfishing. The regional fisheries commissions have not been given sufficient powers to enforce conservation measures. For these reasons, the coastal states claimed the right to establish "exclusive economic zones" (EEZs) of up to 200 miles. Within these they would have sovereign rights to the resources. The third interest the conference had to take into account was that of the landlocked and geographically disadvantaged states, so called. These,

---

[8]For the text of the articles of the 1982 convention, see United Nations, *The Law of the Sea: Official Text of the United Nations Convention on the Law of the Sea with Annexes and Index* (New York: United Nations, 1983).

numbering fifty-five altogether, would either have nothing to gain or would have something to lose if these EEZs were established by coastal states. Then there was a fourth interest: that of the distant-water fishing nations. These countries had large sums of money invested in their fishing industries and, in some cases, had been fishing in certain fishing grounds for a considerable length of time.

The provisions of the 1982 Convention dealing with the EEZ represent an attempt to reconcile these competing interests. Every coastal state is entitled to establish such a zone of up to 200 miles (Articles 55 and 57), within which it has sovereign rights to the living resources (Article 56). The coastal state is, however, under obligation to the international community to undertake conservation measures in order to ensure that these resources are not over-exploited. At the same time, the coastal state is obliged to fix the total allowable catch of different species in order to ensure the optimum use of the resources (Article 61). If the state is unable to harvest the entire allowable catch, it is under an obligation to allocate the surplus to third states (Article 62). The first priority will go to landlocked and geographically disadvantaged states, the second priority to developing countries, and the third priority to other countries, including the traditional fishing nations (Articles 62, 69, 70). The arrangement is an intricately balanced one, with which most states are satisfied.

A third issue concerns the mineral resources of the seabed and ocean floor. The main form of these resources is polymetallic nodules, also known as manganese nodules. In 1967 Dr. Pardo called the world's attention to the existence of these resources and proposed that the seabed and ocean floor outside the then prevailing limits of national jurisdiction, as well as the resources themselves, be declared a common heritage of mankind. In 1970, the UN General Assembly adopted a declaration of principles governing the seabed and ocean floor, and subsoil thereof, by a vote of 108 to 0, with 14 abstentions. (The United States voted for the declaration.) Although the Soviet bloc abstained in the vote, its members subsequently stated their support for the declaration. That declaration says, inter alia, that the sea-floor area shall not be subject to appropriation by states, or by other entities, and that no state shall claim or exercise sovereign rights over any part thereof. It also declares that no state, or other entity, shall have rights with respect to the area or its resources incompatible with the international regime to be established. All activities regarding the exploration and exploitation of the resources of the area shall be governed by that international regime.[9]

In the negotiations on this question, the conference had to reconcile the following competing interests. There was the interest of the international community as a whole in promoting the development of the seabed's resources.

---

[9]United Nations, General Assembly, Declaration of Principles Governing the Sea-Bed and the Ocean Floor, and the Subsoil Thereof, beyond the Limits of National Jurisdiction, Resolution 2749, December 17, 1970, in Lay et al., *New Directions*, 2:740–41.

There were also more special interests: those of potential consumers of the metals that could be extracted from the mid-ocean polymetallic nodules; those of the countries that had invested funds, or were planning to invest funds, in mining the nodules; those of the developing countries that, as co-owners of the resource, wished to benefit not only as consumers but also as participants in its exploitation; and, finally, those of the countries that produced in their land territories the same metals that are contained in the polymetallic nodules. It should be mentioned that, owing to the high cost of the necessary technology as well as the fact of existing surpluses, the future profitability of seabed mining was highly uncertain.

The provisions of Part XI of the convention, Annex III, and Resolution II, taken together, contain compromises that seek to accommodate these prospectively competing interests. In view of the continuing controversy over the seabed settlement, these provisions merit close consideration. Under Resolution II, the consortia and states that have already invested research-and-development funds in the exploration of specific mine sites have been recognized as "pioneer investors." If the state to which a consortium belongs signs and ratifies the Law of the Sea Convention, that consortium may be formally registered as a pioneer investor. In the case of a consortium that is unincorporated and that consists of partners from a number of different countries, the consortium may be registered as a pioneer investor if only one of those countries accepts the convention. Upon being registered as a pioneer investor, the consortium acquires the exclusive right to explore a specific mine site. When the convention comes into force, following completion of the ratification process, the registered pioneer investor gains an automatic right to contract actually to mine that specific mine site, so long as it complies with the requirements of the convention and so long as its sponsoring state is a party to the convention. Thus, the troublesome question about guaranteed access to the resources of the deep seabed has been largely resolved by Resolution II.

In order to give land-based producers some protection against the possible adverse economic consequences of seabed exploitation, the convention contains a formula for limiting the amounts of metals which can be produced from the seabed for a period of twenty-five years (Article 151). Resolution II states that the pioneer investors shall have priority in the allocation of the production authorization calculated under the formula. According to the experts, the production limitation in the convention poses more of an ideological than a pragmatic problem for the seabed miners. This is because, given the economic prospects of the mining industry in the foreseeable future and the limited number of actors that are likely to enter the industry, any reasonable projection will give us a number of mine sites adequate to accommodate all those who are likely to want to enter this arena.

Consistent with the concept of the common heritage of mankind, a seabed miner will have to pay to the International Seabed Authority either a royalty payment, or a combination of a royalty payment and a share of his profits (Annex III, Article 13). The seabed miner may choose either one of the two schemes. If he chooses the latter, he will find a tax structure that is more progressive than any to be found in land-based mining contracts. The tax that a seabed miner pays to the International Seabed Authority will vary, depending upon the profitability of his project, calculated annually, as well as over the life span of the project. The tax system uses the internal rate of return as the measurement of the project's profitability.

Under the terms of the convention, a seabed miner may be required by the International Seabed Authority to sell his technology to the authority (Annex III, Article 5). This transfer-of-technology provision has caused great concern to industrialized countries. It should be borne in mind, however, that this obligation cannot be invoked by the authority unless the same or equivalent technology is not available in the open market. An internal study carried out by the U.S. Department of Commerce shows that, for every component of seabed mining technology, there are at least four sellers on the market. If this is true, then the precondition cannot be met, and the objectionable obligation can never be invoked. Moreover, it should be noted that the convention contains elaborate provision for the resolution of disputes over its terms.

These examples, the territorial sea and straits questions, the fisheries issue and creation of the EEZ, and the problem of access to the resources of the seabed and ocean floors, all illustrate how the Law of the Sea conference managed to reach agreement. The procedures followed by UNCLOS III and its negotiating process also contain many interesting, even unique, features. The conference committed itself from the very start to work by the procedure, pioneered over the years in committee meetings at the United Nations, of "consensus." Progress was made by this method, which puts a premium on skillful and scrupulously fair chairmanship, because delegates could tacitly consent by waiving their right of disagreement. Typically, a chairman would declare, "If there are no objections, the proposal is adopted." An appendix to the Rules of Procedure states, "The Conference should make every effort to reach agreement on substantive matters by way of consensus and there should be no voting on such matters until all efforts at consensus have been exhausted."[10] The conference placed such an emphasis on consensus for two major reasons: it wanted to adopt a convention that would enjoy the widest possible support in the international community, and the consensus procedure was intended to protect the interest and views of minorities at the conference.

The commitment of the conference to consensus was strongly buttressed by its formal Rules of Procedure. The rules made it very difficult to vote on a proposal or an amendment; they also make it difficult for such a proposal or amendment to be adopted by a vote. For example, when a matter of substance came up for voting for the first time, either the president or fifteen delegations could request a deferment for a period not exceeding ten days (Rule 37,2a). During this period, the president was obliged to make every

---

[10]United Nations, *Law of the Sea*, p. 165.

effort to facilitate the achievement of general agreement (Rule 37,2c). At the end of the period, the president was to inform the conference of the results of his efforts. A vote on a proposal could be taken only after the conference had determined that all efforts at reaching agreement were exhausted (Rule 37,2d). During the first eight years of UNCLOS III not a single vote was taken, either by roll call or by ballot, on any of the substantive issues it had been initially called to resolve.

At the last session of the conference, some thirty amendments were submitted for attachment to the Draft Convention. I ordered a cooling-off period of ten days. During this time, I found that there was general support for only four of the amendments. These were adopted by the conference without a vote. I managed to persuade the proposers of all but three of the remaining amendments to withdraw. All three amendments were put to the vote and rejected by the conference. One of them obtained the required two-thirds majority of those present and voting but failed to satisfy the second requirement of a majority of the delegations attending the conference.

There were two other important procedural understandings that advanced the work of the conference. The conference agreed to work on the "package deal" principle. This meant that the conference would adopt one comprehensive convention instead of several conventions, as happened at the 1958 conference. The instrument of this integrating, balancing process was the Single Negotiating Text, which, after going through a number of transformations, became the formal Convention on the Law of the Sea. The other understanding that reinforced the building of consensus was the rule that the convention would permit no reservations (Article 309).

Another interesting and important feature of the conference was the emergence of new interest groups. The traditional ones, such as regional groups, played a very minor role in the work of the Law of the Sea conference. Instead, groups were formed by countries that had kindred interests, such as coastal states, landlocked and geographically disadvantaged states, straits states, archipelagic states, broad-continental-shelfed states (the "margineers"), and many others. One particularly important group, the Group of Five (irreverently dubbed the "Gang of Five" by a Canadian representative), was composed of the industrialized states of Great Britain, France, Japan, the United States, and the Soviet Union.

The group system played both a positive and a negative role at the conference. On the positive side, it enabled countries to join forces with other countries with which they shared a common interest. In this way, a country could acquire a bargaining leverage that it would not have had if it had operated alone. It proved to be impossible to conduct serious negotiations at UNCLOS III until these special-interest groups were formed. It was only after their formation that the competing groups were able to formulate their positions in concrete texts and to appoint representatives to engage in negotiations. On the negative side, it must be admitted that once a group had adopted a common position, it was often difficult for the group to modify its position. This often meant that the negotiators were given a mandate and had little or no flexibility.

Yet another feature of our negotiating process was the fact that there were two parallel structures of negotiations at the conference. On the one hand, there were the officially established committees and negotiating groups. Because these were generally forums of the whole, they were too large to function effectively for negotiations. The need for small but representative negotiating bodies was filled by the establishment of informal and unofficial negotiating groups. Most of these groups were established on the initiative of individuals; for example, the Evensen Group of juridical experts was set up at the personal initiative of Jens Evensen, leader of the Norwegian delegation. The Evensen Group did extremely valuable work on the EEZ. The Castañeda Group, convened by the leader of the Mexican delegation, Jorge Castañeda, succeeded in resolving the controversial question of the legal status of the economic zone and its related issues. There was also a private group on dispute settlement, convened on the initiative of Professor Louis B. Sohn of the United States. Sometimes, an unofficial negotiating group was even formed on the initiative of two competing ones. This happened when the group of coastal states and the group of landlocked and geographically disadvantaged states agreed to establish a negotiating body comprising ten representatives from each group and approached Ambassador Satya Nandan of Fiji to be its chairman. Personal leadership at UNCLOS III did not always coincide with the size of the country of the individual who offered it, or was asked to give it. Sometimes it did, however, as in the noteworthy case of Elliot L. Richardson, the effective chairman of the U.S. delegation.

Toward the later stages of the conference, the other presiding officers and I gradually miniaturized the size of the negotiating groups. It was absolutely essential to transform a large, unwieldy conference of approximately 140 delegations into small, representative, and efficient negotiating groups. Although the efforts to miniaturize the official negotiating forums inevitably encountered resistance, they were essential and ultimately successful.

Another lesson I have learned is that a conference needs the full range of formal, informal, and even privately convened negotiating groups. As a general rule, the more informal the nature of the group, the easier it is to resolve a problem. However, secrecy must be scrupulously avoided. In addition, if the results of a negotiating group are to have any chance of winning the support of the conference, then the group must include all those who have a real interest at stake, as well as the acknowledged conference leaders.

What is the significance of the new Convention on the Law of the Sea? I would draw attention to the fact that it is the first comprehensive convention governing all aspects of the uses and resources of the world's oceans. Unlike the four Geneva conventions of 1958, the 1982 convention represents an attempt to respect the interrelationships between different aspects of the law of the sea. We also tried very hard to live up to Dr. Pardo's exhortation to view ocean space as an ecological whole.

The new Convention on the Law of the Sea is also important because it will contribute to the promotion of international peace, by replacing a plethora of conflicting claims by coastal states with universally agreed limits for the territorial sea, the contiguous zone, the exclusive economic zone, and the continental shelf. The convention represents a victory for the rule of law. It is the first major multilateral treaty which contains mandatory provisions for the settlement of disputes. Moreover, the convention affirms the possibility for countries of North and South, and East and West, to cooperate for their mutual benefit. Finally, the successful outcome of UNCLOS III vindicates the United Nations as an institution that, given the necessary exercise of political will by its member states, can be used to conduct serious negotiations on matters of vital importance to the world.

FOR FURTHER READING

On the various aspects of the Third UN Conference and the Law of the Sea Convention, see Tommy T. B. Koh, "The Third United Nations Conference on the Law of the Sea: What Was Accomplished?" *Law and Contemporary Problems* 46, no. 2 (Spring 1983): 5–9, as well as other articles in this issue. See also James K. Sebenius, *Negotiating the Law of the Sea* (Cambridge, MA: Harvard University Press, 1984); Barry Buzan, "Negotiating by Consensus: Developments in Technique at the Third United Nations Conference on the Law of the Sea," *American Journal of International Law* 75, no. 2 (1981): 324–48; Roderick C. Ogley, *Internationalizing the Seabed* (Brookfield, VT: Gower, 1984); and David A. Ross and John A. Knauss, "How the Law of the Sea Treaty Will Affect U.S. Marine Science," *Science* 217, no. 4564 (September 10, 1982): 1003–08. A fascinating reportorial account of the negotiations and personalities at the conference appeared in *The New Yorker*, August 1 and August 8, 1983, under the title, "The Law of the Sea."

For more general treatments of law of the sea problems, see Juraj Andrassy, *International Law and the Resources of the Sea* (New York: Columbia University Press, 1970); Elisabeth Mann Borgese, ed., *Pacem in Maribus* (New York: Dodd, Mead and Company, 1972) and her concise article, "The Law of the Sea," *Scientific American* 248, no. 3 (March 1983): 42–49; Ross D. Eckert, *The Enclosure of Ocean Resources: Economics and the Law of the Sea* (Stanford, CA: Hoover Institution Press, 1979); Judith T. Kildow, ed., *Deepsea Mining* (Cambridge, MA: MIT Press, 1979); D. P. O'Connell, *The International Law of the Sea* (Oxford: Clarendon Press, 1982); R. R. Churchill and A. V. Lowe, *The Law of the Sea* (Manchester: Manchester University Press, 1983); Louis B. Sohn and Kristen Gustafson, *The Law of the Sea in a Nutshell* (St. Paul, MN: West Publishing Company, 1984); Bradley Larschan and Bonnie C. Brennan, "The Common Heritage of Mankind Principle in International Law," *Columbia Journal of Transnational Law* 21, no. 305 (1983): 305–37; Jacques G. Richardson, ed., *Managing the Oceans: Resources, Research, Law* (Mt. Airy, MD: Lomond Publications, 1985); Ken Booth, *Law, Force and Diplomacy at Sea* (Winchester, MA: Allen and Unwin, 1985).

On the evolution of U.S. policy, see Ann Hollick, *U.S. Foreign Policy and the Law of the Sea* (Princeton, NJ: Princeton University Press, 1981); Bernard H. Oxman, David D. Caron, and Charles L. O. Buderi, eds., *Law of the Sea: U.S. Policy Dilemma* (San Francisco: Institute for Contemporary Studies, 1983); Finn Laursen, *Superpower at Sea: U.S. Ocean Policy* (New York: Praeger, 1983); Jon M. Van Dyke, ed., *Consensus and Confrontation: The United States and the Law of the Sea Convention* (Honolulu: Law of the Sea Institute, University of Hawaii, 1985); and David L. Larson, "The Reagan Rejection of the U.N. Convention," *Ocean Development and International Law: The Journal of Marine Affairs* 14, no. 4 (1985): 337–61.

The basic documentary record of the recent developments in the international law of the sea is contained in S. Houston Lay et al., eds., *New Directions in the Law of the Sea, Documents*, a multivolume collection, and United Nations, *The Law of the Sea: Official Text of the United Nations Convention on the Law of the Sea with Annexes and Index*, both cited in the footnotes.

International Communications and World Order

LEONARD H. MARKS

In most areas of international concern, the problem of creating a worldwide order has arisen only in recent decades, or is only now becoming fully apparent. The field of communications is an exception. Although in some respects the most futuristic of all organized international activities, revolutionized almost daily by developments in electronics and space exploration, it is also the most historical. Indeed, it is generally accepted by scholars that the oldest true intergovernmental, international organization is the International Telecommunication Union (ITU), whose forerunner, the International Telegraph Union, was founded in Paris in 1865.[1]

More than a hundred years ago, therefore, the nations of the world came to the realization that there had to be order or there would be no systemic communication among them. To some extent, this realization resulted from developments in technology. When the telegraph was invented, it became apparent that, if one were to transmit a message, there had to be someone at the other end to receive it. In order to have communication, there had to be an arrangement whereby one party would be transmitting and the other party would be receiving. There had to be cooperation; there could be no unilateral communication. People entering this field had to understand that, unless there

---

[1]The International Telecommunication Union, a specialized agency of the United Nations, was created in 1932 by the merger of the International Telegraph Union and the signatories of the 1932 International Radiotelegraph Convention. The definitive history of the formation of the ITU is George A. Codding, Jr., *The International Telecommunication Union: An Experiment in International Cooperation* (Leiden: E. J. Brill, 1952). See also George A. Codding, Jr., and Anthony M. Rutkowski, *The International Telecommunication Union in a Changing World* (Dedham, MA: Artech House, 1982), and David M. Lieve, *International Telecommunications and International Law: The Regulation of the Radio Spectrum* (Leiden: A. W. Sijthoff, 1970).

were rules of the road, there would be chaos. Accordingly, the nations with the use of the telegraph decided to meet, form a union, and adopt rules and regulations.

It should be stressed at the outset that the ITU, like its antecedent organization, is based upon the principle of the sovereignty of each country. There is no judge who will say a member country has violated the law; since there are no penalties, no country can be fined for failure to observe the regulations. Frequently, this situation has caused difficulty. When two countries desire to use the same communications facility, and neither is willing to yield to the other, an impasse results. Such negotiating deadlocks have often occurred in the history of the ITU. Nonetheless, we do have order with regard to telegraph, telephone, radio, and satellite communication, but the tradition of cooperation that we have developed is based on voluntarism, rather than on imposed regulation or enforced adjudication.

In explaining the international order that has evolved in the communications field, I would draw attention to three stages of historical development, related to the technical characteristics of the media of communication. The story progresses from the time when the telegraph was introduced, through the advent of the radio, to the era of the communications satellite. Despite the radical changes in communications technology in this historical sequence of more than a century, the basic principles of international organization, I would emphasize, have remained very much the same.

Let us first consider the international cooperation required by the telegraph and telephone, for conceptually that is the easiest to grasp. Certain requirements for the transmission of telegraph and telephone messages arise from the very nature of these forms of point-to-point communication. These requirements include frequency and volume, the amount of power used, the transmission time needed, and, in close correspondence, the exchange of revenues. Messages are sent either via cable, such as by the cables buried under the Atlantic and Pacific oceans, or by microwave beamed through the air. For the privilege of using these facilities, people must be compensated; there has to be an arrangement whereby money is exchanged. That exchange has, in fact, been worked out through the deliberations of ITU economic and technical committees.[2]

Radio broadcasting, the second phase in the history of modern international communications, is an entirely different concept. Country A decides to send a message to country B. No money is exchanged. No point at the other end exists at which cooperation is necessary in order for the message to be received, other than that of the listener. The listener, in his home or office, has the right to turn off the switch and not receive the communication, or he can hear a part of it or listen to all of it. Thus, broadcasting is an entirely

---

[2]The principal organ of the ITU for this purpose, with respect to telegraph and telephone communication, is the International Telegraph and Telephone Consultative Committee (CCITT).

different notion from sending a telegram or making a telephone call. Broadcasting involves the wide dissemination of messages, for the receipt of which there is no direct compensation.

When radio broadcasting was introduced, it was a means of communicating domestically. People living within the borders of a country were better enabled thereby to understand what their parliaments, and also business entities, wanted them to know. As countries' geographical areas of concern expanded, radio broadcasting became an instrument of regional and, finally, global international communication. Today, radio communication within and across national borders is commonplace. To a greater or lesser degree, the shortwave spectrum, high-frequency (HF) broadcasting, is used virtually by every country of the world.[3]

The countries that dominate this field are, first of all, the Soviet Union, which uses its shortwave facilities for domestic purposes (to extend to its enormous land boundaries), for regional purposes (to communicate with Eastern Europe, within its political orbit), and for broader international purposes (to inform and influence populations around the globe). The United States is the second largest user, with the Voice of America, Radio Free Europe, and Radio Liberty all involved in broadcasting internationally. (The HF band is not used by the U.S. government for domestic programs.) Then there are the BBC, Deutsche Welle, and Radio Cairo, as well as the Vatican, which broadcasts its views, religious and otherwise, throughout the world. Ten large users probably take up more than three-fourths of the shortwave spectrum. The others, more than a hundred countries, use a very small proportion of the HF band.

Given the fact that the frequencies in the shortwave band are limited, and that these frequencies are the best ones for communicating over long distances, competition inevitably develops between countries for their use. Brazil, a vast country with many remote areas that are only thinly settled, provides a good example of this problem. Brazil uses the same frequencies for domestic broadcasting, to explain its own policies, as the United States uses, to tell the people of Latin America about U.S. policy. How, then, is a collision averted? How does the Voice of America get to communicate in the 6-megahertz band while Brazil uses 11 megahertz? The solution is reached by cooperation. Keeping in mind that whatever is done must be done on a voluntary basis, the engineers of the respective countries convene at bilateral, regional, and world meetings and agree to use certain frequencies during certain times of the day, certain weeks of the year, and certain sunspot cycles. Functional necessity is the most important reason for these adjustments.

The smaller countries, until recent years, have had neither the broadcasting facilities nor the engineering capabilities to compete for the most

---

[3]HF is the range of frequencies from 3 to 30 megahertz (MHz). The desirability of these frequencies arises from the fact that they can have global reach. Unlike medium frequencies (from .3 to 3 MHz), used for AM broadcasts, they are refracted downwards by charged layers in the ionosphere, bouncing between earth and sky all around the planet.

desirable frequencies. In 1979 an ITU World Administrative Radio Conference (WARC) was held in Geneva to deal with the complaints of smaller and less developed countries that they were served too small a part of the spectrum pie. Some of these countries asked for a systematic redistribution of frequencies; this request became a part of a broader program calling for a New World Communications and Information Order. A planning conference to consider these proposals for a redistribution of the wealth of the high-frequency portion of the spectrum was ordered to be held in 1984.

The U.S. delegation, of which I was asked to serve as chairman, approached the 1984 High-Frequency WARC with grave misgivings. The international atmosphere was highly charged. The Soviet Union, after altercations over its invasion of Afghanistan and imposition of martial law in Poland, recently had ended a period of détente in the airwaves, as it had in East-West diplomatic relations, and had resumed the jamming of American, British, West German, and other foreign radio transmissions. These broadcasts, the USSR believed, were incompatible with the welfare of its citizens and also with the best interests of its East European neighbors. Meanwhile, the Third World countries were voicing their requests for more and better frequencies, a demand that had grown insistent since a 1982 plenipotentiary ITU conference in Nairobi.

When the conference opened in Geneva at the beginning of 1984, certain problems of a political nature were uppermost in the minds of everyone present. First, the matter of credentials arose. At an earlier meeting of the ITU in 1982, there had been an attack on the credentials of certain countries, notably Israel, despite the fact that the organization was a technical body which had traditionally avoided entanglements in politics. Would we face that kind of problem during this conference?

No such confrontation took place at the 1984 WARC. Indeed, no challenge was made to any of the credentials. All of the participating countries, all the countries interested in order, should be proud of that fact. Why did nothing happen? The answer, I think, is that the attacks made in other international forums had illustrated clearly that such attacks would destroy the foundation of practical activity in the communications field. Everyone recognized that there had to be universality if there was going to be a functioning system of international communications. Wiser heads prevailed, and the credentials of every country were accepted.

The second concern of the participants was: Would there be an East-West confrontation? Would the USSR and the East European countries complain about the nature of the radio programs which the West was directing at them? Would the West argue that the jamming of those programs violated international law? As Article 19 of the Universal Declaration of Human Rights provides: "Everyone has the right to freedom of opinion and expression; this right includes freedom to hold opinions without interference and to seek, receive and impart information and ideas through any media and regardless of frontiers."[4] This principle is also stated in Basket III of the Helsinki Agreement and in other international documents.[5] It has been accepted throughout the world; and yet, contrary to the provisions of Article 19, many nations today do not want to have their citizens exposed to messages from outside sources.[6]

How did the Soviet government respond to the complaints about jamming? It did not deny that the practice exists, but it took refuge in a 1936 treaty adopted by League of Nations members to which it had adhered in October 1982, forty-six years after its enactment. This treaty—the International Convention Concerning the Use of Broadcasting in the Cause of Peace— was designed to curb Nazi propaganda directed by the Hitler regime at neighboring countries. It outlawed radio broadcasts which transmitted propaganda aimed at creating racial hatred or inciting people to violence and war. Many European nations subscribed.[7]

The Soviet argument presented a basic confrontation between Article 19 of the UN Declaration of Human Rights, asserted by the West, and the provision of the 1936 League of Nations treaty, asserted by the Soviet Union as justification for its jamming. This issue had the potential for preventing any agreement at the 1984 WARC in Geneva. Contrary to expectation, no controversy arose over the issue. Why? The explanation is relatively simple. Behind the scenes, the leaders of delegations from East and West met and decided that these political questions were not relevant to a determination of the technical issues at stake at the Geneva conference. Moreover, these political differences had been debated in Madrid from 1980 to 1983 as part of the Helsinki process. They had been discussed and debated at the UN General Assembly and, to some extent, at UNESCO. Why then, it was reasonably asked, should these same political questions become part of the agenda of a technical forum such as the WARC meeting of the ITU? The principal countries of the world decided against it and determined that the ITU should remain a technical body discussing frequency allocation and problems related to the orderly use of the spectrum. Of course, the technical fact of jamming—

---

[4]Universal Declaration of Human Rights, signed December 10, 1948, G.A. Res. 217 A (III), U.N. Doc. A/810, at 71 (1948), in Richard B. Lillich, *International Human Rights Instruments: A Compilation of Treaties, Agreements and Declarations of Especial Interest to the United States* (New York: William S. Hein, 1985), pp. 440.1–440.7.

[5]See the Conference on Security and Cooperation Final Act, signed at Helsinki on August 1, 1975, in U.S., Department of State *Bulletin* 73 (September 1, 1975): 323–50, especially pp. 325, 341–42.

[6]Interference with communication is not limited to the Soviet and East European governments' jamming of programs coming from the United States, Great Britain, West Germany, and the Vatican. The problem also exists, for example, between Tibet and India, Libya and Tunisia, and Surinam and the Netherlands.

[7]The text of the International Convention Concerning the Use of Broadcasting in the Cause of Peace, signed at Geneva on September 23, 1936, may be found in United Kingdom, *Treaty Series*, no. 29 (1938).

intentional interference—had an important bearing on the WARC meeting, and it was discussed thoroughly. A resolution was adopted condemning the practice as a violation of ITU regulations and providing for practical steps to assess its impact on the allocation of frequencies. The rhetoric of the Helsinki Conference, however, was avoided.

What else was agreed upon at Geneva? In light of the congestion that had developed in HF communication and the reality that there never would be enough frequencies to accommodate everyone, the conference decided that the status quo could no longer be maintained. The large "have" countries which had dominated the use of this band of frequencies since before the Second World War could no longer do so and would be required to make adjustments. The needs of the small countries—the so-called Third World—lacking established access had grown, and their needs had to be recognized.

I should like to stress an important fact about these countries. One frequently hears about a "Third World position." To be sure, at a plenipotentiary conference of the ITU in 1973 at Malaga-Torremolinos, a group of seventy-seven nonaligned and developing countries had formed a voting bloc. In the field of international communications, however, there is no one Third World position. While Third World viewpoints range from the extreme right to the extreme left, from the most conservative to the most radical, from the most corporatist to the most statist, one preoccupation does predominate: the small countries, the "have-not" countries, all want to improve their communications facilities. They want more transmitters; they want better-trained people; they want the opportunity to express themselves clearly, without technical restriction.

The key problem was the use of frequencies. How was it to be decided who was to get which frequency, how much power could be used, and how high the antennas could be? The engineers from 112 participating countries met and for five weeks discussed these questions. They came up with the idea that modern technology offered the opportunity for a solution. The processes of the computer, they thought, might extend the range of what could be comprehended by the human mind, working in a manual way. A collaborative effort was agreed upon whereby during the next two years, in preparation for a second, follow-up WARC session on high frequencies in 1986, an appropriate software program would be devised. All of the desires and requirements of the participating countries would be fed into the computer, and out of it would come, it was hoped, a better, more rational distribution of facilities, more accommodating for more parties at more times. This work will be conducted under the ITU's International Frequency Registration Board, which has invited all ITU members—developing countries and developed countries alike—to contribute. It will be a fair process.

Let us suppose that the program does not work. If it does not, the alternative may be to take frequencies adjacent to those now being used and thereby to "expand" the bands. How is this possible, if somebody is already transmitting in those portions of the spectrum? The tentative current thinking is that fixed services—the telephone companies throughout the world—would in those circumstances have to give up a portion of the frequencies they use in order to accommodate broadcasting use. The fixed services then would have to go elsewhere. This change would entail great expense and would cause a major dislocation, particularly for the smaller countries using these frequencies for domestic purposes. This result is, in part, a consequence of their demand for more shortwave broadcasting, however. One equity thus has to be balanced against another.

The Geneva delegations, by consensus, arrived at a judgment that modern technology can permit a better distribution of frequencies than now exists, and they authorized a scientific effort, to be conducted under ITU supervision, to devise a program. If the scheme does not work, it will be necessary to come back and try something else. The controlling concept will be, however, that order should prevail. No party has said to the others: "I do not like what you are doing; I am going to do what I want to do; I am going to broadcast on such frequencies as I think are desirable." Were the participants to take such an attitude, a communications Tower of Babel would ensue. That has not happened and, on the basis of the past history of the ITU, I do not think it is likely to occur in the future. In the field of international communications at least, everyone has agreed that there must be cooperation. We have to recognize our neighbors' desires, respect their wishes, and make the best of a situation in which everybody gets something, but not all that is desired.

Let me now move to the third phase in the technological history and policy evolution of the communications field: international communication via space satellites. This phase has combined some of the features of the first two eras, both of point-to-point transmission and of broadcasting, but it also exhibits unique characteristics. These include the exceptionally wide span of satellite-based systems—communications satellites are in sight of 42.4 percent of the earth's surface—and also to the peculiarly restrictive nature of the geostationary orbit. This orbit is 22,300 miles in altitude above the line of the equator, where the combined effect of the satellite's momentum and the earth's gravitational pull keep the craft in the desired circular path.

In April 1965 the United States launched Early Bird, the world's first commercial communications satellite, and with it a new era of immediate, and potentially more intimate, global relationships. I had the privilege of being an incorporator of the Communications Satellite Corporation (COM-SAT), conceived under the Communications Satellite Act of 1962.[8] President John F. Kennedy had the vision to see that the new era of space would bring great progress to mankind, and he appointed to the board public and private members who could help the country enter it. When we launched Early Bird in 1965, the United States had a virtual monopoly on all of the required technology. We knew how to make the satellites; we had the launching

---

[8]Background information may be found in Jonathan F. Galloway, *The Politics and Technology of Satellite Communications* (Lexington, MA: Lexington Books, D. C. Heath, 1972).

facilities. The Soviet Union had launched *Sputnik* almost a decade earlier, and both countries had orbited manned spacecraft, but in the communications area we had the edge. COMSAT had a mandate to internationalize the American effort. The original 1962 act provided for a system which was to be established "in cooperation and conjunction with other countries" and to be "part of an improved global communications network." It would be "responsive to public needs and national objectives serving the communications needs of the United States and other countries," and it would "contribute to world peace and understanding."[9]

The COMSAT board, in meeting this responsibility, had a choice. It could put up the satellites and, in effect, say to the rest of the world: "If you want to use them, here are the prices and here are the terms." Or it could turn to the rest of the world and say: "We want you as actual partners, because it takes two to communicate; it takes cooperation." We decided on the latter course. We invited the principal West European countries to join with us in an entity to be called the International Telecommunications Satellite Consortium (INTELSAT). The Europeans initially were skeptical. They thought this was a hare-brained American invention, but they agreed to go along with it, if the United States would put up the money. So we did, while they put in token amounts. Today, INTELSAT has 110 members from all regions of the world, both in developed and less-developed areas. In my judgment, the venture has been singularly successful. It is not beset with political quarrels, and it has been extraordinarily successful as a business enterprise. Every participating country has access to a global array of satellites. The post, telegraph, and telephone administrations of the member countries make enormous profits. Most importantly, the public receives the benefit of the service: the opportunity for instantaneous telegraph, telephone, radio, and television service worldwide. This has occurred only because there is cooperation.

Today, the ITU faces what could be a crisis. The emergent issue before its members is the allocation of space services and frequency bands involving the use of satellites in geostationary orbit.[10] Some countries, particularly those located on the equator and hence situated directly below the geostationary orbit, have taken a proprietary, exclusive view of it. They assert: "We own everything from the ground to infinity, and you must not put a satellite in our sector of sky." Some have further insisted: "We are entitled to three satellites, whether we need them at present or not; we want certain frequencies for our satellites; and we want advance guarantees that these frequencies will be available whenever we wish to use them." If that position—referred to as

---

[9]U.S., Congress, Senate, Committee on Commerce, Science, and Transportation, *Long-range Goals in International Telecommunications and Information: An Outline for United States Policy*, 98th Cong., 1st sess., March 11, 1983, p. 113.

[10]This issue is being addressed by a two-part ITU administrative conference called the "Space WARC." The first session, held in 1985, addressed the problem of identifying which satellite services and frequency bands should be subject to "planning." The second session, to be held in 1988, will attempt actually to devise and implement these planning methods.

a priori assignment, or preassignment—should come to prevail, then all of the order, all of the cooperation, all of the success that I have described would immediately crumble. The present system has evolved on a first-come, first-served basis, a case-by-case approach reflecting actual experience and demand. It relies on continuous coordination among interested parties. This method, sometimes called the *a posteriori* approach, is not necessarily rigid. It can allow for a wider, fairer, and more equitable distribution in response to subsequent actual changes in demand. It also can accommodate future advances in technology.

A successful system of allocation has to be flexible. One cannot have a truly efficient *a priori* distribution. If the frequencies are fixed, then in effect the opportunity for use is narrowed. The answer to maximum utilization, therefore, is flexibility. It is conceivable that, through further scientific progress, orbital positions, frequencies, and satellites can be used more intensively and carry larger payloads than hitherto expected. Nonetheless, it is clear that not every country of the world will be able to have its own geostationary parking space or its own reserved set of frequencies. There has to be sharing. Even at 22,300 miles there is congestion, especially over the Western Hemisphere and the Atlantic Ocean; it will not be possible for every country to have its own little orbital niche. There will have to be regional satellites. Some countries, with relatively little traffic as yet (or ever), may have to be content with ground-based transponders. The determining factor should be actual need and use, rather than theory.

If deliberations of the ITU should break up because of the rigid positions taken by countries that insist upon *a priori* distribution, we are going to face a serious new problem in the international communications field. On the basis of the historical record and institutional legacy that I have described, I do not believe this will happen. I am confident that the same respect for orderliness, the same good judgment, and the same practical outlook that prevailed at the 1984 WARC session on high frequencies will also be present, and predominate, at subsequent conferences of the International Telecommunication Union.

FOR FURTHER READING

Standard, informative works on the organizational history and international law of world telecommunications, cited in the footnotes, are George A. Codding, Jr., and Anthony M. Rutkowski, *The International Telecommunication Union in a Changing World*, and David M. Lieve, *International Telecommunications and International Law: The Regulation of the Radio Spectrum*. For a recent examination of U.S. policy, incorporating an interview with Leonard H. Marks, see Robert A. Kinn, "United States Participation in the International Telecommunication Union: A Series of Interviews," *The Fletcher Forum: A Journal of Studies in International Affairs* 9, no. 1 (Winter 1985): 37–68.

On the political utility of foreign radio broadcasting, see Julian Hale, *Radio Power: Propaganda and International Broadcasting* (Philadelphia: Temple University Press, 1975); David M. Abshire, *International Broadcasting: A New Dimension of Western Diplomacy* (Beverly Hills, CA: SAGE Publications, 1976); and Sig Mickelson, *America's Other Voice: The Story of Radio Free Europe and Radio Liberty* (New York: Praeger, 1983). On its technical aspects, see Leonard Lewin, ed., *Telecommunications: An Interdisciplinary Text* (Washington, DC: Artech House, 1984). Broader issues are discussed in Wilson P. Dizard, *The Coming Information Age: An Overview of Technology, Economics, and Politics* (New York: Longman, 1982); Oswald H. Ganley and Gladys D. Ganley, *To Inform or To Control? The New Communication Networks* (New York: McGraw-Hill, 1982); Jerry L. Salvaggio, ed., *Telecommunications: Issues and Choices for Society* (New York: Longman, 1983); and Ithiel de Sola Pool, *Technologies of Freedom* (Cambridge, MA: Harvard University Press, 1983).

On the development of communication throughout the Third World, see Elihu Katz and George Wedell, with Michael Pilsworth and Dov Shinar, *Broadcasting in the Third World: Promise and Performance* (Cambridge, MA: Harvard University Press, 1977); Philip C. Horton, ed., *The Third World and Press Freedom* (New York: Praeger, 1978); and Robert J. Saunders, Jeremy J. Warford, and Bjørn Wallenius, *Telecommunications and Economic Development* (Baltimore: Johns Hopkins University Press, 1983). Satellite broadcasting is discussed in Jon T. Powell, *International Broadcasting by Satellite: Issues of Regulation Barriers to Communication* (Westport, CT: Greenwood Press, 1985), and Larry Martinez, *Communication Satellites: Power Politics in Space* (Dedham, MA: Artech House, 1985).

COOPERATIVE AND STRATEGIC BASES OF WORLD ORDER

The United Nations, Collective Security, and International Peacekeeping

BRIAN URQUHART

The word "pragmatic" has been emphasized in connection with the Negotiating World Order Project, and, if I may be forgiven, I will make a rather informal and pragmatic set of remarks. As usual, Shakespeare has put our difficulty in a nutshell. In *Henry IV, Part 1* he has Owen Glendower say, "I can call spirits from the vasty deep"; and Hotspur, who is a pragmatic man, replies, "Why, so can I, or so can any man; but will they come when you do call for them?"

Getting the spirits to respond is just as much the issue in modern diplomacy. We in the United Nations run a resolution-producing factory that has now reached industrial proportions. We deluge the world with an enormous number of resolutions. Most of them are reasonably benevolent, but I really do not know what influence they have. Other organizations do the same. There are numerous missions and groups and bodies that have all the right ideas and know all the answers. The trouble is that they and their recommendations mostly do not connect with the political process. We have to address this problem, because good intentions are simply not good enough.

The truth of our dilemma is embarrassingly simple: What we need is a change in attitude, especially on the part of the leaders of the superpowers. Early in this century we muddled into a disastrous world war after which we created what was supposedly a world organization to keep the peace, the League of Nations. After a very promising start, although with certain built-in terrible weaknesses such as the absence of the United States, the participating governments began to give up. They moved far enough away from World War I and the horror of it that they began to give up on the necessity for making the League work. They failed to make a number of decisions they could have made. Effective sanctions were not imposed against Italy in 1935 over its invasion of Ethiopia, just to name one case. Slowly the League fell to bits through a lack of political will, with the ultimate decline into another devastating world war.

After World War II, the same process occurred. Another international organization was created amid tremendous enthusiasm, though with some skepticism in Europe. It was created as the brainchild of the leaders of the victorious alliance—Roosevelt, Churchill, and Stalin—and as the organization that was to save succeeding generations from the scourge of war. I hope very much that we are not going through the process that I grew up with in the 1930s. The laziness, the lack of persistence, the cynicism, the easy scape-goating that destroyed the League are all fatal tendencies. Sometimes when I read the newspapers in the West, I wonder if we are not drifting into such disintegration now, in regard to the United Nations. If we are doing that, we run a very considerable risk of descending eventually into World War III, in a time of nuclear weaponry. After that—it seems likely that the experience will be fairly terminal—there will not be too many people around to set up a third world organization. The lesson in all of this is simple enough: Either we try to make the United Nations work, or we find an alternative to it, which, as it turns out when we examine the causes of the problem, may not be so easy.

The building of a world organization capable of collective action for peace is an extremely complicated matter. Because international security is obviously vital in itself in our dangerous, overcrowded planet, and also the precondition for disarmament and economic development, we should know more about on what it really depends. It would be wise to pay far more attention, however complex and difficult the matter appears, to the insti-tutions, habits, and other necessities that might make a system of international security function. Much of the discussion of this problem is, at present, superficial.

People often make several recommendations regarding collective secu-rity. They recommend the strengthening of the United Nations; they rec-ommend adding to its peacekeeping capacity; and they recommend that the secretary-general be more active and engaged in global peace missions. This approach simply begs the question. It is not the problem. I think that these bland recommendations that we so often hear about strengthening the United Nations are misleading. Dag Hammarskjöld used to say that the UN secretary-general in some respects was a sort of a secular pope, but the trouble was that most of the time he was a pope without a church. It seems to me that it is in the gathering and organizing of the church, the membership, and not in the good intentions that we all keep expressing, that the real interest and the actual challenge lie.

We need to touch the springs of motivation and political action in the real world. It has been done sometimes. It was done to some extent over the nuclear problem; the United Nations was the pioneering institution in that field.[1] It was done by my colleague, Maurice F. Strong, over the rather new problem of environmental pollution.[2] It was done to some extent in this country in bringing about an end to the Vietnam War. However, the problem is to transform these isolated efforts into a consistent, long-term, constructive effort, to get into the political machinery and the international system in such a way that all these good ideas become, in fact, the start of sustained, organized global action.

We had something of a case history of this problem at the United Nations late in 1982. The then new secretary-general, Javier Pérez de Cuéllar, who is an extremely thoughtful and serious person, in his first annual report on the work of the organization departed from previous custom and devoted it entirely to examining why the United Nations did not work in the field of international peace and security as it was intended.[3] Everybody greeted this report with a kind of masochistic pleasure. They said yes, indeed, it is terrible; things aren't as they should be; governments are to blame; the Security Council must discuss what to do about it; and so on. We had made some specific suggestions as to how, for a start, the Security Council itself might do a little better.

We had more than a year of discussions on these and other proposals with an almost total lack of accomplishment. The expedient caution of the governments of the world, as represented in the fifteen members of the Security Council, is clear. Nothing basically has changed.

Why should this be so? Much depends on the commitment by the members to the terms of their initial agreement to cooperate, the Charter.[4] It should not be difficult to have concerted action in certain specified situations among the world's nations, no matter how much they might happen to dislike each other. Because of the unanimity rule on nonprocedural matters, nothing affirmative can be done by the Security Council unless all of its five permanent members concur. This is a guarantee against divisive partisan action by the council; however, it is also an implicit promise that there *be* action. Special

---

[1]United Nations, Department of Political and Security Council Affairs, *The United Nations and Disarmament, 1945–1970* (New York: United Nations, 1970); Brian Urquhart, *Hammarskjöld: A Comprehensive Biography of the Second Secretary-General* (New York: Alfred A.Knopf, 1972), pp. 322–27.

[2]Maurice F. Strong, "Alternative Courses for the Human Future," *Behind the Headlines* 33, no. 1 (April 1974): 1–18; United Nations, Environment Programme, *In Defence of the Earth: The Basic Texts on Environment—Founex, Stockholm, Cocoyoc* (Nairobi: United Nations Environment Programme, 1981).

[3]United Nations, General Assembly, 37th Session, September 7, 1982, *Report of the Secretary-General on the Work of the Organization* (A/37/1).

[4]On the genesis of the UN Charter, see Leland M. Goodrich, Edvard Hambro, and Anne Patricia Simons, *Charter of the United Nations: Commentary and Documents* (New York: Columbia University Press, 1969); Ruth B. Russell, assisted by Jeannette E. Muther, *A History of the United Nations Charter: The Role of the United States, 1940–1945* (Washington, DC: Brookings Institution, 1958).

rights entail special responsibilities. All council members, large and small, share a sacred trust. In 1945 when the Charter was drafted at San Francisco, there were some matters affecting international peace and security regarding which the membership, starting with the greatest powers, had an obligation really to work together. The whole UN system presupposes this collaboration.

If we look at various international situations today, I do not see why this should not again be possible. Look at the Iran-Iraq war. It is a war that everyone, except perhaps the two participants, thinks is crazy. Everybody, including the Arab states, the Gulf states, the USSR, and the United States, is nervous about its possible repercussions. However, the differences between the USSR and the United States, East and West, and their distrust of each other is such that they have failed so far to take any of the measures under the Charter that would have been possible at the beginning, and might even still be possible, to restrict the course of that war, such as arms embargoes, trade boycotts, or communications cutoffs. This is presumably because governments are afraid that, if they support one of these measures, somebody else will take advantage of it. The common interest, though felt, is not effective.

Even the problem of Lebanon could be susceptible to this shared-interest approach. There really are not very great differences in the ultimate interests of everybody outside Lebanon as to what happens within Lebanon. They want the fighting there to end, so that they and their resources will not be drawn into it. Nevertheless, their distrust of each other is so great that they have been unable to articulate that common interest.

If we could get a limited range of activity in such situations as the Gulf and Lebanon in which it was axiomatic that all the countries of the world, and particularly the great powers, would cooperate, then it might be possible to begin to use the full capacity of the United Nations, a capacity that has not really been used to the fullest in forty years. It should be possible to use its peacekeeping capacity, in particular, better than has recently been the case. The technique of peacekeeping is a distinctive innovation by the United Nations. The Charter does not mention it. It was discovered, like penicillin. We came across it, while looking for something else, during an investigation of the guerrilla fighting in northern Greece in 1947.[5] It could be much more effective than it now is. The traditional instruments of mediation, good offices, and conciliation are underused too. Furthermore, it should be possible in extreme cases even to use the enforcement capacity built into the Charter. It should be possible, in cases threatening war, for the nations of the world to agree that the situation is so serious that they will muster sufficient force to deal with it. The enforcement procedure has been used once, in Korea in 1950. It could be used again.

---

[5]On the history of UN peacekeeping operations, see Rosalyn Higgins, *United Nations Peacekeeping: Documents and Commentary*, 4 vols. (Oxford: Oxford University Press, 1969–1981).

The central problem is the relationship between the most powerful countries, the Soviet Union and the United States. The recurrent Cold War between them polarizes international politics. It is a little bit like the contests between the feudal barons of the late Middle Ages.

The chronic medieval problem of baronial warfare was solved in two ways. First, the majority of the community—the bourgeoisie, peasantry, and clergy—finally got together and expressed their common interest in order and in some reasonable degree of peaceful society. Second, they found a respite from incessant war by backing the monarchy. Until then, the monarchy had been more or less of a figment of central authority, rather like the United Nations; everybody paid lip service to it, but in fact no one wanted to pay for it. They cared little for it, because the action was elsewhere. But by backing the monarchy they did create strong central states with strong central governments and, for the first time in Europe, systems of law and also bureaucracy (which is very necessary although it has become a derogatory word). This is when the nation-states of Europe finally came of age.

Today, the way in which the superpowers are super is that they hold the fate of everybody else in their hands. Nothing less than the future of the planet depends on their relationship. It is not a very enviable reason for being called super.

It is worth reminding ourselves how that phrase originated, and how misleading it can be as to the true potency of the superpowers. People are always lamenting our inability to control wars in the Third World, of which there are several going on at any time. The superpowers obviously cannot order these to halt. As long as there is no consensus for conflict control among the most powerful nations, however, there will be very little control over those situations from the international level. I believe there must be a new reaffirmation by the superpowers that questions of international security and threats to the peace are overriding, that they override the normal differences and dislikes of nation-states. That was the concept of the UN Charter. It must now be reaffirmed, but I do not see too much sign of such a move in either Washington or Moscow at present.

Upon all of us, there lies the responsibility of clear thinking, of seeing our situation with detachment. We seem to have an immense capacity in this century for rather casually and mindlessly unleashing very powerful forces, notably as in the arms race, that then turn out to be uncontrollable. Nuclear weapons are only one aspect of this.

A related need is for greater willingness to deal with questions on their merits. There is a prevailing expediency in the way in which governments now tackle international problems. There is a great reluctance to adopt a policy simply because it is the right, or the sensible, policy. It is extremely rare now for any country, or any leader, to make a great initiative simply because it seems the forward-looking thing to do.

I believe that if we look at the reasons why actions are taken in the Middle East or Central America, for instance, we can detect a dangerous trend of thought. It is not simply that one issue is being related to another, in one scheme or other of linkage. It is that specific problems are being subsumed under general stereotypes. A far more pragmatic approach is needed.

The United Nations is supposedly the alternative to international paralysis caused by the mutual suspicions of nations, especially the superpowers. As I have stressed, it has yet to be used properly by governments and with the minimum of confidence needed for such an organization to become fully effective. It has yet to be pushed over the political threshold from being a mere institutional mechanism into being something persistent, consistent, and recognized as a constitutional instrument. There is, for the time being, little sign of any great interest in bringing about such a transformation.

Admittedly, the United Nations is extremely valuable as a last resort, as a scapegoat, and sometimes as a fig leaf. However, it is not being used in the way the authors of the Charter had in mind, although it serves as the only diplomatic channel on certain key issues. It is now the only channel of negotiation on Afghanistan, for example. It has become the only channel of negotiation left open on the Iran-Iraq war. It is also the only channel of negotiation and peacekeeping for Cyprus, which is potentially still an inflammable problem.

Peacekeeping certainly could be far more effective than it has been allowed to be so far. However, tinkering with peacekeeping is not enough; a fundamental change of attitude is needed. One way to strengthen UN peacekeeping is for the two most powerful countries on earth, the United States and the Soviet Union, to participate in peacekeeping under directives from the UN Security Council. This would be very much in the spirit of the Charter. Until that happens, we will tend to have overtones of the East-West struggle, as we know from the experience of some thirteen peacekeeping operations over a period of nearly forty years. The vibrations caused by that contest can be destructive. That was the case, for example, in the early 1960s in the Congo,[6] and it is an important part of the problem now in the Middle East. The UN organization has been based since its inception on a geopolitical fault, rather like the city of San Francisco, where it was born. When that fault—the East-West divide—slips, the organization trembles.

Lebanon is a case study of many of the points I have been discussing. I do not think very many people really understand the Lebanese problem itself. I had an ancestor who wrote a book called *The Lebanon*, published in 1860 in two volumes. Open it at almost any page and discover a striking description of many of the problems we are still up against there.[7] The Jumblatts were going strong; the Shuf was a place where endless fighting was

---

[6]A detailed account of the Congo crisis will be found in my *Hammarskjöld*, pp. 380–456, 472–93, 499–518, 544–89.

[7]David Urquhart, *The Lebanon (Mount Souria): A History and a Diary*, 2 vols. (London: Thomas Cautley Newby, 1860).

taking place; there was a massacre of the Christians in Deir al Qamar, as there would be again in recent years, followed by a countermassacre of the Druse, with all the continuing problems that entails. The emir, like the government today, hoped he had a broad political base but found it continually narrowed until he had to call in outside support to maintain his position. People worried about what the Russians were up to. And this was in 1860. Nothing seems to have changed all that much.

Since 1978 a 6,000-man UN peacekeeping force (UNIFIL) has been laboring hard against very heavy odds in southern Lebanon. A larger role for the United Nations in the Beirut area was also suggested at various times, both before the Israeli invasion of June 1982 and afterwards. There was a belief in the West that something different was needed, so a non-UN multinational force, including U.S. Marines and troops from Britain, France, and Italy, was formed. Predictably, it encountered the manifold complications of the Lebanese situation and was withdrawn in 1984.

One element in the confused situation was not realizing that the local problem, although something in itself, was precipitating other, wider problems onto it, and then trying to interpret it in this broader, region-wide, even global way. There was also a mistaken belief that more force could resolve it. Military power in a situation that does not require it is counterproductive. In our UN peacekeeping operations, our troops have only defensive weapons. We have always discouraged the desire for tanks, heavy artillery, and actual fighting. The reason is very simple: to achieve a military objective by military means, one has to go 100 percent, but a peacekeeping operation can never use maximum force.

The object of peacekeeping is never to enter into a conflict situation, but rather to stay above the conflict and to accept, if necessary, harassment and abuse. It is not a very popular position because peacekeepers are not on anybody's side; they are in the middle. In the end, they get respect, which is all they should have anyway. Once they exchange fire in a conflict or in the reprisal game, they are lost. Self-defense is not to be confused with executing reprisals. I think that this distinction was not appreciated sufficiently during the Lebanon crisis. Aircraft carriers standing offshore will not help much in Beirut, where everybody is armed.

Another important point that has not been appreciated sufficiently about peacekeeping is that, in order to be effective, it needs to have a broad political base in the world community. In one way that is a very constraining factor; in another way it is a great strength. Once Security Council approval is given, none of our UN operations can be interpreted as favoring one side or the other. That gives them considerable durability.

All of these points need to be considered very carefully for the future. It is essential that people address the basic, long-term problem of Lebanon and not just one part of it. The problem of Lebanon was not how to get the Marines out with honor, which obviously had to be done. The underlying problem was to create the circumstances in which internal peace could be restored in that country. Peacekeeping, by itself, can only provide the atmosphere within which negotiations can go forward. Peacekeeping is basically a palliative; it does not solve the actual problem. All it can do is keep people from killing each other. To achieve an enduring settlement, rather than just a cease-fire, one has to know the Lebanese situation itself thoroughly. One has to know all the parties concerned and what would induce them to take a more constructive line. Probably only the Lebanese can do that.

The key to collective security and international peacekeeping and peacemaking is identifying the common interest and building upon it. That takes a great deal of work. It means one has to talk to people and not dismiss them. In situations like Lebanon, Cyprus, Iran-Iraq, or the Middle East problem as a whole, there is a considerable degree of common interest, even between the superpowers, but it is overshadowed by hostility and lack of confidence. It should not be beyond the reach of human ingenuity and practical statesmanship to find ways to translate that latent common interest into cooperative action. What is at stake is whether there is going to be some tolerable degree of order and expectation in the world, or anarchy, cynicism, and despair. That is the objective of our efforts in peacekeeping and peacemaking.

FOR FURTHER READING

On the founding of the United Nations as a collective-security instrument, see the magisterial volume by Ruth B. Russell, *A History of the United Nations Charter: The Role of the United States, 1940–1945*, cited in the footnotes; also Inis L. Claude, Jr., *Swords Into Plowshares: The Problems and Progress of International Organization*, 4th ed. (New York: Random House, 1984); and Evan Luard, *A History of the United Nations* (New York: St. Martin's Press, 1982). Other authoritative works are Ernest A. Gross, *The United Nations: Structure for Peace* (New York: Harper, 1962); Ruth B. Russell, *The United Nations and United States Security Policy* (Washington, DC: Brookings Institution, 1968); Arthur Rovine, *The First Fifty Years: The Secretary-General in World Politics, 1920–1970* (Leiden: A. W. Sijthoff, 1970); John F. Murphy, *The United Nations and the Control of International Violence: A Legal and Political Analysis* (Totowa, NJ: Rowman and Allanheld, 1982); and Leo Gross, *Essays on International Law and Organization*, 2 vols. (Dobbs Ferry, NY: Transnational Publishers, 1984). Much institutional history also is contained in Brian Urquhart, *Hammarskjöld: A Comprehensive Biography of the Second Secretary-General*, cited in the footnotes. A later secretary-general, Kurt Waldheim, has published *Building the Future Order: The Search for Peace in an Interdependent World* (New York: Free Press, 1980) and *The Challenge of Peace* (New York: Rawson, Wade, 1980). The annual reports of the UN secretaries-general, especially the outspoken reports of recent years, are also worthy of note.

For critical commentary on the United Nations, see Shirley Hazzard, *The Defeat of an Ideal: A Study of the Self-Destruction of the United Nations* (Boston: Little, Brown, 1973); Daniel Patrick Moynihan, with Suzanne Weaver, *A Dangerous Place*

(Boston: Little, Brown, 1978); Peter R. Baehr and Leon Gordenker, *The United Nations: Reality and Ideal* (New York: Praeger, 1984); and Thomas M. Franck, *Nation Against Nation: What Happened to the U.N. Dream and What the U.S. Can Do About It* (New York: Oxford University Press, 1985). The increasing influence of the non-aligned countries is discussed in Richard L. Jackson, *The Non-Aligned, the UN and the Superpowers* (New York: Praeger, 1983). For an analysis of UN decision-making procedures, see Johan Kaufmann, *United Nations Decision Making* (Alphen aan de Rijn, The Netherlands: Sijthoff and Noordhoff, 1980).

On UN peacekeeping, see the multivolume record by Rosalyn Higgins, *United Nations Peacekeeping: Documents and Commentary*, mentioned in the footnotes. Specialized studies of peacekeeping, based on the experience of practitioners, are Indar Jit Rikhye, Michael Harbottle, and Bjørn Egge, *The Thin Blue Line: International Peacekeeping and Its Future* (New Haven: Yale University Press, 1974); Indar Jit Rikhye, *The Theory and Practice of Peacekeeping* (New York: St. Martin's Press, 1984); and Henry Wiseman, ed., *Peacekeeping: Appraisals and Proposals* (New York: Pergamon Press, 1983). For an account of the personal involvement of Brian Urquhart in UN peacekeeping, see Madeleine G. Kalb, "The U.N.'s Embattled Peacekeeper," *New York Times Magazine*, December 19, 1982.

The Great Illusion: "Star Wars" and World Order

GERARD C. SMITH

In this imperfect world there is little prospect for a secure international order, unless nuclear weapons are first regulated and eventually outlawed. I use the ambiguous word "regulated" advisedly, because much more is involved than just superpowers' agreements to put quantitative and qualitative ceilings on their strategic weapons. Regulation also must include restraints on their use, such as those foreshadowed by the "no first use" proposal that several colleagues and I have made.[1] It should encompass as well limits on nuclear weapons' spread, which now is only loosely controlled by the 1968 Non-Proliferation Treaty. Nonetheless, the U.S.-Soviet race to build more and more complex instruments of strategic warfare is the dynamic that most seriously challenges stability.

Unfortunately, the fact is that *de*regulation of strategic nuclear arms is now taking place. The latest move in this direction is the commitment by the U.S. government to an effort to make Soviet offensive missiles impotent by building nationwide defensive screens in violation of that most important agreement, the 1972 Anti-Ballistic Missile (ABM) Treaty. The ABM Treaty, the only strategic arms treaty which has been ratified and which is legally in effect, has become the symbol of Soviet-American arms control. I worked to negotiate it and I consider it, in fact, to be the centerpiece of the whole nuclear relationship with the USSR. This tilt toward a defensive strategy is fundamentally inconsistent with arms control and would destabilize the strategic balance, on which international order rests.

In the 1960s and 1970s some progress was made on the beginnings of nuclear arms regulation by Washington and Moscow. The high point was the

---

[1] McGeorge Bundy, George F. Kennan, Robert S. McNamara, and Gerard C. Smith, "Nuclear Weapons and the Atlantic Alliance," *Foreign Affairs* 60, no. 4 (Spring 1982): 753–68.

69

1972 treaty banning *nationwide* ballistic missile defenses by either party and sharply limiting other kinds of missile defense.[2] The ABM Treaty was based on a recognition by the superpowers that defenses against ballistic missiles could only weaken the deterrent effect of their retaliatory forces and, by destabilizing the military balance, make nuclear war more likely. The ABM Treaty has been reviewed twice by the parties—the second time as recently as 1982, under the current administration—and found to be in their mutual interest. The treaty was based, it is important to note, on the expectation that the interim agreement limiting offensive forces (SALT I) accompanying it would soon be followed by a more long-term treaty further limiting strategic offensive systems. It was understood that, in the long run, limits on both kinds of weaponry were needed if a stable balance were to be maintained. Nothing has happened technologically or politically in the meantime to change the validity of these assumptions.

In 1979 a treaty (SALT II), limiting offensive strategic systems, was signed but not ratified by this country. Both the United States and the USSR, however, declared that they would live up to its terms. Unfortunately, it expired in 1985. Two other arms control treaties were also signed but not ratified by the United States: the Threshold Test Ban Treaty and the Peaceful Nuclear Explosions Treaty, both of which limit the size of underground nuclear weapons tests. In late 1983 the USSR withdrew from the two principal arms negotiations then taking place: the Strategic Arms Reduction (START) and the Intermediate Nuclear Forces (INF) talks. The United States has refused to resume negotiations for a comprehensive ban on nuclear testing and on antisatellite systems. This looks very much like deregulation.

The most ominous sign that the arms control regime is unraveling is the proposal made by President Reagan on March 23, 1983, for the development of nationwide antiballistic missile defenses for the United States and its allies (popularly and accurately called "Star Wars").[3] Such systems are explicitly banned by the ABM Treaty. The president then proposed, also for the long term, a reversal of U.S. strategy of relying on survivable retaliatory forces to deter aggression, and in place thereof he foreshadowed a strategy of relying exclusively on antimissile weapons. War presumably would be prevented because each side's defenses would be so impenetrable as to make both immune from nuclear retaliation.

What, then, is so wrong about trying to develop defenses? Is not the purpose of high-technology "strategic defense" weaponry to destroy missiles and not people? Admittedly, this is the stated purpose of the administration's Strategic Defense Initiative (SDI). But nuclear weapons have upset classical concepts of the relationship between offense and defense. For decades the

---

[2]*Arms Control and Disarmament Agreements: Texts and Histories of Negotiations* (Washington, DC: U.S. Arms Control and Disarmament Agency, 1982), pp. 137–47.

[3]Ronald W. Reagan, "Peace and National Security," address to the nation, March 23, 1983, in U.S., Department of State *Bulletin* 83, no. 2073 (Spring 1983): 8–14.

United States and the Soviet Union have both assumed, however paradoxically, that their existence depended on a state of mutual insecurity—somewhat like two scorpions in a bottle, each unwilling to sting the other lest it in turn be stung to death. If one or the other came to believe that it was sting-proof, it might be tempted to attack. And that is what is dangerous about a nationwide defense which the president envisions. If we go for defenses, the Soviets will do the same; then both sides' concerns about being attacked will rise. We ourselves may not begin to think offensively simply because we assume we have an effective defense. But what if the other side believes that we actually are aggressive and thus itself begins to contemplate a first strike, lest it be subjected to sudden attack?

This is not just abstract game theory. It is actual history. In the late 1960s the Soviet government deployed the "Galosh" ABM system to defend Moscow. In addition, concern was expressed that even the Soviet antiaircraft systems might be able to destroy our retaliatory missiles. One of the main justifications for the subsequent great increase in U.S. offensive strategic warheads—multiple independently targetable reentry vehicles (MIRVs)—was to assure a capability to penetrate such Soviet defenses. The American MIRV programs were quickly followed by similar Soviet systems. For some years, partly as a result, we have lived with a destabilizing threat to our land-based missiles by "heavy" many-warheaded Soviet missiles, a condition called "a window of vulnerability." Although this notion now is seen to have been largely illusory, it has led to new strategic requirements for U.S. force modernization. We see how the logic of strategic defense, in this case initiated by the Soviet Union, evokes strategic-offensive reactions.

An optimist might think that, when the dire possibilities of defenses on both sides sink home in the minds of the leadership in Washington and Moscow, an effort will be made to abort a new arms race. The best that can probably be hoped for, then, is a return to the present status—a mutual ban on nationwide defenses. Is such an irrational process of regaining what we already have an inevitable step in human progress?

Since the beginning of the nuclear era, as I know from personal conversations with them, there have been scientists, engineers, politicians, and academics who have speculated about escaping from the horrors of the nuclear standoff by mounting such effective defenses that attack would no longer be feasible. This is utopian, however well-meaning. It does not take a moralist to see that a purely defensive strategy would be much more humane and consistent with civilized standards than the present Soviet and American threats to destroy each other. These promises of retaliation, if fulfilled, could "winterize" the planet and leave it uninhabitable.[4] Unfortunately, there has never seemed to be a practicable way to achieve this switch from an offensive to a defensive strategy. Quite apart from the many technological difficulties

---

[4]Carl Sagan, "Nuclear War and Climatic Catastrophe: Some Policy Implications," *Foreign Affairs* 62, no. 2 (Winter 1983/84): 257–92.

involved, there remains the problem of adjusting inherited thinking and altering basic psychology, now conditioned to accept the paradoxical logic of the nuclear age. The task for diplomats would be formidable. How can Moscow be persuaded that this sudden move toward an American strategic defensive capability—threatening the condition of mutually assured destruction (MAD)—does not cloak a purpose of seizing an advantage: if not to attack, then to negotiate from a position of power to attack?

The president's concept of moving toward a nationwide defense is said by its proponents to be consistent with the ABM Treaty, presumably because that treaty permits some research and development on ABM systems. Nothing in the ABM Treaty prevents research on new systems, although development of air-, sea-, or space-based systems or land-based mobile systems is outlawed. In negotiating the ABM Treaty, it was anticipated that exotic directed-energy systems like lasers and particle-beam accelerators would be coming over the horizon. "Star Wars" research is now legitimate. However, a presidential announcement of an intention to develop systems banned by treaty seems quite inconsistent with the traditional American respect for international law.

The most immediate threat to arms control is this prospective termination of the ABM Treaty. No legal training is needed to predict that a program to mount a nationwide defense will soon violate a treaty that expressly bans such a defense (in Article 1). Only two ABM systems—one centered on the nation's capital and another at an intercontinental ballistic missile (ICBM) site—were permitted to each party by the treaty, and a 1974 Protocol to the ABM Treaty reduced this to only one apiece.[5] Nothing in the treaty suggests that a country can prepare for a nationwide defense and not be in violation until such spatially extended defenses are actually deployed. Perhaps the United States, for a few years, can continue to hold to the position that its "Star Wars" programs are consistent with the treaty. But all informed observers are in no doubt that we are on a collision course with it. Some advocates, appropriately, speak of amending the ABM Treaty to permit a "Star Wars" system. That would be like amending the Volstead Act of Prohibition days to permit the sale of alcohol.

Only a totally impenetrable defense would warrant abandoning our present deterrent weapons and strategy. The president has had in mind such a perfect defense, although with the passage of time less ambitious goals are being cited by administration officials. Reagan would go even further, beyond protecting the United States. Once such defenses were operational, he has said, an American president might well offer to give such defensive weaponry to the Soviets to prove to them that there was no longer any need for retaliatory missiles. He would have a future president say, "I am willing to do away with all my missiles. You do away with all of yours."[6] One may reasonably

---

[5]*Arms Control and Disarmament Agreements*, pp. 161–63.

[6]Reagan interview with journalists at White House, March 29, 1983, in *New York Times*, March 30, 1983.

ask why defensive systems would be needed at all if one could trust the USSR, at some point, to do away with its offensive missiles. Lest one attribute the president's rather fantastic statements to some random whim, it is worth noting that the secretary of defense, Caspar Weinberger, said that "the defensive systems the President is talking about are not designed to be partial. What we want to try to get is a system which will develop a defense which is thoroughly reliable and *total*. I don't see any reason why that can't be done."[7] He enthusiastically endorsed the president's utopian appeal, arguing that he hoped and assumed the Soviets would develop a similar defense which then would have the effect of completely removing these missiles from the earth. While our leaders would, in fact, never agree to a complete ban on strategic nuclear weapons because they do not trust the Soviets—and correctly so— they are holding out this prospect of offensive weapons disappearing from the face of the earth when new defensive weapons systems will have neutralized them. This strikes me as a cruel illusion to put in the minds of the American people.

In this lecture, I am concentrating largely on the prejudice to arms control that would result from this move toward strategic defenses, but a few observations about their technical feasibility may be in order. I make no claim to "hardware" expertise, as opposed to knowledge of the diplomacy of nuclear weapons. But, having been acquainted for about a third of a century with leading nuclear scientists and engineers, I prefer the judgment of those who conclude that a full "Star Wars" capability is an impossibility. One Nobel laureate with great nuclear expertise called it "science fiction." Any conceivable system could be neutralized by countermeasures, and a defensive strategy to replace the present mutual retaliatory strategy is just not feasible. They point out that, for an effective nationwide defense, not just ballistic missiles but bombers and cruise missiles, which would enter our airspace at low altitudes, must be rendered impotent. They believe that, after spending many hundreds of billions of dollars, we will have an imperfect defensive system. It may supplement, but not supplant, offensive systems. Can't America's security dollars be more prudently spent?

There are deep divisions in the Pentagon about the wisdom of the new course, and estimates of its cost vary widely. Dr. George Keyworth II, former science adviser to the president, has said, "There's no reason to believe that the technology would cost any more than what we're spending today on offensive nuclear weapons."[8] But former Under Secretary of Defense Richard DeLauer testified that eight areas of new technology are required, each one of which would demand at least an effort of the size of the Manhattan Project for the atomic bomb. That could cost more than a trillion dollars. And DeLauer

---

[7] NBC, "Meet the Press," March 27, 1983.
[8] "Can Reagan's 'Star Wars' Plan Really Work?" *U.S. News and World Report* 94, no. 14 (April 11, 1983): 24–25.

did not help the president's case by saying, "There's no way an enemy can't overwhelm your defenses if he wants to badly enough."[9]

Although President Reagan seems genuinely committed to the idea that eventually the superpowers can forsake offensive weapons, it seems that some of the supporters of this initiative have a less idyllic future in mind. Instead, they see a time when America's superior technological and economic power will allow us to have both massive offensive forces and sufficient aerospace defenses to permit regaining some degree of the strategic superiority we held in the past. These people are aiming for defenses *in addition to* offensive forces, not in lieu of them. They do not see defensive systems as means of rendering offensive forces impotent, but rather as very useful adjuncts for limiting damage in nuclear hostilities. Although the president rightly foresaw the dangers of such a partial defense nuclear strategy, he has not yet drawn the necessary conclusions. In his March 1983 speech he said, "I clearly recognize that defensive systems have limitations and raise certain problems and ambiguities. If paired with offensive systems, they can be viewed as fostering an aggressive policy; and no one wants that."[10] No one may want it, but that is what a "Star Wars" strategy necessarily entails. The accuracy of the president's statement was quickly shown by the Soviet reaction. The late Soviet President Yuri Andropov said of Reagan's proposal: "This deserves special comment. . . . At first glance, this may even seem attractive to uninformed people. . . . In fact, the development and improvement of the U.S.'s strategic offensive forces will continue at full speed, and in a very specific direction—that of acquiring the potential to deliver a nuclear first strike."[11]

However benign the president's motives, if we proceed to mount a nationwide defense the Soviets, whether they fear the worst or simply want justification for their own programs, will quickly follow suit. We will face a new arms race to see which side can more effectively deploy defensive systems, and that race will accelerate the competition in offensive systems too as both sides try to deploy forces capable of penetrating the new defensive screens.

There is good historical precedent for estimating that the U.S. foreshadowing that it will not be bound by the ABM Treaty will likely cause a severe Soviet reaction. In 1958 both sides informally agreed to a moratorium of further nuclear testing, while negotiation for a Comprehensive Test Ban Treaty was proceeding. In late 1959, President Eisenhower publicly stated that the United States would feel free to resume testing after January 1, 1960. The Soviet Union reacted with a massive test series in 1961. Folklore has it that the USSR broke this informal moratorium, but the U.S. declaration that it would no longer be bound must be considered partially to blame.

---

[9]"Developments in a Ballistic Missile Defense: We're Already There . . . in a Decade or So," *Government Executive* (July-August 1983): 17.

[10]Reagan, "Peace and National Security," p. 14.

[11]From interview in *Pravda*, March 27, 1983, as reprinted in *Current Digest of the Soviet Press* 35, no. 13 (April 27, 1983): 4–5.

A similar escalation could well result from the new American missile defense program. The USSR surely will not disappoint Secretary Weinberger's hope, cited above, that they too will deploy massive defensive systems. This will generate concerns about the adequacy of our offensive forces as well as suspicions about basic Soviet intentions, once Moscow possesses both offensive and defensive capabilities.

Contrary to the president's idealistic hopes, we would then be engaged not just in one arms race, as at present, but in two: defensive as well as offensive. And there is also likely to be a third competition, one in which the Soviets will have a solid advantage. That is for civil defense. Soviet society can accept the constraints inherent in defending their population much better than American society can. Since, regardless of present hopes, no defense will prove to be impenetrable, it must be assumed that some missiles will explode on American and allied targets. It will be impossible to predict which places will be hit, so civil defense systems will take on central importance. Experience suggests that Americans will be very resistant to burrowing underground in order to make a defensive strategy seem credible. Will our allies be any more willing to take on this burden accompanying American "defense" of their lands?

An especially pernicious rationalization for "Star Wars" is that, rather than stimulate the arms race, it will have a beneficial effect on arms control. Not surprisingly, this claim is frequently made by officials whose main interests lie in getting on with new weapons systems. It is curious to read statements by administration officials that, once we have demonstrated a national resolve to deploy massive defenses, the USSR will begin to take seriously our present proposals to reduce offensive arms. As if a demonstrated intention to end one form of arms control would encourage the adversary to agree to another! This calculation is not unlike the administration's repeated estimates that, once the United States started to deploy Pershing missiles in Europe, the Soviets would start seriously to negotiate at the Geneva INF talks. The Soviets did not oblige and instead suspended that negotiation. The rationalization that "Star Wars" is an instrument of arms control is merely the latest in a series of misleading claims that our building new weapons will encourage the Soviet Union to negotiate. It generally has not worked that way.

Some people dismiss the "Star Wars" concept as a rhetorical stunt and expect that little will come of it. That may be wrong. Increases in research and development funding are very large, and the program continues to gain momentum. It could be the greatest bonanza ever for defense industries. Now that the Soviet Union has been put on notice that we are setting a course in conflict with the ABM Treaty, their future policies and programs too may well differ from those based on a presumption of continuance of that agreement. This will provide a justification for still larger American defense appropriations and the search for ever more exotic technologies.

Almost two decades ago, the prospect of the superpower military rivalry spilling over into outer space was foreseen, and a treaty was entered into in

1967 banning the orbiting of nuclear weapons and their placement on celestial bodies.[12] One technique now being considered for many-layered defense against ballistic missiles involves nuclear weapons in space. It thus seems probable that the Outer Space Treaty would be another casualty of the "Star Wars" program. And since it is quite unlikely that the Pentagon will be willing to rely on an untested defensive system, requirements may arise for testing nuclear weapons' effects in space. This would end the Limited Test Ban Treaty of 1963.[13]

In addition to losing existing treaties and the still-hoped-for results of negotiations that were long suspended (START and INF), there also must be included in the likely-to-be-lost column two other important agreements which have long been declared goals of American policy. Any life that is left in the Comprehensive Test Ban (CTB) negotiation would be extinguished if the Limited Test Ban Treaty were breached by testing nuclear defensive systems in space. With the demise of hopes for a Comprehensive Test Ban, in my judgment, there would depart the world's best hope to get the nuclear proliferation problem under some control.

A further example of the prejudicial effect of "Star Wars" on arms control possibilities will be its influence on the resumption of negotiations for a ban on Anti-Satellite Systems (ASATs). Since the United States depends greatly on space satellites for its military operations, one would naturally suppose that we shared the Soviet interest in banning systems to destroy satellites in space. The Soviet Union has even tabled a treaty which, some experts believe, forms the basis for a serious negotiation. However, under this administration (unlike the Carter administration) no real interest has been shown. Definitional and verification questions have been cited as reasons for not negotiating. The United States has begun ASAT tests on a new system expected to be much more efficient than the current Soviet system. The former chief of the Advanced Space Programs of the U.S. Air Force, Dr. Robert M. Bowman, has written: "Whether they are called experiments, demonstrations, or whatever, weapons-related testing in space should be prohibited. This would prevent erosion of the ABM Treaty's prohibition on testing ABM components. It would prevent the perfection of new dedicated ASAT systems which could threaten stabilizing military early-warning and communications satellites."[14] Fortunately, Congress is sufficiently unsure of the wisdom of ASAT testing that it has attached a condition to the program's appropriation banning testing against objects in space, unless the United States is genuinely negotiating with the USSR to control space weapons, or unless the tests are necessary "to avert clear and irrevocable harm to the national security."[15]

---

[12]*Arms Control and Disarmament Agreements*, pp. 48–58.
[13]Ibid., pp. 34–47.
[14]Robert M. Bowman, "Star Wars and the Geneva Arms Talks," Issue Brief (Potomac, MD: Institute for Space and Security Studies, March 1985).
[15]U.S., Congress, House, *Department of Defense Authorization Act, 1985: Conference Report to Accompany H.R. 5167*, 98th Cong., 2d sess., 1984, H. Rept. 1080, p. 20.

The arms control regime gradually set up over the last twenty years has become an important part of the military relationship between the United States and the USSR. The spheres of defense and of disarmament have become inseparable. For example, operations which would have been considered espionage before are now blessed by arms control treaties—permitted "national technical means." Reconnaissance satellites are essential to verification of arms control agreements, and interference with them is appropriately banned by treaty. One good reason for trying permanently to ban ASATs is that they threaten those very space satellites on which the life of strategic arms control, as well as national military security, depends. If these technical means of verification are compromised, the viability of the treaties will be sharply reduced.

Common sense may yet spare us the aberration of "Star Wars." There are already signs of second thoughts among better informed administration officials. Claims of possibilities for perfection are being scaled back. The president's dreams are beginning to come up against reality. The urgings of zealots for early deployments, involving existing technology, have been resisted. Despite the resources being allocated to SDI, an operational "Star Wars" system is not likely to exist during President Reagan's lifetime.

Nonetheless a continuing effort is called for to keep the full "Star Wars" concept in a prenatal condition of research and development. The sole purpose of such a controlled, confined program should be to hedge against a serious Soviet breach of the ABM Treaty—a "breakout"—involving their deployment of a regional or nationwide defense. An important dividend of such research and development would be to gain information, which is needed to permit adequate understanding of intelligence which we obtain about the Soviet program. Arms control negotiations themselves, it should be noted, are a source of such knowledge, as well as being an opportunity to apply it.

As perceptions sharpen about the planetary effects of a nuclear war and public pressures rise for change in official attitudes regarding nuclear weapons, is it too much to expect that leaders will realize that the way to reduce the risk of war is not to build new weapons systems like "Star Wars," but instead to put more faith, interest, and energy into their international regulation and control? Perhaps faith in deregulation will give way to the new conditions of the nuclear world.

FOR FURTHER READING

For the documentary record of East-West strategic nuclear arms talks, see U.S. Arms Control and Disarmament Agency, *Arms Control and Disarmament Agreements: Texts and Histories of Negotiations*, cited in the footnotes, and also its annual volume, *Documents on Disarmament*. An unofficial monitor of the arms control process is *The Arms Control Reporter: A Chronicle of Treaties, Negotiations, Proposals*, published since 1982 by the Institute for Defense and Disarmament Studies. For the history of nuclear weapons and attempts to regulate them, see Bernard C. Bechhofer, *Postwar Negotiations for Arms Control* (Washington, DC: Brookings Institution, 1961); Stockholm International Peace Research Institute, *The Arms Race and Arms Control* (Cambridge, MA: Oelgeschlager, Gunn and Hain, 1982); Lawrence Freedman, *The Evolution of Nuclear Strategy* (New York: St. Martin's Press, 1983); and Paul B. Stares, *The Militarization of Space: U.S. Policy, 1945–1984* (Ithaca, NY: Cornell University Press, 1985). Detailed accounts vividly reflecting the perspectives of individual participants in recent nuclear discussions are Gerard C. Smith, *Doubletalk: The Story of the First Strategic Arms Limitation Talks* (Garden City, NY: Doubleday, 1980); Henry A. Kissinger, *White House Years* (Boston: Little, Brown, 1979) and his *Years of Upheaval* (Boston: Little, Brown, 1982); and Strobe Talbott, *Deadly Gambits: The Reagan Administration and the Stalemate in Nuclear Arms Control* (New York: Alfred A. Knopf, 1984).

For information and argumentation concerning the issue of "Star Wars," see the following articles and books: McGeorge Bundy, George F. Kennan, Robert S. McNamara, and Gerard C. Smith, "The President's Choice: Star Wars or Arms Control," *Foreign Affairs* 63, no. 2 (Winter 1984/85): 264–78; Robert Jastrow, "Reagan vs. the Scientists: Why the President is Right About Missile Defense," *Commentary* (January 1984): 23–32, and his book, *How to Make Nuclear Weapons Obsolete* (Boston: Little, Brown, 1985); Ben Bova, *Assured Survival: Putting the Star Wars Defense in Perspective* (Boston: Houghton Mifflin, 1984); Keith B. Payne, ed., *Laser Weapons in Space* (Boulder, CO: Westview Press, 1983) and his more recent *Strategic Defense: "Star Wars" in Perspective* (Lanham, MD: Hamilton Press, 1986); Ashton B. Carter and David N. Schwartz, eds., *Ballistic Missile Defense* (Washington, DC: Brookings Institution, 1984); John Tirman, ed., *The Fallacy of Star Wars* (New York: Vintage Books, 1984); Bhupendra Jasani, ed., *Space Weapons—The Arms Control Dilemma* (London: Taylor and Francis, 1985); and Sydney D. Drell, Philip J. Farley, and David Holloway, *The Reagan Strategic Defense Initiative: A Technical, Political, and Arms Control Assessment* (Cambridge, MA: Ballinger, 1985). Also useful are two recent issues of *Daedalus*, Spring and Summer 1985, on the theme, "Weapons in Space."

The Diplomacy of Nuclear Nonproliferation

JOSEPH S. NYE, JR.

The spread of nuclear weapons is one of the most challenging issues, if not the most challenging issue, for any conception of negotiating world order, or multilateral regime making. International politics is essentially an anarchic order. Anarchic need not mean chaotic, but it does mean a world without government, without a central hierarchical governmental structure. International politics is the realm of self-help, and self-help means the right of self-defense. Implied in that is the ability to have whatever form of defense one wishes. In that sense a few countries have availed themselves of the most devastating form of self-help possible, and that has pro-

duced, oddly enough, an international balance in military terms which has been stable for longer than many balances of previous eras. It is important to remember that there has been no use of nuclear weapons since 1945 despite the fact that, as we are always reminded, the United States and the Soviet Union have between them approximately 50,000 nuclear weapons and all the rest of the countries in the world, lumped together, probably less than 1,000.

It is sometimes argued—indeed my colleagues and I in *Living with Nuclear Weapons* argued—that one might attribute this remarkable stability to a "crystal ball effect."[1] Any leader contemplating a major nuclear war has, in a sense, a crystal ball handed to him; he knows what the effects of unleashing the weapons would be. We used in that book the analogy of August 1914, in which one could imagine a meeting among the czar, the kaiser, and the emperor of Austria-Hungary, where each would be handed a crystal ball with a picture of 1918 within it and told, "Look at the end of the war. You will

---

[1]The Harvard Nuclear Study Group (Albert Carnesale, Paul Doty, Stanley Hoffmann, Samuel P. Huntington, Joseph S. Nye, Jr., Scott D. Sagan), with a foreword by Derek Bok, *Living with Nuclear Weapons* (New York: Bantam Books, 1983), pp. 43–44.

have lost your throne; your empire will be dismembered and millions of your people will have been killed. Do you still want to go to war?" Most of those leaders had in their minds the last great war in Europe, the short, sharp war of 1870. It is not unreasonable, therefore, to think that such a crystal ball vision, if truly vivid, might have induced an additional degree of prudence.

Given the knowledge that exists of the scientific effects of nuclear weapons, now dramatized even more by the recent arguments about a "nuclear winter," leaders have become extraordinarily prudent in the way they deal with these weapons.[2] The fact that nuclear weapons have created such a degree of prudence has led some people to say, "Why not generalize the effect? Why not, in fact, think of a world order constructed upon a generalization of nuclear deterrence? Why could not that be the basis of a better international order?" A world of porcupines, as it is sometimes called. Kenneth Waltz, of the University of California at Berkeley, has even entitled a recent pamphlet, *The Spread of Nuclear Weapons: More May Be Better*. Shai Feldman recently published a book about the Middle East situation, arguing that Israel might feel more relaxed about coming to terms with its Arab neighbors if it had an overt nuclear weapons capability.[3] So there is a line of thought that says that perhaps proliferation is not a problem, but rather a solution. According to it, we should think about the possibility of a world order constructed on the progressive spread of this technology in its military form.

There are certain dangers, however, in trying to base a general order on the crystal ball analogy, with an expectation of prudent behavior on the part of more and more nations. Crystal balls can be shattered. They can be shattered by accident, by miscalculation, or by irrational actions. It seems to me that it is quite unlikely that nuclear deterrence will last forever, even in the U.S.-Soviet relationship. To believe it would last forever means that we can assume that Murphy's Law has been repealed and that humans are no longer fallible. That leads me to the conclusion that even the great powers, the superpowers, have to take steps gradually to reduce their reliance on nuclear technology over the long run, and to take steps to reduce the risk of relying on that technology in the meantime. I am speaking about very long periods, of many decades, but nonetheless I think the argument is correct. Though I do not agree with all the details of their position, I think the Catholic bishops recently came to essentially the correct overall conclusion about nuclear weapons. Nuclear deterrence is only conditionally moral, conditional upon taking steps to reduce our reliance upon it in the long run and to negotiate forms of reducing the risks of having it in the short run.[4]

---

[2]See Carl Sagan, "Nuclear War and Climatic Catastrophe: Some Policy Implications," *Foreign Affairs* 62, no. 2 (Winter 1983/84): 257–92.

[3]Kenneth N. Waltz, *The Spread of Nuclear Weapons: More May Be Better*, Adelphi Paper no. 171 (London: International Institute for Strategic Studies, 1981); Shai Feldman, *Israeli Nuclear Deterrence: A Strategy for the 1980s* (New York: Columbia University Press, 1982).

[4]National Conference of Catholic Bishops, *The Challenge of Peace: God's Promise and Our Response: A Pastoral Letter on War and Peace*, Publication No. 863 (Washington, DC: United States Catholic Conference, 1983).

We have to think about nuclear weapons in relation to world order as a question of probability and time. We must use the time we have bought to reduce the probability of nuclear weapons ever being used. From that perspective we can see one of the flaws in the argument of a world order deliberately built on furthering proliferation. The probability of use of nuclear weapons for many of the new countries that would have them is, I believe, considerably higher than the probability of use between the superpowers. Very often the nuclear optimists will make an argument that assumes, roughly speaking, that other things are equal. In other words, if deterrence has produced prudence in the superpower relationship, then, other things being equal, it should also do so between India and Pakistan, Israel and its Arab neighbors, Argentina and Brazil, or whatever other pair. The trouble is that other things rarely are in fact equal.

Among those that are least equal are the procedures for command and control of nuclear weaponry. The control problem has two dimensions: a political side and a technical side. Politically, a case can be made based on the statistics of where coups, civil wars, and other disruptions have occurred. It leads to the conclusion that there is a higher probability of disruption of governmental processes in many of the new countries which would be seeking nuclear weapons than there is in the USSR or the United States. Now, I am not arguing that nuclear weapons are all right because we are white and they are not, which is a travesty of an argument sometimes attributed to people making the case I am making. What I am arguing is that, looking at the problem in probabilistic terms, there is some chance of governmental processes breaking down and rash decisions being taken, anywhere. Many people believe that Richard Nixon's state of mind just before his resignation in 1974 is a phenomenon that should be thought about before attributing absolute stability even to us in the United States. We can have a failure of the government processes that affect the control of nuclear weapons in any country. But I would argue that the historical statistics of coups and civil wars show that the probabilities are much higher in countries like Pakistan, Nigeria, or Argentina.

The other dimension concerning the problem of command and control of nuclear weaponry is the unevenness of countries' technical capacity. Over the years the United States and the USSR have built up elaborate processes for the control of nuclear weapons in a technical sense. There are permissive action links which would inhibit unauthorized use of nuclear weapons, and special safety devices which keep a weapon from going off inadvertently if it is dropped or shot at, or damaged in an explosion of a nonnuclear sort. These technical capabilities are usually beyond the skills of new entrants into nuclear weapons status. This does not mean that they will not be developed over time, but that improvement of capacity is by no means certain. Ironically, it is easier to make a crude fission device than it is to make the safety catch that prevents the unauthorized use of that crude device. Now the answer to that is to give out safety catches, so to speak, but who among the recipients would trust the safety catches they had been given? And what about the technology and information that would be transferred in trying to present an acceptable solution? The matter is very complex. The quick fixes, the idea that we will simply transfer the necessary technology to remedy the technical deficiencies of the new countries' command-and-control systems, and in that way make "other things equal," strikes me as implausible.

A further problem with the optimists' proliferation argument, and a further reason why it is hard to generalize the spread of nuclear weaponry as a basis for world order, is the problem of timing or transition, of getting from here to there. It is very difficult to imagine how to move from a situation of current intense regional rivalry between pairs of countries to a more relaxed situation of second-strike capability, in which neither side would be vulnerable to a preemptive attack by the other. It is one thing for the leader of a country to say, "I am this secure now without nuclear weapons. If I could add nuclear weapons on top of that I would be that much more secure." He is thinking rather one-dimensionally up one scale. If time is put into the graph, it may well turn out that, if he is at present secure to a degree with conventional weapons and tries to add nuclear weaponry, his security will first go down before it eventually goes up. The reason is that, by starting out on a nuclear weapons program, he will have offered a big incentive for his neighbor to preempt now, rather than later, while his nuclear facilities are still soft and vulnerable. For stability to be maintained, both sides in such a rivalry would have to be able to believe that there was going to be stable nuclear deterrence at the end of it all, rather than to conclude that it makes more sense to preempt now rather than to risk destruction later. The Israeli attack on the reactor in Iraq in 1981 was not a nuclear preemption, but it was a case of a preemption designed to prevent the growth of a nuclear capability. I have sometimes called this "the valley of vulnerability," an illusory situation in which a country's leader, thinking he is going up the mountain to greater security, actually goes down into a valley of greater insecurity before he and his countrymen are able to climb out again.

For these three reasons, the problems of political and technical control and the difficulty of transition, it strikes me that the people who are trying to make an argument for building a type of world order on the spread of nuclear weaponry do not have a very convincing case. Thinking in terms of the probability of risks answers these theorists. It may be that, in some cases, stable deterrence within pairs of countries will result. The overall effect is a matter of degree. We have to do a careful assessment of whether, on balance, the idea of a proliferated world order would produce stability. We must look at all the pairs of relationships. The conclusion that proliferation would provide a basis for a general world order, whatever it might do to stabilize relations within a particular pair of countries or another, strikes me as implausible.

Thinking in terms of probability of risk also helps to answer the diplomats who often argue, in such settings as the United Nations, that nuclear nonproliferation is a hypocritical policy and a morally blinkered approach because it assumes that nuclear weapons are all right for the great powers but not for the smaller ones. If the reader has followed what I have presented so far, he will appreciate that I have not used two standards. I have used a single standard. I have argued that, in fact, nuclear weapons are dangerous for all countries and over the very long run are not an adequate basis for a common world order. I have also argued, however, that this realization has to be coupled with an understanding of degrees of risk, which can be based on factual analyses of the circumstances of the superpowers in comparison with the vulnerabilities of some of the new entrants into nuclear weapons status. Basically, my argument is that there is not a basis for a sound or stable world order based on the spread of nuclear weaponry among any class of countries and that a policy of nonproliferation does not rest on a hypocritical, double standard or on immoral logic.

With that stated, let me turn to a consideration of the immediate problem I would like to discuss: the practical diplomacy of building the nonproliferation regime that we live under today. We live in the presence of a variety of international regimes: some strong, some weak, some very broad, some quite narrow and specific, and most far from perfect. They vary in their coherence and degree of adherence. Generally, we measure their existence in terms of the normative constraints that they put on international behavior. For non-proliferation, the main regime norms and practices are found in the 1968 Non-Proliferation Treaty (NPT) and its regional counterparts like the Treaty of Tlatelolco, and the safeguards, rules and procedures of the International Atomic Energy Agency (IAEA).[5] While there are a few important exceptions, the large majority of states in the world today adheres at least to a part of this set of norms. That is really quite remarkable. Essentially, what we have is a world in which the large majority of states adheres to a presumption against the spread of nuclear weaponry. That most states adhere to a regime in which they forswear the right to use the ultimate form of self-help in technological terms is quite an extraordinary situation.

The beginnings of this current nonproliferation regime date back to 1953. In the aftermath of the failure of the Baruch Plan, and with it the international effort to be totally restrictive with the control of nuclear technology, President Dwight D. Eisenhower launched his famous Atoms for Peace Program.[6] Its aim was to assist countries in the development of nuclear civil energy in return for their guarantees that such assistance would be used only for peaceful purposes. The policy was oversold, and it was poorly thought through in its execution at a time when too little was known about the likely

---

[5]For the texts of the Treaty on the Non-Proliferation of Nuclear Weapons, the Treaty for the Prohibition of Nuclear Weapons in Latin America, the Agreement Between the United States of America and the International Atomic Energy Agency for the Application of Safeguards in the United States, and other relevant documents, see *Arms Control and Disarmament Agreements: Texts and Histories of Negotiations* (Washington, DC: U.S. Arms Control and Disarmament Agency, 1982).

[6]On the history of the Baruch and Eisenhower proposals, see Bernard G. Bechhofer, *Postwar Negotiations for Arms Control* (Washington, DC: Brookings Institution, 1961).

pace and cost of peaceful nuclear development. It did, however, serve to create an initial consensus on which to build. Essentially, the most powerful state in the nuclear field had used its power in a way to attract others to a normative framework. More specifically, the central accomplishment of the Atoms for Peace Program was the creation of a system of international safeguards and an institutional framework in the form of the IAEA, established in 1957 with headquarters in Vienna. Under the IAEA safeguard systems, nonweapon countries agree to file with the agency regular detailed reports on nuclear civilian activities and agree to allow international inspectors to visit their facilities to verify the reports and ensure no materials have been diverted from peaceful to military purposes. The safeguard system is central to the basic bargain of the international regime, in which other countries are assisted in their peaceful nuclear energy needs in return for their accepting the intrusion of safeguards and inspection.

This regime was further developed and strengthened by the signature in 1968 of the NPT, which had originated in an Irish proposal in the United Nations early in the 1960s. Nine significant countries—Argentina, Brazil, China, France, India, Israel, Pakistan, South Africa, and Spain—have refused to sign the nuclear nonproliferation treaty, usually on grounds that it is discriminatory. Of the nine, France, it is worth noting, has indicated it will not undercut the purposes of the treaty. In Latin America a regional agreement limiting nuclear weapons, the 1967 Treaty of Tlatelolco, helps to fill the normative gap. Skeptics have dismissed the NPT as a modern equivalent of the infamous Kellogg-Briand antiwar pact, since any state can simply quit on three months' notice. Other detractors have argued that the treaty is imperfectly drafted and involves promises that cannot be kept. Nonetheless, by establishing a normative presumption against proliferation and by creating procedures to verify intentions, the NPT has helped to build confidence and a degree of predictability in states' behavior. It helps to strengthen the international nuclear regime by symbolizing a common interest. The NPT is not, as some enthusiasts tended to believe in the 1960s, sufficient or the same as the international nuclear regime, but, with some 130 adherents, it has certainly become the central focus of the regime.

By the early 1970s there was a good deal of complacency about the nuclear nonproliferation system. Such complacency was shattered, however, by three events that occurred in the mid-1970s. The first was the Indian explosion in May 1974 of a so-called peaceful nuclear device, using plutonium derived from a Canadian-supplied research reactor and U.S.-supplied heavy water. The second event was the oil embargo of 1973–74 and the fourfold increase in oil prices, which created widespread insecurity in energy supplies and also highly exaggerated expectations about the importance of nuclear energy in remedying those energy insecurities. The net effect of the oil embargo was, specifically, to accelerate governments' plans for the early commercial use of plutonium fuels which, unlike the low-enriched uranium currently used as fuel in most reactors, is a weapons-usable material. The IAEA then projected that some forty countries might be using plutonium fuels by the end of the 1980s. At the same time, safeguards and institutions for dealing with such a flood of weapons-usable materials were not adequately developed. Finally, the third event was a spate of proposals to sell facilities for producing weapons-usable materials without regard to their economic justification or proliferation implications. Subsequently it was disclosed that, in at least three cases, the recipients were attempting to develop nuclear weapons. I refer to South Korea, Taiwan, and Pakistan. Had the proposed sales gone through, there would almost certainly have been violations or abrogations of safeguards. In such circumstances there was grave danger that the whole international regime for the containment of nuclear weaponry might collapse.

These threats to stability were reinforced by trends in the power position of the United States both within the context of the nuclear issue and outside it. Outside the nuclear issue, the United States suffered during this period its disastrous defeat in Vietnam, with an accompanying turn in its cycle of foreign policy attitudes in an inward direction. Inside the nuclear issue, America's share of world nuclear exports had begun to decline, as strong industrial competition developed for the sale of light-water reactors (the current type of reactors developed in the United States and Europe). Concomitantly, American leverage over nuclear fuel supplies eroded. Whereas in the period when Eisenhower was promoting his Atoms for Peace Program there was a virtual U.S. monopoly in the nuclear fuel-supply area, by the mid-1970s an oligopolistic structure of exports had developed.

The years 1976 and 1977 saw a series of American initiatives in response to these events. First, the Nuclear Suppliers Group, a fifteen-nation body including the Soviet Union, was established in London to prevent commercial competition from undercutting safeguards obligations. Second, late in 1976 President Gerald Ford announced a more cautious policy toward the use of plutonium in America's own nuclear programs. And third, with the Carter administration in 1977, there was a tightening of both of these measures.

These new restrictions tended to create a degree of rancor internationally, yet maintaining and refurbishing the international regime was going to require a general approach around which a broad group of nations could rally. The process of rethinking the conditions of the regime had to be shared beyond the United States alone. A confrontational approach which threatened to isolate this country would further disrupt the regime. In those circumstances, in the job that I filled as deputy under secretary of state for Security Assistance, Science, and Technology, I had to think of some device in diplomatic terms that might reduce the degree of tension between having American leadership and gaining the multilateral solution required by the nature of the problem. The device that I designed to meet these various policy needs was the International Nuclear Fuel Cycle Evaluation (INFCE), essentially a special type of conference diplomacy. It has been described by Harvey Brooks, a Harvard professor of technology and public policy, and others as a pioneering effort at international technology assessment. Officially, it provided a two-year period in which nations could collectively reexamine assumptions in a search for ways to reconcile their different assessments of the energy and nonproliferation risks involved in various aspects of the nuclear fuel cycle, which was the dimension from which the most recent challenges had come.

While INFCE was officially given a predominantly technical rationale, it was in fact a means of attracting broad participation into what was really part of a political process of providing a basis of stability for the international nuclear regime. The sixty-six countries and organizations that came together in Vienna in those two years, 1977–1979, included both consumer countries and supplier countries in the nuclear area, and both rich and poor countries, East and West; most important, they included a dozen countries that had not signed the NPT. In all, some 519 experts from forty-six countries participated in sixty-one meetings of eight working groups that produced 20,000 pages of documents! The common denominator of this diverse gathering was the final plenary conference finding that INFCE had "strengthened the view that effective measures can and should be taken to minimize the danger of proliferation of nuclear weapons without jeopardizing energy for peaceful purposes."[7] The participants were determined to preserve the climate of mutual understanding and cooperation in the nuclear energy field. This is one of the major accomplishments of INFCE.

As a diplomatic device, INFCE helped to reestablish a basis for consensus on a refurbished regime for the international nuclear fuel cycle. The very process of engaging in international technology assessment helped to heighten awareness of the nonproliferation problem and the threats to the regime. In that sense, INFCE helped the U.S. government to set the agenda for other governments. It was not so much that the outcome was exactly what we wanted in every detail; it was that everybody was looking at the problem in the terms in which we defined it. Moreover, it affected the bureaucratic processes inside other governments. Foreign offices, rather than just nuclear energy agencies, became more involved. As anyone who has looked carefully at the problems of international order realizes, transgovernmental associations between parts of governments are extremely important in determining what is do-able and not do-able in the international ordering. When one finds a transgovernmental coalition such as the tight coalition among nuclear energy agencies, one of the solutions to the problem of rigidity that develops is to bring in more attention from the top levels of the government and more of a role for the foreign ministries. INFCE helped get other governments' top officials and foreign ministries more actively engaged in areas that had previously been delegated solely to energy agencies.

---

[7]Communiqué of the Final Plenary Conference of INFCE, International Atomic Energy Agency, Vienna, February 27, 1980.

Most important of all, attention to the proliferation problem and to regime maintenance was spread beyond the United States. While the U.S. government did not always agree with all the details of INFCE's answers, the most important point was that INFCE focused other countries' attention on our objective: nonproliferation. INFCE's success in defusing some of the sharp conflicts over the tension between the suppliers' interest and the NPT was clear at the 1980 NPT Review Conference, at which fuel-cycle issues proved far less contentious than general disarmament questions.

INFCE is an example of a device of multilateral diplomacy that can be used to solve a particular type of problem. It would be a mistake to think of it as the only device necessary in trying to organize the diplomacy of maintaining the nonproliferation regime. In fact, one of the central questions in maintaining the nonproliferation regime, and the nuclear-control regime generally, is the issue of using different types of diplomacy at the same time. Let me start at the most primitive, or simplest, level with bilateral diplomacy and then move on to the more general level of multilateral diplomacy, followed by a discussion of the IAEA.

First, bilateral diplomacy is extraordinarily important in running a nonproliferation regime. There have to be bilateral contacts with all sorts of countries. One sort of relationship is with potential entrants into nuclear weapons status. It was bilateral diplomacy with countries such as South Korea and Taiwan that helped to persuade them they were unwise to continue with their pursuit of the nuclear weapons option. Bilateral diplomacy also is important in the U.S.-Soviet dimension. On nonproliferation, one does not have the same kind of confrontational approach between the United States and USSR that one has on other issues. Another dimension of bilateral diplomacy is with other key critical supplier countries. In the nuclear nonproliferation area, probably the most important country to work with closely is France, which has an active nuclear program and a significant nuclear supply potential. Regular bilateral meetings were held between the U.S. and French governments. Similar sessions were held with a number of other supplier governments, particularly when hard cases arose such as the supply of so-called gray-area materials that could be used for nuclear weapons or for other purposes. This problem is often best dealt with in quiet, bilateral diplomacy with the supplying country. Indeed, one could argue that, in these bilateral meetings, "the quieter, the better." There remains an important role for quiet, bilateral diplomacy even when dealing with a multilateral issue.

One cannot, of course, always control what can be done by means of quiet diplomacy alone. Sometimes it is not even possible to keep it quiet—or bilateral. As a member of the transition team for the Carter administration, I wrote a paper for the incoming secretary of state which looked at the difficulties arising from the German sale of sensitive nuclear materials to Brazil and the French sale of the same to Pakistan. These issues are intensely sensitive, I said. If we raise them publicly, I argued, they are bound to get people's backs up and nothing will be accomplished. The only way to deal with such matters is to go about resolving them through quiet diplomacy. Yet within a few days of the new administration's coming into office, I found myself on an airplane to Rio de Janeiro, with newspaper reporters in attendance before I went and newspaper reporters present after I got there and the attitude of the Brazilian government exactly as I had predicted. The reason was that the German government, in an effort to forestall a difficulty they saw coming in bilateral relations, had sent a private emissary to call on the not yet inaugurated Carter administration. The emissary was trying to deliver a message of conciliation, saying that Germany would hold off a bit before actually delivering the sensitive technology, though of course it would eventually deliver it. When he called on the officials and transition staff at the White House, they heard the part of the message that Germany was going to deliver, but they did not really hear the first half. The word very quickly came over to the State Department that the Germans were "playing hardball" and that we were to respond in kind—hence my highly reported journey. So much for planning papers and the avoidance of publicity in dealing with what are best treated as quiet, bilateral issues. The result in this case was not very successful.

Contrast that, however, with the French-Pakistan case where, for a year and a half, despite the leaky climate of Washington, we managed to work very quietly with our French counterparts and were able to convince them that their sale of a reprocessing plant to Pakistan indeed would be used for military purposes. Fortunately, the French government, looking carefully at the evidence we presented, agreed that the plant was going to be misused for military purposes and changed its policy. It changed its policy a long time before it announced it in the summer of 1978, and we managed to keep that absolutely quiet. The French government was not embarrassed, and gradually it withdrew its participation in that particular program without totally disrupting its relationship with Pakistan, which it had been worried about. So, in bilateral diplomacy, the quieter the better, but that works sometimes and not at other times.

The second type of diplomacy needed in trying to maintain the nonproliferation regime is what might be called small multilateral diplomacy. Essentially this means setting up subgroups of the total which have particular interests and foci. The best example of that is the Nuclear Suppliers Group (NSG). The credit for beginning its negotiations goes to the Ford administration which, in rather belated response to the Indian explosion, nonetheless began in 1975 to organize the fifteen key supplier countries to come together and talk about ways in which they could prevent their commercial competition from undercutting the international nonproliferation regime and its safeguards. The group eventually grew to fifteen countries. The formal diplomacy of the NSG was carried out at meetings with a hundred or so people, if one counted all the spear carriers behind the chiefs of delegations. It was small only in comparison with UN diplomacy. Much work was done during NSG conferences in a series of revolving bilateral meetings, but the fact that they were conducted at the same time in the same city—London—allowed the participants to register what was happening and to figure out what positions they would take so that they could get things accomplished even when there were a hundred people in the room.

The NSG was a successful venture. We did manage to establish a framework for organizing competition in such a way so as not to undercut safeguards. We published those guidelines in January 1978 through the IAEA, so that it would not look as though we were trying to divorce ourselves from it but rather were trying to work through it in support of the IAEA system.[8] At that point, it was decided that the NSG would not meet again in plenary but would instead serve as a framework by which we would organize bilateral consultations, if necessary. The reason for that decision is that there is a certain danger when one organizes a small subset of any larger organization: namely, those who are not there resent it. There also was a shared concern that, if we tried to organize all the diplomatic activity inside the NSG, it was going to wreck the IAEA and the nonproliferation treaty. It would look as though the big countries were ganging up on all the rest. Now that we had our published framework through the IAEA, we would continue with the private bilateral meetings, where the heart of the action was anyway. When issues have arisen about dual-use technology being sent to countries with dubious records, the necessary bilateral consultations have gone on within the NSG framework.

The third type of diplomacy used in maintaining the nonproliferation regime is the discussion that occurs within the IAEA, as a specialized agency of the United Nations. An IAEA board meeting normally is composed of several hundred people, with a formal procedure, which lends itself to more rhetorical statements than might be heard in NSG meetings. The IAEA meetings are supplemented by having a set of bilaterals with the key countries. Again, the network of quiet diplomacy develops within the context of a larger organization. This larger specialized agency diplomacy is still important. The IAEA secretariat plays an important role in preparing reports, keeping track of what is happening, bringing together committees, and reinforcing the formal norms and procedures of the organization. While the effective work may be done in private bilaterals, the resolutions passed and the votes taken in the large IAEA board setting are necessary and useful.

There has been a tendency in the IAEA in recent years toward a greater degree of politicization, along the North-South cleavage, than in the past. Formerly, the IAEA structure reflected the U.S.-Soviet domination of the nuclear issue area. Gradually that structure was popularized as more countries became technically competent in the nuclear area. Perhaps more important

---

[8]International Atomic Energy Agency, "Communications Received from Certain Nuclear States Regarding Guidelines for the Export of Nuclear Material, Equipment, or Technology," Information Circular no. 254, February 1978.

than that has been the intrusion of larger issues from the UN debates, not only the North-South issues but also the Arab-Israeli dispute. For instance, after the Israeli bombing of the Iraqi nuclear reactor, a resolution was passed to penalize Israel within the IAEA. At one point, it appeared that the United States might have to withdraw over the issue. To have done so would have cut off our nose to spite our face.

In these concentric circles of diplomacy, the largest and most encompassing diplomacy is that of the UN system, both in the form of General Assembly discussions and, every five years, the NPT Review Conference. A very different type of diplomacy is found in these very large organizations, with much more oratory. The same people whom you might meet in a private bilateral session will often say something much more aggressive or strike a much more grandiose pose in the larger forums of conference diplomacy. Nonetheless, the larger forms of conference diplomacy cannot be ignored, because nonproliferation is a problem that is multilateral by its nature. Keeping a broad consensus, preserving a general interest, is essential to maintaining the overall nonproliferation regime. At the NPT Review Conference meetings there will be arguments about whether the large countries have lived up to their promise in Article VI of the NPT to take steps to reduce what is called vertical proliferation, the growth of total numbers of nuclear weapons, or complaints about the willingness to supply equipment according to the terms of Article IV of the treaty. Long and rhetorical flourishes can be expected on both of these issues, Nonetheless, it would be foolish to ignore these complaints, because there is some merit in each of them. It would be even more foolish to take every speech exactly at face value. The reasoning behind countries' membership in the nonproliferation regime is not fully developed in the speeches of their delegates at NPT Review Conferences. The reasons for maintenance of the regime go back to the basic interests of each country in terms of security. Only if we were so foolish as to ignore the exercise of large conference diplomacy and to flaunt our own disinterest in it would we create a pretext, for others, that could lead to the unraveling of the process that is so often threatened at such meetings.

We find, then, as we consider the diplomacy of maintaining a nuclear nonproliferation regime, that we have to think of aligning four concentric circles or, perhaps more apt, keeping four hoops in the air at the same time without having one bump into the other or fall. Keeping all these types of diplomacy going at the same time is not easy. It is particularly not easy in a democracy, where there is more than one juggler trying to pretend that he is the main show. The difficulties of managing the necessary coordination between the executive and legislative branches have made this problem of diplomatic juggling more difficult than it otherwise might be. The Nuclear Nonproliferation Act passed by Congress in 1978 particularly complicated our efforts in the administration to develop the INFCE to smooth over the confrontations that had arisen early in the NPT regime. Diplomacy had to go in two directions:

it had to be practiced with other countries and conducted with Congress simultaneously.

In conclusion, let me briefly address the question of prospects for the future. A central paradox in the nonproliferation regime goes back to what I said at the beginning about the basic principles of the anarchic world system in which we live: sovereignty, legal equality, and self-defense. There is always going to be some tension between the general norm of separate states, with the right of self-help, and the basic purpose of the nonproliferation regime, which is to prevent the further spread of nuclear weaponry and therefore must distinguish between some states having nuclear weapons and others asked to forswear nuclear weapons. That tension is always going to be present, and it is always going to affect the practical implementation of the various rules to prevent the diversion of fissionable materials and the organization of procedures and institutions necessary for inspection.

The real question then is: Is this basic tension sustainable? Or, how can it be sustained? First, during the initial phases of the regime, the tension was sustainable partly because of the great concentration of power in this area between the United States and the Soviet Union. The superpowers were able to cooperate in dealing with this particular issue. Second, at the initiation of the regime there was a carrot as well as a stick: the incentives and lures of the peaceful uses of nuclear technology, which helped to get others to play the game. Third, in the maintenance of the regime, the basic tension, or balance, has been sustained by the self-interest of the smaller states who have wanted constraints on their neighbors. They want to be able to have stable expectations for their own security planning, their own economic planning. They must know what their neighbors are going to do, or are not going to do. You might not like being constrained yourself, they think to themselves, but you surely do like having your potential rival constrained. You might not like the intrusiveness of the inspectors coming into your own country, but you certainly do want to know what the inspectors found out when they went into the country next door. So, in that sense, the self-interest of rival smaller states has helped to maintain the regime.

A fourth point about how equilibrium has been maintained is that some of these informal norms of the regime take on a life of their own. The norms may originate in a particular power structure of some countries having more than others, but gradually they become accepted and are made explicit, not only internationally in the form of the treaties but also domestically in government policies. Again, think transnationally and transgovernmentally. Governments are not monoliths; they are collections of people vying for their own interpretations of policy and their own ways of implementing it. International regimes may reinforce some parts of governments against others. In domestic debates, the fact that there is a treaty, that the country has a reputation for not violating its treaty commitments, and that a network of people inside the country is committed to certain procedures becomes very important in maintaining the presumption against the spread of nuclear weapons. Again, such a constraint is not an absolute; it can always be broken, and it can always be changed. The important point, however, is that when a state of tension exists between the norms of what one thinks is typical of the self-help system overall and the particular norms of the nonproliferation regime, the presumption toward one pole rather than the other can be the basis of stability.

In short, the nonproliferation regime makes a difference to how states define their self-interests both internationally and in terms of domestic expectations. It creates a certain inertia in favor of one way of approaching a problem in the future. It puts the burden of proof on proponents of nuclear weaponry rather than on those who favor nonproliferation. It works against those who may want to be free riders, who may want to say, in giving up the responsibility for maintaining the NPT regime, "Let the treaty constrain others but not us." It operates against the dissenters from the nonproliferation norm, who say they have such an impossible security dilemma that they would rather go it on their own with nuclear weapons than maintain participation in common controls. Countries such as Israel, South Africa, and Pakistan may fall into this category.

Can the existing nonproliferation regime be maintained against their doubts and the questions of other such insecure states? An occasional breach of law does not destroy a normative order. (Anyone familiar with driving a car in Massachusetts knows that well.) But there are, sociologists tell us, tipping points with regard to the degree of observance of norms, after which a certain amount of noncompliance leads everybody not to comply. When does a certain form of behavior or amount of noncompliance become so great that virtually everybody stops complying? The key questions about the future of the regime—whether it can be perpetuated—depend, then, on the rate and the degree of proliferation.

The question of rate is: Can we keep the curve flat? Can we keep it creeping up only very slowly along the bottom of the graph as we go out in time, as opposed to becoming suddenly exponential? So far, we have done this relatively well, but unless we make the effort and invest in keeping the curve flat, a sudden change or upward movement in the rate of proliferation could quickly reach a point at which the whole regime would topple.

The other question is the degree of proliferation. Proliferation is like a staircase; there are many steps before a first explosion and many steps after an explosion that have political significance. The difference between Israel, which probably has nuclear weapons but has not exploded them, and India, which has had an explosion but has not made nuclear weapons, makes a blur about where some of these steps actually lie. Some people would argue that the future in this area is going to be a "bomb in the basement" phenomenon: that is, more and more countries, realizing that there is a certain penalty for crossing the explosion threshold, will creep right up to it and take a position such as the Israeli one of saying, essentially, "We are one screwdriver turn away from having nuclear weapons, but we will not be the first to introduce nuclear weapons in the Middle East." The issue then is: "What difference does it make if everybody does go up to that point? It is basically a proliferated world, in any case." Well, it does make a difference.

It makes a difference that we pay attention to that first explosion and try to inhibit it, for several reasons. First of all, the initial explosion is what is written into the normative structure. The existing treaties define proliferation in terms of a first explosion. If we think of proliferation as a staircase, the first explosion is a wider stair. It is a landing. So there is some reason to keep a focus on the salient point at which there is already some normative structure built. Second, if there has not yet been an actual explosion, probably leading to a series of explosions, it is much harder to weaponize—to reduce the size and increase the useability of weapons. There are essentially terror devices or anti-city devices, but not effective nuclear war-fighting devices. Third, there is much less political symbolism, I believe, from the bomb in the basement than there is from the overt nuclear explosion, in terms of generating the reciprocal political passions that may drive countries to neglect their larger or longer term security interests. So, I think that, with regard to the degree of proliferation as well as its rate, a lot may be said for trying to keep things low on the staircase and moving slowly, while continuing to maintain public concern about the critical landing, that is, the first explosion.

If I were to be asked for my predictions for the future, I would say that there might be eleven or so countries with nuclear weapons by the end of the century. If I had to make a bet, I would bet on twelve, just because I never trust my own judgment and I throw in a wild card. Such a development has to be contrasted not with the perfect world in which we stop all further spread of nuclear weapons (because I do not think we can), but with the world that John F. Kennedy described in 1963 when he predicted as many as twenty-five nuclear weapons countries by the time of the age we live in right now.[9] In other words, we are doing a lot better than was expected a generation ago. In light of this accomplishment—the fact that we have controlled the rate of proliferation, that we have kept it flat along the bottom of the curve rather than letting it go exponential, that we have arrested some nuclear programs before they resulted in the deployment of weapons—I am myself able to conclude that we can maintain this regime, and the world order it represents. We can indeed continue to inhibit the rate of growth of nuclear proliferation, but only if we are willing to pay a cost.

We have to pay a price of leadership, and we must realize that both nuclear proliferation and the diplomacy of nuclear nonproliferation are costly. If we place too high a priority on the proliferation issue, we can, for instance, really complicate relations with Pakistan, which inhibits our ability to deal with Afghanistan, which in turn affects the way we relate to the USSR. But if we do not, if we say instead, "I will make an exception for Pakistan," what

---

[9]President Kennedy, quoted in Glenn T. Seaborg, *Kennedy, Khrushchev and the Test Ban* (Berkeley: University of California Press, 1981), p. 199.

is the signal we are then giving to the nth-plus-one country with regard to maintaining the overall nuclear regime? The willingness to invest in nonproliferation is essential to keeping the rate of proliferation low. And it is not cheap to have such a diplomacy. Partly for that reason, I think it is important for the United States to continue to try to encourage a sharing of leadership—to involve the USSR, to involve France, and probably also to involve the rising tier of potential supplier nations (India and Argentina, to name two). In addition, the success of maintaining the present nonproliferation regime will depend on our ability to use various forms of diplomacy, often quite contradictory in their modalities and sometimes their effects, at the same time—the four concentric circles, or four hoops, that I mentioned. Before accepting my basically hopeful prediction too easily, please keep in mind the difficulty involved in conducting such a four-ring diplomacy within and for a democracy. But the potential cost of failure obligates us to try.

FOR FURTHER READING

For an introduction to most aspects of the nuclear question, including the issue of nonproliferation, see Harvard Nuclear Study Group, *Living with Nuclear Weapons*, cited in the footnotes; also Graham T. Allison, Albert Carnesale, and Joseph S. Nye, Jr., eds., *Hawks, Doves, and Owls: An Agenda for Avoiding Nuclear War* (New York: W. W. Norton, 1985), and Joseph S. Nye, Jr., *Nuclear Ethics* (New York: Free Press, 1986). Studies by Joseph Nye dealing specifically with the proliferation problem include "Nonproliferation: A Long-term Strategy," *Foreign Affairs* 56, no. 3 (April 1978): 601–23; "Maintaining a Nonproliferation Regime," *International Organization* 35, no. 1 (Winter 1981): 15–38; "Nonproliferation in the '80s," *Bulletin of Atomic Scientists* 38, no. 7 (August/September 1982): 30–32; "Nonproliferation Policies," in Warren Hecrotte and John C. Smith, eds., *Arms Control in Transition* (Boulder, CO: Westview Press, 1983); and "NPT: The Logic of Inequality," *Foreign Policy*, no. 59 (Summer 1985): 123–31.

Other informative recent works on the development of this subject are the following: Joseph A. Yager, ed., *Nonproliferation and U.S. Foreign Policy* (Washington, DC: Brookings Institution, 1980); Amy Finkelstein, "Brazil, the United States and Nuclear Proliferation: American Foreign Policy at the Crossroads," *The Fletcher Forum: A Journal of Studies in International Affairs* 7, no. 2 (Summer 1983): 277–311; Leonard S. Spector, *Nuclear Proliferation Today* (Cambridge, MA: Ballinger, 1984) and an article, "Silent Spread," *Foreign Policy*, no. 58 (Spring 1985): 53–78; James A. Schear, ed., *Nuclear Weapons Proliferation and Nuclear Risk* (New York: St. Martin's Press, 1984); John Simpson and Tony McGrew, eds., *The International Nuclear Non-Proliferation System: Challenges and Changes* (New York: St. Martin's Press, 1984); Rodney W. Jones et al., eds., *The Nuclear Suppliers and Nonproliferation* (Lexington, MA: Lexington Books, 1985); Sadruddin Aga Khan, ed., *Nuclear War, Nuclear Proliferation and Their Consequences* (Oxford: Clarendon Press, 1985).

The Lessons of the Madrid
CSCE Conference

MAX M. KAMPELMAN

The first public-policy question to face me after I was asked, in the late spring of 1980, to join the American delegation to the Madrid follow-up meeting of the Conference on Security and Cooperation in Europe (CSCE) was whether the United States should even participate in that meeting. This was in the aftermath of the December 1979 Soviet invasion of Afghanistan, an event that had shocked the world and caused the cancellation of American participation in the Moscow Olympic Games. The preparatory meeting to arrange for the agenda and modalities was scheduled to open in September 1980. During this period, one of the presidential candidates, Ronald Reagan, agreed with the position of nationally syndicated columnist William Safire that, since we were not sending our athletes to Moscow, we should not be sending our diplomats to Madrid.[1] Also, two former senior American diplomats, both of whom had participated in the development of the 1975 Helsinki Final Act, privately urged me not to go to Madrid.

Their case was a good one. More than just the fate of Afghanistan was at issue. The very unity of the Western alliance was at stake. The origins of the Helsinki Final Act could be traced to the Soviet Union's 1969 proposal for a "European Security Conference"; when the Soviets proposed a European Security Conference, they meant a meeting that would exclude the United States and Canada. An important objective of Soviet leaders since the end of the Second World War had been to separate the United States from Western Europe, the argument being that European countries, including the USSR, have more in common with one another than they have with non-European

---

[1] William Safire, "Doing It Ourselves," *New York Times*, May 22, 1980; "An Interview with Reagan," *Time* 115, no. 26 (June 30, 1980): 15–16.

countries. This was one of the major objectives of the Soviet proposal for a European Security Conference, as well as for its successor meetings. The Soviets also wanted such a conference to provide legitimacy for their postwar boundaries, which had been established at the wartime Teheran and Yalta conferences. Because there was no formal peace treaty at the conclusion of World War II, these boundaries, which certainly were not the same as they had been prior to the war, had no legitimacy. Both of these Soviet goals were to go unrealized. The Soviets had been able, however, to sell the idea of the Helsinki conference on the premise that the East and West were moving decisively into an era of détente, and this too was a very important Soviet objective.

When the Soviet proposal for a conference at Helsinki was first made, we in the United States were quite cool to it. Our European friends, though having more at stake, did not react to it with much greater enthusiasm. However, as the Nixon foreign policy developed a warmer relationship with the Soviet Union, the momentum grew for entering into the negotiation the Soviets had proposed.[2] We Americans were, in a sense, both in and out of those negotiations. The brunt of the negotiating effort was really the responsibility of our Western European allies. Our allies were able, with our encouragement, to introduce a major humanitarian component into the deliberations at Helsinki.

In our country, when we think of the Helsinki Final Act, we tend to identify it as a human-rights agreement. In Europe, the security component has for many an even greater significance, although for some Europeans, Helsinki has the same significance as it does for us. The fact that the West as a whole was able to inject into this negotiating process a major humanitarian component has really made this instrument an expression of Western values.

The Helsinki Final Act assumed the process of détente. The 1975 agreement was a reflection of all that could be done at that time. However, the delegates also provided for follow-up meetings in order to advance the Helsinki process, the hope being that, as relationships between East and West matured, it would be possible to improve upon the Final Act and move forward. Insofar as the military-security component was concerned, this continued diplomatic effort was looked upon by many of our European allies as likely to lead to important further steps.

The first follow-up meeting took place in Belgrade, from October 1977 to March 1978.[3] Madrid, the meeting which I attended initially as cochairman with former Attorney General Griffin B. Bell and then as American chairman, was the second follow-up meeting. At the time the Madrid conference was

---

[2]On the genesis of the Conference on Security and Cooperation in Europe, see Henry A. Kissinger, *White House Years* (Boston: Little, Brown, 1979), pp. 412–16.

[3]See the concluding statement by Justice Arthur J. Goldberg, chairman of the U.S. delegation, March 8, 1978, U.S., Department of State *Bulletin* 78, no. 2013 (April 1978): 40–44.

preparing to meet, some of us were giving serious consideration to whether we should even go. It was unmistakable by that time that the Soviets were acting as if the humanitarian provisions of the Helsinki Final Act were non-existent. Why, therefore, dignify the agreement and Soviet participation in it by acting as if its commitments were really genuine? There were other, even larger factors we had to consider. The most important consideration was related to the issue of peace.

Peace is a complicated idea. The basic Western notion has been that lasting peace means more than the absence of war. Peace is the supreme achievement of statesmanship. In order to be lasting, it must constitute a network of relations based on order, cooperation, and law. The West had successfully argued that peace had to encompass the totality of the relationships among states. The Helsinki Final Act, signed by thirty-five nations, reflected that concept. In addition to the provisions dealing with vital issues of security, there were provisions for stimulating international trade; for the exchange of ideas, information, and peoples; and for cultural exchanges. Then there were the provisions committing us to human rights. The passage under Principle VII of the text, concerning "respect for human rights and fundamental freedoms, including the freedom of thought, conscience, religion or belief," was unique in its breadth, and it became a major component of our search for peace.[4] Its underlying premise was that a state which declares war against its own people cannot be trusted not to declare war against its neighbors. Our nonattendance in Madrid would possibly have ended international consideration of the Helsinki Final Act and, with it, the force of these Western values. We thought that this was a responsibility which we should not take on.

To absent ourselves, furthermore, would have made us appear disinterested in the wider negotiating process with the East. It would have separated us in this respect from our European allies, whose political requirements were such that East-West talks had become an indispensable part of their diplomacy. We, rather than the Soviets, would have been blamed for destroying the Helsinki process, despite the fact that it was their disdain for it that was undermining the integrity of the accords.

At the same time, we knew that we could not permit our attendance at the Madrid meeting to serve in any way as a form of implicit toleration of Soviet behavior. We appreciated that it would be shortsighted for us to deny ourselves the use of Madrid as an effective forum to state our case. I felt very strongly about that. Our decision, therefore, was to prove at Madrid, and use our energies vividly to demonstrate, that Soviet violations of what were indeed noble Helsinki standards were threatening the peace and stability of Europe.

---

[4]For the text of the CSCE Final Act, signed at Helsinki on August 1, 1975, see Department of State *Bulletin* 73, no. 1888 (September 1, 1975): 323–50. The passage mentioned is on p. 325.

On the eve of the Madrid preparatory meeting in September, a deep desire for liberty gave birth to the Solidarity movement in Poland. As we were preparing to leave Washington for Madrid, we learned that among the first demands of the striking workers in Szczecin was that the Helsinki Final Act be republished in the Polish press so that the Polish people could be reminded of their human rights under the accords. Indeed, throughout the three years of the conference direct appeals reached us from Helsinki monitors in the East. We knew, as a result, that we belonged in Madrid—that the Helsinki process was important to the aspirations and morale of the men and women behind the Iron Curtain.

The Soviet government also recognized the challenge posed by the continuation of the Helsinki process. As Yuri Andropov, the Soviet leader, later told his Communist party cadres, there was a vital battle under way "for the hearts and minds of billions of people on this planet."[5] We in Madrid never forgot the existence or the importance of that battle.

The Madrid conference provided an opportunity for the most thorough review of the Soviet Union's actions and its crimes against humanity that has ever occurred in any international forum. A united group of Western nations, speaking in many languages but with one voice, documented the Soviet record. This included, besides armed aggression in Afghanistan and Poland, slave labor camps; the use of psychiatric hospitals as political punishment; government-sponsored anti-Semitism; religious persecution of evangelical Christians, Baptists, Seventh-Day Adventists, Pentecostals, and Catholics; the constriction of scientific freedom; the erosion of peoples' cultural and national heritage; the denial of the right to emigrate; and defiance of agreements against the use of chemical and biological weapons. There were also the violations of provisions of the Helsinki Final Act itself, including suppression of the Helsinki Watch Groups which had been formed in the Soviet Union to monitor the Soviet government's adherence to its commitments.[6]

Our statements were made in the first instance to the representatives of the thirty-five states at our sessions. There were thirty-three European states, plus the United States and Canada. We made our statements not only to these representatives, but our speeches and comments were also disseminated widely through the electronic and print media, particularly in Western Europe. In this battle for hearts and minds, we had to reach people. We were not content with making allegations; we provided evidence for our conclusions. Detailed stories from Madrid reached Eastern Europe on a daily basis through various Western radios, including the Voice of America, Radio Liberty, and Radio Free Europe. My own appearances on the BBC and Deutsche Welle were

---

[5]Andropov speech at plenary session of the Central Committee of the Communist Party of the Soviet Union, June 15, 1983, in *Pravda* and *Izvestia*, June 16, 1983. An English translation may be found in *Current Digest of the Soviet Press* 35, no. 25 (July 20, 1983): 1–8.

[6]For details on the suppression of the Watch Groups, see the formal opening address of Attorney General Griffin Bell on November 13, 1980, in *World Affairs: A Quarterly Review of International Problems* 144, no. 4 (Spring 1982): 311–18.

almost constant. These were frequently supplemented by appearances on radio and television stations elsewhere in Europe. The communications that we received from the East, as well as the West, proved the effectiveness of this activity. There was a uniform message: the Soviet Union and the other Warsaw Pact states had to comply with the agreements they had made in 1975 if they wished to be accepted as responsible members of the international community.

The question might now well be raised as to whether confrontation, which is exactly what I have been describing, is consistent with serious negotiation. Our side has not always been clear on this question. When the U.S. delegation at Belgrade in 1977 mentioned the names of six victims of Soviet repression—and we were one of only two of the thirty-five participating states to mention names—there was great concern about the propriety and the desirability of such an approach. (The Netherlands, incidentally, was the other state that did so.) In Madrid, however, the United States was but one of fourteen states to mention names. Not merely six, but a total number of 123 victims of repression was identified at our meetings.

I might note that the first state at the Madrid conference to cite a person by name was a neutral country, Sweden, whose delegation talked about Raoul Wallenberg, the Swedish diplomat whose heroic intervention during World War II saved thousands of Jews in Hungary from annihilation. Wallenberg was subsequently imprisoned by the Soviets and, despite periodic unofficial reports that he was still alive, has never been heard from since.[7]

When a negotiation takes place without confrontation, where the objective facts require blunt talk, and yet that blunt talk does not take place, it is a charade. The purpose of negotiation is obviously to reach agreement. Where difficult issues are involved, however, agreement may not be possible in the short run. An equally important use of the negotiating process is to communicate concerns that exist, so as to lessen the likelihood of ambiguity and resultant miscalculation. Such clarity, in turn, can lead to desirable changes in subsequent behavior. Without this clarity, there is no reason for the other side to take seriously the depth of our commitments and the strength of our perceptions.

Three illustrations from Madrid demonstrate this point. My first substantive presentation was made in November 1980, at the beginning of the main meeting. I then spoke of the fact that the United States and Russia had never fought a war against each other. I discussed the cultural and historical similarities between our two peoples, both occupying continental countries, and I remember specifically referring to "cossacks and cowboys." In going on to analyze the deterioration of the Soviet-American relationship, I spoke firmly and critically of the Leninist threat to world stability and of Soviet

---

[7]In 1982 the United States, by act of Congress signed by the president, made Raoul Wallenberg an honorary American citizen—the second person in history, following Winston Churchill in 1963, to be awarded that status. For my own tribute to this moral giant of a man, see my statement to the conference on November 6, 1981, in *World Affairs*: 446–50.

aggression and repression.[8] A few weeks later, just before Christmas, a dinner was sponsored by the head of the Finnish delegation. At that dinner, a member of an Eastern European delegation, whose discretion had obviously lost the battle against vodka, quietly took me aside to talk about that speech. He referred to the speech of November 17th. I had quickly to dig back in my mind to recall what speech he was referring, because I did not think of it in terms of a particular date. Far from having been offended by it, he went on to say that he was taking the speech home at Christmas to share with friends and family members.

On another occasion, early in 1981, I spoke with great specificity about the Soviet arms buildup and its potential threat to peace in Europe. I used exact numbers to describe how many tanks and other armored vehicles they had. I went through these matters in great detail, raising serious questions as to whether these arms were truly defensive.[9] (They obviously were not.) At the end of that morning session, the head of another Eastern European delegation came up to me and said: "I never knew these facts, Max, until this morning." He did not question the accuracy of the data.

Later in 1981, the head of the Soviet delegation in that period, Leonid F. Ilichev, and I engaged in the most serious confrontation that yet had taken place between us. It later got worse, but this was the most serious clash so far. He started in with abuse of our government, which I thought was totally inappropriate. I had a feeling he must have just received blank instructions to attack. Out of the blue came this diatribe against our government, and I could not tolerate it. Since my briefcase was usually filled with data to be used when needed, I responded fully, and in what a friend later characterized as a devastating fashion. Ilichev became very angry and, in replying in anger, he acted unusually. It is quite common at a conference to respond and then to leave it at that. In this case, he spoke and I responded, and, instead of leaving the matter, he came back. I then decided that I too would come back, with sharpness and with further facts from the briefcase. That ended the exchange. At that point, I could see out of the corner of my left eye the head of the delegation of Austria, a neutral country, coming toward me, and out of the corner of my other eye, from my right and behind, the head of the Finnish delegation coming toward me. Both neutrals knew I had not started the exchange, and they knew I had been provoked, but they showed grave concern. The question in their minds was: What would all this mean? Would the Soviets now walk out of the meeting? They were worried. This implied threat that the Soviets might walk out was always of great concern to the neutrals and nonaligned countries at the conference, and even to some of our NATO allies. In response to their legitimate query of "What did this mean?" I informed them that I was due at the Soviet ambassador's residence for lunch

---

[8]Statement on November 17, 1980, ibid.: 318–24.
[9]Statement on February 11, 1981, ibid.: 386–93.

in about an hour, and that I would learn then if they were indeed angry by noting if the door was locked against me.

The lunch took place, and it was pleasant and even constructive, which was not always the case. I can remember having lunch at critical moments with the head of the Soviet delegation and hearing lectures about Chinese cooking. He had spent eleven years negotiating with the Chinese—without agreement, as I had pointed out to him. On this occasion, ours was a serious talk. My host made no reference to our argument. Since I was his guest, and mine had been the last word in the morning, I did not bring the matter up, either. At the very end, as he walked me to the door, he put his arm around me and said to me in Russian, which had to be translated, that what he liked about dealing with me was that he could "exchange pleasantries" in the morning and then engage in serious, businesslike discussion in the afternoon.

The existence of a united Western group in Madrid was an indispensable condition for whatever effectiveness we had at the conference. Prior to its opening, I made two trips to Europe to meet with our allies and to discuss the approach we would together take at the Madrid meeting. Among the points I made was our own decision to mention the names of victims of repression. As a lawyer, I explained, I knew of no better way to illustrate a point than to use examples. I hoped that, unlike the experience at Belgrade, we would be supported and emulated in this approach. Most of our allies said only they would consider it, but at least they knew what we were planning. Indeed, we did get a tremendous amount of help and support. To a great extent, this mentioning of names was a joint effort.

However, there was one colleague, a West German, who said to me that he could not join. His country's approach, which he insisted had been effective with the Soviet Union, was to negotiate quietly. His government had been able, in this manner, to obtain the release of many whose freedom it had sought. We talked, and I remember saying that I did not want to recommend any policy which would keep a single human being in bondage, anyone who would otherwise be released. However, as in a symphony orchestra, someone must bang the drums and blow the trumpet, and somebody else has to play the harp and touch the piano keys softly. What was important was that we make music together.

We did make music together at Madrid. This required an effort on the part of all of us. Our NATO group (fifteen, then sixteen when in June 1982 Spain joined the alliance) normally met three or four times a week. There were many occasions when we met three and four times a day when necessary. We consulted on all aspects of the conference, and we kept one another fully informed. We worked closely with our neutral and nonaligned friends, as well, because we knew they shared our values. This high degree of coordination was itself one of the main achievements of the Madrid meeting. The West is stronger in dealing with the Soviet Union when it speaks with one voice and gives one consistent message.

There is today, nonetheless, still much mutual sensitivity within the NATO alliance. Crises in our relations have seemed inescapable. There have been disputes over whether or not to participate in the Moscow Olympics, whether or not to complete the Soviet natural gas pipeline, whether or not to install Pershing II and cruise missiles in Europe. There is always the potential for divisiveness when sixteen free and sovereign states, governed by democratic principles and shaped by different historical and cultural backgrounds, attempt to formulate common policy. What is necessary is for the sixteen constantly to keep in mind that it is our values, indispensable to our being, that tie us together. It was those values that were under attack at the time of the Madrid conference and had to be preserved. In a real sense our task at Madrid, as it would be again thereafter, was to raise the vision of the West above the minutiae of our relationships, important as these minutiae may appear at any given moment.

The Soviet Union respects military strength. Its incentive for negotiating an agreement is greater when the positions taken by its negotiating partner have the added dignity of being supported by a physical capacity to resist. The leadership of the Soviet Union is serious. Its diplomats are serious people. They are well-trained people, and they appear to be ideologically committed to Leninism. The comment of one Soviet diplomat to one of our arms control negotiators—"We Soviets are neither pacifists nor philanthropists"—tells much of that seriousness of purpose.[10] Their negotiating posture toward any issue is motivated by one primary consideration: how well does that position protect the perceived interest of the Soviet Union?

The word "negotiating" is the dominant one in this series of lectures. Negotiation means more than talking; it also means listening, as well. It is particularly important for the United States to understand, and to let others know that it understands, that our superpower status does not necessarily confer super wisdom on us. We have national interests as they do, and we define and advance them as we think best. We have views, and it is our right to assert them. Nevertheless, other countries, our friends as well as our enemies, have their own interests. These must be respected if we are to achieve understanding with them.

I mention this because a major difficulty in the diplomatic relationship between the United States and the Soviet Union is a feeling on the part of both of us that the other side is not listening. The Soviets want us to listen to their security needs, and we want them to appreciate ours and to understand as well that no country's national security interests can be fostered through aggression or lack of respect for the sovereignty of one's neighbors. In Madrid, I spent more than 350 hours in private discussion and negotiation with my Soviet counterparts outside of our formal meetings. I listened a great deal, and I believe I understood more as a result of that listening. I believe they

---

[10]The quoted comment was made by Academician Aleksandr N. Shchukin to Lt. Gen. Edward L. Rowny. Editor's telephone conversation with General Rowny, March 4, 1985.

finally began to listen also. Of course, one of the difficulties is that Soviet negotiators are not decisionmakers, but they did cable home for instructions. We were able, by the end of the conference, to come to an agreement on words, and these words were ones that were in our interest and, presumably, in theirs as well. Let me briefly assess the substance of the agreement that we reached.

The Madrid Concluding Document, which derived from a basic nego-tiating text known as RM-39 that a group of neutral and nonaligned states had usefully advanced, went beyond the Helsinki Final Act in a number of specific respects.[11] Given that all decisions had to be made by consensus, which gave the Soviet Union a veto, some of these advances were remarkable. Several of the new provisions directly reflected our immediate concerns about Poland. One provision dealt with the rights of labor to organize, which the Helsinki Final Act did not mention. All the participating states agreed to "ensure the right of workers freely to establish and join trade unions, the right of trade unions freely to exercise their activities and other rights as laid down in relevant international instruments," an implicit reference to the conventions of the United Nations-affiliated International Labor Organization (ILO). This was a legacy of the Solidarity movement. Efforts by the West to secure an explicit reference to Soviet involvement in the denial of liberty in Poland failed to achieve consensus. However, in the Principles section of "Basket I," relating to security in Europe, there is a commitment by all participants reaffirming that "refraining from the threat or use of force, as a norm of international life, should be strictly and effectively observed." Everyone knew what that meant.

The issue of religious expression is also singled out. Among the Con-cluding Document's provisions strengthening the Helsinki Final Act on the subject of the freedom of religion is a stipulation, urged by the Vatican, requiring that governments "favourably consider applications by religious communities of believers practising or prepared to practise their faith within the constitutional framework of their States, to be granted the status provided for in their respective countries for religious faiths, institutions, and organizations."

Among still other important results of Madrid was an agreement, achieved despite Soviet efforts to intimidate some of the neutral and nonaligned states into believing that the Helsinki process would end with the Madrid meeting, on a third follow-up meeting to take place in Vienna in November 1986. Also, a tenth-anniversary commemoration was scheduled for Helsinki in August 1985. In addition, a whole series of other meetings was scheduled by the Madrid conference. For example, a conference on disarmament in Europe (CDE) opened in Stockholm early in 1984 on Confidence- and Security-building Measures in Europe. The United States joined with other Western

---

[11]The text of the Concluding Document is in Department of State *Bulletin* 83, no. 2079 (October 1983): 50–60.

governments in supporting a French proposal aimed at ensuring that such a post-Madrid security forum on the issue of surprise military attack be practical and constructive, and not degenerate into an occasion for rhetorical statements on disarmament. Fortunately, the neutral and nonaligned states agreed with this Western objective, and the Eastern version of the CDE idea, offered by the Polish government, was dropped. Also scheduled for 1984 was an experts' meeting in Athens on the peaceful settlement of disputes and a seminar in Venice on Mediterranean security. In 1985, besides the commemorative session in Helsinki, there was to be an experts' meeting on human rights in Ottawa and a cultural forum in Budapest. Before the third large CSCE follow-up meeting in Vienna in 1986 there would be another experts' meeting, in Bern, to deal broadly with the subject of human contacts, including marriage and reunification of families, emigration regulations and procedures, and access to diplomatic missions and consular posts.

There is an obvious risk that these many and varied specialized meetings will detract somewhat from the publicity that unified sessions, such as the Madrid conference, can command. At the same time, because no enforcement mechanism is provided under the Helsinki Final Act, the factor of continued attention to implementation of Helsinki principles in a range of specialized fields, even without major publicity, is important. What we have tried to do, in short, is to substitute accountability for enforcement.

There is a responsible view in our society, which questions the effectiveness and desirability of our negotiating with the Soviet Union at all. Those of this persuasion hold, with good reason, that the Soviet Union remains committed to the Leninist principle that violence is both necessary and justified in the pursuit of Communist destiny. The Soviet Union thus is seen as the major threat to our security and values: an aggressive society seeking, with massive military and police power, to expand its influence. The USSR is also seen as a repressive society, determined to defend its totalitarian power within its own borders, whatever the human cost. This view places no confidence in the bona fides of the Soviet Union when it protests its love of disarmament and peace. It does not forget that after World War II, when we and our allies rapidly demobilized, the Soviet Union preferred to keep many of its troops on a wartime footing, maintaining a large conscript army and large reserve forces. It also realizes that, as we let the pace of our armament slacken in recent years, the Soviets engaged in the most massive buildup in the history of the world.

It is not useful to deny these realities. The task is how to face them constructively. I suspect that we, and our friends who value freedom, will pay a heavy price and suffer great anguish as we come to grips with the Soviet challenge in years ahead. However, we must come to grips with it. The integrity, character, and strength of our society, and of our people, will undergo the greatest testing in our history as we learn how to face up to Soviet military power, challenge it, and simultaneously strive to maintain peace with it even as we remain constant in our ideals.

In some ways, Americans are not well equipped for the task. We still look upon ourselves as a young and developing society, even though we now have one of the oldest, most stable political systems in the world. Our relative geographic isolation, our bountiful natural resources, our productive people, and our pursuit of liberty have made us strong. At the end of the Second World War, we found ourselves in the position of something like a giant among nations. Being a giant is not easy. It is hard to find shoes to fit, and the bed is always too short. Nor is it easy living with a giant. Our friends are learning that. Being strong, however, the giant can afford to be gentle, even if he is awkward at times.

We in the United States have made mistakes because we have not adjusted to the fact that our mistakes may have great consequences. We have been hesitant about, as well as unaccustomed to, the responsibilities of world leadership. As a result, our foreign policy is at times one of fits and starts, which can confuse others. In this context, it is worth emphasizing again the relative continuity of the CSCE process. The Madrid follow-up meeting itself lasted two years and ten months, formally opening on November 11, 1980, and concluding on September 9, 1983. Except for a long recess in 1982, owing mainly to the imposition of martial law in Poland, the sessions were almost continuous. (The initial expectation had been that the conference would last only for about six months.)

It has been said that the test of negotiating with the Soviets is a readiness to remain one day longer than they are prepared to remain. That was a reality that I had to face personally. It was possible for me to do so because of an unusual expression of nonpartisanship in foreign policy. I had been appointed by Secretary of State Cyrus Vance in the Carter administration and was later reappointed under the Reagan administration, which tells you something about our political system.

We talk in America a great deal about values and about aspirations to liberty. Some of our more sophisticated friends in the world see our linkage of idealism with global Realpolitik as a form of naïveté. We talk about the values of freedom because, to us, they are not abstract. Neither are they abstract to millions of people elsewhere who are unable to enjoy them, as we know from our own immigrant heritage. Our beliefs are what distinguish us from the totalitarians and authoritarians of this world. They are our strength. They are also what gives our diplomacy its basic continuity.

This is our faith, and we should talk about it. However, as we talk about it, we must understand that we may thereby implicitly threaten the Soviet Union. This is a large part of our difficulty in negotiating with Moscow. Like any dictatorship, the Soviet ruling class is deeply concerned about the subversion of its power, which has been accumulated not by agreement or consent, but by military force and political influence alone. Where there is no legitimacy, there is repression, working together in the Soviet case with traditional national and cultural oppressions. This combination of factors obviously contributes to the Soviet Union's insecurity. The fact that there are free societies nearby creates a powerful draw and attraction to those who live under totalitarian rule. By their example, the democracies inevitably tend to subvert the Soviets' authority, and the Soviets know it.

Thus, we have the dilemma, the challenge, the danger, the threat, but also the opportunity. It is necessary to find a formula under which we can live in dignity together with the Soviet Union. We share the same globe. All responsible people understand that we must define our objectives consistently with Hobbes's first law of nature, "to seek peace and to follow it." We must engage in the pursuit of peace without illusion, but with persistence, regardless of the provocation. Thus, in Madrid, we attended, talked, debated, negotiated, argued, dined, condemned, and talked some more. We achieved some results in words. We have not yet achieved a basic alteration in other patterns of Soviet behavior. That will only come, if it ever does come, when the Soviet Union concludes that it is in its interest to change, and when its leadership decides that it can best keep itself in power if its patterns of conduct do change.

In the meantime, we must not be misled into negotiating false agreements. My experience as a lawyer—a different background from that of most other heads of delegation at Madrid—has taught me that "success" should not be defined as a piece of paper. As a lawyer, I have often advised clients *not* to sign a piece of paper. "Agreement" is perhaps not so important to me as it is to those engaged in professional diplomacy. This includes some of the professionals in our own State Department, whose competence and commitment I greatly respect.

The Soviet leadership will likely neither soon undergo what was called in the time of Jonathan Edwards a "great awakening" nor, like Saint Paul earlier, see a blinding light on the road to Damascus. Yet the imperatives for survival in the nuclear age require a new perspective. Through the deterrence that comes from military strength, through dialogue, through mutual criticism, through diplomatic negotiation, we must continue the search for understanding, agreement, and peace.

We must also be prepared to visit. I mention this because I have repeatedly been struck by the fact that, to date, neither of the present leaders of the superpowers has set foot in the country of the other. We must never forget the impact on Nikita Khrushchev of the sight of an American grain field and the demonstration of how it was tilled and managed. Peoples must know one another in order to judge one another.

I believe that the "correlation of forces," in the broadest sense, has been moving against the Soviet Union. The credibility of its system as a viable alternative has collapsed for sensible people. The gas has largely escaped from its ideological balloon. It is time for the Soviet authorities to comprehend that in our day repressive societies cannot achieve inner stability or true security. We hope they will come to understand the need to show the rest of us, through their behavior, that cruelty is not an indispensable part of their system, as it is, indeed, thoroughly counterproductive to what they want to do. A government that is unrestrained by public opinion tends to ignore the popular good and be blind to the misery experienced by those who do not receive honors and privileges from the state. Such people will eventually grow impatient. Just as the Leninist aim of achieving world communism has no relevance in this nuclear age, so must it be understood by an evolving Soviet leadership that in the long run it cannot survive without humanizing its controls and the image it presents to the world.

Included in our own message and program must therefore be an understanding that new opportunities exist for cooperation with us on all levels. These are unlimited, if the leaders in Moscow will live up to their international responsibilities, so clearly delineated in the Helsinki Final Act and in the Madrid Concluding Document, whose words they freely accepted. We have nothing to fear and everything to gain from an open and frank relationship with the Soviet Union. This is what we offered for three years in Madrid, during a period when most other Western relationships with the Soviet Union, including the arms control talks, were in suspension or at a standstill. This is what we must be prepared to continue to offer wherever the opportunity for exchange and negotiation is available to us.

FOR FURTHER READING

For the major statements by Max M. Kampelman before the Madrid Conference on Security and Cooperation in Europe, with an introduction by Alexander M. Haig, see the collection, "Negotiating with the Soviets in Madrid," in *World Affairs: A Quarterly Review of International Problems* 144, no. 4 (Spring 1982), referred to in the footnotes. The staff of the Commission on Security and Cooperation in Europe, a congressional-executive supervisory body, compiled and edited *The Madrid CSCE Review Meeting* (Washington, DC: 1983), a useful summary with documents. See also Dante B. Fascell, "Helsinki, Gdansk, Madrid," *Washington Quarterly* 7, no. 4 (Fall 1984): 170–80; Geoffrey Edwards, "The Madrid Follow-up Meeting to the Conference on Security and Cooperation in Europe," *International Relations* 8, no. 1 (May 1984): 49–72; Jan Sizoo and Rudolph Th. Jurrjens, *CSCE Decision-making: The Madrid Experience* (The Hague: Martinus Nijhoff, 1984).

For general studies of human rights and American foreign policy, see Vernon Van Dyke, *The United States, Human Rights, and World Community* (New York: Oxford University Press, 1970); Arthur M. Schlesinger, Jr., "Human Rights and the American Tradition," America and the World 1978, *Foreign Affairs* 57, no. 3 (1978): 503–26; Sandy Vogelgesang, *American Dream, Global Nightmare: The Dilemma of U.S. Human Rights Policy* (New York: W. W. Norton, 1980); Barry M. Rubin and Elizabeth R. Spiro, eds., *Human Rights and U.S. Foreign Policy* (Boulder, CO: Westview Press, 1979); Natalie Kaufman Hevener, ed., *The Dynamics of Human Rights in U.S. Foreign Policy* (New Brunswick, NJ: Transaction Books, 1981).

On international humanitarian law, see Arthur Henry Robertson, *Human Rights in the World, Being an Account of the United Nations Covenants on Human Rights, the European Convention, the Permanent Arab Commission, the Proposed African*

Commission and Recent Developments Affecting Humanitarian Law (Manchester: Manchester University Press, 1972); Myres S. McDougal, Harold D. Lasswell, and Lung-chu Chen, *Human Rights and World Public Order: The Basic Policies of an International Law of Human Dignity* (New Haven, CT: Yale University Press, 1980); Paul Sieghart, *The International Law of Human Rights* (Oxford: Clarendon Press, 1983); and Philip Alston, "Conjuring Up New Human Rights: A Proposal for Quality Control," *American Journal of International Law* 78, no. 3 (July 1984): 607–21.

REGIONAL BASES OF WORLD ORDER

The North Atlantic Alliance as a Form of World Order

ALAN K. HENRIKSON

While it is common to speak of the North Atlantic Alliance as supporting or reinforcing order among nations, it is not at all conventional to discuss NATO, the organization built upon the North Atlantic Treaty of April 4, 1949, as an international order itself. Indeed, the concepts of "alliance" and "order" have generally been thought of as polar opposites, as antitheses. The one, alliance, implies a formation directed against a country or group of countries for purposes of aggression or for defense. The concept is intrinsically exclusive. The other, order, implies a more general form of international organization, relatively open and inclusive in character. At a deeper level, the two terms suggest fundamentally different concepts of world politics. An alliance presupposes an essentially anarchic world, in which aggressive power is controllable only by countervailing power. A system of international order, by contrast, suggests a more harmonious political universe, governed not merely by force but also by voluntary adherence to principles and norms.[1]

Despite the apparent inconsistency in logic, it has in fact historically not been uncommon for an alliance, conceived initially as an exclusive arrangement, to evolve into a more inclusive form of organization and thus become a component of international order itself. An excellent example of this process is the transformation of the Quadruple Alliance against Napoleonic France into the inclusive, ostensibly impartial Quintuple Alliance. After Napoleon's defeat at Waterloo in 1815, France (under a Bourbon king, Louis XVIII) was admitted, somewhat self-contradictorily, into membership in what

---

[1]Compare the concept of "order" discussed in Hedley Bull, *The Anarchical Society: A Study of Order in World Politics* (New York: Columbia University Press, 1977).

hitherto had been essentially an anti-French combination. This wider agreement, although in its origins only a limited, defensive union and a result of the disharmony of European politics, was the basis of the Concert of Europe, which established for a time an effective system of diplomacy by conference among the European great powers.[2] Similarly, the winning coalitions of World Wars I and II—the Triple Entente, plus the United States and other associated powers, and the worldwide coalition of the United Nations, respectively— are major instances of large alliance formations becoming transformed into emergent general international orders.

This subtle but profound change in the nature of the major alliances of the twentieth century was prophetically envisioned by President Woodrow Wilson in January 1917 when he urged: "There must be, not a balance of power, but a community of power; not organized rivalries, but an organized common peace."[3] A comprehensive international commitment, a universal alliance, would, in his view, paradoxically *disentangle* the powers from their partial, conflicting obligations to each other. This was the genesis of the concept of "collective security," institutionalized first in the League of Nations and later in the United Nations Organization. After both world wars, the defeated peoples, notably the Germans, eventually were included in these newly established international organizations, joining the victorious allies as equals in maintaining the peace they themselves had upset. Collective defense thereby was transformed into collective security.[4] In the experience of modern international relations, the conversion of collective defense into collective

---

[2]Article VI of the Quadruple Alliance (Treaty of Chaumont), as renewed on November 20, 1815, provided for periodic meetings of sovereigns or their ministers to examine measures considered most salutary "for the repose and prosperity of the peoples and for the peace of Europe." See Edward V. Gulick, *Europe's Classical Balance of Power: A Case History of the Theory and Practice of One of the Great Concepts of European Statecraft* (New York: W. W. Norton, 1967), pp. 289–90, 293–94; and Henry A. Kissinger, *A World Restored* (New York: Universal Library, 1964), pp. 221–23. For a documentary record of the Concert of Europe, see René Albrecht-Carrié, *The Concert of Europe, 1815–1914* (New York: Harper and Row, 1968). For a recent theoretical discussion, see Robert Jervis, "From Balance to Concert: A Study of International Security Cooperation," *World Politics* 38, no. 1 (October 1985): 58–79.

[3]Quoted in Arthur S. Link, *Wilson: Campaigns for Progressivism and Peace, 1916–1917* (Princeton, NJ: Princeton University Press, 1965), p. 265.

[4]On the origins of the "collective security" concept, see Richard N. Current, "The United States and 'Collective Security': Notes on the History of an Idea," in Alexander DeConde, ed., *Isolation and Security* (Durham, NC: Duke University Press, 1957), pp. 33–55; Willard Range, *Franklin D. Roosevelt's World Order* (Athens: University of Georgia Press, 1959), chap. 11, "A Collective Security System"; Inis L. Claude, Jr., *Swords into Plowshares: The Problems and Progress of International Organization*, 4th ed. (New York: Random House, 1984); and Roland N. Stromberg, *Collective Security and American Foreign Policy: From the League of Nations to NATO* (New York: Frederick A. Praeger, 1963). The political theorist Arnold Wolfers distinguishes sharply between "alliances, now usually called collective defense arrangements," and "collective security under the United Nations," rhetorically justified as a form of "police action for the world community." He warns that the latter conceivably could oblige the United States to take punitive steps against its closest allies. See Wolfers, *Discord and Collaboration: Essays on International Politics* (Baltimore: Johns Hopkins Press, 1962), chaps. 11 and 12.

security, or alliance into order, thus appears to be the rule rather than the exception. Political theory, in preserving a distinction between these two ideas, has not taken sufficient account of actual history.

The history of the North Atlantic Treaty Organization (NATO), although originating during the Cold War rather than in the transforming crucible of a large-scale fighting war, has also been characterized, I would argue, by a developmental progress from coalition to concert, though not so complete or dramatic as in the earlier cases. This alliance-into-order change has been evident in NATO from its beginning. To an extent, the forms of international order in NATO, as distinct from its alliance features, have already quite clearly emerged. Some further development along these lines is possible, I suggest, and it is that hypothesis that I would like herein to present, drawing upon the historical experience of NATO and projecting its current patterns, actual and potential, into the future. The North Atlantic Alliance of today is a greater international achievement than is commonly recognized. When the fullness of its nature is more clearly understood, it may be enabled to make an even larger contribution to international stability and peace.

In order to explain how a regional military bloc—for that is how NATO is commonly regarded—can have the broad stabilizing, equilibrating, and even mediating role that I believe it has, I should like to consider three problems pertaining to the North Atlantic Alliance: first, the problem of the relationship of NATO to the United Nations Charter and, more generally, to universal collective security; second, the problem of using the NATO structure to adjust differences and settle disputes within the Atlantic community itself, defined to mean all countries within the geographical area of the treaty; and third, the problem of adapting NATO, a military organization, for nonmilitary purposes, above all the purpose of negotiating détente and disarmament arrangements with the Soviet Union and its allies of the Warsaw Pact. Briefly restated, the issues I shall address are those of NATO's universality, complexity, and flexibility—each of these being essential qualities for a world-ordering regime.

As the three characteristics of universality, complexity, and flexibility have emerged at different times in the history of the North Atlantic Alliance, my discussion will coincide, to an extent, with major stages of NATO's evolution, from its early, formative period through its present mature phase and beyond it into an uncertain future. Going beyond historical analysis, I shall attempt to suggest ways by which the alliance-into-order transformation that I perceive in NATO might be made more perfect and more productive.

My specific argument regarding NATO and world order will have three interrelated parts: 1) that the legal and political premises on which NATO was built in the late 1940s logically permit and encourage a change of the alliance into a broad ordering system; 2) that the structure and processes of the alliance, as it actually has developed during the years since 1949, demonstrate a capacity for such an international ordering role; and 3) that the current condition of global affairs, particularly the East-West deadlock, urgently necessitates a bold effort to use the North Atlantic Alliance to promote a more comprehensive, more capacious international order.

First of all, then, let us consider the question of the basic compatibility of the North Atlantic Treaty with the UN Charter and, more generally, the ideal of worldwide collective security. What did the founders of the alliance themselves think about the problem of the relationship of their pact to such a larger order? Their own words, which do not necessarily reveal their innermost thoughts, tell us something. When President Harry S. Truman signed the North Atlantic Treaty in Washington on April 4, 1949, he observed: "To protect this area against war will be a long step toward permanent peace in the whole world."[5] Today, in the aftermath of Nixon-Kissinger Realpolitik diplomacy, we might be inclined to interpret Truman's words mainly in balance-of-power terms, that is, as a geopolitical statement. We might assume that all he wanted was for the United States, Canada, and the leading countries of Western Europe to declare their unity, proclaim their values, and concert their policies. This would create such a bloc of strength at the world's center (for this is what the Atlantic undeniably was in those days) that the problems on the world's periphery, where many of the North Atlantic partners still had colonial interests, and also on the fringes of the Soviet empire, notably in Eastern Europe, would take care of themselves. To have strength at the center would, by the very fact of it, impose a kind of structure, or order, on relationships at the margin of world affairs, whether in the oceanic realm or on the Eurasian landmass. As President Truman himself emphasized, the North Atlantic area had been "at the heart" of the last two world conflicts.

There is, however, quite a different way of understanding Truman's remarks. They can be interpreted not geopolitically but, rather, normatively, as a declaration that the establishment of freedom from aggression and any threat of force in the area of the North Atlantic would set a universal example and constitute part of a global cooperative order, specifically that established, in principle, by the UN Organization. "Through this treaty," Truman stated at the signing ceremony, "we undertake to conduct our international affairs in accordance with the provisions of the United Nations Charter. We undertake to exercise our right of collective or individual self-defense against armed attack, in accordance with Article 51 of the Charter, and subject to such measures as the Security Council may take to maintain and restore international peace and security." He did not, and most of the founders of NATO did not, I submit, think of their creation merely as a traditional alliance, as a classic defensive arrangement. It was an alliance with a difference. "This is more than a treaty for defence," said Canadian Minister for External Affairs Lester B. Pearson at the signing ceremony. "We must, of course, defend ourselves, and that is the first purpose of our pact; but, in doing so, we must

---

[5]Address of the President of the United States, U.S., Department of State *Bulletin* 20, no. 511 (April 17, 1949): 481–82. All Truman quotations that follow in the text are taken from this address.

never forget that we are now organizing force for peace, so that peace can one day be preserved without force."[6]

There were, in fact, two dominant ideas at the end of the Second World War regarding creation of a cooperative international order. One was the idea of four-power collaboration among the United States, the United Kingdom, France, and the Soviet Union. The practical focus of this concept, which emerged from the Yalta and Potsdam conferences and related deliberations, was the joint postwar occupation and long-term control of Germany. This was the preferred American solution to the German problem, and it seemed for a time also the Soviet preference. The British and, especially, the French governments too favored it. U.S. policy on the subject was stated most explicitly when, in April 1946, Secretary of State James F. Byrnes proposed a twenty-five-year Four Power Draft Treaty on the Disarmament and Demilitarization of Germany. The scheme was meant to be not only a method for administering Germany but also a basis for peace between Eastern and Western Europe, as well as, in more symbolic terms, between East and West globally. A comparable arrangement, including China, also might have been worked out for the long-term management of relations with Japan in the Far East.[7]

Owing to numerous differences with the Soviet Union over the substance of German occupation policy, and probably also to a provision in the Byrnes draft for action by majority decision (thus depriving the Soviet Union of a veto), the proposed treaty never was concluded. The American, British, and French control zones were amalgamated into what became the Federal Republic of Germany. The Soviet zone eventually became the German Democratic Republic. The four-power idea did not completely die, however. A vestige of it survives today in the American, British, French, and Soviet supervision of the city of Berlin. Even when other East-West talks are in suspension, quadripartite bodies such as the Berlin Air Safety Center normally have continued to function, albeit with some friction. As institutional mechanisms for resolving practical disputes in times of difficulty, they remain very important. It should be emphasized that there is nothing in the North Atlantic Treaty, or subsequent NATO agreements, that is fundamentally inconsistent with the original four-power model of postwar world order. From one perspective, in fact, NATO can be viewed as a kind of truncated three-power version of it.[8]

---

[6]Remarks by Lester B. Pearson, Department of State *Bulletin* 20, no. 511 (April 17, 1949): 473.

[7]Proposal by the U.S. delegation at the Council of Foreign Ministers, April 30, 1946, *Papers Relating to the Foreign Relations of the United States, 1946* (Washington, DC: Government Printing Office, 1970), 2: 190–93 (hereafter cited as *FRUS*, followed by the appropriate year). See also James F. Byrnes, *Speaking Frankly* (New York: Harper and Brothers, 1947), pp. 171–76.

[8]Bernard Gwertzman, "3 Western Powers Protest on Berlin," *New York Times*, April 5, 1984; Hervé Alphand, "The Atlantic and European Policy of France" (speech delivered at *New York Herald Tribune* Forum, October 20, 1953), Speech Series No. 46, North Atlantic Council Information Service; Alan K. Henrikson, "The Creation of the North Atlantic Alliance," in John R. Reichart and Steven R. Sturm, eds., *American Defense Policy*, 5th ed. (Baltimore: Johns Hopkins University Press, 1982), pp. 296–320, especially p. 308.

Similarly, nothing in the North Atlantic Treaty itself or in the things NATO has since done violates the UN Charter, which articulates another more multilateralist postwar concept of international order. Indeed, the text of the pact was carefully written so as to be fully consistent with that master document. The North Atlantic Treaty's preamble emphasizes: "The Parties to this Treaty reaffirm their faith in the purposes and principles of the Charter of the United Nations and their desire to live in peace with all peoples and all Governments."[9] In the operative parts of the treaty, there are even more specific commitments to uphold the Charter. In Article 1 the signatories undertake, as stipulated in the Charter, to settle any international disputes in which they may be involved by peaceful means and to refrain from the threat or use of force in any manner inconsistent with the purposes of the United Nations. Article 5, the so-called heart of the treaty, specifically mentions Article 51 of the Charter, affirming "the inherent right of individual or collective defense" of nations. Any measures taken by the treaty partners in exercise of this right would "immediately be reported" to the UN Security Council and "terminated" when the United Nations itself successfully had acted to restore peace. For good measure, Article 7 of the North Atlantic Treaty declared that nothing in it in any way affected the parties' existing rights and obligations under the Charter or "the primary responsibility of the Security Council for the maintenance of international peace and security." Finally, in the review of the treaty after ten years which Article 12 permitted, the factors to be taken into account included "the development of universal as well as regional arrangements under the Charter of the United Nations." In other words, the North Atlantic Treaty Organization, in theory, could find itself superfluous.

In retrospect, these provisions regarding the United Nations might seem quite unrealistic. Historical skeptics have pointed out that the universalist language of the Atlantic treaty was chosen calculatedly in order to ward off attacks by American isolationists, who hoped that UN membership would make individual and collective defense unnecessary, and by Asia-firsters, who wanted comparable U.S. military commitments to be made to Chiang Kaishek's China.[10] The founders of the North Atlantic Alliance themselves were candid in expressing their disappointment in the United Nations, whose development as an organ of collective security seemed stunted by the Soviet Union's abuse of the Security Council veto. Various plans were offered to try to circumvent this obstacle by using Article 51, enabling community-minded states to take action "within the Charter but outside the veto." One such proposal for a security pact supplementing the UN Charter was made by the

---

[9]The text of the North Atlantic Treaty and other basic alliance documents can be found conveniently in North Atlantic Treaty Organization, *NATO: Facts About the North Atlantic Treaty Organization* (Paris: NATO Information Service, 1965), *NATO Handbook* (Brussels: NATO Information Service, February 1976), and *The North Atlantic Treaty Organization: Facts and Figures*, 10th ed. (Brussels: NATO Information Service, 1983).

[10]Compare Lawrence S. Kaplan, *The United States and NATO: The Formative Years* (Lexington: University Press of Kentucky, 1984), pp. 42–43.

Canadian statesman Louis S. St. Laurent. Another widely discussed scheme was proposed by the editor of *Foreign Affairs*, Hamilton Fish Armstrong. He envisaged "a sort of protocol, or 'optional clause,' open to all," by which members of the United Nations could bind themselves to carry out the Charter's obligation to resist armed aggression, if 1) two-thirds of the signatories decided that collective action was called for and 2) the Security Council failed to act.[11]

The North Atlantic Treaty was the result of these discussions and, even more directly, of the precedent of the Inter-American Treaty of Reciprocal Assistance, concluded in Rio de Janeiro in September 1947. The Rio Pact, a regional arrangement aimed both at joint peacemaking within the Western Hemisphere itself and at collective defense against extrahemispheric aggression, proved that effective multilateral action, consonant with the UN purposes, was still possible. As President Truman stated when the North Atlantic Treaty was signed in April 1949, the United States and other countries had hoped to establish "an international force" for the use of the United Nations, but their efforts had been "blocked" by one of the major powers. "This lack of unanimous agreement in the Security Council does not mean that we must abandon our attempts to make peace secure."

Far from intending to subvert the United Nations, substituting partisan collective defense for impartial collective security, the founders of NATO appear to have believed that they were doing what they could to strengthen the UN Organization, *in the only way possible* in the international circumstances of the deepening Cold War. Their action in forming the North Atlantic Alliance was not a washing of the hands of the United Nations and its ideals. Secretary of State Dean G. Acheson said of the treaty, "It is designed to fit precisely into the framework of the United Nations and to assure practical measures for maintaining peace and security in harmony with the Charter."[12] Of course, no one can know for sure whether administration officials were entirely sincere in uttering such statements in support of the world body and the promise of world order. Certainly statesmen like Truman and Acheson were realistic, and they recognized the difficulties in the path of cooperation with the USSR, whether through four-power control or through a more global, multilateral structure such as the United Nations. Nonetheless, it is important to keep in mind that, on the formal record, these leaders, even in effectively bypassing the Soviet Union, espoused a more inclusive conception of international cooperation. Their words helped to sustain principles and norms that,

---

[11]On the various proposals to strengthen the United Nations, using Article 51, see Arthur H. Vandenberg, Jr., ed., *The Private Papers of Senator Vandenberg* (Boston: Houghton Mifflin, 1952), chap. 21; Escott Reid, *Time of Fear and Hope: The Making of the North Atlantic Treaty, 1947–1949* (Toronto: McClelland and Stewart, 1977), pp. 30–34; Hamilton Fish Armstrong, *The Calculated Risk* (New York: Macmillan, 1947), pp. 57–58.

[12]Dean G. Acheson, "The Meaning of the North Atlantic Pact," *Department of State Bulletin* 20, no. 508 (March 27, 1949): 384–88.

if adhered to intellectually and spiritually, could only exert an influence toward a more inclusive order.[13]

The North Atlantic Alliance was not, in sum, just a classic defensive pact, with a specified opponent and military preparations made only with it in mind.[14] It did not mention the Soviet Union, nor did it name Germany, against which the French, particularly, desired guarantees almost as much as they sought protection against the USSR. It was the specter of the Soviet Union in Germany, commanding its position and controlling its manpower and resources, that truly frightened them. Both the bilateral Anglo-French Treaty of Dunkirk (1947) and the Brussels Pact (1948), which included Belgium, the Netherlands, and Luxembourg, provided explicitly for mutual assistance in the event of a renewal of aggression from Germany. The genius of the North Atlantic Pact, by contrast with these agreements, is that, following the wording of the Rio Treaty before it, it was completely neutral in regard to the source of aggression. It was inspired by the idea of creating an international security *system* for North America and Europe, not merely a politico-military coalition of states. Article 5 stated simply that "an armed attack against one or more" of the signatories "shall be considered an attack against them all." The recognized merit of this general formulation—the famous one-for-all, all-for-one pledge—was that the Germans could one day be accepted as coparticipants in it. They could be welcomed as allies under the North Atlantic Treaty and might themselves be willing to sign it, without depriving the French and other neighboring Europeans of the treaty's implicit security guarantee against the possibility of a resurgent Germany.

Even more noteworthy is the fact that nothing existed in the North Atlantic Treaty that precluded participation by the USSR or by any of the East European satellite states. The only possible obstacle, in theory, to an eastward extension of the transatlantic system was an ideological one: namely, the reference in Article 2, the so-called Canadian article, to the "free institutions" of the parties.[15] In the minds of some of the European makers of the alliance, especially, the treaty was not merely an assurance of American participation in another European war but also a nucleus of a continent-based, Europe-wide security system, somewhat analogous (except in not being nominally directed against Germany) to the concept behind the Byrnes Four Power

---

[13]Words used and ideas invoked by public leaders often constrain them in the future, regardless of what they inwardly intended by them at the time. The very fact that they said the things they did (and not other things) suggests, moreover, that these specific points then "needed" to be made, that political circumstances and the ideological climate "required" their making. Such necessitating factors and imperative forces, if they continue, become sustaining influences, "holding" statesmen to their words.

[14]Wolfers, who considered NATO a traditional alliance, regarded it as merely a "peculiarity" of so-called collective defense arrangements that they did not name their opponents and identified the source of aggression only in abstract geographical terms. Wolfers, *Discord and Collaboration*, p. 183.

[15]On the Canadian government's promotion of Article 2, emphasizing the "community" aspects of the North Atlantic relationship, see Reid, *Time of Fear and Hope*, passim.

Draft Treaty. That idea was politically passé, however. For U.S. officials, the most relevant analogy was the new inter-American security system. John D. Hickerson, director of the State Department's Office of European Affairs and probably the strongest advocate of a formalized U.S.-European multilateral security arrangement, carefully explained the virtues of the Rio Treaty model to British Ambassador Lord Inverchapel. The "real strength" of the inter-American defense system, he pointed out, was the fact that "automatic action against aggression whether from without or within" was provided for. If based upon this pattern,

> the European defense system would not seem specifically directed against the Soviets and might make it easier of acceptance by states whose geographical position rendered them more vulnerable to Soviet pressure, such as Sweden. Conceived in these terms *it would be even possible for the Soviet Union to join the arrangement* without detracting from the protection which it would give the other members.[16]

Even if this remarkable statement was insincere, or was made by Hickerson largely for illustrative purposes, the fact that a new Western security was formally being structured in such a way as to admit of membership by the Soviet Union, as well as participation by neutrals and presumably also the satellite states, is a reality too significant completely to discount. It was of considerable political importance in Europe at the time not to conclude an agreement that would alienate half of the continent. The hope was not abandoned by makers of the alliance that other European countries would join the association being born. Besides envisioning the membership of Germany, the great, acknowledged prize, the leading Western powers specifically intended that the treaty remain open to states distributed around the Western European core. Norway, Denmark, Iceland, Portugal, and Italy finally joined as original members along with the three small, centrally located Benelux countries. In 1952, Greece and Turkey acceded to the treaty. There was even some thought during this time that Tito's Yugoslavia, having broken with Moscow in 1948, might become an additional Mediterranean member, or at least tacitly accept dependency on NATO. The Federal Republic of Germany was admitted in 1955. Following the demise of the Franco dictatorship, with which the United States has maintained a bilateral security relationship since 1953, Spain finally became a member in 1982.[17]

The inclusion in the North Atlantic Alliance of countries bordering the Mediterranean Sea indicates that the scope of the treaty was not of necessity

---

[16]Hickerson memorandum, January 21, 1948, U.S., Department of State, *FRUS, 1948* (Washington, DC: Government Printing Office, 1974), 3: 9–12. Emphasis added.

[17]On the Mediterranean dimension of the Atlantic Alliance, see Lawrence S. Kaplan, Robert W. Clawson, and Raimondo Luraghi, eds., *NATO and the Mediterranean* (Wilmington, DE: Scholarly Resources, 1985). An authoritative account of Spanish membership is Leopoldo Calvo-Sotelo, "NATO: The Spanish Debate in 1981" (Address, The Fletcher School of Law and Diplomacy, Tufts University, Medford, Massachusetts, April 4, 1984).

confined narrowly to one geographical region. Care was taken by the governments, in fact, not officially to publicize the treaty as a "regional" arrangement. The reason is not simply that such a designation would be spatially limiting and make distant countries wonder whether or not they would be protected. There was a technical reason as well. Chapter VIII (Articles 52, 53, and 54) of the UN Charter, which permitted regional arrangements, required that any enforcement action taken under them be authorized by the Security Council, where the Soviet veto could be employed.[18]

Despite these antiregionalist considerations, the drafters of the North Atlantic Treaty did, with Article 6, formally define a "treaty area"—roughly, the territory of the signatory states and the intervening Atlantic Ocean space, limited on the south by the Tropic of Cancer—within which an aggressor's attack would constitute a *casus foederis*. This did not limit the view of the alliance, however. That the North Atlantic allies expected to be able to rely on their partnership as a basis for possible coordinated operations in other parts of the world is made quite clear by Article 4 of the treaty, which promises that the parties "will consult together whenever, in the opinion of any of them, the territorial integrity, political independence or security of any of the Parties is threatened." In a set of confidential "agreed minutes of interpretation," the parties recorded their common understanding that "Article 4 is applicable in the event of a threat in any part of the world," including a threat to the "overseas territories" of any of the parties.[19] This reflected not only the colonial interests of Great Britain and France, but also those of Belgium, the Netherlands, and Portugal. Despite the tension that existed between the colonial involvement of the European partners and the historic anticolonialist bias of the U.S. government, there was thus no disclaimer whatever of the Western allies' worldwide concerns in the North Atlantic Treaty. "Its conclusion," President Truman rightly and emphatically stated on April 4, 1949, "does not mean a narrowing of the interests of its members."

In principle, it was even possible that countries lying far outside the North Atlantic area might become attached to the treaty. Logically, if the pact was not "regional," limited by Chapter VIII of the UN Charter, it was universal and open to all, for Article 51 of the Charter implied no spatial limit or membership list. Only the arbitrary "Tropic of Cancer" restriction would have to be lifted, or redefined. Some of the earliest Western plans for security cooperation, under Article 51, were in fact global in geographical scope. The United Kingdom originally had contemplated associating the Dominions—not only Canada but also South Africa, New Zealand, and Australia—with a transatlantic defense pact with the United States, making

---

[18]For a good discussion of the issue of the alliance's geographical scope by a participant in the drafting, see Nicholas Henderson, *The Birth of NATO* (Boulder, CO: Westview Press, 1983), pp. 101–05. For a legal analysis, see Hans Kelsen, *Collective Security Under International Law* (Washington, DC: U.S. Government Printing Office, 1957).

[19]The text of the "agreed minutes" is in Henderson, *Birth of NATO*, pp. 103–04.

it thereby an "English-speaking" alliance. The French also envisioned a wider cultural association. They demanded, with success, that much of Algeria, organized as *départements* of metropolitan France, be covered by the treaty (Article 6). The United States considered that its detached territory of Alaska was encompassed by its protection as well. Some thought was even given, especially by U.S. officials who were intent upon "containment" of the Soviet Union, to bringing strategically located Iran within its purview, or within a Mediterranean-Middle Eastern security arrangement linked to NATO. For related strategic reasons, as well as for sentimental ones, the British government imagined associating the three countries of the "new" Commonwealth— Pakistan, India, and Ceylon—with a Western alliance.[20] It thus should not be forgotten that, historically and ideologically, the North Atlantic Treaty emerged from a set of traditional imperial orders as well as from an idealized concept of global order. The text of the treaty, by itself, did not prohibit security cooperation among the North Atlantic allies to protect their geographically scattered interests. Even if not in practical terms truly a universal security system, neither was it, in the minds of its originators, a narrowly constrained, or inwardly constraining, North Atlantic regional order.

This brings us to the second issue I would like to discuss: the internal ordering role of the alliance, i.e., the problem of its complexity, or its inner variety and the management of it. The tendency of critics today, especially in Europe, is to view NATO as a rigid bloc, whose governments are so preoccupied with military defense and political solidarity that the individual nations supporting this heavy structure can scarcely breathe. At the time the North Atlantic Treaty was signed, however, the dominant fear in the West was that the alliance might not prove cohesive enough, that the traditional rivalries of pluralistic Europe, particularly that between France and Germany, would re-emerge, defeating the dream of Western unity and world peace. The problem for NATO, in its internal workings, has been therefore to maintain a balance between these two extremes: preserving international unity, without becoming an oppressive monolith, and respecting national diversity, without breaking apart into unruly and useless pieces.

For this complex purpose, a concept of "world order" has been indispensable to the alliance. Paul H. Nitze, a longtime senior official in the U.S. State and Defense departments, has explained why:

> It is my suggestion that a concept of world order is necessary both to hold the alliance system together and as a basis for harmonizing the relations between the alliance system and the "coalition of free nations."
>
> A concept of world order makes it possible to raise the debate between members of the alliance system above a mere discussion of whose interests in a given situation should be controlling. With such a concept it is possible, at least in principle, to deduce criteria for judging the answers

---

[20]Ibid., p. 106; Reid, *Time of Fear and Hope*, p. 100.

to most of the more divisive problems—criteria that are based upon a higher set of interests than those of any single country or group of countries. No such supervening criteria can be found in the narrow interests of England, of France, of Germany, or of the United States. Even the interests of the NATO nations as a group constitute an inadequate basis on which to advance convincing arguments in a situation where the interests of non-NATO members of the coalition are also involved.

Although such an elevating concept of world order is not a "cure-all," Nitze admitted, it nonetheless is an essential element in an alliance or coalition structure "sufficiently flexible, powerful, and directed to compete successfully with the Soviet-Communist system."[21]

No problem was more divisive for the North Atlantic Alliance and the free-world coalition of which it was the core during the early Cold War years than the issue of the rearmament of Germany. With the beginning of the Korean War in June 1950, however, even the suspicious French began to see that the long-term stability of Europe and its territorial integrity vis-à-vis the USSR required exploitation of Germany's military potential as well as economic resources. The U.S. government had been urging this recognition upon the French and other European governments for several years. Its own plans regarding Europe—to draw most of its forces there into reserve, rather than keeping them on the front line—were premised on the German Federal Republic's ultimate rearmament and, in a sense, its replacement of the United States in the postwar European international balance. Americans had landed in Europe in 1944 to restore the European balance, not to become a part of it.

The French thus were moved to accept a degree of German remilitarization as inevitable, however painful the idea was for them. In order to exercise control over the process, the French government in October 1950 proposed the Pleven Plan, later developed into a scheme for a European Defense Community (EDC). The complicated EDC proposal envisioned the functional integration of West German forces into a European whole—a European army and defense council, led by a European minister of defense. It was meant to be the military counterpart of the European Coal and Steel Community (ECSC), or Schuman Plan. No German high command or general staff or even any large, division-sized German units would be allowed under it. The German soldiers in a European army would be so dispersed throughout it that they would scarcely be aware of their national identity. This was France's price for allowing any German remilitarization at all. According to a French saying of the day, the German forces within an EDC should be strong enough to impress the Soviet Union, but weak enough not to threaten

---

[21]Paul H. Nitze, "Coalition Policy and the Concept of World Order," in Arnold Wolfers, ed., *Alliance Policy in the Cold War* (Westport, CT: Greenwood Press, 1976; originally published in 1959 by Johns Hopkins Press, Baltimore), pp. 15–30, quotations on pp. 26–27.

Luxembourg. The EDC's authors thought they had found just the right balance with this plausible but impractical scheme.

In August 1954 the French National Assembly itself defeated the EDC proposal, largely because of an inability to overcome fear of Germany's militarism.[22] One European leader, British Foreign Secretary Anthony Eden, whose country itself had held aloof from the EDC, had the glimmer of an idea for a creative response to this awkward situation: "If such fear of Germany persisted, it could not be met in E.D.C.; N.A.T.O. was the place for this." He subsequently developed this line of thinking, proposing that the Federal Republic not only be incorporated into NATO but also be accepted, along with ex-enemy Italy, into the 1948 Brussels Pact. "If we could bring Germany and Italy into it and make the whole arrangement mutual," Eden reasoned, "we should have a new political framework for Europe, without discrimination."[23] The Brussels Pact also subtly could be converted from an alliance into an order. At a conference in London at the end of September 1954, seven European nations, plus the United States and Canada, met to confirm the new arrangements. They were formalized by a meeting in Paris the following month. According to the so-called Paris agreements, the expanded Brussels Treaty was renamed the Western European Union (WEU), the occupation regime in Germany was brought to an end, and the Federal Republic of Germany was invited to join NATO. A West German scholar, Josef Joffe, recently has written, "Long forgotten, the London Conference of 1954—the closest equivalent to a postwar settlement in Europe—provided the capstone for a West European order that has endured until this day."[24]

The ideological, political, and institutional context that made this imaginative reordering possible was the security afforded by the North Atlantic Treaty Organization. Embodying the continuing commitment of the United States to their safety, NATO gave to the West European partners a reassurance they needed. It thus changed the terms of their interaction. As Joffe points out, the entry of the United States into Europe—that is, U.S. influence carried through the vehicle of NATO—resolved the current European security dilemma. The prospect of a collective gain in security overcame the logic of historic rivalry and relative individual advantage. Joffe interestingly goes so far as to

---

[22]On the complicated motivation behind the French decision, see Henri Brugmans, "The Defeat of the European Army," in F. Roy Willis, *European Integration* (New York: New Viewpoints, 1975), pp. 38–49.

[23]Anthony Eden, *The Memoirs of Anthony Eden: Full Circle* (Boston: Houghton Mifflin, 1960), pp. 44, 169.

[24]Josef Joffe, "Europe's American Pacifier," *Foreign Policy*, no. 54 (Spring 1984): 66–84, quotation on p. 75. For the texts of the London final act and the Paris agreements, see Chatham House Study Group, *Britain in Western Europe: WEU and the Atlantic Alliance* (London: Royal Institute of International Affairs, 1956), app. 2, and North Atlantic Treaty Organization, *NATO: Facts*, apps. 6 and 10.

reverse the traditional direction of thinking about the relationship of alliances and international order. Conventional doctrine holds that states coalesce in order to assure their security. In the case of West Germany's entry into NATO, Joffe suggests, they coalesced because their security was assured by a powerful outsider, whose involvement provided them not only with external protection but also with internal confidence. Order, in this instance, was thus the pre-condition of alliance, rather than its result.[25]

One of the first fruits of this new Western accord was an agreement on the vexatious issue of the Saar, legally still a part of Germany but detached by France at the end of the war. One of the specific agreements signed at Paris in October 1954 was a French-German arrangement to give the Saar a European statute within the framework of the WEU. When, in 1955, the Saar electorate voted against "Europeanization," France accepted this judgment and, after tense negotiations concerning appropriate economic compensations to France, the Saarland was in 1957 reunited with Germany. It is unlikely that, without prior WEU/NATO-facilitated agreement between France and Germany and the other Western allies on basic security issues, a solution would have been worked out so smoothly or so quickly.

The integration of the Federal Republic of Germany into the West, on terms acceptable to France and the Low Countries as well as Great Britain and the United States, is by far the most important contribution NATO has made to the internal stability and peace of the Atlantic world. It is possibly the greatest historical achievement of the Atlantic Alliance in general. There have been, to be sure, other attempts at interallied conflict resolution that are also worthy of note. One is the role that NATO periodically has played, both through the intervention of the NATO Secretariat and the intercession of individual NATO members including the United States, in the nettlesome British-Icelandic fishery dispute. Another is the active part that NATO has occasionally taken, in support of UN efforts, in trying to solve the Cyprus problem involving the interests of three allies: Great Britain, Greece, and Turkey. Although the local contest between the Greek majority and Turkish minority has not been resolved, at least the issue has not been allowed to drive either Greece or Turkey out of their common defense commitment. The NATO framework has helped to contain the problem and to ensure the sympathetic concern of nations whose distance might otherwise have made them indifferent to it. At the other end of the Mediterranean, there is another ancient dispute, over Gibraltar, whose resolution one day could be facilitated within a NATO setting. "The tricky problem of Britain's Gibraltar garrison might be overcome by running up a Nato flag over it in place of the union jack," the London *Economist* recently has suggested. "This would give Gibraltarians the reassurance of a British presence, while soothing Spanish national pride. Spain's membership in Nato would allow it to claim a little jurisdiction over

---

[25]Joffe, "Europe's American Pacifier": 75, 76.

what it treats as foreign soldiers on its soil." Some such solution, within the NATO context, surely could be negotiated, and should be.[26]

The most notable failure of interallied consultation—the 1956 Suez crisis, pitting Britain and France, which landed forces in Egypt to protect the canal, against the United States, which disapproved of their intervention—should not obscure the considerable potential of the North Atlantic Alliance as an instrument of stabilization and pacification. Of course, the formal relationship among the allies could always be ignored. As major alliance decisions are made through the rule of unanimity, with any member able in effect to prevent a formal alliance-wide policy or decision, care is taken by the allies to preserve their right to act unilaterally, or in small groups of allies with shared interests. This is what occurred in October 1956, despite the fact that NATO just then was engaged in an institutional effort to improve the quality of consultation among its members. This normative commitment (Article 4) was, in a negative way, highlighted by the Suez débâcle.

Following it, the representatives of the NATO Council, sobered by what had happened, approved a report by a Committee of Three—Canada's Pearson, Norway's Halvard Lange, and Italy's Gaetano Martino—on nonmilitary cooperation within NATO. Admitting the "severe strains" that the alliance had undergone, the "three wise men" stressed that the Atlantic community could develop greater unity "only by working constantly to achieve common policies by full and timely consultation on issues of common concern." Invoking Article 33 of the UN Charter and Article 1 of the North Atlantic Treaty itself, dealing with peaceful resolution of disputes through negotiation, the three addressed intermember disputes, recommending specifically that alliance members henceforth "submit any such disputes, which have not proved capable of settlement directly, to good offices procedures within the NATO framework before resorting to any other agency." The NATO secretary-general was empowered to bring such issues to the attention of the council and to offer his services to resolve them. Besides thus strengthening the political coherence of the alliance and the office of the secretary-general, the wise men sought, in an original and bold move, more explicitly to globalize the scope of alliance consultation, thereby building upon the implications of Article 4. "NATO should not forget," they advised,

> that the influence and interests of its members are not confined to the area covered by the Treaty, and that common interests of the Atlantic Community can be seriously affected by developments outside the Treaty area. Therefore, while striving to improve their relations with each other,

---

[26]For an account of the Icelandic fisheries and Cyprus problems by a NATO secretary-general, see Paul-Henri Spaak, *The Continuing Battle: Memoirs of a European, 1936–1966,* trans. Henry Fox (Boston: Little, Brown, 1971), chap. 34. On the Gibraltar question, dating from the Treaty of Utrecht (1713), see "Howe now," *Economist* 294, no. 7380 (February 9, 1985): 14–15.

and to strengthen and deepen their own unity, they should also be concerned with harmonizing their policies in relation to other areas, taking into account the broader interests of the whole international community; particularly in working through the United Nations and elsewhere for the maintenance of international peace and security and for the solution of the problems that now divide the world.[27]

This brings me to the third problem I would like to discuss: NATO's suitability for negotiations with its adversaries, principally the Soviet Union and its Warsaw Pact allies. The apparent success of the Western alliance in providing for deterrence and defense, which has made the alliance seem to have an overly rigid, military emphasis, has given rise to public demands in the West for a comparable effort by the NATO governments in the spheres of détente and disarmament. The better ordering of diplomatic relations with the Soviet bloc, it was argued, also would contribute to the collective security of the societies of the Atlantic community.

The capacity of the alliance for negotiation with its adversaries—that is, its flexibility—was very much in question, however. Its disposition had been partially tested in the mid-1950s when a number of proposals were floated, by the American diplomat George F. Kennan and several European statesmen, for a mutual "disengagement" of forces from Germany or even a larger zone in central Europe. None of these schemes was taken very seriously. Most Western leaders remained convinced of the logic of "negotiation from strength," the strategy Acheson had propounded in the late 1940s.[28] The growing popular realization, heightened by the 1962 Cuban missile crisis, that this doctrine of building up streng*'* .irst, and negotiating only later, could mean the indefinite postponeme· of meaningful talks with the Soviet Union, put pressure on the Weste··· .vernments to take steps toward peace. French President Charles de G· ., after taking his country out of NATO's integrated military structure (f· .igh not its commitments in the North Atlantic Treaty), ceremoniously visi .a the Soviet Union in 1966. The German Social Democratic leader, Willy Brandt, initiated his policy of Ostpolitik. Even smaller countries like Be'gium began commercial and other exchanges with some of the nations of Eastern Europe. The Belgians developed especially close ties with Poland for example.

The individu· character of these initiatives, sometimes prompted by the needs of dom·· .ic politics, caused confusion and exhibited the need for

---

[27]For the ·   see North Atlantic Treaty Organization, *NATO: Facts*, app. 11. For the background, see   .ak, *Continuing Battle*, chap. 31.

[28]George   Kennan, *Russia, the Atom and the West* (New York: Harper and Brothers, 1958); George · Kennan, "Disengagement Revisited," *Foreign Affairs* 37, no. 2 (January 1959): 187–210; Hu·· Gaitskell, "Disengagement: Why? How?" *Foreign Affairs* 36, no. 4 (July 1958): 539–56; De· . G. Acheson, "The Illusion of Disengagement," *Foreign Affairs* 36, no. 3 (April 195· 371–82; Coral Bell, *Negotiation from Strength: A Study in the Politics of Power* (New Yor· . Alfred A. Knopf, 1963).

coordination. The North Atlantic Alliance was the obvious framework in which this could be done. Accordingly, the NATO Council set in motion the "Harmel exercise," led by the Belgian foreign minister, Pierre Harmel. The Harmel group's report, *Future Tasks of the Alliance*, appeared at the end of 1967.[29] This council-approved document emphasized that the North Atlantic Alliance had two main functions, the second having been given insufficient attention. The two functions were defense and détente, which henceforth should be considered inseparable. "Military security and a policy of detente," it stated, "are not contradictory but complementary." Collective defense was a stabilizing factor in world politics; it was the necessary condition for effective policies aimed at a relaxation of tensions. However, "the way to peace" in Europe rested on the constructive use of the alliance in the interest of détente. "The ultimate political purpose of the Alliance is to achieve a just and lasting peaceful order in Europe accompanied by appropriate security guarantees," the report declared. Henceforth nobody could miss the point, as the American ambassador to NATO at the time, Harlan Cleveland, later put it, that "the North Atlantic Alliance was now in the peacemaking business."[30]

Recognizing that the alliance afforded "an effective forum and clearing house" for exchanging views and information, *Future Tasks of the Alliance* urged that each ally play its full part in promoting an improvement of relations with the Soviet Union and countries of Eastern Europe, "bearing in mind that the pursuit of detente must not be allowed to split the Alliance." If the allies' diplomacy proceeded "on parallel courses," the report suggested, it would be "all the more effective." So far, contacts with Eastern countries or the Eastern bloc had developed "mainly on a bilateral basis." However, certain subjects required "by their very nature a multilateral solution." One such area was the problem of German reunification and its relationship to a European settlement; this had been the special responsibility of three Western powers—France, Great Britain, and the United States—and the Soviet Union. A second was the newer field of "disarmament and practical arms control measures, including the possibility of balanced force reductions." A third important focus for the alliance was the urgent matter of improving the defenses of "exposed areas," particularly NATO's southeastern flank in the Mediterranean and Middle East.

The Harmel report, by fastening the concepts of defense and détente together, established the "two pillar" doctrine of alliance unity. Although the impetus behind the emphasis given to the relaxation of tensions with the Eastern bloc countries came from the European side of the alliance, much of the analytical content of the new policy, particularly in the technical sphere

---

[29] The text is in North Atlantic Treaty Organization, *NATO Handbook*, app. 1.
[30] Harlan Cleveland, *NATO: The Transatlantic Bargain* (New York: Harper and Row, 1970), p. 146.

of arms control, came from the American side.[31] The principal expression of
the new alliance commitment to multilateral arms control so far has been the
Mutual and Balanced Force Reduction (MBFR) talks, which have been proceeding intermittently, and inconclusively, in Vienna since 1973.

The objective of the Vienna talks is an enhancement of stability by a
reciprocal lowering of force levels in "the area of reductions," consisting of
the Benelux countries, the Federal Republic of Germany, the German Democratic Republic, Czechoslovakia, and Poland. These seven countries, plus
Canada, Great Britain, the United States, and the Soviet Union, are the "direct
participants." The remaining Warsaw Pact states with no troops in the reduction area (i.e., Bulgaria, Hungary, and Romania) are designated "special
participants," as are NATO members Norway, Denmark, Italy, Greece, and
Turkey. Iceland, with no armed forces, chose not to participate. Portugal,
whose importance to NATO lay mainly in the maritime sphere, did so as
well. France, with its ambiguous relationship to NATO, has stayed out of
the negotiations, although its forces were a major factor to be taken into
account in them. The newest ally, Spain, also has held itself aloof from the
MBFR process, just as it has avoided integrating its military forces into the
NATO structure.

Owing in part to inability of the two sides to agree on how many troops
the two sides actually have in the area of reduction, and thus by what exact
numbers they must be reduced, the MBFR talks have long been in a stalemate.
Yet a recent concession by the NATO side in agreeing to accept the Warsaw
Pact's figures as the basis for negotiations seems not, so far, to have produced
the long-awaited breakthrough.[32] Because of the imbalance in favor of the
Warsaw Pact side, the Western proposals, which includes not only large
reductions but also insistence upon close verification of the large Soviet
withdrawals that are requested, presumably still are unacceptable to Moscow.
For some defenders of the Vienna talks, a continued deadlock is not critically
important, as "the MBFR process" itself is the real value to be preserved.
Behind-the-scenes consultations, including even the allied governments not
directly involved in the Vienna process, have maintained a political consensus
in the West on the subject of conventional arms levels. Through the MBFR
negotiations, ill-considered unilateral efforts to withdraw national troop contingents, such as proposed by former Senator Mike Mansfield and other
American legislators, have been defeated. The talks, though unsuccessful in
achieving their primary purpose of reduction, have also served as confidence-
building measures, assuring both sides that the forces deployed probably will

---

[31]According to Harlan Cleveland, the report of a subgroup of the Harmel group headed
by the former U.S. ambassador to the Soviet Union, Foy D. Kohler, "provided the first full
rationale for a major effort by NATO in the arms control field, suggesting more intensive
consultation on Western disarmament positions, thinking of arms control as the other side of the
coin of NATO force planning." Ibid., p. 145.

[32]John Tagliabue, "Soviet Cool to Western Proposal at Vienna Talks on Troop Cuts,"
New York Times, December 6, 1985.

not be used. In significant part because of this systematic diplomacy in which the Eastern and Western alliances have been participating for so many years, the military situation in central Europe is today perceived, fairly accurately, to be basically stable. As one U.S. veteran of the MBFR talks, John G. Keliher, has written, "Such military stability has accomplished what, when all is said and done, is the basic objective of any successful arms control agreement—preservation of peace."[33]

The NATO doctrine of defense-cum-détente, the result of which has been diplomatic as well as military engagement with the Soviet Union and the Warsaw Pact, has established latently a kind of order—at least stability and predictability, if not also equity and justice—not only in western Europe but also on the continent of Europe as a whole. NATO and the Warsaw Pact have been locked in an orderly relationship since the latter's formation. Established in 1955, ostensibly in reaction to the incorporation of the Federal Republic of Germany into NATO, the Warsaw Pact is in some respects a mirror image of NATO. Like the Western alliance, it purports to be a fragment of a larger, more comprehensive international security system. Article 11 of the Warsaw Pact stipulates in fact that, should "a system of collective security" eventually be established in Europe and "a General European Treaty of Collective Security" concluded for that purpose, the treaty would cease to be operative. In other words, a willingness of the Western countries to negotiate away their NATO commitment might make possible a mutual dissolution of alliances. Until then, the Warsaw Treaty Organization offers a mutual non-aggression pact.[34]

What the NATO-Warsaw Pact symbiosis amounts to is an inchoate Europe-wide security system. Another part of this system, begun at Helsinki in 1975, is the continuing Conference on Security and Cooperation in Europe (CSCE).[35] In December 1979 a further major step was taken with the celebrated "two-track" decision of the NATO allies, meeting in Brussels, to deploy Pershing II and cruise missiles on the territory of some of the members and at the same time to try to negotiate an arms control agreement regarding these

---

[33]John G. Keliher, "Does MBFR Have a Future?" in David S. Yost, ed., *NATO's Strategic Options: Arms Control and Defense* (New York: Pergamon Press, 1981), pp. 85–109, quotation on p. 106.

[34]For further background on the NATO-Warsaw Pact relationship, see Malcolm Mackintosh, "The Warsaw Treaty Organization: A History," in David Holloway and Jane M. O. Sharp, eds., *The Warsaw Pact: Alliance in Transition?* (Ithaca, NY: Cornell University Press, 1984), pp. 41–58, and Lawrence S. Kaplan, "NATO and the Warsaw Pact: The Past," in Robert W. Clawson and Lawrence S. Kaplan, eds., *The Warsaw Pact: Political Purpose and Military Means* (Wilmington, DE: Scholarly Resources, 1982), pp. 67–91. For recent proposals of the Warsaw Pact-NATO nonaggression pact idea, see Serge Schmemann, "Warsaw Pact Jogs NATO on a Treaty," *New York Times*, April 8, 1983, and the text of a *Pravda* interview with Soviet leader Yuri V. Andropov, *New York Times*, January 25, 1984.

[35]See the essay in this volume by Max M. Kampelman on "The Lessons of the Madrid CSCE Conference."

theater nuclear weapons, or intermediate nuclear forces (INF). The 1979 dual-track decision was consciously made in the tradition of the Harmel report, approved by the NATO Council a dozen years before. An important difference between the two situations, however, is that, whereas the conventional weapons and other military reductions contemplated during the Harmel exercise were to be multilateral and involve most of the allies, any negotiations regarding theater nuclear weapons presumably would be conducted by the United States, independently, on behalf of the alliance. The nature of the weapons, which are capable of strategic missions, is such that Washington wished to have the talks, like the earlier Strategic Arms Limitation Talks (SALT), under its direct control. The Brussels communiqué did provide, however, for a high-level "special consultative body" to be formed within the alliance "to support the US negotiating effort."[36]

Stirrings were heard in Western Europe against this American hegemonic presumption. Christoph Bertram, a West German who was then director of the International Institute for Strategic Studies in London, has reflected upon the novelty of the December 1979 decision: for the first time, the alliance has been asked (by the Federal Republic of Germany as much as by the United States) to take collective responsibility for the procurement and installation of nuclear weapons. As he noted, the dual-track approach meant that the military program would be pursued "as far as necessary," and arms control "as far as possible." This was acceptable. "But while the first track constituted the Alliance's first *multilateral* nuclear production decision, the second was put firmly in the context of *bilateral* Soviet-American talks and agreements." To Bertram this procedural incongruity could not much longer be tolerated, especially as the Reagan administration seemed to be proceeding fast along only one track, that of rearmament. "We owe to the avowed skepticism of the Reagan Administration toward arms control that the built-in contradiction between multilateral arming and bilateral arms control has been brought into the open. It is an awkward one for European domestic, for East-West, and for West-West relations."[37]

It has long been the received wisdom of the alliance, in the face of such appeals for a more collective Western diplomacy, that NATO cannot negotiate. Kennan, writing in 1958, elaborated the reasoning behind this conventional assessment:

> Not only can the strengthening of NATO *not* be a substitute for negotiation, but NATO cannot itself provide either the source of authority or the channel for the negotiating process. The governmental structures of the individual NATO members are already of such ponderous and frightening complexity in themselves that it sometimes seems to me questionable when they would be capable of providing the imagination,

---

[36]For the text, see U.S., Department of State *Bulletin* 80, no. 2035 (February 1980): 16.

[37]Christoph Bertram, "The Implications of Theater Nuclear Weapons in Europe," *Foreign Affairs* 60, no. 2 (Winter 1981/82): 305–26, quotations on p. 313.

the speed of decision, and the constancy of style necessary for the pursuit of any delicate diplomatic undertaking, even if they were not encumbered with their obligations to allies.[38]

This sounds rather like a mandate for the kind of virtuoso diplomacy subsequently practiced by Henry Kissinger, who himself in the past has judged NATO an institution wholly unsuited for diplomatic negotiation. Commenting on the theory that the organization is "as much an instrument of detente as it is of defense," the former secretary of state has stated bluntly: "I think that is simply not correct. NATO is not equipped to be an instrument of detente."[39] The traditional American statesmanly proclivity has always been toward the conclusion that, no matter how desirable interallied consultation might be, there must always be a "leader."

Against this view, Europeans have increasingly begun to ask the question, as Bertram optimistically phrases it: "Would the situation now be improved by a more direct participation by European governments in the negotiating process?" Acknowledging the logical force of the objections to European participation, including the disparity between the nuclear superpowers and the West European states and an added degree of complication that would result from their more direct involvement, Bertram nonetheless urges reconsideration of the bias against alliance-wide negotiation. The Vienna MBFR negotiations, he argues, have shown "a remarkable degree of cohesion within the Alliance, over an unprecedented period of time." They have indicated that even the primarily bilateral issue of Soviet and American conventional force withdrawals can be addressed in a multilateral forum, through the device of a first (superpower) stage and a second (European) stage of reduction, without uncontrollable "slippage" from one negotiating area to the other. The MBFR experience further demonstrates that interallied political differences are "more effectively reduced when West European governments have a seat at the table than when they have not." The MBFR talks, and the CSCE process as well, thus appear to have disproved earlier fears about aggravating interallied dissonance through attempts at common negotiation. In fact, as Bertram points out, the direct participation of West European delegates in these forums has led "not only to highly effective Alliance coordination but also to the determination of all Western governments concerned to sort out their differences *in camera* and not in the public political arena."[40]

If multilateral consultation and negotiation have proved advantageous in the MBFR and CSCE settings, why not also try this method in the INF negotiating context? A combined NATO delegation thus could be formed in Geneva as well. The European allies, after all, are the ones principally affected

---

[38]Kennan, *Russia, the Atom and the West*, p. 95.

[39]Henry A. Kissinger, "The Future of NATO," in Kenneth A. Myers, ed., *NATO, The Next Thirty Years: The Changing Political, Economic, and Military Setting* (Boulder, CO: Westview Press, 1981), pp. 3–19, quotation on p. 10.

[40]Bertram, "Theater Nuclear Weapons in Europe": 314–15.

by the intermediate nuclear weapons being stationed on their soil. There does occur, of course, a considerable amount of discussion within the alliance of these matters, even nuclear issues, already. The NATO Nuclear Planning Group, composed of defense ministers, has existed since 1966. The American delegates to the MBFR and INF talks, as well as to the conferences dealing with strategic nuclear weapons and space defense, regularly meet with the members of the NATO Council in Brussels. The U.S. chairman of the allied delegation to MBFR actually receives his instructions from the NATO Council, after informal bilateral and multilateral deliberations among the national governments. Recognizing the merits of a more collaborative style of diplomacy, no less a Western strategist than Kissinger lately has proposed, in effect, an American-European role reversal. As part of a larger plan, involving the unprecedented appointment of a European as the Supreme Allied Commander Europe (SACEUR) and an American as NATO secretary-general, he would have the MBFR and the INF negotiations both "Europeanized," with each to have "a European chairman, an American deputy and a mixed, though predominantly European, delegation."[41]

Although such proposals as these run the risk of appearing more symbolic than substantive, they do accurately reflect the reality that the balance of influence and competence in NATO is changing. My own judgment is that, although the military defense of the West should still be left primarily in American hands, the diplomatic functions of the alliance should be managed much more jointly. Therefore, I would favor a "Europeanized" MBFR delegation and a U.S.-headed, but alliance-wide, INF negotiating team.

The basic purpose behind these suggestions of Bertram, Kissinger, and some other knowledgeable Europeans and Americans is to create a greater uniformity of outlook within the Western alliance, replacing a quasi-hegemonic order with a more cooperative one. The United States thereby can be reassured more completely of the commitment of Europeans to collective defense, and Europeans can be convinced more thoroughly of the American interest in collective arms control. The result would be a stronger North Atlantic Alliance, more estimable in its own eyes and surely also in the sight of others. There would be a broader "collective" purpose behind this multilateralizing of the Western alliance as well. Through the force of common example and through the influence of joint diplomacy, the Soviet Union and its Warsaw Pact associates might be drawn into a more cooperative and civilized modus vivendi, with each other and with the West. In the terms I have earlier used, the Eastern bloc, too, might be made more universal, more complex, and more flexible.

What has been built up over the years, I would conclude, is a de facto international order between the Western and Eastern alliances, to some extent substituting for the outmoded system of four-power control and supplementing

---

[41]Henry A. Kissinger, "A Plan to Reshape NATO," *Time* 123, no. 10 (March 5, 1984): 20–24.

the imperfect collective security system of the United Nations. It has evolved from a series of ad hoc decisions and improvised practices. It has as well derived strength and purpose from programmatic institutional arrangements and generalized policy statements. Alliances, assumed to be short-lived marriages of convenience, tend to be underestimated. They are associated with disorder. Napoleon rejoiced at being able to face an international coalition, which he expected to collapse from its members' own quarreling. Instead, the anti-Napoleonic alliance became the first institutionalized European international order. Order does not always require the appearance of orderliness. "In NATO," as one ambassador to it has written, " 'disarray' is sometimes another way of saying 'Alliance at Work.' "[42] A lively, open alliance is an attractive force as well as a strong one. Others can be drawn into it and into sympathy with it. As conventionally defined, an alliance is an international formation opposed to another grouping of states. To a considerable extent, this has been the character of NATO, especially since its formal juxtaposition to the Warsaw Pact after 1955. Its original purpose, however, was larger than this. NATO remains, in principle, a fragment of a wider security system, a section of a general world order. So, nominally speaking, does the Warsaw Treaty Organization. While in substance these institutions are not comparable, they have much in common: at bottom, an interest in European security.

The two sides increasingly have generated between themselves a systemic, working relationship, a mutual ordering role, that conceivably might be transformed one day into an actual Europe-wide security system. Obviously, to repeat, the Warsaw Pact is not a NATO. The North Atlantic Treaty is dedicated, as its preamble states, to "the principles of democracy, individual liberty and the rule of law." The Warsaw Pact, by contrast, is often viewed as an organized instrument of Russian tyranny and Soviet oppression. Through exchanges with it, including arms control discussions as well as commercial and cultural interchanges, it nonetheless has been made more open.

Rather than proposing, as was done in the 1950s, a mutual "disengagement" of the blocs, I would suggest contemplation of ways by which the two halves of Western civilization, NATO and its Eastern counterpart, can further develop their interdependence. Even formal links between the two organizations might be forged. These would include, as to some extent already have been developed in Europe, visits of military inspection teams, reciprocal observations of maneuvers, and other such confidence-building contacts. At present, owing to a carry-over of the hostile climate created by the Soviet invasion of Afghanistan, military repression in Poland, and other untoward episodes, East-West ties of this sort have been reduced to a minimum.[43]

---

[42]Cleveland, *NATO*, p. 7.

[43]General Bernard M. Rogers, current SACEUR of NATO, has recommended that an earlier practice of limited military visits, interrupted by the 1979 Soviet invasion of Afghanistan, be resumed. Steven Erlanger, "NATO Head Urges East-West Talk," *Boston Globe*, September 27, 1985.

Ultimately, more ambitious cooperative relationships will have to be devised. One worthwhile project would be to establish a formal crisis-prevention regime, with permanent crisis-control centers located in Europe as well as in the United States and the Soviet Union.[44] A formal Warsaw Pact-NATO nonaggression treaty, if premised on a substantive improvement of East-West relations, also merits serious consideration. Even some form of actual institutional association of the one organization with the other, or joint membership in a newly devised security entity, is worth contemplation. It should not be forgotten that, as was pointed out during the preparation of the North Atlantic Treaty in 1948, "it would be even possible for the Soviet Union to join the arrangement." The North Atlantic Alliance originated as an open, not a closed, system—as an allied order. Although its potential as a model for a larger pattern of security and peace may never fully be realized, the very idea enables us to address the problem of regional alliances and world order in a new way: not alliance versus order, but alliance as order itself.

FOR FURTHER READING

On the historical background and official diplomacy of the creation of the North Atlantic Alliance, see, especially, the participant accounts by Nicholas Henderson, *The Birth of NATO*, and Escott Reid, *Time of Fear and Hope: The Making of the North Atlantic Treaty, 1947–1949*, cited in the footnotes. Historical detail also may be found in two other works cited: Alan K. Henrikson, "The Creation of the North Atlantic Alliance," in John R. Reichart and Steven R. Sturm, eds., *American Defense Policy*, and Lawrence S. Kaplan, *The United States and NATO: The Formative Years*, which includes an extended bibliographical commentary. Other works on facets of NATO's early years are Timothy P. Ireland, *Creating the Entangling Alliance: The Origins of the North Atlantic Treaty Organization* (Westport, CT: Greenwood Press, 1981); Lawrence S. Kaplan, *A Community of Interests: NATO and the Military Assistance Program, 1948–1951* (Washington, DC: Historical Office, Office of the Secretary of Defense, 1980); Geir Lundestad, *America, Scandinavia, and the Cold War, 1945–1949* (New York: Columbia University Press, 1980); and Olav Riste, ed., *Western Security: The Formative Years, European and Atlantic Defence, 1947–1953* (New York: Columbia University Press, 1985).

Postwar American-European relations are treated comprehensively by A. W. DePorte in *Europe Between the Superpowers: The Enduring Balance* (New Haven: Yale University Press, 1979) and Alfred Grosser in *The Western Alliance: European-American Relations Since 1945*, trans. Michael Shaw (New York: Vintage Books,

---

[44]Alexander L. George, *Towards a Soviet-American Crisis Prevention Regime: History and Prospects*, Arms Control and International Security Working Paper No. 28 (Los Angeles: Center for International and Strategic Affairs, University of California, Los Angeles, November 1980); and William Langer Ury and Richard Smoke, *Beyond the Hot Line: Controlling a Nuclear Crisis*, A Report to the United States Arms Control and Disarmament Agency (Cambridge, MA: Nuclear Negotiation Project, Harvard Law School, 1984).

1982). More specifically focused on NATO are Robert E. Osgood, *NATO: The Entangling Alliance* (Chicago: University of Chicago Press, 1962); Timothy W. Stanley, *NATO in Transition: The Future of the Atlantic Alliance* (New York: Frederick A. Praeger, 1965); Henry A. Kissinger, *The Troubled Partnership: A Re-appraisal of the Atlantic Alliance* (New York: McGraw-Hill, 1965); David Calleo, *The Atlantic Fantasy: The United States, NATO, and Europe* (Baltimore: Johns Hopkins Press, 1970); Lawrence Freedman, ed., *The Troubled Alliance: Atlantic Relations in the 1980s* (New York: St. Martin's Press, 1983); Robert W. Tucker and Linda Wrigley, eds., *The Atlantic Alliance and Its Critics* (New York: Lehrman Institute, 1983); Clive Rose, *Campaigns Against Western Defence: NATO's Adversaries and Critics* (New York: St. Martin's Press, 1985); Gregory F. Treverton, *Making the Alliance Work: The United States and Western Europe* (Ithaca, NY: Cornell University Press, 1985); and Edwina Campbell, *Consultation and Consensus in NATO: Implementing the Canadian Article* (Lanham, MD: University Press of America, 1985).

The Lyman L. Lemnitzer Center for NATO Studies at Kent State University has produced a number of relevant works: Lawrence S. Kaplan, Robert W. Clawson, and Raimondo Luraghi, eds., *NATO and the Mediterranean*, and Robert W. Clawson and Lawrence S. Kaplan, eds., *The Warsaw Pact: Political Purpose and Military Means*, mentioned in the footnotes, and also Lawrence S. Kaplan and Robert W. Clawson, eds., *NATO After Thirty Years* (Wilmington, DE: Scholarly Resources, 1981) and Robert W. Clawson, ed., *East-West Rivalry in the Third World: Security Issues and Regional Perspectives* (Wilmington, DE: Scholarly Resources, 1986).

On the work of the NATO secretariat and individual secretaries-general, see Robert S. Jordan, *The NATO International Staff/Secretariat, 1952–1957: A Study in International Administration* (London: Oxford University Press, 1967) and *Political Leadership in NATO: A Study in Multinational Diplomacy* (Boulder, CO: Westview Press, 1979). On alliance nuclear discussions, see Paul Buteux, *The Politics of Nuclear Consultation in NATO, 1965–1980* (Cambridge: Cambridge University Press, 1983). Conventional arms control deliberations are well described in William B. Prendergast, *Mutual and Balanced Force Reduction: Issues and Prospects* (Washington, DC: American Enterprise Institute for Public Policy Research, 1978), and John G. Keliher, *The Negotiations on Mutual and Balanced Force Reductions: The Search for Arms Control in Central Europe* (New York: Pergamon Press, 1980).

The Organization of American States and International Order in the Western Hemisphere

ALEJANDRO ORFILA

Peace is the tranquility of order. This is the definition of peace which has inspired Western culture for over fifteen centuries, since the time of Saint Augustine. Living as he did at the end of the ancient Roman Empire, the bishop of Hippo was deeply conscious of the turmoil and tragedy caused by the violent breakup of the classical civilization of Rome. He saw that there could be no peace unless a tranquil order was restored. This did not mean imposing order by any means, just or unjust; rather, it implied promoting a civic order that respected human dignity. In Augustine's cosmic view, peace could be achieved only as the City of Man approximated the City of God. Humanity, in other words, could not find either peace or perfection within itself. It had to ground its pursuit of peace in transcendent principles. These would illuminate, guide, and serve as a measuring rod for the course of action. We, as citizens of the West, are heirs to this transcendent, universalist tradition. Our heritage encourages us to try to agree upon higher principles of political and economic order so that our peoples, and societies in other parts of the world as well, might live in harmony.

It is essential for us to recognize that, as a consequence of various historical and cultural circumstances, the regions of our constantly shrinking planet also have separate traditions. Each of our regions contributes to the world culture, but each views this unity from its own distinctive perspective and horizon. The political, economic, and cultural institutions that unite sovereign states in common causes differ considerably from region to region. It is in the light of this reality that I address the present theme, with particular reference to the Western Hemisphere, of the relationship between regional order and world order.

We, in the Americas, possess the world's oldest regional international organization, the Organization of American States (OAS), evolved from earlier hemispheric institutions and now stretching toward its centenary year.[1] In addition, we have created the first of the existing legal and political frameworks for maintaining international order—the Inter-American System.[2] The Western Hemisphere's political traditions derive from the general inheritance of the West, but they also originate in the specific experiences of the thirty-five independent states of this hemisphere. What is so remarkable about the hemispheric community today is that its members are still inspired by the principles that, in embryonic form, were proclaimed long ago, at the moment when the New World broke off from the Old, by statesmen such as José de San Martín, Simon Bolívar, and Henry Clay. These historic norms include: respect for the equality of sovereign nations, old and new; a mutual desire to resolve disputes by peaceful means; and the expectation that regional states should seek to build up a system of friendship, harmony, and cooperation among themselves.

When the OAS Charter was adopted at Bogotá in 1948, the founders of this organization attempted to blend into one document all of the basic ideas regarding democracy, human rights, nonintervention, and development that are common to the inheritance and aspirations of all of the states in our hemisphere. The vision they held was that of a hemisphere united from the Bering Sea to the Beagle Channel, from Alaska to Patagonia. They were confident that "the true significance of American solidarity and good neighborliness can only mean the consolidation on this continent, within the framework of democratic institutions, of a system of individual liberty and social justice based on respect for the essential rights of man." The OAS Charter was updated in 1967, but its essential principles remain intact.[3]

It is almost self-evident that agreement on principles is frequently not accompanied by concrete action to put them into effect. The folly of human beings, the excessive pride and blindness of would-be leaders, and the conditions of any given moment in history inevitably restrain mankind from living fully in accordance with the high ideals and principles it proclaims. Yet a most remarkable feature of human culture is the fact of ever-renewed and

---

[1]For an excellent account of the evolution of the OAS, see M. Margaret Ball, *The OAS in Transition* (Durham, NC: Duke University Press, 1969). The OAS now has thirty-two member countries. Guyana and Canada are Permanent Observers. Belize, formerly British Honduras, is not yet formally associated with the OAS.

[2]A thorough analysis of the structure, functions, and activities of the Inter-American System, including texts of the basic instruments, may be found in Inter-American Institute of International Legal Studies, *The Inter-American System: Its Development and Strengthening* (Dobbs Ferry, NY: Oceana Publications, 1966).

[3]*Charter of the Organization of American States, As Amended by the Protocol of Buenos Aires in 1967*, Treaty Series 1-C (Washington, DC: Pan American Union, General Secretariat, Organization of American States, 1968), p. 1.

incessant efforts by men and women everywhere to seek to live by the principles they cherish and honor. In their inmost being, both individuals and societies innately sense that, if peace and justice are to be promoted, action must follow words, as night follows day.

During the twentieth century no doubt the paramount impulse of mankind has been to give priority to global, over regional, order. The 1907 Hague Convention, the League of Nations, and the United Nations all testify to this dynamic orientation toward order on a world scale. This tendency was accelerated as a consequence of the breakdown of the world economy into regional trading blocs during the 1930s and of the failure of the League of Nations itself, an organization that one of the most powerful nations of the world, the United States, had never joined. Sovereign states came to believe, during that period, that the global system's regional hegemonies had led to the evils of the Second World War. They were also convinced that the economic autarchy of the 1930s could not be repeated if the world were to prosper, benefiting poor and rich countries alike. As a result, after 1945 the general tendency among nations and their leaders was to pin their hopes for a peaceful and prosperous world order on a politically and economically strong central world organization.

Events were to dictate, however, that these hopes would be disappointed. Many of the worldwide institutions under the aegis of the United Nations have become only pale shadows of what their founders, in the immediate aftermath of the Second World War, expected them to be. In these circumstances, during the Cold War between the two superpowers, the vision of regional order in the Americas gained in attractiveness. It should be recognized that this vision, grounded in history, was not put into effect overnight. It came into existence, rather, by slow and halting degrees over a long period. At various moments in history, difficulties within the Western Hemisphere threatened to undermine the alliance that was gradually being formed, thereby fragmenting, or Balkanizing, the region's international system.

It is appropriate briefly to recall these stages of limited progress. Bolívar's call for a regional congress of nations led in 1826 to the convening of the Congress of Panama. Attending that meeting were delegates from Colombia, Mexico, Peru, and Central America (an independent confederation from 1823 to 1839). President John Quincy Adams nominated two U.S. commissioners to attend the Panama meeting, but they failed to arrive before it adjourned, and the instruments resulting from it were never ratified. During the mid-nineteenth century, some of the Southern Cone nations engaged in alliances of cooperation, but these proved abortive. With the first Pan American Conference, held in Washington, DC, in 1889–90, a definitive and continuing step toward a truly transcontinental Pan American system was finally initiated, with the creation of the Commercial Bureau of the American Republics. From small beginnings, this agency was to lead through a series of further meetings to establishment in 1910 of the Pan American Union, located at Washington. At subsequent inter-American conferences, a large network of legal instruments and treaties for the whole region was built, eventually resulting in 1947 in the collective-defense provisions of the Rio Treaty and in 1948 in the OAS Charter.

With acceptance of the historic and flexibly designed Charter, the signatory American states agreed to abide legally by a whole series of interrelated principles: respect for the sovereign equality of each OAS member country, large or small; nonintervention by one regional country in the affairs of another; the peaceful resolution of conflicts within the region; democracy as the ideal form of government for the hemisphere; the strengthening of policies to guarantee the protection of human rights within the region; and, perhaps most innovatively, cooperation by all member OAS nations to promote the region's economic, cultural, and social development (*desarrollo integral*).

These principles, it should be recognized, have not been put into effect to the same extent, or in the same manner, by all signatories. For its part, the United States has tended to emphasize the political and geostrategic side of the regional association, whereas the Latin American nations consistently have urged that the OAS give equal weight and force to cooperative action for economic development. From time to time, these divergent conceptions of the regional relationships have led to clashes regarding both the day-to-day activity of the OAS and the basic structuring of the organization. This divergence was particularly noticeable during the 1970s, as most OAS members supported a Peruvian initiative to give the principle of "collective economic security" equal stature with the geopolitical principles found in the Rio Treaty and OAS Charter. The United States, skeptical, responded in 1976 with a proposed OAS Assembly on Cooperation for Development. Now, a decade later, this assembly has not taken place.

The regional inter-American association is not, we must note, the only instrument whereby states in the hemisphere have attempted to regulate and order their relationships with each other. At subregional levels (but outside the formal framework of the Inter-American System) there also exist other arrangements designed to perfect the cause of peace and cooperation. These include the Guarantor Pact of 1942 by which Argentina, Brazil, Chile, and the United States assisted in maintaining stability on the border between Peru and Ecuador.[4] Argentina and Chile, with the assistance of mediation by the Holy See, now have finally succeeded in signing a treaty that settles their prolonged dispute over the Beagle Channel. In the strictly economic field, much work has been done to establish greater Latin American autonomy in making international decisions and to increase the impact of Latin America on world economic policy. These efforts have led to the formation of regional

---

[4]Protocol on Peace, Friendship, and Boundaries Between Peru and Ecuador, signed at Rio de Janeiro, January 29, 1942, in Charles I. Bevans, comp., *Treaties and Other International Agreements of the United States of America, 1776–1949*, 12 vols. (Washington, DC: U.S. Government Printing Office, 1968–76), vol. 3, *Multilateral, 1931–1945*, pp. 700–03.

integration and market arrangements, not only in the Andean Common Market area but also in Central America. They also have resulted in the creation of the Latin American Economic System (SELA) and of the Organization for Latin American Energy Development (OLADE).

Finally, a more recent example of Latin America's determination to develop its own course, independent of the United States and in a subregional context, is the current effort by the Contadora states (Colombia, Mexico, Panama, and Venezuela) to promote peace in Central America.[5] While all citizens of the Americas must applaud the Contadora initiatives, it should not be overlooked that these came about because the troubled Central American situation was never placed on the agenda of the OAS. The only thing that we received from the different parties at the OAS was a series of letters of information. No request for real action was received. Why? It is difficult to say. I imagine that one of the reasons is because the several parties concerned made a judgment that the forum of the OAS was not a place in which to win—to get complete support for partisan positions. Since the parties evidently decided that success was not possible, there came into existence the four-nation Contadora group. I sincerely hope the group succeeds. They are Latin Americans and, as Latin Americans, they tend to think similarly to the Central Americans. They are well equipped to make a contribution. A great deal of time has passed, however, and that passage may degrade the possibility of a solution. In the meantime, the OAS is seen to be inactive, although it has sent a fact-finding mission to Costa Rica to investigate border tensions with Nicaragua and has issued a report. I believe that the OAS has paid a terrific price in terms of public opinion within the hemisphere, and also outside it, because of the existence of the Contadora group. People have come to believe, accurately or not, that the OAS is no good because it was unable to act in the face of a situation that, according to its Charter, it should have been able to deal with, but did not. It may still be possible for the organization to help compose peace in the Central American region, but the task will be very difficult.

Turning to the global context, one may observe that the international horizons of Latin America today extend far beyond the regional association into the North-South dialogue, resulting in involvement with movements such as the Group of 77 and the Lomé Convention. By participating in these broad international forums, the nations of Latin America and the Caribbean are searching for measures to reduce their severe economic vulnerability to every shift in the tides and fortunes of the world economy, as well as for ways to strengthen their political autonomy.

It is now clear, even to the most forceful advocates of the OAS, that the traditional regional relationship, of which the OAS is the apex, is not

---

[5]For a detailed commentary on the September 7, 1984, proposals of the Contadora group, named after the Panamanian island on which they first met, see "Contadora: A Text for Peace," *International Policy Report*, Center for International Policy, Washington, DC, November 1984.

being used by the member nations to the extent that it once was. The organization remains in existence; its legal and political foundations are secure; and its previous contributions to hemispheric security and peace, such as during the 1962 Cuban missile crisis, the aftermath of the 1965 Dominican Republic intervention, or the 1969 border conflict between El Salvador and Honduras, are adequately recognized. The many technical activities of the OAS, in the fields of health and education and other areas, continue to be available to the member states. Yet, at present, the OAS is not the dominant force in working to resolve the severe difficulties that periodically emerge in the hemisphere. By both the political right and left, the regional institutions are, in fact, frequently ignored or given only pro forma recognition.

A major instance of this was the 1982 clash between the United Kingdom and Argentina over the Malvinas Islands. This was a great crisis for the OAS, which found its hemispheric role eclipsed by the United Nations in New York and by the individual mediation efforts of U.S. Secretary of State Alexander M. Haig. The crisis within the OAS went even deeper, however. One consequence was to make one of the protagonists, Argentina, more "Latin American." This is extremely important to recognize. The Argentines became much more part of Latin America because of the reaction of other Latin American countries, which tended to favor Argentina's basic position. A related product, unfortunately, was the widening of the gap between the two areas of the OAS: Latin America and the Caribbean. There are now thirty-two members of the Organization of American States. (St. Kitts-Nevis was admitted early in 1984; Cuba, although still listed as a member, has been suspended since 1962.) One-third of the OAS membership is now from the Caribbean, an area with traditions somewhat different from those of most of Central and South America. It has been observed, as by Bernard Weinraub in the *New York Times*, that the Caribbean tradition is to a large extent derived from "a British parliamentary system of debate and a concept of majority rule with minority rights," and that this tradition is perceived as "anathema" to the Latin American countries whose political style is one "in which decisions are agreed to privately and then publicly rubber-stamped amid considerable theatrics."[6] It would be wrong to deny that there is some truth in this differentiation. Nonetheless, the gulf that exists need not have emerged. Cooperation within the OAS should be a matter not of geography and history, but of a common civility. We all belong to the same club, the inter-American club.

Despite the division that occurred during the Malvinas crisis, this sense of hemispheric community survives. What the Caribbean states felt during the struggle over the Malvinas was not so much favoritism toward Great Britain on the territorial issue, I believe, as it was resentment that force was used by Argentina in order to try to resolve it. The Malvinas were, without

---

[6]Bernard Weinraub, "O.A.S.: Feeling of Bewilderment at the Future," *New York Times*, November 17, 1982.

doubt, a profound cause of misunderstanding. For every Argentine, the Malvinas *are* Argentina. They are as much a part of Argentina as my home state of Mendoza. The way in which the Argentine government went about trying to regain that part of the national territory put the whole country on the spot in view of public opinion abroad. Whoever it was, exactly, who took the decisions leading to the invasion did so on the basis of assumptions that were incorrect. As a result, the entire hemisphere suffered a great setback, from which it is slowly recovering. Not the least of the casualties, one hopes only a temporary one, was the sense of effectiveness of the OAS.

For a decade now, numerous proposals have been made for the purpose of ending this situation of drift in the regional association. One such measure was the Peruvian call for a commitment to collective economic security in addition to, and equal to, military collective security. In 1983, during discussions at OAS regional meetings in Caracas and Asunción, certain courses were agreed upon that were intended to assist in dealing with the severe economic and financial crises afflicting Latin America. These deliberations perhaps have made some contribution to recent cooperation within the region in handling the debt problem, without formation of a debtors' bloc. Such steps were not under the direct authority or supervision of the OAS, however. For the most part, our organization has continued to be gripped by inertia and indecision.

As a way of making the OAS an institution more directly responsive to Latin America's concerns, it has even been suggested that the OAS establishment be relocated. One may hear Latin Americans say that we should move the OAS out of Washington and put it in San José or Panama. For what practical, political purpose? Whom would we arrange to lobby in San José or Panama? Who? The great merit of the OAS, in my view, is the organization itself. Should we not use this marvelous institution-for-lobbying, legalized and available to all OAS members? Within the organization there are some people who believe that everything must be done through the U.S. State Department exclusively. Any ambassador who thinks that is so misuses 90 percent of the facilities, including the media, that this great country, the United States, offers to a good ambassador working to protect the interests of his country. The OAS, as currently situated, is from a realistic Latin American point of view an ideal center of dialogue between thirty-one developing countries and one developed country. The procedures of the organization are favorable. No veto; one vote; one voice.[7] Despite the location of the OAS within the United States, Washington does not use it in a domineering manner. I can testify as an Argentine, as a Latin American, that I have not seen the influence of the United States exercised unduly in the OAS. On the contrary, I have seen the United States sometimes mistreated at the OAS, as for instance

---

[7]On the OAS voting system, see Ann Van Wynen Thomas and A. J. Thomas, Jr., *The Organization of American States* (Dallas: Southern Methodist University Press, 1963), pp. 111–12.

during the controversy over the Panama Canal (satisfactorily settled by a U.S.-Panamanian treaty approved by the U.S. Senate in 1978).

It is understandable that the big states in the hemisphere, not only the United States, sometimes do not approach multilateral discussions within the OAS with much interest. Bilateral diplomacy, in which the larger state can more easily exercise its weight, in truth often seems more attractive to U.S. officials, especially in a military context. Reflecting upon the history of diplomacy within the Western Hemisphere, I have often thought that there is a permanent fight between bilateralism and multilateralism. The two methods of diplomacy ought to be regarded as complementary. During the Panama Canal Treaty negotiations, the government of Panama in fact combined bilateral negotiations and multilateral discussions quite effectively. The United States can do the same. Sometimes the U.S. government has been very supportive of the OAS and has freely participated in multilateral decision making. The brief but golden period of the Alliance for Progress in the 1960s was such a time.[8] In other circumstances, Washington has preferred, many times for good reasons, to deal with Latin American countries bilaterally.

In the last several years, something new has been entering the U.S.-Latin American relationship, I believe. For the first time, the United States and the Latin American countries need each other. In the past, the Latin nations needed the United States; the United States did not need us. I believe now that the United States requires Latin American support as much as the Latin American states must have U.S. assistance. The October 1983 Grenada episode illustrates the point. For legal and political, as well as moral, purposes, the administration of President Ronald Reagan wanted to have Latin American support for its occupation of that island—an action that on the face of it contravened the OAS Charter principle against intervention. That principle is in truth fundamental to OAS members, but it is not their only basic principle. The Charter contains Articles 18 and 19 concerning nonintervention, to be sure, but it also includes Articles 21 and 22 reflecting the basic right of a country to defend itself. The prime minister of Dominica, Eugenia Charles, explained in effect that the Eastern Caribbean is a nation divided into seven states and that one of those states (Grenada) was going in a direction detrimental to the rest. Having no means of their own, the majority of the Organization of Eastern Caribbean States called on the United States for help. They also requested military contingents from Barbados and Jamaica, fellow members of the Caribbean Community and Common Market (CARICOM).[9] The OAS did hold a meeting, one meeting only, on the issue of the U.S. occupation of Grenada. Eighteen members supported the principle of nonintervention in differing degrees; but the reaction of Latin America as a whole

---

[8]Jerome Levinson and Juan de Onís, *The Alliance That Lost Its Way: A Critical Report on the Alliance for Progress* (Chicago: Quadrangle Books, 1970).

[9]For the October 25, 1983, statement by the Organization of Eastern Caribbean States and various U.S. government statements, see "Grenada: Collective Action by the Caribbean Peace Force," U.S., Department of State *Bulletin* 83, no. 2081 (December 1983): 67–82.

changed, I believe, when the discoveries of Soviet weapons were made. Public opinion against intervention then lost some of its pressure. I think this happened within the United States, too. It would be incorrect to say that the OAS supported the U.S. action, but a certain amount of realistic understanding was evident. Despite this helpful acquiescence, the principle of nonintervention remains very important. Undoubtedly, there was damage done when the invasion occurred.

If the OAS as a body is itself going to take action regarding pressing issues in the hemisphere, there must be a greater willingness on the part of governments to use the organization. The OAS reflects the governments. It is an instrument through which their political wills are shown. When the political will exists, the OAS is effective; when political will does not exist, neither does the OAS.

Who actually is the leader of the OAS? Is it the secretary-general? No, it is not. According to the Charter, the secretary-general is strictly an administrator of the organization, and not a political figure. Then who *is* the leader? The leader would have to be the Permanent Council, but the Council is a group of thirty-two ambassadors, and they naturally represent thirty-two points of view. The Council has a chairman, but that position, once held for a one-year term, now changes every three months—partly to give the ambassadors an increased chance of holding that post during their tenures. It is difficult to be leader of a body in a position that rotates by alphabet in three months' time. Where, then, can the political leadership come from? How can the vacuum be filled? In order to solve this problem, it would be necessary to change the Charter, perhaps by lengthening the term of the Council chairmanship. Alternatively, greater authority and initiative could be given to the General Secretariat. I myself believe that the secretary-general must be the leader of the OAS. One cannot ask of oneself to be such a leader, and happily remain in that role.

My criticism, I wish to stress, is not meant to suggest that I believe the OAS has outlived its usefulness, or that it will be any less important in working toward peace and development in the hemisphere in the future. The basic principles of the OAS, indeed, retain both their validity and their value. The OAS member states must produce the will and the skill to preserve and modernize their system, however. It is evident that the shape and direction of the organization must be adapted to current realities, both economic and political. Such adaptation will require decisive and transforming action by the member governments that, together, make up and give life to the organization.

I wish to underscore one point: it is not the principles standing behind the regional association that have been found wanting or defective. In the past, these standards, however difficult of application, have contributed to the creation and evolution of a progressive regional order in the Americas. They should continue so to serve in the future, far beyond the centenary of the OAS. However, even as we recognize the difference between ideals and reality, we must inquire more deeply into whether we possess the instruments to deal with the worsening situation of Latin America. Consider again the Grenada episode and the turbulent situation in Central America, as well as the chronic international debt problem and slow pace of economic development in our region. Would not these matters be more susceptible to solution, on an organized regional basis, if the political attention and economic resources of our hemisphere were not so committed to a globalized East-West struggle?

We will not overcome the existing malaise of the OAS, caused partly by preemptive global issues, through inaction. Member governments must search for and find ways to turn inter-American institutions in new and more promising directions. Such a renewed emphasis on regionalism was attempted to some extent in the report of the U.S. National Bipartisan Commission on Central America, chaired by former Secretary of State Henry A. Kissinger.[10] The OAS, unfortunately, was virtually ignored in that report (suggesting, incidentally, the value of more active and effective diplomatic lobbying by members of the institution). Time alone will tell whether the findings and recommendations of the Kissinger Commission can be related to a future enlarged role for the OAS, or even for major OAS members, in bringing about peace in Central America and, as needed, elsewhere in the hemisphere.

As a prelude to creation of a more stable international order on a global scale, the experience of regional international systems, such as that of the Western Hemisphere, ought be given closer study. Such regional systems can serve as a model for fostering international peace and stability, not only for what they have done but also for what they have been unable to do. In diplomacy we must learn from our failures as well as from our successes. In this measured, modest way, we can perhaps derive some benefit from the hard and brutal lessons of history, rather than merely endure them.

The OAS and the Inter-American System have not produced the same level of international integration as has been achieved, for example, by the European Community. The hemispheric system has contributed to regional and even world order in another manner. From its inception, it has contributed to a reduction, admittedly not a complete elimination, of intervention by states in the affairs of others. Even though it has not led to the functional integration of states on the pattern of Western Europe, it has brought about increases of positive international cooperation as well. Moreover, it has done so on a truly transcontinental scale, encompassing nearly all of the diversified subregions of the Americas and involving almost every dimension of cooperation— political, military, economic, and cultural. One day the cooperative realm of the Western Hemisphere may completely include Canada, itself a mosaic of subregions and cultures.[11]

---

[10]*Report of the National Bipartisan Commission on Central America*, January 10, 1984 (Washington, DC: U.S. Government Printing Office, 1984).

[11]Canada accepted Permanent Observer status at the OAS in 1972 and participates in a number of OAS-affiliated specialized organizations, e.g., the Inter-American Development Bank. On the growing Canadian-Latin American relationship, see D. R. Murray, "The Bilateral Road: Canada and Latin America in the 1980s," *International Journal* 37, no. 1 (Winter 1981–82): 108–31; and "Canada Looks South," *Canada Today/D'Aujourd'hui* 14, no. 6 (1983).

In the Western Hemisphere, we know that international peace cannot be defined simply as a negative thing or merely, as it was for so long, the tranquility of order. We in the Americas have, in a real sense, expanded upon the concept of Saint Augustine to incorporate the modern ideal of development into the traditional definition of peace, thereby expanding the nature and meaning of the term for statesmen the world over to use. Experience has taught us that the true name for peace today is, in fact, development: integral human development in every society and nation. Anything less than pursuit of this complete objective will contribute to peace only in limited ways.

This transformed conception of peace should become more widely recognized as the foundation principle upon which the peoples of the Americas, in particular, can revitalize their traditional regional relationship. Only as we rely on this modernized concept of international order can we build upon our previous achievements—relative peace and geographical inclusiveness—and strive toward a community of nations that can be a shining hope for all mankind: a regional international commonwealth committed to protecting freedom and human rights and ensuring social justice for each and every human being in the Americas.

FOR FURTHER READING

Basic works on the Organization of American States, referred to in the footnotes, are M. Margaret Ball, *The OAS in Transition*, and Ann Van Wynen Thomas and A. J. Thomas, Jr., *The Organization of American States*. Other useful studies are Gordon Connell-Smith, *The Inter-American System* (London: Oxford University Press, 1966); Jerome Slater, *The OAS and United States Foreign Policy* (Columbus: Ohio State University Press, 1967); G. Pope Atkins, *Latin America in the International Political System* (New York: Free Press, 1977); and Tom J. Farer, ed., *The Future of the Inter-American System* (New York: Praeger, 1979). See also Alejandro Orfila, *The Americas in the 1980s: An Agenda for the Decade Ahead* (Lanham, MD: University Press of America, 1980). For a more formal record, with texts, consult Inter-American Institute of International Legal Studies, *The Inter-American System: Its Development and Strengthening*, cited in the footnotes, and *Inter-American Treaty of Reciprocal Assistance*, a series of volumes describing applications of the Rio Pact published by the General Secretariat, Organization of American States.

On the Alliance for Progress, see Harvey S. Perloff, *Alliance for Progress: A Social Invention in the Making* (Baltimore: Johns Hopkins Press, 1969) and Jerome Levinson and Juan de Onís, *The Alliance That Lost Its Way: A Critical Report on the Alliance for Progress*, cited in the footnotes. On the problems of Central America and OAS and Contadora peacemaking activities there, see Mary Jeanne Reid Martz, *The Central American Soccer War: Historical Patterns and Internal Dynamics of OAS Settlement Procedures* (Athens, OH: Center for International Studies, Ohio University, 1978); Robert S. Leiken, ed., *Central America: Anatomy of Conflict* (New York: Pergamon Press, 1984); Tom J. Farer, "Contadora: The Hidden Agenda," *Foreign Policy*, no. 59 (Summer 1985): 59–72; and Bruce Michael Bagley et al., eds., *Contadora and the Central American Peace Process: Selected Documents* (Boulder, CO: Westview Press, 1985).

The International Role of the
Association of Southeast Asian Nations

LEONARD UNGER

In the 1950s and 1960s, five nations lying at the southeastern extremity of the Asian landmass gradually worked out a pattern of special association to bring themselves together into an increasingly close relationship. This collaboration took concrete form on August 8, 1967, in a ceremony at the Saranrom Palace, the home of the Thai Ministry of Foreign Affairs in Bangkok, as the Association of Southeast Asian Nations (ASEAN). The new association was not, and is not, a military alliance. It is not yet a common market. It is not—nor will it probably ever be—a political federation, a United States of Southeast Asia.

Nonetheless, ASEAN is actually and potentially a significant means of promoting world order through international consultation and negotiation. As an organization bringing together originally five, now six, countries, it enables this extensive regional grouping of states (Thailand, Malaysia, Singapore, Indonesia, the Philippines, and, since January 1984, the newly independent country of Brunei) to achieve what could not be accomplished by the five or six nations acting separately. "It is because ASEAN speaks in unison that the world listens to ASEAN," the deputy director-general in Thailand, Tej Bunnag, has said.[1]

In its first years, ASEAN's formal expression was limited to the annual meetings, and sometimes special additional meetings, of the five ASEAN foreign ministers. Since then it has acquired a limited amount of central machinery, but ASEAN's organizers have long been persuaded that it would be a serious mistake to build up yet another large international bureaucracy.

---

[1]Tej Bunnag, remarks at conference, "Thailand: National Development and International Role," The Fletcher School of Law and Diplomacy, October 1–2, 1982.

In recent years, it has been considered desirable to establish a central sec-retariat for ASEAN. This is housed in an elegant building on the outskirts of Jakarta, where the ASEAN secretary-general, now Phan Wannamethee from Thailand, has his permanent office and where there is space for a considerable expansion of the association's activity. In the capitals of each member state there is a national secretariat, headed by a director-general, for coordination of ASEAN relations within that country. However, the emphasis on "small is beautiful" persists, and there is still a determination to avoid a large per-manent establishment.

The ultimate goal of ASEAN, in the view of the five original govern-ments, was, as later expressed in the 1971 Kuala Lumpur Declaration, to create a regional "zone of peace, freedom, and neutrality" (ZOPFAN).[2] While Thailand, alone in the region, had never come under foreign domination, the other ASEAN nations had all been under colonial rule, European or American. The *freedom* of ZOPFAN reflects the determination of the ASEAN countries to preserve their hard-won independence, which came during the years after World War II. There is a further commitment to settle their own problems without resort to arms and involvement in superpower contests that would jeopardize the *peace* of the region. Finally, a policy of *neutrality*, while defying precise definition in this context, reflects a desire on the ASEAN members' part to keep their distance from the East-West struggle. Two of the ASEAN nations, Thailand and the Philippines, are in fact bound to the United States and other powers through a mutual security treaty, the Manila Pact (1954). Malaysia and Singapore also have security ties, albeit looser ones, with Australia, New Zealand, and the United Kingdom. At the same time, however, most ASEAN countries are associated, in greater or lesser degree, with the Third World, the Nonaligned Movement, the Group of 77, the South, and other such formal and informal groupings of the developing countries. Some ASEAN members belong to the Islamic League. Today, nonetheless, the commitment to cooperation in ASEAN transcends any of these other associations. This is, I believe, a remarkable fact.

My own first experience with ASEAN may serve to illustrate the emer-gence of this novel form of regional self-reliance and diplomatic cooperation. In this series of lectures at the Fletcher School of Law and Diplomacy, many of the speakers have been "leading figures who have worked as 'negotiators of world order' in various major fields of international activity."[3] I should emphasize that my role at the time of the birth of ASEAN was rather con-sciously and carefully to play no role at all! I had just returned to Bangkok after having been assigned there earlier as deputy to the U.S. ambassador,

---

[2] For the text signed in Kuala Lumpur on November 27, 1971, see Alison Broinowski, ed., *Understanding ASEAN* (New York: St. Martin's Press, 1982), app. E.

[3] The phrase is from the initial project description, "Negotiating World Order: A Project in Celebration of the Fiftieth Anniversary, 1983–1984, of the Fletcher School of Law and Diplomacy."

from 1958 to 1962. Immediately upon my return in September 1967, as ambassador, I was in touch with the Thai foreign minister, Dr. Thanat Khoman. This was virtually at the moment of birth of ASEAN, and the diplomatic corps in Bangkok was invited to attend one of the ceremonies. It was subtly suggested to me, and I understood and honored the suggestion, that, as the representative of the U.S. government, I not seek to play any special role. In other words, "please come as one of the diplomatic corps, have a benign and approving look," but do nothing more. At that moment in history, if one thinks back to 1967, the United States was very deeply involved in Thailand. It had major programs in the economic sphere and also had close to 40,000 military people in that country, related primarily to the still growing U.S. role in Vietnam. Inevitably, any American ambassador played an active part in the situation in Thailand. Nevertheless, I took the suggestion, accepting that I should not be any more involved in the birth of ASEAN than any of my diplomatic colleagues, whether from Saudi Arabia or Switzerland. (Washington did not always see it this way, incidentally, and had its impatient moments with "the Asian way," which I thought should be respected.)

This initial acquaintance with ASEAN was not a case of negotiating world order. Even for the direct participants it was not, if the phrase is taken in the sense of a finite, rule-making negotiation or the establishment of a regime. Rather, the story of ASEAN is an account of the creation and evolution of a new organism, which has subsequently "grown." Through the processes of diplomatic consultation and negotiation, a habit of acting together has been formed. This has introduced some order into the otherwise loose and sometimes chaotic theater of international relations of Southeast Asia. In this way, through relations with other organizations and through emulation, ASEAN can perhaps make a significant contribution to international order on an even wider scale.

The history of ASEAN really opens with the end of World War II and a Southeast Asia, with the exception of Thailand, that had for the past century and a half been under Western colonial domination. Owing to this colonial condition, most of the ties that might have bound the countries of this region to each other had for a long time been weakened. These affinities were primarily cultural, historical, and religious. There had been only very limited economic links. Whether it was the Dutch East Indies, the Federated Malay States, the Philippine Commonwealth, or French Indochina, external connections were usually with the metropole rather than with each other. For example, in Bangkok, if one wanted to send a cable to Rangoon or Saigon, one had to route the message via London or Paris, halfway around the world, despite the fact that Burma and Indochina were next-door neighbors to Thailand. Only slowly, as these countries became independent following 1945, did they discover the sense of identity and kinship that had been so long repressed in the region. They began an intercourse among themselves that grew rapidly. It is worth mentioning that this intraregional interchange has been greatly facilitated by the development of modern communications, including the use of satellites. Since the completion of Satellite Earth Station projects in Indonesia in 1969 and Malaysia in 1970, every original ASEAN member nation has had its own satellite ground receivers and senders.

The explicit emphasis of the founding fathers of ASEAN was on economic, social, and cultural issues. Their commitment was to enhance mutual cooperation in Southeast Asia in those realms. This choice has been characterized as nothing less than a stroke of genius, for they "knew that it was economic, social, and cultural cooperation which would keep ASEAN together and launch it into the future."[4] In their pragmatic way, the founders said nothing of security and defense questions, which they feared would be divisive. Instead, through the work of eleven permanent committees encompassing the social and economic goals of the new association, the members focused, in the words of a later Malaysian foreign minister, on "getting to know each other's systems, their strengths and weaknesses and their procedures."[5]

At the same time, however, the five ASEAN partners, all of which were basically free-enterprise oriented and non-Communist in outlook, kept a wary eye on the aggressive expansion of the Soviet Union and the People's Republic of China (PRC). Their worry was not only Vietnam but also Communist insurgencies in some of their own countries. Communist subversion was a long-standing regional concern, going back to the late 1940s. The Western policy of containment, articulated by George F. Kennan in *Foreign Affairs* in July 1947, also had its lesser known expression in Southeast Asia.[6]

This threat of Communist expansion and infiltration became more serious as the colonial powers were obliged to give up their colonies and exit the area, leaving what could have been a dangerous vacuum. Following the collapse of the French regime in Indochina in 1954, the Southeast Asia Treaty Organization (SEATO) was formed, with headquarters in Manila. This new arrangement provided great-power assurances to two members in the immediate region, Thailand and the Philippines, and also to Pakistan in South Asia. Cambodia, Laos, and "the free territory under the jurisdiction of the State of Vietnam" (i.e., South Vietnam) also were protected by means of a special protocol.[7] This was one of the first mutual associations of some future members of ASEAN, although very different from the organization that was to follow.

---

[4]Bunnag remarks, "Thailand" conference.

[5]Tan Sri M. Ghazali Shafie, "ASEAN: Contributor to Stability and Development," *The Fletcher Forum: A Journal of Studies in International Affairs* 6, no. 2 (Summer 1982): 356–73, quotation on p. 363.

[6]"X" [George F. Kennan], "The Sources of Soviet Conduct," *Foreign Affairs* 25, no. 4 (July 1947): 566–82; also printed in George F. Kennan, *American Diplomacy, 1900–1950* (Chicago: University of Chicago Press, 1951), pp. 107–28; Robert M. Blum, *Drawing the Line: The Origin of the American Containment Policy in East Asia* (New York: W. W. Norton, 1982); and Michael Schaller, "Securing the Great Crescent: Occupied Japan and the Origins of Containment in Southeast Asia," *Journal of American History* 69, no. 2 (September 1982): 392–414.

[7]For the text of the Southeast Asia Collective Defense Treaty and its protocol, see George McTurnan Kahin and John W. Lewis, *The United States in Vietnam* (New York: Delta, 1967), app. 3.

The largest country in the region, Indonesia, under the leadership of its flamboyant President Sukarno, pursued a very different course from those followed by most of the other countries of Southeast Asia. Rather than linking himself with the United States or any European power and seeking protection from an alliance, Sukarno became one of the leaders of the Asian-African Nonaligned Movement. Sukarno's companions in this initiative were Jawaharlal Nehru of India, Zhou Enlai of China, and Gamal Abdel Nasser of Egypt, with moral support from Josip Broz-Tito of Yugoslavia. A conference in Bandung, Indonesia, in April 1955 brought the Nonaligned Movement together for the first time.[8] Thus Southeast Asia was divided by a sharp difference in orientation between the "committed" nations of the area, on the one hand, and "nonaligned" Indonesia, on the other hand. This situation made for strained relationships, recriminations, and, in some cases, even border conflicts and guerrilla warfare. Much of this tension was the result of the effort by Indonesia, with some help at various times from the Philippines, to try through a policy of "confrontation" (*Konfrontasi*) to frustrate the formation of the new Malaysia, and especially to deny it possession of territory on the island of Borneo (Kalimantan).

Even in this period, there were some seeds of regional cooperation and association that had been planted and had started to grow in Southeast Asia. Some of these were in part inspired and nurtured by outside help. There was SEATO which, though a military alliance initiated largely by the United States, also sponsored economic and social regional development programs. These efforts brought together mainly Thailand and the Philippines and, by looser association, the non-Communist governments of Indochina. The new Commonwealth countries in the region, Malaysia (1963) and Singapore (1965), were linked to each other partly through association with the more distant Commonwealth members, Australia and New Zealand.

Modest measures were made in this period to try to bring together ministers of education, finance, and so on from as many of the countries of the region as were interested, with the thought in mind that they had many common problems; they could benefit from "comparing notes" and from developing cooperative programs. This collaborative work extended to developing and refining techniques for teaching English (Southeast Asia's lingua franca) as a foreign language. The United States provided leadership in organizing these programs. Its reasoning was that, if feelings of regional identity and solidarity could be heightened in Southeast Asia, there would be less susceptibility to penetration and subversion from Communist sources. Moreover, if neighboring countries would work together, they might make the

---

[8]For background on Indonesia's policy, see Ide Anak Agung Gde Agung, *Twenty Years: Indonesian Foreign Policy, 1945–1965* (The Hague: Mouton, 1973); Donald E. Weatherbee, *Ideology in Indonesia: Sukarno's Indonesian Revolution*, Monograph Series No. 8, Southeast Asia Studies, Yale University (1966); and Rex Mortimer, *Indonesian Communism under Sukarno: Ideology and Politics, 1959–1965* (Ithaca: Cornell University Press, 1974). The thirtieth anniversary of the Bandung meeting was held at its original site in April 1985. See Barbara Crossette, "Nonaligned Nations to Mark Founding Conference of 1955," *New York Times*, April 2, 1985.

need for outside assistance somewhat less. Simultaneously, there were non-aligned efforts, some of which had Southeast Asian regional aspects, in which Indonesia played an important part.

Finally, and most pertinent to the present discussion, there were preliminary efforts—mostly abortive—by some of the Southeast Asian countries to develop international associations entirely on their own initiative. One of these was the Association of Southeast Asia (ASA), an entity formed in Bangkok in 1961 by Thailand, Malaya, and the Philippines. The Thai foreign minister of that time, Thanat Khoman, found that other countries in the region to which he paid visits to discuss the project were "caught by the nonaligned fever" and were apprehensive lest membership in ASA make them appear to have joined a pro-Western front. "Born under an unlucky star," as it seemed to him, ASA was plagued by territorial as well as ideological disputes, such as that between the Philippines (joined later by Indonesia) and Malaya over North Borneo, or Sabah, which was incorporated into the Federation of Malaysia in 1963.[9] Another self-initiated regional organization was called Maphilindo, which amalgamated Malaya, the Philippines, and Indonesia. This emerged in 1963 from a proposal by Philippine President Diosdado Macapagal for a Greater Malay Federation. The racial connotations of the Maphilindo concept did not commend it to the other nations in Southeast Asia, however, and it lapsed. I stress these two regionalist experiments because, although short lived, they reflect an impulse on the part of these countries themselves to develop a pattern of association. They did not wish to find themselves in a situation like the predicament of the Balkan countries in which hostilities might develop that would be very hard to suppress or, once broken out, to forget. Southeast Asians hoped that, having been isolated from each other during generations of colonial rule and having in part for that reason developed mutual suspicions, they could now find ways of working together more effectively.

These initial attempts at association did not get very far. A large part of the reason is that the Southeast Asian country with the greatest weight, Indonesia, had been following a nonaligned course and had developed affiliations that lay principally outside the region. However, in 1965, the left-leaning Sukarno was replaced as president by General Suharto, ably assisted in foreign relations by Dr. Adam Malik. Indonesia then embarked upon a different course. The new policy was particularly different with regard to Indonesia's Southeast Asian neighbors. Thus 1965 is a year of significant positive transition for the entire region. Southeast Asian intraregional relationships then began to move toward the cooperative mode that has so strongly characterized them in the years that followed. The events in Indonesia, combined with the increased presence of the United States in Vietnam, are generally considered the catalyst of the historical process that produced ASEAN.

---

[9]Thanat Khoman, address, October 1, 1982, "Thailand's Role in Forging Regional Cooperation," *Thailand: National Development and International Role*, Conference Report (Medford, MA: The Fletcher School of Law and Diplomacy, 1983), app. B.

The idea of nonalignment that was abroad in Southeast Asia, and still has its impact today in many realms, was certainly not thrown overboard, however. Indonesia and Malaysia still label themselves nonaligned.[10] Nonetheless, there was growing strength in the idea among the Southeast Asian nations that they had more in common with each other than with anyone else, whether superpower or nonaligned country, and that they could benefit from closer cooperation among themselves. Their thinking suggested an association that would bring into being some kind of regional political order, provide for fruitful collaboration in pertinent fields, and bring to an end the antagonisms that until then had characterized some of their relationships. A positive rather than a negative concept of regional identity began to predominate.

When the future ASEAN members first began to talk seriously about this idea of cooperative association, there was a prevailing pessimism about the prospects. Some governments feared their action might be misunderstood; particularly they thought it would be unwise for them to seem to be setting up a new bloc. It was partly for that reason that they talked little about security matters or political issues, believing such matters should be frankly approached only after it had been demonstrated, in less sensitive and controversial fields, that the five nations could work together successfully. Moreover, they did not want to give any superpower an excuse for exerting pressure or for intervening. Thus they gave their attention, initially, to cultural and economic cooperation.

They were five rather remarkable figures, the five foreign ministers, who set up ASEAN in 1967. The founding fathers, besides the indispensable Thanat Khoman and Malik, were, for the Philippines, Fidel Ramos and later Carlos Romulo; for Singapore, S. Rajaratnam; and for Malaysia, Tun Razak, who was strongly supported by the prime minister at that time, Tungku Abdul Rahman. It was these men, acting somewhat autonomously, who were principally responsible for the formation of ASEAN and for giving the group its first look as primarily a cultural and economic organization. They agreed on the need to develop, through association, a way to make common cause regarding issues that were of importance to them. However, at the same time, they were emphatic that there should be no implication of an alliance.

In the Negotiating World Order Project there is a tendency to make a distinction, and also a separation, between the architects and the practitioners. The men I have mentioned were certainly practitioners, all of them with much experience. Acting in their capacities as skilled ministers and diplomats, however, they also became architects of a new international structure, ASEAN. There are certainly times when traditional diplomacy, usually conducted on the bilateral level, has a major role to play. At other times, the building of something new is required, something supranational. It is the practitioners in office who can, and must, do it. ASEAN is a case in point.

---

[10]Mochtar Kusumaatmadja, minister of foreign affairs, address, October 6, 1983, *Indonesia*, Final Report (Medford, MA: The Fletcher School of Law and Diplomacy, 1984), p. 11; Tan Sri M. Ghazali Shafie, address, November 19, 1984, *A Conference on Malaysia*, Final Report (Medford, MA: The Fletcher School of Law and Diplomacy, 1985), p. 16

The situation in Southeast Asia in the fall of 1967 did not seem conducive to achieving such regional unity. Besides the war in Vietnam, which was growing graver, there was an upheaval going on in China. The PRC, beginning its Cultural Revolution, adopted a generally aggressive posture with regard to the new ASEAN partners. It sponsored subversive activities that were particularly disturbing in Thailand, Malaysia, and Indonesia. The so-called Emergency in Malaysia was related to the presence of a small but tightly organized Chinese rebel group which received assistance from the PRC. In Thailand there was an insurgency, particularly serious in the northeast and north, that received support from the PRC and North Vietnam. Indonesia had passed through an acute crisis brought about by a leftist bid for power, considered by many to have received Chinese help.

In these circumstances, stresses and strains among the five ASEAN countries themselves could ill be afforded. This was recognized by the foreign ministers and other leaders I have mentioned. They knew that, if their countries were going to survive, the last thing that could be countenanced was further division and dissension within the region. Their objective, therefore, was to create an area of stability that would free their countries from any of the recurring internal crises that would give outside powers control over them. This would enable them to devote their energies to nation building.

ASEAN, as it was announced in Bangkok, would aim at economic and cultural cooperation. This was a wise tactic, for the political realm was too dangerous a sphere until mutual trust and a habit of cooperation had been developed. The Bangkok Declaration of August 8, 1967, therefore included references to mutual assistance in the form of training and research facilities in the educational, professional, technical, and administrative fields. It also mentioned collaboration among the members in agriculture and industry, expansion of trade in commodities, improvement of transportation and communication, and, generally, a raising of living standards. In addition, it encouraged the promotion of Southeast Asian studies. This was the practical vision of the people who were putting ASEAN together at that time. Better to start with modest steps, they believed, and go from there.

The Bangkok Declaration, however, also pledged its signatories in more general and abstract terms to "maintain close and beneficial cooperation with existing international and regional organizations with similar aims and purposes, and explore all avenues for even closer cooperation among themselves."[11] This foreshadowed political collaboration and an active diplomacy. It became clear very early that one of the important advantages of ASEAN was the leverage that it gave this new collective entity in dealing with the superpowers, with Japan, with China, and with the European Community. When all five ASEAN states adopted a unified position and presented a united front, they had to be taken seriously.

---

[11]The text of the Bangkok Declaration may be found in *10 Years ASEAN* (Jakarta: Association of Southeast Asian Nations, 1978), pp. 14–16; also in Broinowski, *Understanding ASEAN*, app. A.

The value of ASEAN cohesion became clear when, in April 1975, South Vietnam collapsed and North Vietnam established its rule throughout the entire country, and subsequently Kampuchea and Laos. These events gave urgent point to ASEAN and its role, and ASEAN's top-level deliberations henceforth became more formal and substantive. In February 1976 in Bali, Indonesia, the heads of government of the ASEAN countries met for the first time. At the Bali summit, three important documents were signed: the Declaration of ASEAN Concord, the Treaty of Amity and Cooperation in Southeast Asia, and the Agreement on the Establishment of the ASEAN Secretariat, whose chairman would be appointed by the ASEAN foreign ministers on a rotational basis.[12]

A further practice developed out of the ASEAN foreign ministers' meeting. When their own annual deliberations were over, they met with the foreign secretaries of Japan, the United States, Canada, Australia, and New Zealand, and also with representatives of the European Economic Community (EEC). These postministerial dialogues provide a valuable means by which the ASEAN countries and leading nations of other regions can inform one another, reach agreed assessments, and adopt coordinated approaches to common problems.

An illustration of the ASEAN countries' diplomatic methods is provided by their handling of the issue of Kampuchea. This is a matter of acute concern, especially to Thailand. ASEAN deliberately has eschewed any military confrontation with Vietnam, even though this possibility has been real several times when Vietnam's forces have approached, or even breached, the Thai frontier. Instead, ASEAN consistently and forcefully has put its case before the United Nations. This seizure of the initiative on the international level has prevented Hanoi from securing recognition by the United Nations, and world opinion at large, of its occupation of Kampuchea by force in February 1979. ASEAN's resolution condemning the Vietnamese invasion, though vetoed by the Soviet Union in the Security Council, has won increasingly large majorities in the General Assembly. Through lobbying at the United Nations and by exploiting the affiliations that some of its members have with the Nonaligned Movement, ASEAN has resisted Soviet bloc efforts to oust the representatives of Democratic Kampuchea (the coalition of Prince Norodom Sihanouk, Son Sann, and Pol Pot) from the United Nations and to replace them with representatives of the Victnam-backed regime of Heng Samrin. ASEAN diplomatic collaboration, formally authorized by Article 9 of the 1976 Treaty of Amity and Cooperation, has been remarkably effective in maintaining at least the status quo regarding Kampuchea. Its objective is a compromise negotiated settlement.[13]

As a reflection of its wisdom in general and a cold assessment of the military balance, ASEAN has kept open the door for a direct dialogue with

---

[12]For the texts see *10 Years ASEAN*, pp. 111–16, 118–23, 125–32. The texts of the ASEAN Concord and Treaty of Amity and Cooperation are in Broinowski, *Understanding ASEAN*, app. B and C.

[13]Kishore Mahbubani, "The Kampuchean Problem: A Southeast Asian Perception," *Foreign Affairs* 62, no. 2 (Winter 1983/84): 407–25.

Vietnam. Earlier, before Hanoi's move into Kampuchea, it had even offered Vietnam accession to the Treaty of Amity and Cooperation, Article 18 of which includes the pointed statement: "It shall be open for accession by other States in Southeast Asia." Hope remains that a solid ASEAN position, backed by a UN majority, eventually will persuade Hanoi to accept a Kampuchean solution that accords that tragic country real independence. In a word, the ASEAN objective has been to internationalize the Kampuchean issue, and thereby to contain Vietnam's belligerence and bring security to the entire region.

What does ASEAN represent beyond this diplomatic front? As a geopolitical entity it has enormous potential. In total area, it is about the same size as the United States east of the Mississippi, plus Texas and Oklahoma. Its members range in size from the city-state of Singapore, through little Brunei, all the way to Indonesia, an archipelago of some 735,000 square miles with a population of nearly 170,000,000. The total population of the ASEAN nations is now the fourth largest such region-based grouping in the world today, with close to 275,000,000. It seems quite clear that by the end of the century only China and India will be more populous. In terms of resources and production, Southeast Asia is a major source of the world's tin, rubber, rice, tropical hardwoods, and vegetable oils. It also is a producer of petroleum, sugar, coffee, and tapioca. For some time, it has manufactured textiles as well as some relatively simple machinery and basic electronic products. More sophisticated enterprises, however, are already well established in Singapore and are beginning to appear in most other countries in the region. The prospect is good for the growth of labor-intensive industries, no longer so profitable as they once were in Japan, Korea, and Taiwan. In addition, there is now the basis in the ASEAN area for a petrochemical industry, with all of the downstream products that could bring.

Especially since the February 1976 Bali summit, followed in March of that year by a meeting in Kuala Lumpur of the ASEAN economic ministers, collaboration among the members in the industrial field has intensified. It must be admitted, however, that the economic dreams of ASEAN's founders have not been achieved. Among the reasons for this are the chronically depressed levels of world prices for many commodities and also the tendency toward protectionism on the part of many of the industrialized countries, on which ASEAN heavily depends for markets. A fundamental fact, difficult to overcome, is that the ASEAN economies are more competitive with each other than they are complementary. Despite the establishment of a preferential trading arrangement among them in 1977, intra-ASEAN trade accounts for less than 15 percent of the group's total trade.[14]

The Southeast Asian region, nevertheless, does have basic advantages. A factor of major importance, never to be ignored, is the geographical position

---

[14]"ASEAN," *Far Eastern Economic Review Asia 1984 Yearbook* (November 30, 1983): 103–06, 108.

of the ASEAN countries lying astride the routes between the western Pacific, encompassing Japan, Korea, Taiwan, and China on the one side, and the nations bordering the Indian Ocean, Persian Gulf, Red Sea, and Mediterranean on the other. Theirs is a strategic location, controlling, and presumably capable of blocking, the vital economic and military routes through that geographically irregular area. Through the Strait of Malacca and other straits pass enormous quantities of Middle Eastern oil, to Japan and elsewhere. The region is also strategically important to the two naval superpowers, the United States and the Soviet Union. It provides them with the optimum route to be taken for moving their fleets back and forth between the Indian Ocean and the western Pacific. These circumstances give the ASEAN countries leverage, diplomatic and legal if not military. It also, however, exposes them to the risk of intervention.

It was partly for this reason that, several years after ASEAN was created, it declared itself to be a zone of peace, freedom, and neutrality. The initiative for this declaration of ZOPFAN, issued in 1971, came mainly from Malaysia. Although Malaysia itself, along with Singapore, has a security arrangement with Australia, New Zealand, and Great Britain, and although Thailand and the Philippines as signatories of the Manila Pact have security relations with the United States, the idea of ZOPFAN has great appeal in the region. I have become persuaded that ZOPFAN is essential to the ASEAN philosophy, however hard it is to define in specific terms. It rests on the basic principle that these six countries are going to go their own way and seek their own pattern of political and economic development. They mean not to be caught up in the East-West struggle and thus speak of their "equidistance" from the superpowers, even though they have an orientation that is basically friendly to the United States, Japan, Australasia, and the Western European countries. However willing they may be to trade and conduct other relations with the Communist powers, they remain generally apprehensive of their intentions. This apprehension, incidentally, has grown more acute with the increasing military presence of the Soviets on the shores of the South China Sea, at Da Nang, at Cam Ranh Bay, and possibly even Kompong Som (Sihanoukville). Nonetheless, the ASEAN countries adhere to the objective of ZOPFAN, of neutrality.

In order to pursue this elusive concept a little further, I have talked about ZOPFAN with Southeast Asian friends and with Americans familiar with the region. There is general agreement that the concept is deeply rooted. It has primarily Malay origins, but also Buddhist sources. While a non-Asian might be tempted cynically to dismiss the concept as "eating your cake and having it too," Southeast Asians themselves consider it to have a more consistent and positive meaning. From one careful Malaysian scholar, I heard it spoken of as "national resilience, a not-enforced neutrality." His emphasis was on maintaining independence, keeping a middle way. According to other Malaysians, however, ZOPFAN might involve a guarantee of neutrality in which the great powers could play a role. By contrast, Indonesians, partly because of their nonalignment tradition and also the larger size of their country, resist any idea of giving such a role to the powers. They consider ZOPFAN to be related primarily to Southeast Asia's regional solidarity and favor keeping the external powers, particularly the superpowers, out of the region.

The modalities of ASEAN are sometimes as ambiguous as their purposes. As our theme is Negotiating World Order, we should not fail to discuss how ASEAN negotiates. The processes of ASEAN illustrate a method that is something of a departure from earlier patterns of negotiating world order. In the West, where most such patterns have been developed, organizations have generally been structured so as to operate on the basis of majority vote, or sometimes even unanimity. In keeping with these procedures rooted in classical and medieval legal systems and institutional history, he who musters a majority vote, even if only a majority of one, carries the day. His program becomes the program of all, loyally followed even by those who are opposed.

ASEAN, rooted in South and East Asian traditions, seeks to negotiate consensually. Consensus is often discovered by scholars to be the best term to describe the psychological bases of an Asian nation, particularly one with a Buddhist background in which the Middle Way is always the ideal. Specifically, this has been said of Thailand but would have pertinence throughout ASEAN. Thailand's foreign policy thrives on compromise and alliance rather than confrontation. Malay culture has its counterpart process, called *musyawarah*. This is the idea that a leader should not arbitrarily impose his will but rather make gentle suggestions of the path a community should follow; the conclusions he delivers, following discussion, are in the nature of syntheses. It is indicative that at ASEAN meetings *musyawarah* is employed, rather than Western-style debate and majority voting. This is a process, a species of dialogue, that traditionally leads to consensus. Southeast Asians are persuaded that, for themselves at least, their nonabrasive way of functioning yields more benefits in the long run and risks fewer confrontations than would a more mechanical way of proceeding.

The solidarity ASEAN members thereby achieve gives them more weight than they might otherwise have in some of the large international commodity, monetary, and trade meetings in which they participate. They are able not only to take common positions in the Group of 77 and other gatherings of the developing countries but also to negotiate as a single entity with Japan, the United States, and the EEC. This habit-confirming mode of consensus has also increasingly produced benefits for the institution of ASEAN itself. This is evident even in the difficult economic field. While most of ASEAN's collaborative economic projects are but hopes of the six countries and have not become at all concrete, some success has been achieved. Given the predominantly agricultural character of the ASEAN economies, except for that of Singapore, the development of agribusiness in the region has received particular emphasis. The first ASEAN industrial project to come on stream is an Indonesian ammonia-urea plant in northern Sumatra, intended to help make the region more self-sufficient in fertilizer. ASEAN is also pursuing a scheme of industrial complementation, involving complementary trade exchanges of specified processed or manufactured products within an agreed package. The resulting combinations qualify for intra-ASEAN tariff preference. The initial arrangement involves a steel firm in Thailand and an automotive company in the Philippines, which are cooperating to market auto parts. An ASEAN industrial joint-ventures agreement also has been drafted.[15]

There is an even more ambitious ASEAN goal of forming a free-trade area or a common market in the region. Several thousand items have been identified and entered in that program, although few are significant factors in international trade. The obvious model for an ASEAN economic union is the EEC, which, however, was founded at a higher level of economic development and integration. Precisely because the ASEAN nations still have basically competing economies and are still nurturing infant industries, they are going to have an uphill struggle to find items that would be advantageous for them to produce and market collectively. The fact that they are associated and recognized as such, means that they can negotiate from strength with outsiders even on economic matters.

ASEAN today is perceived as being at a crossroads, one theoretical route being political union and the other economic unity. ASEAN'S uncertainty is expressed by a leader of the ASEAN Chambers of Commerce and Industry, Anand Panyarachun, of Thailand: "To be very candid, ASEAN is in a dilemma." One school of thought holds that ASEAN's having progressed as far as it has is already a major achievement and that no radical policies or measures should be instituted that would bring out fundamental differences. This would result in a division of political unity and regional harmony. The other school expresses grave reservations about the overcautious, step-by-step approach adopted by the pragmatists, and it advocates a more forward-looking attitude, with meaningful measures of economic cooperation to turn ASEAN into a credible regional economic organization.[16]

To some extent, this division reflects a difference in perspective between ASEAN's governments, viewed by economic commentators as often too timid and too slow, and that of the region's private business enterprises, seen to be more venturesome. On these issues, Indonesia and Singapore are frequently at opposite ends of the spectrum. The former has a vast domestic market that its government wants to protect, and the latter, with scarcely any hinterland, relies on foreign trade led by the private sector. "Unless such differing priorities, and a general protectionist attitude, can be substantially reconciled in the name of economic cooperation," the *Far Eastern Economic Review* has stressed, "ASEAN will remain primarily a political union, which is not what it was originally intended to be."[17]

---

[15]Ibid.
[16]Quoted in ibid.
[17]Ibid.

In truth, ASEAN has had a dual identity, political and economic, from the start. The picture of a fork in the road, with diverging futures, is therefore an illusion. ASEAN's initial focus in 1967 on the cultural and economic fields, though entirely sincere, was indirectly a manifestation of the political preoccupations of Southeast Asia at the time. When, following the collapse of South Vietnam in 1975, the ASEAN partners were left alone with a single, Moscow-backed Communist regime in Vietnam, their cooperation had to take on a more overtly political form. At the same time, however, it gained a more substantively economic character. Political development and economic development are inseparable in the region.

The external challenge under which ASEAN has lived from the beginning has had a generally stimulating effect. In this respect, the history of the association has not been so different from that of the EEC, with which Southeast Asians are tempted to compare it. "Perhaps the EEC is too advanced to be our model," Singapore's prime minister, Lee Kuan Yew, has observed. "But, in one respect, we have a situation vaguely analogous to theirs. What gave birth to the EEC was the pressure of a competing and different political system, COMECON, the Soviet Union and the countries of Eastern Europe." Since April 1975, the ASEAN countries have had "to face up to competition from the Marxist-socialist systems of Vietnam, Laos and Cambodia."[18] This they have succeeded in doing. The former "dominoes" have, as a group, shown extraordinary strength and resilience.

Does ASEAN's unity actually depend on this competition from a hostile neighboring political and economic system? Is the enduring Indochina conflict the raison d'être of the association? If an international reconciliation were somehow achieved in the region, so, too, would there be a resolution of the conflicting factors that have been essential to ASEAN's being? Or, to the contrary, would a definitive end to the Indochinese struggle liberate new cooperative energies that have hitherto been mostly latent in Southeast Asia?

One cannot be sure, but the record of diplomatic experience during the nearly twenty years since the association's birth suggests that it will still continue to grow. ASEAN as an organization has far transcended, in the scope of its activity and the range of its interests, the circumstances of its origins. Particularly in its international role, as a regional mediator and as an interlocutor between the six member countries and the United States, Japan, the European Community, and global international organizations such as the United Nations, ASEAN has found a distinctive personality. A new identity exists in the region, a collective consciousness that never existed previously, either in the colonial period or in the years of early nationhood. The roots of ASEAN lie very deep in the culture of Southeast Asia. Thus firmly established,

---

[18]Lee Kuan Yew, statement at opening of ASEAN heads of government meeting, February 23, 1976, at Denpasar, Bali, Indonesia, *10 Years ASEAN*, pp. 99–101.

the institution is likely to survive and, as an example of regional order, be a factor for order in the world.

FOR FURTHER READING

On the background of the current international political relations of Southeast Asia, see Evelyn Colbert, *Southeast Asia in International Politics, 1941–1956* (Ithaca, NY: Cornell University Press, 1977); Russell H. Fifield, *The Diplomacy of Southeast Asia, 1945–1958* (New York: Harper and Row, 1958); George McTurnan Kahin, ed., *Governments and Politics of Southeast Asia*, 2nd ed. (Ithaca, NY: Cornell University Press, 1964); George McTurnan Kahin and John W. Lewis, *The United States in Vietnam*, rev. ed. (New York: Delta, 1969); and Estrella D. Solidum, *Towards a Southeast Asian Community* (Quezon City: University of the Philippines Press, 1974).

On the formation and functions of ASEAN, see Alison Broinowski, ed., *Understanding ASEAN*, and Association of Southeast Asian Nations, *10 Years ASEAN*, cited in the footnotes. See also Patricia Lim, *ASEAN Bibliography* (Singapore: Institute of Southeast Asian Studies, 1984), containing an informative introductory essay, "The Constellation of ASEAN Institutions." On ASEAN in its international context, see Russell H. Fifield, *National and Regional Interests in ASEAN: Competition and Co-operation in International Politics*, Occasional Paper No. 57 (Singapore: Institute of Southeast Asian Studies, 1979); Sheldon W. Simon, *The ASEAN States and Regional Security* (Stanford, CA: Hoover Institution Press, 1982); Lawrence B. Krause, *U.S. Economic Policy Toward the Association of Southeast Asian Nations: Meeting the Japanese Challenge* (Washington, DC: Brookings Institution, 1982); Donald K. Crone, *The ASEAN States: Coping with Dependence* (New York: Praeger, 1983); Jun Nishikawa, *ASEAN and the United Nations System* (New York: UN Institute for Training and Research, 1983); Chin Kin Wah, "Regional Attempts at International Order: ASEAN," *Australian Outlook* 38, no. 1 (April 1984): 16–20; and Donald E. Weatherbee, ed., *Southeast Asia Divided: The ASEAN-Indochina Crisis* (Boulder, CO: Westview Press, 1985).

ECONOMIC BASES OF
WORLD ORDER

Creating a Framework to Strengthen and Stabilize International Commodity Markets

GAMANI COREA

The United Nations Conference on Trade and Development (UNCTAD) from its inception has been the forum in which the international consideration of commodity issues has taken place. UNCTAD's role in that area is now, I believe, well established. The commodity agreements that are negotiated in UNCTAD are legal instruments. Similar contributions in other fields have been more of an ad hoc nature, but in respect to commodities our responsibility is continuous.

The international consideration of commodity issues has origins that extend well beyond the creation of UNCTAD in 1964. Even before the Second World War, there were restriction schemes for some products. I know tea and rubber well because they involve my own country of Sri Lanka. After the war, commodities loomed large in the discussions that resulted in the 1947 Havana Charter, even though that ambitious agreement to create an international trade organization, owing to protectionist pressures and nationalism, never came to be implemented in all its dimensions.

Beyond this institutional history, there was a basis for commodity intervention in economic thought. Classical economic theory had given some blessing to the concept of governmental action to regulate commodity markets. The idea of intervention did not come from the socialist attack on market forces, but rather from those who recognized the lack of symmetry in the way the market operated in the field of agriculture, in contrast to the area of manufactures. Because of the peculiar nature of the responses of supply to price in the field of primary products, the market was not seen to be self-correcting. It called, therefore, for a certain degree of regulation not to replace it, but to improve upon it.

167

The actual actions that have been taken originated in the political processes of individual countries and, in particular, in the pressures brought by producers of agricultural products on their governments. This was especially evident in the case of domestic price-support schemes. Even in the international arena, when commodity agreements were first established, there was a direct link between producers and governments; the governments were those of the consuming countries. In colonial periods, commodity production was organized with the capital and the enterprise provided by the metropolitan countries, and the production located in the colonies. Nonetheless, producers of primary products exercised political influence over important governments, an example being the control scheme established in 1922 by the British government to cover both Malayan and Ceylonese exports of natural rubber.[1]

After World War II, there was a dichotomy between producers and consumers because a large number of the primary producing territories attained their independence. The political influences that favored commodity agreements therefore took on a different character. Commodities became more a part of the North-South dialogue than an aspect of the identity of interests among the colonial powers vis-à-vis former colonies.

This change of relationship is one reason why a certain loss of momentum occurred in the consideration of commodity issues in the early postwar era. In the immediate post-Havana Charter period, there was but little to show in the way of progress in the area of the regulation and stabilization of commodity markets.[2] The record then was not totally blank, however; there were commodity agreements for coffee, sugar, tin, and subsequently for cocoa. Even these agreements, when successful, had at least some of their genesis in a sense of political identification on the part of the important consuming countries with the producing territories. The coffee agreement had a great deal to do with the perception, particularly on the part of the United States, of the importance of stability in Brazil within the Western Hemisphere. The cocoa agreement, too, had something to do with Britain's interest in stability in Ghana and Nigeria and other cocoa-producing territories in Africa.

Several early UNCTAD conferences did focus to some degree on commodities, but the results were not substantial. At UNCTAD III in Santiago, Chile, in 1972, for example, there was a resolution calling for intensive consultations on as many as fourteen products of interest to developing countries. These consultations took place, but they achieved practically nothing. This was the background to the historic UNCTAD IV meeting in Nairobi in 1976.

Before this, some frustration had been experienced in the effort to set up commodity agreements, despite a widespread recognition of their importance

---

[1]For more on such control schemes and the structure of commodity markets generally, see J. W. F. Rowe, *Primary Commodities in International Trade* (Cambridge: Cambridge University Press, 1965).

[2]An excellent source of information on these matters is Fiona Gordon-Ashworth, *International Commodity Control: A Contemporary History and Appraisal* (London: Croom Helm, 1984). See also Rowe, *Primary Commodities*.

as instruments for international economic cooperation. In Nairobi there was a new constellation of forces. One will recall that UNCTAD IV took place in the aftermath of the 1973 oil price increase and the 1974 Special Session of the General Assembly, which adopted the Declaration and Program of Action on the New International Economic Order (NIEO). When the Nairobi Conference convened there was a feeling of a new international alignment, resulting largely from the bold actions of the Organization of Petroleum Exporting Countries (OPEC); it was a feeling that commodities as a whole were assuming a new importance. Developing countries thought that one way of meeting the increased charges on their import bills as a result of the rise in the price of oil was to have recourse, not only to emergency aid and to borrowing, but also to increasing their export earnings through strong and stable commodity markets. They also thought vaguely that the oil-producing countries would help them achieve this objective, and that some further commodities might display some of the elements of oil power, even if not to the same degree.

The developed countries, which are the main consuming countries, also had new perceptions. They were sensitive to the predicament of the nonoil-producing developing countries and to the need to strengthen their situation by means other than aid. They too had an apprehension, however tentative and weak, that other commodities might follow the role of oil and encourage the creation of other producer cartels, if a cooperative response on their part were wholly absent. All these forces and thoughts were never clearly defined or expressed. They were in the background, however, and contributed to the political climate that made it possible for the commodity issue to receive the attention it did at Nairobi.

It was in the context of this new negotiating environment that the UNCTAD secretariat proposed its Integrated Program for Commodities. We sought to introduce some new elements into the discussion in order to help break the impasse of the earlier UNCTAD meetings. These new elements consisted primarily of the concept of looking at commodities as a whole, which is the reason why we use the term "Integrated." In the past, commodity negotiations were approached in a fragmentary and ad hoc fashion, with each commodity problem being considered on its own. There had been no overall framework of principles and policy objectives to knit them together.

We thought also that commodity negotiations had failed in the past because of the inability to use the management of stockpiles as an important instrument of stabilization. The main reason was the paucity of finance. We thought that, if a new instrument were created to remedy this defect, there could be a new stimulus to commodity negotiations. This was the origin of our proposal for a Common Fund.[3] We described it as "the integrating element"

---

[3]The Common Fund will have two main areas of activity: the "first window" of the Fund will raise finance for commodity agreements based on stocking as an instrument of stabilization; the "second window" will raise finance for commodity agreements aimed at improving structural conditions in commodity markets via research and development and other nonstocking measures.

of the Integrated Program because it would support a number of commodities and make possible new agreements as a result of the possibility of financing. We added as well a third dimension to the Integrated Program, the strategy of bringing within its ambit other elements of commodity policy: compensatory financing, to provide loans for shortfalls of export earnings from expected levels; measures for the marketing, distribution, and processing of primary products; and long-term contracts for the supply and sale of commodities. The Integrated Program sought to inject all of these new elements into commodity negotiations by creating a framework within which the discussions could proceed more smoothly.

We succeeded at Nairobi in putting in place this basic framework of principles. As a result, we now have a facility in UNCTAD to treat commodity problems, to initiate studies, to call meetings, and to convene negotiations. Many people are disappointed with the degree of progress achieved in the post-Nairobi phase, however. I share that disappointment. I want to reflect a little on the causes of our dissatisfaction, but before doing so I want also to underline some of the positive results that emerged from the Nairobi Conference.

We now have a framework for dealing with commodity issues, which did not exist before. That framework continues to be available. We have convened a great number of meetings and activities to deal with problems of more than a dozen major commodities, ranging from copper and iron ore to bananas and tea.[4] We have made other fundamental advances. We did succeed, after long and difficult and sometimes dramatic negotiation, in bringing about unanimous agreement on the Common Fund, a major step in the international negotiation process in North-South issues. The Common Fund remains now to be established after the completion of a ratification process.

Since the Integrated Program was launched, we have succeeded in negotiating three new commodity agreements, for natural rubber, jute, and tropical timber. However, only the natural rubber agreement has provisions for price stabilization.[5] For jute and tropical timber, we have set up commodity organizations with research and development programs and the possibility of expanding into agreements with economic provisions. Also, we have succeeded in renegotiating a number of the existing agreements for sugar, cocoa, and tin. The continuation of these agreements has been very useful in maintaining an environment of existing norms for the international community regarding trade in primary commodities.

We also have succeeded in clearing the way for commodity negotiations in many other commodities. We have undertaken numerous activities in respect to bauxite, copper, iron ore, phosphates, cotton, hard fibers, vegetable oils, and tea. Progress has varied in each of these cases. In some of them we are

[4]For a comprehensive review of these meetings, see UNCTAD document TD/B/C.1/223, and references cited therein.

[5]Kabir-Ur-Rahman Khan, "The International Natural Rubber Agreement, 1979," *Resources Policy* 6, no. 3 (1980).

far from even being able to visualize a state of negotiation. This is particularly true in the area of minerals. In others, such as tea, some distance has been covered, and I would not rule out altogether the possibility of future agreements, even though there are problems to be overcome.

Some other aspects of the Integrated Program received attention after Nairobi beyond these discussions of particular commodities. UNCTAD V in Manila in 1979 and UNCTAD VI in Belgrade in 1983 both passed resolutions on marketing, distribution, and processing of commodities: UNCTAD has been called upon to start new activities leading to the negotiation of frameworks of international cooperation in this area. Furthermore, the subject of compensatory financing of export earnings, also an element of the Integrated Program, has received increased attention. It was viewed in light of the experience of the arrangement of the European Economic Community (EEC) for the African, Caribbean, and Pacific (ACP) countries, the STABEX scheme.[6] At the Belgrade meeting, I was asked to convene an expert group on the question of how a commodity-specific system of compensatory financing, as against the more general balance-of-payments compensatory financing system of the International Monetary Fund, could evolve. This group's report and recommendation will be studied by governments with a view toward further progress on this front.

Although there has been some movement, it has not been enough. The Common Fund has yet to come into being, because the ratification process has dragged on. We should have had more commodity agreements. We might have made more progress in the areas of marketing, distribution, and processing, and also in that of compensatory financing. For those who express impatience, I must say that I myself share in that sentiment.

A number of powerful factors lying behind the evolution of the commodity issue in the post-Nairobi period need to be understood in order to project greater success. These factors relate both to environment, or the climate of opinion, and to attitudes, which are more deep-seated and entrenched. The international environment for negotiations in the aftermath of Nairobi was not congenial. After 1976 in particular, the developed countries were preoccupied with the problem of internal inflation. They were engaged in an effort to evolve adequate domestic policy responses to this problem. For that reason, they were somewhat less inclined to give attention to the building of longer term international structures, such as a regime for commodity markets.

---

[6]Compensatory finance involves the lending to a country of all (or a portion) of the shortfalls of its actual export earnings in a given year from the expected, or "normal," level in order thereby to avoid an interruption in the country's development program. The loans are to be repaid later, when export earnings presumably have recovered from their temporarily depressed level. The International Monetary Fund operates such a scheme, based on total merchandise export earnings ("balance-of-payments compensatory financing"). The EEC scheme is based on export earnings of a country from an individual commodity ("commodity-specific compensatory financing"). It applies to the sixty-four ACP countries associated with the EEC in the framework of the Lomé Convention, originally signed in 1974 and twice renegotiated in 1979 and 1984.

In fact, in the context of powerful inflationary forces, commodity negotiations were not seen as helpful. On the contrary, they were seen as constituting a danger, for many of these negotiations were aimed at establishing floors to prices.

A commodity agreement has to start at the lower reaches of the cycle because it is only in that phase, when there are surpluses, that the instruments for defending the limits can be created and made available, whether those instruments be quantitative restraints and their relaxation or the acquisition of stocks and their release. Since one cannot release stocks not yet accumulated, or remove export restraints if they have not previously been imposed, one cannot start a commodity agreement at the top of the price range. One has to build it from the bottom. In an inflationary period, the laying of such a foundation was not a prospect which the major consuming countries found appealing.

The developing countries also found their own responses influenced by the climate of the period. In the late 1970s, there was a boom in commodities, at least in some commodities, that relieved their position. At the same time, the liquidity of the developing countries improved as a result of the new-found access to borrowing in the private capital markets. These countries, therefore, did not feel the acute pressure that would have impelled them to participate in negotiations with any sense of urgency. In addition, some of the élan of OPEC was beginning to fade. The idea of oil power buttressing other commodities was becoming less of a realistic prospect. In fact, during that period the price of oil was beginning to decline in real terms.

Even more important was the question of basic attitudes. The adoption of the Integrated Program for Commodities at Nairobi marked a new departure. How significant was that departure? It created a new framework of principles and objectives to guide future negotiations. It also provided for the mechanisms and logistical support needed for these activities. To what extent, I ask myself, did it represent a genuine change of heart and thinking in the world's approach to commodity problems? Sometimes I believe that the shades of an answer to this question were in the course of the Nairobi negotiations themselves. These negotiations were extremely difficult and tense. At every stage, the developed consumer countries of the Organization for Economic Cooperation and Development (OECD), which negotiated as a group against an equally coherent group of more than a hundred developing countries, were insistent on the merits of the case-by-case approach.[7] They were less than convinced by the logic of the Common Fund. When they finally agreed to

---

[7]From UNCTAD's inception in 1964, member countries aligned themselves into four basic groups for negotiating purposes, with one spokesman per group carrying the main burden of actual negotiations. These groups were: 1) the Western industrial countries of the OECD, known in UNCTAD as "Group B"; 2) the socialist countries of Eastern Europe, known as "Group D"; 3) the developing countries en bloc—the Group of 77, which now numbers over 120 members; and 4) China, which has acted as a group unto itself.

the resolution on it in Nairobi, they agreed to launch future negotiations without, necessarily, a commitment to their outcome. This basic hesitation, this lack of total identification with the objectives of the Integrated Program, was reflected in their behavior throughout the period after Nairobi when we were grappling with the implementation process. The consumer countries came to commodity negotiations not with a political decision behind them to arrive at an agreement to stabilize this or that commodity market, to take the necessary actions; they came more as agnostics.

There were specific technical problems as well that loomed large. These problems regarding particular commodities assumed extraordinary proportions, however, because of the dilution of the political will to overcome them. In the course of our negotiations on commodities, many of the old and familiar demons had free run of the conference room, including the idea of interference with the workings of the free market, the idea of giving encouragement to producer cartels, and the idea of actually raising, rather than stabilizing, prices in the long run. There was also a general antipathy, if not hostility, on the part of the private grain and minerals trade to market intervention. All these considerations conditioned the attitude of the consuming countries, particularly when, in individual negotiations, the wider dimensions of the Integrated Program and basic rationale of international commodity policy receded into the background, and the more narrowly commercial aspects of each commodity issue came to the fore. For these countries, the assurance of continued supplies at the lowest possible price assumed a preponderant importance.

There were problems of attitude on the part of the developing countries as well. Despite the commitment of these countries to commodity stabilization through UNCTAD, my suspicion is that the idea of an international solution to commodity problems did not come naturally to many officials in the capitals of developing countries. They are more familiar with the day-to-day aspects of commodity production and trading—the agronomic and immediate commercial aspects—rather than with their overall economic and international characteristics. A further difficulty is that developing countries tend to be at least as much concerned with volume as they are with price. They do not respond easily to any scheme for commodity stabilization that involves a cutback in volume, with all of the implications of this for production, employment, and government revenues, even though such cutbacks hold the promise of significantly improved long-term export earnings as prices rise in line with reduced supply. Moreover, many of the smaller countries have not felt confident that they could influence a commodity negotiation undertaken internationally. The developing countries have tended to come to commodity negotiations relatively unprepared; they do not have the facilities of the OECD or the EEC to reinforce their preparation; there is no Third World secretariat to provide the appropriate assistance. They came to these commodity negotiations, therefore, in a relatively passive frame of mind, hoping that satisfactory agreements would be provided for them by the consumers or by the secretariat of UNCTAD. They did not see these negotiations as instruments they had to grasp, by their own initiative, their own organization, and the mobilization of their own strength.

There were other complications as well. In commodity negotiations, there is often a situation, particularly in the area of minerals, in which developed countries are present as commodity exporters rather than as importers. These countries usually have their own domestic price-support schemes for commodities produced domestically and also a higher degree of vertical integration between the production of raw materials and the final manufactured output. These nations' interest in commodity price stabilization was powerfully shaped by these features of their own domestic commodity production. As a result, national attitudes often played a perverse part, since the logic of extending to the international level the mechanisms used to protect commodity producers at the national level seemed not to dominate.[8]

The failure to establish fully the Common Fund was an important factor in the slow and unsatisfactory tempo of progress in the period following the Nairobi Conference. The Common Fund was conceived as the instrument to bring about a breakthrough. It was expected to be the catalyst in helping to establish various specific commodity agreements. If one has a process of commodity negotiations without the Common Fund, then one has not introduced anything new into the negotiating process. Those of us who believed that the Common Fund was vital to bringing about a new regime cannot be very surprised that, in the absence of the Common Fund, progress has been slow.

What conclusions can we draw from this experience for the future? I believe that there are now two basic options: one road is that of making a continued and resolute effort to fulfill the objectives of the Integrated Program; the other is to step back from its objectives. Some have suggested, to some extent understandably, that there be a retreat. Such people have questioned the efficacy, if not the desirability, of price stabilization and its proposed alternatives. They have contended that not only has it been difficult to bring new commodity agreements into being, but also even those agreements that already exist have proved to be difficult to maintain effectively. I do not subscribe to this view. I am convinced that these existing agreements, despite their weaknesses, play an important part, and that more can be done.

It must be remembered that the agreements we have now were designed to deal with a cycle of fluctuations specific to each individual commodity, and not to a synchronized global recession, which has been an unprecedented occurrence in the postwar period. None of the existing commodity agreements

---

[8]This may have been due in part to the perception by the industrial country policymakers that "foreigners" do not vote in national elections, but domestic farmers and mining interests do. Therefore it is "necessary" to do at the national level things one would not wish to do, and to accept the proliferation of measures which at the international level one would ideally wish to prevent.

for natural rubber, tin, cocoa, coffee, and sugar, for example, was meant to be able to cope with the problems of a global recession in the commodity markets. Where there are already agreements, the activities of the commodity organizations have played a part in moderating the decline in prices so far in the 1980s. Rubber has been purchased under the terms of the agreement for the rubber stock; tin and cocoa have been purchased also. The only constraint on the scale of this activity in support of prices is the lack of finance. In each of these instances, the commodity organizations exhausted the limits of the finance available to them. Nonetheless, they proved to be a source of some support in a situation that would have otherwise been worse.

It has been suggested that other attacks on the commodity problem should be explored. I have already mentioned compensatory financing. There are people who argue that this solution would be a preferable alternative to price stabilization; they point out that it has the advantage of overcoming the complexities of the negotiation of price stabilization agreements, that it does not involve market interventions, and that it could extend to all countries. I myself think that compensatory financing can be an important instrument of international commodity policy. We included it, therefore, as one of the basic elements of the Integrated Program for Commodities. I do not believe, however, in the juxtaposition of compensatory financing and price stabilization as alternatives. A compensatory-financing scheme should be considered as a supplement to, rather than a substitute for, price stabilization. If one had tried solely to compensate for the total loss of commodity earnings during the depression years of 1981, 1982, and 1983, for instance, the cost would have run into several billions of dollars. We must remember that commodity earnings declined by $50 billion during 1981–1983 for the developing countries as a whole. The effectiveness of compensatory financing, in terms of cost, would be much enhanced if prices themselves fluctuated less. If we had a price stabilization scheme to impart some measure of strength and stability to commodity markets, the feasibility of compensating the shortfalls would be greater to that extent. I welcome compensatory financing as an instrument, but I do not see it as an alternative to the effort to strengthen and stabilize commodity markets themselves. Compensatory financing would not alter the incorrect signals that widely fluctuating markets give to investors and producers.

Lately there also have been those who argue that, in the future, more attention should be given to commodity agreements that concentrate on the "second-window" type of activity of the Common Fund; that is, commodity agreements designed to support research-and-development activities for particular commodities, as in the cases of the recently concluded agreements for jute and tropical timber. This kind of action is helpful, but only as an interim measure. If it proves difficult to enter into full-fledged agreements, replete with all the economic provisions, then I would encourage the creation of the easier type of agreement, which sets up an international commodity organization that then can provide a foundation on which to build in the future. I therefore welcome second-window type agreements, but, again, as supplements rather than as substitutes, and as the first step rather than the last in moving toward international commodity arrangements.

If we insist on continuing with the thrust for commodity agreements, how can we avoid the experience of recent years and achieve a genuine and wider breakthrough? There are several elements of a possible answer. To begin, I insist on the importance of finally bringing the Common Fund into existence. Although the ratification process has been slow, it is encouraging to see that, since the UNCTAD VI meeting in Belgrade in 1983, there has been some momentum toward its ratification. More than eighty governments have now ratified the Common Fund. We need a total of ninety ratifications in order to bring the Common Fund into being, but not merely ninety ratifications alone; they must be by countries that represent two-thirds of the subscribed capital of the fund. I am reasonably hopeful that the requisite number will be reached. There are certain least developed countries whose subscriptions have been financed, or are capable of being financed, by the OPEC Fund; and there are a number of other developing countries for whom Norway has offered financing. These countries are in the process of negotiation and have not yet ratified the Fund. There are still other countries where the negotiation of the ratification instruments is caught up in the legislative process. Taking everything into consideration, I feel reasonably confident that the required number of ratifications eventually will be secured.[9]

What remains is the other objective, the two-thirds subscriptions. The countries that have ratified the Common Fund so far account for only about 50 percent of the subscribed capital. It is thus possible to have ninety ratifications but still fall short of the necessary two-thirds of the subscribed capital. The United States has signed the instrument of the Fund but has not yet completed the ratification process. Most of the other OECD countries, including Canada, Japan, the EEC, and the Nordic countries, have either completed the ratification process or are in the course of doing so. The U.S. ratification would really be decisive and would ensure the two-thirds target.[10] Ratification by the socialist countries of Eastern Europe also could be decisive. These countries have not even signed the agreement on the Common Fund, despite the fact that they participated in the consensus achieved during its negotiation.[11] They have not declared their unwillingness to ratify the Fund, but they have indicated that they are undergoing a process of assessment. If they were to ratify the Common Fund, then, again, the two-thirds target would be reached. In one way or another, the Fund will be established, but it is essential that either the United States or the socialist group of countries—preferably both—ratify the Common Fund as it comes into being.

---

[9] The figure of ninety ratifications was reached on January 14, 1986. —Ed.

[10] The U.S. government announced in 1985 that it would not ratify the Common Fund Agreement. —Ed.

[11] In UNCTAD we strive to achieve positions to which all our members can subscribe, which we call reaching a consensus; only very rarely does an issue require to be taken to a vote.

Whatever happens to the Common Fund, if we are to have a new experience in commodity negotiations there needs to be a change in attitude toward commodity stabilization, because the experience of the past attests to the power of conventional thinking and established interests. For that reason, we must provide, in addition to the old arguments, a new rationale that would make governments, both of the developed and developing countries, more responsive to the commodity issue. There are at least three factors that might help bring about a new consensus.

The first of these points arises from a consideration of the changing dynamics of the commodity situation in the contemporary world. It is a fact that commodity markets have increased in instability in recent years and are likely to continue to be unstable because of supply fluctuations in the context of a sluggish demand. This instability is a matter of vital consequence even to the industrialized countries, because upward movements in commodity prices feed the cost-push inflationary process, while downward movements do not provide comparable and symmetrical relief.[12] For the industrialized countries, this consideration must be an important element of domestic macroeconomic policy. Concern about the inflation-causing effects of commodity price fluctuations was absent from the rationale of international commodity policy at the time of the Havana Charter, but it is of considerable importance and relevance today.

The second element relates to the need for structural change in the world economy in light of apparent long-term trends facing world commodity markets. Even though these markets are showing an increasing susceptibility to upward fluctuations in the short run, the long-term picture does not suggest a very strong and vigorous upward course. The prospect of relatively slow overall growth in the industrialized countries, of the growing substitution of synthetic for natural products, of the increasing economies achieved in the raw material content of new products, and of the shift away from industries that are intensive in raw materials are factors tending to impart a downward pressure on the long-term trend for commodity prices. This might be compensated to some extent by the possible increase in demand for raw materials and primary products on the part of the developing countries themselves, as they bring about the industrial transformation of their economies. Although this should not be underestimated, this basic process will take time. The main conclusion one must draw from the long- or medium-term prospect is that commodity-producing countries will need to enter into a process of diversification and structural adjustment if commodity markets are to remain healthy and vital. International commodity policy and the members of UNCTAD will

---

[12]On this point, see Richard N. Cooper and Robert Z. Lawrence, "The 1972–75 Commodity Boom," *Brookings Papers on Economic Activity*, no. 3 (1975): 671–723; Nicholas Kaldor, "Inflation and Recession in the World Economy," *Economic Journal* 86, no. 344 (December 1976): 703–14; and S. M. R. Kanbur and D. Vines, "North-South Interaction and Commodity Control," Discussion Paper No. 8 (London: Centre for Economic Policy Research, March 1984).

need to respond to this necessity, not only by imparting greater strength and stability to commodity markets themselves, but also by taking this matter of structural adjustment into account directly in the design and composition of new commodity arrangements.

The third element of a possible new rationale derives from the presence of commodities in the international economy in the new context. Commodities are losing their importance in the total trade of developing countries. This fact emerges, however, in the aggregate statistics of these countries, which are increasingly dominated by the fuels and manufactured goods exports of a handful of the developing countries. For a large number of the developing countries, commodity exports are still of preponderant importance. The commodity issue will continue to be an important international issue, because the functioning of the economies of the developing countries is now a part of the functioning of the world economy as a whole. The recent recession in commodity prices, by playing an important part in weakening the capacity of many important developing countries to service their debts, has clearly demonstrated this. The linkages between some of the important economic issues of today, such as debt and overall growth (increasingly generated by the positive impulses imparted by the developing countries to the industrialized countries), give new relevance to a focus on commodities as part of global economic progress. In this regard, I want to stress the important role that the commercial banks, which have so much at stake in the developing countries, could play in stimulating further efforts toward stabilization of commodity markets. Unfortunately, the presence of the banks in this field has so far been extremely limited, so their potential for positive action has not been realized.

These are all reasons not only to continue our efforts but also to give a new impetus to the handling of commodity issues in the international field. This new impetus may not come in the near future, because the North-South dialogue is in a kind of impasse, and progress is difficult in almost every field. I am not so naive as to think that, by pure exhortation, we are going to bring about a major new effort to give life to the Integrated Program for Commodities. This impasse, however, is not going to persist indefinitely. The course of events on the world economic and political scenes will once again compel attention to North-South issues. The problems of the developing countries, and the importance of responding to their problems in the interest of the proper functioning of the world economy as a whole, as well as the soundness of international political relations, require broad, cooperative action. From that point of view, I think we are on the threshold of a new phase.

I increasingly see a sensitivity to the need to adapt and to rebuild in international economic affairs. There are initiatives to reexamine the evolution of the monetary system; there are similar initiatives to look again at the international trading system. The network of institutional support for the world economy should be a triad of instruments, dealing not only with money and finance, and with trade, but also with commodities. This was the perception of the Havana Charter, which did have this triad of instruments to regulate the postwar economy, and we must return to that more unified concept.[13]

In the refashioning of the institutional system that might begin in the late 1980s, there is a need to incorporate a new development consensus, comparable to the full-employment consensus that characterized the fashioning of the Bretton Woods system and the General Agreement on Tariffs and Trade (GATT). This is not only because the development process is important to the developing countries, but also because it is increasingly important to the developed countries themselves, and to the proper functioning of the entire world economy. It is impossible today to have a world that is functioning satisfactorily if the developing countries are languishing and the development process is in disarray. In this respect, there is a contrast between the situation that prevailed two decades ago at the time of the founding of UNCTAD and the international predicament of today. What we now have is a situation of increasing unity and complexity in the working of the world economy. The forces of interdependence are gaining in strength. Not only is there the previous dependence of the developing countries on the developed, which is still of extreme importance. There is also a reverse dependence, that of the developed countries on the economies of the developing countries. Upon this broader, more balanced foundation, a new global framework for trade and development can and must be built.

FOR FURTHER READING

For specific studies of the commodity problem, see J. W. F. Rowe, *Primary Commodities in International Trade* and Fiona Gordon-Ashworth, *International Commodity Control: A Contemporary History and Appraisal*, mentioned in the footnotes. Other useful works are Alton D. Law, *International Commodity Agreements: Setting, Performance, and Prospects* (Lexington, MA: Lexington Books, 1975); Jere D. Behrman, *International Commodity Agreements: An Evaluation of the UNCTAD Integrated Commodity Programme* (Washington, DC: Overseas Development Council, 1977); David L. McNichol, *Commodity Agreements and Price Stabilization: A Policy Analysis* (Lexington, MA: Lexington Books, 1978); Louis M. Goreaux, *Compensatory Financing Facility* (Washington, DC: International Monetary Fund, 1980); Geoffrey Goodwin and James Mayall, eds., *A New International Commodity Regime* (New York: St. Martin's, 1980); and Ronald C. Duncan, ed., *The Outlook for Primary Commodities, 1984 to 1995* (Washington, DC: World Bank, 1985).

For a more comprehensive treatment of commodities and other North-South economic issues, see Gamani Corea, *Need for Change: Towards the New International*

---

[13]For a discussion of the Havana Charter, see Clair Wilcox, *A Charter for World Trade* (New York: Macmillan, 1949); and Stein Rossen, *Notes on Rules and Mechanisms Governing International Economic Relations* (Bergen: Michelsen Institute, 1981).

Economic Order (New York: Pergamon Press, 1980); *The History of UNCTAD, 1964–84* (New York: United Nations, 1985); and M. Zammit Cutajar, ed., *UNCTAD and the South-North Dialogue—The First Twenty Years: Essays in Memory of W. R. Malinowski* (New York: Pergamon Press, 1985). See also Branislav Gosovic, *UNCTAD Conflict and Compromise* (Leiden: A. W. Sijthoff, 1972); William R. Cline, ed., *Policy Alternatives for a New International Economic Order: An Economic Analysis* (New York: Praeger, 1979); Robert F. Meagher, *An International Redistribution of Wealth and Power: A Study of the Charter of Economic Rights and Duties of States* (New York: Pergamon Press, 1979); Anthony Sampson, ed., *North-South: A Program for Survival* [Report of the Independent Commission on International Development Issues] (Cambridge, MA: MIT Press, 1980); Stephen D. Krasner, *Structural Conflict: The Third World Against Global Liberalism* (Berkeley: University of California Press, 1985); and Jagdish N. Bhagwati and John Gerard Ruggie, eds., *Power, Passions, and Purpose: Prospects for North-South Negotiations* (Cambridge, MA: MIT Press, 1984).

Especially noteworthy on the processes of negotiation and regime construction in this field are the writings of Robert L. Rothstein, including: *Global Bargaining: UNCTAD and the Quest for a New International Economic Order* (Princeton, NJ: Princeton University Press, 1979); "Regime-Creation by a Coalition of the Weak: Lessons from the NIEO and the Integrated Program for Commodities," *International Studies Quarterly* 28, no. 3 (September 1984): 307–28; and "Condemned to Cooperate: U.S. Resource Diplomacy," *SAIS Review* 5, no. 1 (Winter/Spring 1985): 163–77.

The GATT and the Negotiation of International Trade Rules

GARDNER PATTERSON

There is an honored theoretical justification for world order in international trade. The theory is, of course, that of comparative advantage. But as all economists have long known, this powerful proposition in its simple and strongest formulation rests on a series of heroic assumptions about perfect competition, full employment, complete information, and a minimal role of government in economic life. It also ignores the role of noneconomic considerations in the making of national foreign trade policies. Because these assumptions often do not hold and because governments are often motivated by objectives other than maximizing the amount and variety of goods and services available to their people, the world has found that nations, left to themselves, have a very strong tendency to erect all sorts of trade barriers at their frontiers. These lead to national and world impoverishment, political disputes, and instability and uncertainty: the bane of those who would engage in international economic intercourse. Still, with all of its shortcomings and the limitations on its applicability, the comparative-advantage theory has served as a powerful guide to enlightened policy. Certainly it is a better long-term guide in this field than any other general proposition that has been put forward.

One point about trade policy is clear from past experience. If there is a case, as I firmly believe there is, for fewer rather than more barriers, and for rules to provide order and reasonably firm conditions for those who would trade, then a system to ensure this will have to be negotiated. This is because no single nation, in this century at least, has shown a willingness to bind itself, by itself, to a set of rules and practices and thereby try to establish an ordered general pattern. Each, in my view wisely, has demanded "matching" commitments or, that unfortunate word, "concessions" by others.

181

In the words of those who organized the Negotiating World Order Project at the Fletcher School, accomplishments in the field of international trade now depend primarily on the skill of the master artisans, or negotiators. The architects, the source of the fundamental ideas, did their work a long time ago. This was realized by those who, during and immediately after World War II, were drafting various specific plans, agreements, and arrangements for the postwar international economic system. As they saw it, the needs were for a three-part system: a World Bank, to lend monies for economic reconstruction and development; an International Monetary Fund, to provide for exchange-rate order and stability; and an International Trade Organization (ITO), to deal with problems of trade, foreign investment, employment, business practices, and related matters. Largely for political reasons in the United States, and because of the complexity and contradictory objectives of the scheme itself, the ITO never came into being. Nonetheless, those parts of the proposed structure dealing with trade, in the narrow sense of goods moving across national frontiers, became what is known as the GATT, the General Agreement on Tariffs and Trade.[1]

This agreement, to which some ninety countries that account for over 85 percent of world trade have now acceded (the only major trading countries currently outside the system are the Soviet Union, the People's Republic of China, and Mexico), is a remarkable testimony to international diplomatic negotiation. It is a very complex undertaking, so complex that the then chairman of the Senate Finance Committee, Eugene D. Millikin, observed, when that panel was considering the necessary U.S. implementing legislation, that anyone who read the GATT was likely to have his sanity impaired.

Its principles and its norms are briefly stated in its preamble. The signatories recognized that their relations in the field of trade and economic endeavors should be conducted "with a view to raising standards of living, ensuring full employment and a large and steadily growing volume of real income and effective demand, developing the full use of the resources of the world and expanding the production and exchange of goods." Furthermore, they expressed their desire to contribute to these objectives "by entering into reciprocal and mutually advantageous arrangements directed to a substantial reduction of tariffs and other barriers of trade and to the elimination of discriminatory treatment of international commerce."

---

[1]On the genesis of the GATT, finally signed, after years of negotiation, in Geneva in October 1947, see Claire Wilcox, *A Charter for World Trade* (New York: Macmillan, 1949); William Adams Brown, *The United States and the Restoration of World Trade* (Washington, DC: Brookings Institution, 1950); Kenneth W. Dam, *The GATT: Law and International Economic Organization* (Chicago: University of Chicago Press, 1970); and Gérard Curzon, *Multilateral Commercial Diplomacy: The General Agreement on Tariffs and Trade, and Its Impact on National Commercial Policies and Techniques* (New York: Praeger, 1966). On the defeat of the ITO Charter, see Richard N. Gardner, *Sterling-Dollar Diplomacy: The Origins and the Prospects of Our International Economic Order* (New York: McGraw-Hill, 1969), chap. 17, "The End of the I.T.O."

The document then proceeds to set out a body of rules, often in maddening and tortured language because it was multilaterally negotiated, and both the French and English texts are authentic.[2] The most important of these rules are as follows. Nations shall not discriminate among sources in their treatment of imports at the frontier; that is, unconditional most-favored-nation treatment is required.[3] Once foreign goods have entered a signatory country they are to be extended national treatment subject to the same internal taxes, laws, and regulations as domestic goods. In general, it is stated, nations shall rely only on tariffs and not on quantitative restrictions or quotas to restrict imports. Certain "unfair" trade practices, especially subsidies and dumping, are frowned upon, and provisions are made for taking action against them. In the interest of future trade expansion, the signatories agree to undertake periodic negotiations to reduce trade barriers. Provisions are made for reimposing import restrictions under certain conditions, the so-called "safeguard" article. And finally, procedures are set out for settling disputes.

In 1969 the signatories, called "contracting parties," added a new section, Part IV, to deal specifically with the problems of developing countries. In effect, these articles and institutionalized practices relieve the developing countries of many of their GATT obligations and impose on the developed countries the obligation to provide special and favorable treatment to products of great export interest to the developing countries.

Since 1947, under the aegis of the GATT, there have been seven rounds of multilateral trade negotiations, the last being the Tokyo Round, which lasted from 1973 to 1979.[4] The accomplishments are impressive. Tariffs on goods entering the industrialized countries have been cut, on the average, by at least 80 percent, to the point where, with a few important exceptions, they

---

[2]The two classic studies, especially of the legal aspects of the GATT, are Robert E. Hudec, *The GATT Legal System and World Trade Diplomacy* (New York: Praeger, 1975), and John H. Jackson, *World Trade and the Law of GATT* (Indianapolis: Bobbs-Merrill, 1969). For the text of the General Agreement on Tariffs and Trade (including interpretative notes and Protocol of Provisional Application), see Dam, *The GATT*, or Jackson, *World Trade*.

[3]Under the conditional form of the most-favored-nation (MFN) principle, if country A grants a concession to country B in exchange for a given concession, A extends the concession to another country, C, only if C negotiates a corresponding concession. Under the unconditional form of MFN, C obtains the concession without granting one of its own, but must also automatically extend to A any concession it grants to B.

[4]On the most recent GATT rounds, see The General Agreement on Tariffs and Trade, Report of the Director General, *The Tokyo Round of Multilateral Trade Negotiations* (Geneva: GATT, April 1979), and *Supplementary Report* (Geneva: GATT, January 1980); Ernest H. Preeg, *Traders and Diplomats: An Analysis of the Kennedy Round of Negotiations under the General Agreement on Tariffs and Trade* (Washington, DC: Brookings Institution, 1970); John W. Evans, *The Kennedy Round in American Trade Policy: The Twilight of the GATT?* (Cambridge: Harvard University Press, 1971); William R. Cline, Noboru Kawanabe, T. O. M. Kronsjö, and Thomas Williams, *Trade Negotiations in the Tokyo Round: A Quantitative Assessment* (Washington, DC: Brookings Institution, 1978); and Robert E. Baldwin, "The Tokyo Round of Multilateral Trade Negotiations," in Robert E. Baldwin and J. David Richardson, *International Trade and Finance: Readings*, 2d ed. (Boston: Little, Brown, 1981), pp. 231–61.

are no longer major barriers to cross-frontier traffic. New codes of behavior, sets of rights and obligations, have been negotiated on a wide variety of nontariff measures which, as tariffs are being cut, have become the chief trade-limiting and trade-distorting measures. The most important of these codes deal with the problem of dumping (selling abroad at a lower price than at home), subsidies for exports, government procurement policies, the whole range of customs administration and practices, and the immense and complex field of standards (health, safety, and performance requirements).

This system not only has successfully avoided trade wars (indeed, even isolated retaliatory measures have been rare and contained), but it also has made possible a large expansion of trade. The liberalizing of international trade under the GATT has resulted in a growth of real exports well in excess of the increase of world production of movable goods. This has meant that a significant part of the growth in the world economy, from the end of World War II to the mid-1970s, was export-led. Altogether, this is an impressive record for the already negotiated world order in international trade.

However, all is not well today. Far from it. One need only read any week's issues of the *New York Times, Le Monde*, or the *Financial Times* to know that there are massive protectionist pressures at work in virtually every country. The low rate of economic growth worldwide in recent years and the likelihood that, in many countries, growth will continue to be slow and unemployment high for the rest of the decade has vastly strengthened the ever-present desire of most producers, in whatever nation, to protect them-selves from foreign competition. An especially serious threat to the up-to-now remarkably successful system of trade cooperation and to the world order with which we are concerned is the increasing tendency for the big nations to approach many of their problems on a bilateral and sectoral, rather than multilateral and general, basis. I will come back to this matter in discussing the major areas for future negotiation in the international trade field.

Before doing so, I should like to sketch some of the more important negotiating procedures and techniques that have developed in the GATT during the past forty years, including the period (1966–1981) of my own service in that organization. The specific details vary from issue to issue, but there are certain general characteristics of the GATT negotiating process that can be described usefully.

It must be noted at the outset that, although each member of the GATT has a right to one vote, in practice votes are rarely taken, and never on major substantive issues. The GATT procedure is to reach decisions, such as whether on a new government procurement code, a formula for reducing tariffs, the terms of reference of a working party on trade in services, or instructions to be given a dispute panel—all of which have to be negotiated—by consensus. In the GATT framework, this means that an agreement is reached when those who do not agree either keep quiet, for one reason or another, or are so few or so small in terms of their interest in the issue that their agreement is not regarded by whoever is chairing the negotiations as essential to the successful implementation of the proposed action. Obviously, a great deal of negotiation on the substance of a question is necessary before that state of agreement is reached. Decision making by consensus, rather than by vote, has been found indispensable to international negotiations in trade matters when a large number of countries are involved and when they differ greatly in their economic importance and in their concern with particular issues.

Because of their economic and political importance, and also their active participation in all aspects of the GATT's work, the United States and the European Community have an effective veto power. No decision can be taken if either of these entities actively opposes. However, neither of them can by itself, or even in combination, bring the GATT to take any action in the face of stated and strong opposition by several of the other trading countries.

A major difficulty at the GATT, itself a negotiating problem, is getting a concrete proposal on the table. This can be a complex and delicate affair. On the one hand, it is usually to a country's advantage to have the negotiations start from its own draft, because the first draft often sets the range and the tone of the negotiation. On the other hand, once written, a proposal often limits a party's subsequent freedom of action and so can reduce its bargaining strength. This consideration sometimes leads to proposals being put forward anonymously, that is, "by certain delegations." It also means that on occasion the secretariat of the GATT puts forward proposals. We never did this, however, before carefully and discreetly determining the limits beyond which the major players would not go. "Nonnegotiable" issues must never be tabled by an international secretariat if it wishes to play a substantive role.

Any member can put a proposal forward in the GATT. There is a strong tradition that, before doing so, the member should hold informal and private discussions with a number of other members and obtain assurances from them that they will support at least the major thrust of the proposal. It is common for such advance supporters to reserve the right to offer amendments in light of future developments, including, for many, the possibility that their own governments may alter their instructions.

Furthermore, serious multilateral negotiations on trade matters cannot go forward unless there is a single document before the negotiators. This is commonly accomplished by having a document which incorporates parts of several, often conflicting, proposals, with the disputed paragraphs in square brackets. This editorial device is used to make clear what has not been agreed. It also serves the very useful purpose of pinpointing the areas where further negotiations must still take place. In any event, it is almost always understood in trade negotiations that acceptance of a proposal as a "basis for negotiation" means that any agreement along the way is *ad referendum*. This means that nothing is agreed until all is agreed, and that final approval is in the hands of someone back in the capitals and not those of the actual negotiator. This also means that the final days and hours of a negotiation are intense and full of suspense.

Another major problem in any negotiation that includes many countries— as most world-order negotiations must—is deciding who is able to participate in the discussion at different stages. This is an extremely delicate matter, and many a chairman has suffered much abuse and many a negotiation has been greatly prolonged on this score. In the GATT, the usual procedure is what some of us call the "expanding-and-shrinking-concentric-circle approach."

When a matter is first considered, everyone interested is invited, and each speaks his piece. Thus there is made a record, either for real or simply for those back home to read. In such a meeting, or series of meetings, one gets a rough idea of the aspects of the proposal that have wide support, those that are being pushed by only a few or whose support is not critical, and those on which there is strong and divided opinion. The next step, often requiring months of quiet negotiation, leads to the step of some one party, or several parties, putting on the table (circulating) a specific draft, sometimes anonymously. Often this represents the work of a small group. The large group may be invited back into the room to discuss it. Then the small group goes back into a private, restricted series of sessions to work out a revised version. This back-and-forth process is often repeated many times, with steady and increasing pressure for more delegations to take part in the smaller drafting group, because each successive draft narrows the room for further changes. In order to strengthen their claim for admission, some of the GATT members have developed the practice of joining forces. Several small countries with more or less common interests in the particular matter will form an informal group, select a common spokesman, and then insist, not always successfully, that they are large enough to enter. Thus, in the Tokyo Round, we had a Nordic group, an ASEAN group, a recognized spokesman for some of the developing countries, and, on occasion, a nonmarket-economy group.

Because it is essential that the giants, the United States, the European Community, and Japan, always be in the room, there is a constant threat implicit in this mechanism that the interests of the smaller nations will get lost. One of the greatest tricks to perform in any multilateral trade negotiation is to ensure that the interests of the smaller countries are properly considered. This can be done by several means. The formation of groups is one device. Another, often more effective, is for each small nation to define early on and very carefully exactly what aspects of the matter are central to it and, on these issues alone, to wage a constant campaign outside the room with those who do get into the room. Precision and persistence on what a small country wants can pay off handsomely. Another device is for the secretariat, an international body, which typically services the negotiations, to plead the case for the smaller members. However, as has become increasingly common, if the giants decide they have had enough of the kibitzers and decide to hold a small group meeting session outside the regular venue of the negotiations, in one of their capitals or at a nearby resort, the opportunity for the smaller countries to influence the results is greatly reduced.

Timing in this matter is all-important. It is an inherent characteristic of most trade negotiations that the agreement finally reached by those playing the most active roles represents a compromise and a delicate balancing of very complex trade-offs. Any change after the principals have reached agreement among themselves is very likely to upset the trade-off balance. The consequence is all too often that the agreed compromise is therefore imposed on the other parties. Meeting the clear and acknowledged needs of small nations thus remains a major unsolved problem in negotiating international multilateral agreements that involve many countries.

To end a multilateral trade negotiation, also a timing problem, can be as complex as conducting it in its intermediate phases. On the one hand, the pressure to keep the negotiation going is strong. There is always the hope of obtaining still another concession. There is the difficulty of having to concede on yet one more issue in order to achieve a final agreement. There is the fact that the tough differences are usually left to the end. There is the domestic political consideration that as long as one is engaged in an international negotiation one can more easily fend off protectionist pressures at home. There is also the likelihood that the negotiators really enjoy the work and are reluctant to see it end. On the other hand, the credibility of the exercise demands that there be a conclusion. The benefits of the negotiation cannot be realized until agreement is reached. The negotiators themselves, whatever their basic job satisfaction, may become exhausted and irritable. Finally, there is the very important point that if the negotiation goes on too long the problems can change, and earlier agreements on parts of the package become moot.

In the field of trade negotiations, by far the best device yet found for concluding a negotiation has been a practice of the U.S. Congress: namely, setting a specific date in the law beyond which the negotiators for the United States no longer have legal authority to continue to act. This can result in a veritable orgy of negotiations during the last few days and nights before the date set in U.S. law. A reasonably good alternative, slightly more flexible, is for a senior political official of one of the major parties to state publicly that his delegation will cease to participate after a certain date and to start calling members of the negotiating team home some weeks prior to that date in order to convince others that he is serious.

There are two kinds of substantive problems in this kind of negotiation. The first set of issues arises from those current practices and tendencies that are weakening the present international trading system. The second set pertains to new areas that need to be brought into a system of international rules. Stated otherwise: Where does the existing system need strengthening, and where should it be extended?

Doing anything in either area is made much more difficult because of the dramatic change in the past fifteen years in the leadership of the world trading system. The undisputed leader in the first two decades of the era following World War II was the United States. Its policies were characterized by a firm belief in negotiated multilateral solutions to trade problems, with the double aim of lowering trade barriers and making detailed rules that set out specific rights and obligations to provide stability and certainty for traders. During that period, the United States was rich enough, and trade was small enough, to absorb the domestic political and economic costs of international leadership. The influence of America's vast wealth enticed or compelled others to go along. As is well known and need not be elaborated here, for more than a decade a major relative decline in the power and economic importance of the United States has been occurring. With this decline has come some diminution of the American sense of responsibility for the system. This has meant that the single, confident leader has been replaced by what may be called a cantankerous troika: a United States still influential but far less certain than before of the merits of its earlier policy; a clumsy and often divided European Economic Community (EEC), with strong traditions of protectionism, discrimination, and bilateralism along with its commitment to cooperation; and a sometimes politically powerful but frequently uncertain, disorganized, and suspicious group of developing countries, the so-called Group of 77. What this adds up to all too often is no effective leadership at all.

The greatest specific threat to the present system, which, to repeat, has served the world so well, is not the protectionist pressures that we hear so much about, although these do indeed constitute a serious problem. Even though they are particularly strong at the moment, primarily because of the low rate of economic growth during the past decade (and, in the United States, the overvalued dollar), such pressures are always present. It must not be forgotten that it was the existence of just such forces, and the knowledge that they would always be with us, that led to the negotiation of the GATT in the first place at the end of World War II. The present threat to the system comes rather from the way in which the major trading powers are dealing with the forces of protectionism. I have already mentioned the problem arising from the current strong tendency of governments to settle their problems bilaterally, and in effect to impose the results of their separate agreements on others.

Even more serious, in my view, is the current tendency of the giants, especially the United States, the European Community, and Japan, to approach many of their international trade problems on a sectoral basis. We see this developing in agriculture and in such major industries as steel, automobiles, shipbuilding, electronics, and textiles, which have been treated sectorally for a long time.

This way of handling problems, because of the usual absence of opposing interests and debate from outside the particular sector and countries concerned, almost always develops in the direction of imposing import restrictions of one kind or other, e.g., orderly marketing arrangements and so-called voluntary export restraints. Equally serious from the point of view of ensuring the best use of the world's resources (which is, we sometimes forget, the raison d'être of the multilateral trading system) is that the sectoral approach, whose stated objective is always to relieve the pressure of foreign competition on an industry "temporarily" in trouble, is exceedingly difficult to reverse. This is so because such policies are usually negotiated first between the affected industry and the government in a given country, and then between that government and each exporting country's combined industry-and-government position. A whole set of vested interests is thus created, which makes reversal most difficult. Moreover, such government involvement in helping one sector is highly contagious. In democracies, it is difficult to grant favors to one industry and to refuse them to another finding itself in trouble. Precedents are a powerful force. Thus a sectoral approach to trade policy, attractive as it may seem if one suffers from a very short time horizon and a very narrow view of the national economy, involves recourse to devices that can violate the general rules so laboriously negotiated. These violations are usually not formally protested because those who participate in the arrangements have, in effect, negotiated away their rights. Finally, it must be noted, this resorting to a series of discrete, separately negotiated trade policies for one sector, and then another, cumulatively removes more and more trade from the agreed general rules and thereby makes global and coherent national trade policy that much more difficult. Indeed, each sector comes to have a trade policy of its own. If this becomes the situation in one or more of the dominant trading groups, the whole system is placed in dire straits.

There is as yet no consensus among practitioners about how best to cope with problems of individual sectors. The present rules do not seem adequate for dealing with a major industry in deep and protracted trouble. However, to have all such sectoral negotiations take place within the general GATT framework would go some way in making them less a threat, because this would both open up and make more visible the process by which such decisions are made. This would help ensure that the interests of the nonparticipants could better be taken into account. Negotiations to set rules for terminating such agreements are also needed. In addition, it is probably necessary to have something even more difficult to negotiate: rules, agreements, or agreed practices on structural adjustment.

Beyond sectoral agreements, the United States has also recently been showing considerable interest in general, bilateral, so-called freer trade agreements: the Caribbean Basin Initiative (CBI), the recently approved free-trade agreement with Israel, the Canadian talks, and those with the ASEAN group. While it is always easy to find an immediate justification for such agreements with particular countries or regions (including the doubtful proposition that they can serve as stepping-stones to truly multilateral negotiations), they do represent a serious erosion of the previously negotiated multilateral world trading system. Like the sectoral agreements, they introduce special provisions for selected countries, often at the expense of others against whom there is subtle discrimination. From press reports, one gathers that these proposed bilateral deals will be structured so as not to be "outlawed" by the GATT. But they do run counter to its thrust and certainly fall far short of the previously negotiated GATT provisions for free trade areas and customs unions, which are required to ensure that regional groups have a net effect of creating trade, not diverting it from more efficient to less efficient sources.[5] Moreover, whatever the actual economic effects of the CBI, etc., this recent resort by

---

[5]Article XXIV deals with customs unions and free trade areas. For the text, see Dam, *The GATT*, pp. 431–34.

the United States to the sort of regional arrangements it has strongly opposed in the past further tarnishes its image as a leader in negotiating *world* order. Nonetheless, in the Trade and Tariff Act of 1984, Congress specifically authorized the administration to negotiate a bilateral free-trade agreement with Israel and to do the same with other countries after receiving explicit approval from appropriate congressional committees.[6]

If we can prevent these sectoral, bilateral, and regional agreements from destroying the present world order in the trade field, there will still be a need for negotiated reforms of the present system. Changes are clearly required in some areas. Beyond that, we should ask, where might negotiations be useful for bringing new areas into the system?[7]

A very big deficiency of the present international trading order is that far too many violations go unchallenged, with a resultant erosion of that order. Even when formal disputes do arise from challenges, the time needed to settle them is often far too long, and the disputed practice continues in the meantime. There are two major reasons why so many violations of the rules go uncorrected. First, oftentimes those who know of a violation and who may suffer from it do not themselves have clean hands, and so are reluctant to make formal complaints. Second, many nations, especially smaller ones, hesitate to blow the whistle for fear of retaliation. Moreover, in each individual case, countries may not be able to see much in it for themselves in protesting, even though they realize the system that they support is being nibbled away.

One answer to this problem would be to negotiate an agreement whereby the GATT secretariat, the international civil servants, are instructed, not just authorized—although that too would be a step forward—to place documented cases of violations on the agenda of the GATT contracting parties' monthly meetings. A negotiation would be needed to define the instructions concerning such questions as: What is acceptable evidence? What violations should be covered? How should it be determined which parties are affected? Is concrete injury to others necessary, or is action undermining the established rules and principles enough? Should the notification of the violation only cover established facts or also include recommendations? This innovation would be a major reform and exceedingly difficult to negotiate, given the lack of precedents and repeated refusal of governments to give real power to genuine international civil servants, as distinct from national officials serving on international bodies.

---

[6] For the text of the Trade and Tariff Act of 1984, signed on October 30, 1984, see U.S. *Statutes at Large*, vol. 98 (1984), pp. 2948 ff. For an analysis of the act, see Eliza Patterson, "Features of the Omnibus Trade Act in the United States," *World Economy* 7, no. 4 (December 1984): 407–21.

[7] For two recent studies on which I have drawn that examine these issues, see Miriam Camps and William Diebold, Jr., *The New Multilateralism: Can the World Trading System Be Saved?* (New York: Council on Foreign Relations, 1983) and William R. Cline, ed., *Trade Policy in the 1980s* (Washington, DC: Institute for International Economics, 1983).

In the case of an alleged violation there are likely to be denials; in other words, one has a dispute on one's hands. Therefore, if more cases are to be presented, it would also be necessary to speed up the present dispute-settlement process. One would need to negotiate more stringent time requirements than now exist for filing complaints, giving replies, holding meetings, appointing panels, and rendering and implementing the decisions. Such increased dispute-settlement activity would also require much greater reliance than at present on nongovernmental persons to serve as panel members. This might reduce the likelihood of national bias and political pressure.

A further problem arising from existing GATT policy and practice concerns the "graduation" of developing countries. It would be highly desirable, but exceedingly difficult, to negotiate new rules for increasing the assumption by less developed countries (LDCs) of their full GATT obligations. At the moment there are some countries—Brazil, Israel, Korea, and Singapore come quickly to mind—that are lumped together with Pakistan, Bangladesh, and Chad in being classified broadly as "developing countries" and therefore entitled to the special treatment set out in the various GATT articles. Many of these countries are not now in fact being referred to as developing countries but rather as NICs, newly industrializing countries. The advanced industrialized nations are, one by one and each in its own way, treating these developing NICs differently in trade matters from other developing countries, and so are unilaterally forcing a certain amount of graduation. The problem with this is that there are no general rules; therefore one is seeing a lot of ad hoc action, which inevitably leads to uncertainty, inequities, and resulting political tension. There are no easily agreed-upon criteria as to what constitutes graduation for these purposes, or what obligations are appropriate for various stages of development. The time has come to grapple with this issue, however. Just as dividing the world, for certain economic and political purposes, into developing and developed, North and South, or First World and Third World, has enormous implications for the way we handle international affairs, so too the huge differences in speed with which these developing countries are moving into industrial status has consequences that must be recognized and dealt with if there is to be world order.

Having said this, I must hasten to add that, despite all the derogations from GATT obligation that have been granted developing countries and the commitments the developed countries have assumed to grant them special treatment, many of the LDCs have suffered, and are suffering, from the policies of the developed nations. They are often victims of discrimination, and many of their major exports, such as textiles, clothing, and farm goods, are subject to all manner of restrictions in the advanced nations. Moreover, as noted, they are often kept out of the room when negotiations of significant interest to them are taking place.

Another major area crying for reform is the treatment of the nonmarket economies. Several of these—Yugoslavia, Romania, Hungary, and Poland—are already GATT members. The rules for their participation are proving far from satisfactory, however. This problem is of growing importance because of the evidence that the People's Republic of China may soon seek to enter the GATT. For its participation to be mutually satisfactory there needs to be a negotiation for new rules concerning the so-called entrance fee of a non-market economy, where a lowering of tariffs, the usual fee, has little significance. Other difficulties needing to be resolved concern the provision of economic data, the "transparency" problem; early removal of the discriminatory quantitative import restrictions applied by some Western European countries against imports from the nonmarket economies; and, above all, improved rules on how to treat nonmarket economies' exports when it is alleged they are "unfairly" traded, by being sold at prices that appear to be below cost, whether by being dumped or subsidized or otherwise supported. This last major problem arises because the present rules governing what can be done to offset unfair pricing practices are based on the assumption that domestic prices, the standard of comparison, are determined in an open competitive market, and nonmarket price-formation systems often have little in common with that. There are ideas as to how to meet these various problems of the nonmarket economy participation, but as yet there is no agreement. Clearly, a negotiation is needed. The prospective entry of China makes this need urgent.

Still another major area needing work is the area of safeguards, the terms according to which a country may impose, or reimpose, restrictions on imports causing important injury to domestic producers. Everyone recognizes that the present rules and procedures regarding safeguards (Article XIX of the GATT) are inadequate. It is also agreed that a loophole is necessary if nations are to commit themselves in an international trade agreement to certain standards of behavior. Redefining the conditions under which a nation legitimately may reimpose import restrictions or otherwise be relieved of its international obligations is a matter that has been on the negotiating table for nearly a decade, but agreement has not been reached. As a consequence, the existing rules are at risk. This is not surprising, for the mere act of deciding that there is a need for reform removes a good bit of authority from the existing rules. The particular issue in which this negotiation has foundered is that of "selectivity," the application of safeguard measures in a discriminatory fashion. The present rules provide that if certain strict conditions are met a nation may restrain imports of specified products, but that imports of that product must be restrained from all sources; in other words, the restraint must be nondiscriminatory.

The negotiations that began in the mid-1970s led to considerable progress in redefining and strengthening the conditions justifying the reimposition of restraints, the nature of the permitted restraints, and the duration of them. A number of nations, led by those of the European Community, insisted, however, that the new rules permit in exceptional circumstances the application of restraints only against some exporting countries. The "some" were those that, the EEC argued, could objectively be identified as a source of "trouble." The LDCs were violently opposed to this change, insisting that, as newcomers and as nations with little retaliatory power, they would be the ones selected for restraints. Given the power of the EEC, and because it was adamant on the selectivity principle, the LDCs finally accepted the position that in exceptional cases safeguards could be applied selectively. The negotiations then shifted to the definition of "exceptional." After weeks of intense debate, the EEC concluded that the restrictive definition demanded by developing countries meant "never" and was therefore unacceptable. There the matter rests. The old rules are still on the books, but they are heavily discredited by the fact of the stalled negotiations. Leaving it here is most corrosive of world order. When negotiations resume they will, most likely, have to grapple not only with selectivity but also with the much more difficult problem of whether those who impose safeguards must also undertake adjustment measures in order to make future resort to such safeguards unnecessary.[8]

With such difficult negotiations needed to correct deficiencies in the existing system, one is inclined to be prudent in selecting new areas for negotiation, such as extending the scope of an agreed world order in trade. There are, however, two major areas that cry out for attention: trade in services, and, even more difficult, the coordination of trade policy and international monetary policy, which quickly takes us into the controversial area of industrial policy.

There are now virtually no international rules for trade in services, although the amount of such trade is very large and is rapidly growing. Its value probably comes to $500 billion per year (the statistics in this area are very poor), but its rapid growth reflects basic developments, some of which are readily measured, such as underlying shifts in employment from goods to services. The growing specialization in services, which encourages trading, and the large economies of scale in the production of many of them, which creates a need for world markets, together with the rapid advances in telecommunications, which facilitate internationalization, have made the services market a global one. At the same time, impediments to international trade in services are already extensive. The reasons for this resistance are many. National governments often worry about protecting the privacy both of their citizens and of their corporations. They are concerned about the dependability of access to data stored in foreign countries. Above all, they often want to protect or foster their own service industries and their own telecommunications systems, which are often public monopolies. There is, moreover, deep concern regarding damage to their cultural values by foreign (read: American) television programs.

At the moment, one can still say that this whole field is in a state of flux. Many nations are as yet uncertain about where their exact national interest

---

[8]For a recent analysis by an international group of distinguished "wise men" of ways of improving the system, see The General Agreement on Tariffs and Trade, *Trade Policies for a Better Future: Proposals for Action* (Geneva: GATT, 1985).

lies. There also remains much ignorance about the nature and the scope of the problem. There is, as well, a shortage of ideas about what can be done feasibly in the way of international regulation, although most agree in the abstract with the general proposition that it would be useful to have some rules to the end that traders in services might have some certainty about the treatment they are to expect, and that such trade would continue to grow. Typically, at a GATT ministerial meeting in late 1982 the U.S. government, which has given more study to this problem than any other country, could not even get agreement for a systematic examination of the problem or on setting out possible negotiating options for liberalizing the services trade. All they could achieve was an agreement that each nation could, if it wished, submit national reports or studies on the matter. Two years later, toward the end of 1984, the Americans were off to garner a bit more support for their position, but still no agreement was reached. Why has so little been possible?

First, most governments are so uncertain about their own country's interests that they fear that the terms of reference for even a study of the problem could be prejudicial to them. Second, widespread suspicion persists that the whole thing is a move by the United States, the acknowledged leader in many service areas, to set up rules designed to protect its original, albeit increasingly challenged, leadership position. This suspicion is fed by the fact that the United States itself has not been able to speak with any great specificity about what it really thinks is desirable, or has been hazy about what it presumably has in mind. This is ironic, because this obscurity may have been in part an intentional U.S. effort to offset the concern of others that the United States envisions a scheme to protect its leadership. Third, some countries, including such powerful international negotiators as Brazil and Canada, feared that the discussion was a backdoor effort by the United States to set up rules for safeguarding international investment, currently a very sensitive issue. Fourth, there was great uncertainty and confusion about what is included in the notion of "services." Many have spoken of banking, telecommunications, insurance, shipping, television programs, and professional engineering services as being covered. Shudders went through many developed-country governments, however, when it was proposed that the international movement of unskilled labor be included. Fifth, there was, not surprisingly, also an institutional impediment. The question arose: Should such a study be conducted in the GATT framework, or should it be carried out in the framework of the United Nations and UNCTAD? This is not a trivial matter, because the practices, traditions, and objectives, as well as the secretariats, of these different negotiating forums can heavily influence the results.

We have a major negotiating problem ahead of us in the relatively new and expanding services field. Governments must first agree on the subject of negotiations. They must also agree on an appropriate forum for negotiations. There then must be an agreement regarding the issue of whether, given the great diversity of services, the approach should be through a series of individual sector codes or via the usual GATT method of general rules with exceptions and special provisions. Following that, there must be negotiations on the many difficult substantive issues. How much liberalization is feasible? Should the most-favored-nation rule be applied? What sort of dispute-settlement machinery is needed? Are the national-treatment rules now applied to trade in goods also appropriate for trade in services? Are special rules needed regarding the rights of establishment, i.e., the right to set up a business in a foreign country as distinct from the right to sell a product in the country? Is there a place for reciprocity rules? How is one to handle the federal problem, which arises because the United States and Canada, and to some extent Germany, have systems whereby the central government cannot bind cities, provinces, or states to anything like the same degree as most other national governments can? What concessions are appropriate to meet the infant-industry concerns of the developing countries? What kinds of exceptions are needed for national security interests? One can go on, but that is enough to indicate the complexity of our problem. We have a very long way to go before the international community will have a negotiated agreement on world order, a set of principles and rules, for trade in services, even though few deny the need and importance of such an order.

There is an even tougher problem. In its broadest sense, it is the problem of coordinating, nationally and internationally, far better than we handle it now, all those policies that have a major impact on foreign trade, in goods and services alike. The specific area most urgently crying for attention is the relationship between international financial policy and international trade policy. These are widely seen as separate and distinct problems, the former being concerned with exchange rates, interest rates, and the money supply, and the latter being concerned with such problems as tariffs, quotas, and subsidies. In virtually every government, finance and trade are the responsibilities of different ministries or departments, the Ministry of Finance (or the Treasury) on the one hand, and the Ministry of Trade (or Department of Commerce) on the other. In virtually every government, these institutionalized bureaucracies have surprisingly little contact. On the international level, too, we have a separation: the International Monetary Fund in Washington, and the GATT in Geneva. Our universities even support this division. Most universities have separate courses in international trade and international finance, and different faculty members teach them.

There are serious intellectual reasons for this. Trade policy is concerned basically with the level and composition of trade; it is long-term and microeconomic in approach. International monetary policy is concerned with trade balances, its approach is essentially short-term and macroeconomic. Moreover, huge amounts of technical expertise are required in each area, so some specialization is inevitable. Nonetheless, it is obvious, and becoming more so, that very close interrelationships exist between these subjects. For example, it is quite clear today that high U.S. interest rates are creating large capital inflows into the United States. These are raising the price of the dollar, which in turn increases U.S. imports and creates huge problems for U.S.

exporters, resulting in protectionist pressures and demands for subsidies. If, as is clearly true, exchange rates in the monetary field can and do deviate substantially from "equilibrium" for extended periods of time, then a country ends up with a very big trade policy problem.

What is to be done? I do not pretend to know exactly. Clearly much more intellectual work, as well as diplomatic effort, is needed. We need more economic analysis of the relationships between exchange rates and trade. (Often it is the capital account, not the trade account, that moves exchange rates.) We also need much wider international agreement on just what is the equilibrium exchange rate that should be the goal of objective policy. The need is obvious for a common international institutional framework for effecting closer coordination of trade and monetary policies, within countries as well as between them.

Similarly, there is an intimate relationship between international trade and international investment. The one often creates the other. Sometimes they substitute for one another, as happens when exporters-turned-investors produce goods for sale behind the protection of high tariffs or restrictive quotas. These trade and investment fields are even less well coordinated than are trade policy and exchange-rate policy. In recent years, a growing practice of many countries has been to impose on foreign investors certain "performance requirements": replace imports, expand exports, they are told, as a condition for permission to invest. This has produced disputes in the GATT. More generally, it has increased the awareness of trade and investment as related phenomena, requiring coordination through policy. Thinking along these lines quickly gets one into the whole untidy area of trade and industrial policy. The critical point I wish to make, finally, is that a major requirement for a really first-rate world order in trade is an extension of the present system of cooperation to a wider range of national and international economic policies.

FOR FURTHER READING

On the legal aspects of the GATT, see Kenneth W. Dam, *The GATT: Law and International Economic Organization*, Robert E. Hudec, *The GATT Legal System and World Trade Diplomacy*, and John H. Jackson, *World Trade and the Law of GATT*, cited in the footnotes. Other useful general works are also cited therein. The writings on international trade by Gardner Patterson include: *Discrimination in International Trade: The Policy Issues, 1945–1965* (Princeton, NJ: Princeton University Press, 1966); "Trade Policies of the Developed Countries for the Next Decade," in Jagdish Bhagwati, ed., *The New International Economic Order* (Cambridge, MA: MIT Press, 1977), pp. 236–39; and "The European Community as a Threat to the System," in William R. Cline, ed., *Trade Policy in the 1980s* (Washington, DC: Institute for International Economics, 1983), pp. 223–42.

For additional discussion of current international trade policies and problems, see C. Michael Aho and Thomas O. Bayard, "The 1980s: Twilight of the Open Trading

System?" *The World Economy: A Quarterly Journal on International Economic Affairs* 5, no. 4 (December 1982): 379–406; Robert B. Reich, "Beyond Free Trade," *Foreign Affairs* 61, no. 4 (Spring 1983): 773–804; John H. Jackson, Jean-Victor Louis, and Mitsuo Matsushita, *Implementing the Tokyo Round: Legal Aspects of Changing International Economic Rules* (Ann Arbor: University of Michigan Press, 1983); and Ernest H. Preeg, ed., *Hard Bargaining Ahead: U.S. Trade Policy and Developing Countries* (New Brunswick, NJ: Transaction Books, 1985).

For a more theoretical treatment of international trade, see W. M. Corden, *Trade Policy and Economic Welfare* (Oxford: Clarendon Press, 1974); Richard E. Caves and Ronald W. Jones, *World Trade and Payments* (Boston: Little, Brown, 1981); Edward E. Leamer, *Sources of International Comparative Advantage: Theory and Evidence* (Cambridge, MA: MIT Press, 1984); and John Whalley, *Trade Liberalization Among Major World Trading Areas* (Cambridge, MA: MIT Press, 1985).

For a comprehensive view of the major international economic institutions, including the GATT, see A. I. Macbean and P. N. Snowden, *International Institutions in Trade and Finance* (London: George Allen and Unwin, 1981). On policy making and international economic diplomacy, see David H. Blake and Robert S. Walters, *The Politics of Global Economic Relations* (Englewood Cliffs, NJ: Prentice-Hall, 1976); I. M. Destler, *Making Foreign Economic Policy* (Washington, DC: Brookings Institution, 1980); and Jock A. Finlayson and Mark W. Zacher, "The GATT and the Regulation of Trade Barriers: Regime Dynamics and Functions," *International Organization* 35, no. 4 (Autumn 1981): 561–602.

Dealing with the International Debt Issue

NATHANIEL SAMUELS

The umbrella title that covers this series of lectures, "Negotiating World Order," implies that order is a virtue. This may be right. Any particular order, of course, is not an objective or universal good; its value involves perception and relativity. This is a situation not unknown between faculties and students or between parents and children, for example, or between reactionaries and revolutionaries. In the world in which I work and live, attitudes toward order differ: accountants, lawyers, bankers, and creditors tend to cherish it; speculators find it dull and unrewarding; and debtors find it inconvenient and oppressive.

The negotiating process, as we learn in our separate, individual ways, is itself not unambiguously virtuous. It comprises elements not only of reason and logic but also of emotion and, from time to time, of power, exercised in subtle and sometimes not so subtle forms. The rather neat, modulated, and rational world of international finance, inhabited by bankers, finance ministers, central bank governors, and executive directors of the great official international institutions, does provide an environment generally compatible with the basic, nonviolent nature of the negotiating process.

The renegotiating and rescheduling of debt that has taken place during the last several years contains, in varying measure, all of the elements to which I have alluded. This unfolding drama is not an international debt issue alone. It is a world problem of many facets that has not one but many causes, and that harbors within it potential forces of severe and painful disorder. There is a need for the sovereign states, the international institutional framework, and also the private financial sector, in combination, to negotiate an orderly transition from one set of economic, financial, and political circumstances relating to the debtor-creditor relationships, which cannot long continue, to

199

another set of international circumstances, to which we must adjust. In organized societies, we are in fact frequently engaged in seeking such orderly adjustments, often amid disorderly facts and blurred perceptions. In the current debt crisis, the degree of transition is extreme, and its handling involves painstaking and detailed effort on our part.

The present international debt crisis had its origins in a variety of causes over the past two decades. The critical elements of it, however, may be identified. A large part of the problem was precipitated by the oil price revolution of the 1970s. We may know this or suspect it, but we tend to minimize the consequences of this cause and to look, instead, for villains, as we try to find our way out of the morass. The levels of international borrowing and lending rose markedly in the 1960s, well before the oil shocks were even imagined. The magnitudes of capital involved in trying to cushion and absorb the financial effects of the oil price increases of 1973–74 and 1978–79, however, reached heights beyond anything we in the financial world had ever experienced.

There emerged as a consequence an urgent need to "recycle" huge sums of money that were flowing from the purchasers of oil to the developing oil-exporting countries. Some of this money had somehow to be directed onward to the oil-deficit countries, particularly the nonoil developing ones. Many of these latter countries were rapidly sinking into deep balance-of-payments deficits because they could not sustain themselves without continuing to import oil as well as food and necessary equipment and merchandise. At the same time, the developing oil-exporting countries, having infrastructures with limited absorptive capacity, could, in the short run, use only part of their swelling export revenues. Thus they had to find outlets for these surplus liquidities. The governments, official agencies, international institutions, and private banks in the industrialized countries that were the main recipients of the mounting deposits of the oil-surplus countries all joined in the monetary recycling process. They were not, however, in a position, either singly or together, to sort out a set of national and international economic policies that would be consistent with the changing economic conditions then emerging. There were at least two basic reasons for this difficulty.

The first was the limited time available. During the rush of events, bankers, governments, and international institutions could not think through the ramifications of such large-scale, unprecedented borrowing and lending and at the same time respond to changing trends in the terms of trade, interest rates, and financial and investment flows. Given the immediacy of the problem, little collective heed was given to the capacities of the borrowers to service their debts if the prices of their export commodities should decline significantly, or if the world economic climate in general should take a turn for the worse.

The second was the fact that there were no precedents of a similar nature to help those with decision-making responsibility to measure the magnitude and character of the profound change that was so rapidly taking place. Little consideration was given by the commercial banks, for example, to the practicality of limiting their risks by acting as agents in some of their lending rather than as principals, thus diminishing their risk. In truth, it is quite possible that any broad-scale deviation from traditional procedures might have interfered with and jeopardized the entire recycling process. The ideas that were then put forth to deal with the huge surpluses and deficits received little organized attention, owing to the uncertainties and blurred perceptions of an unprecedented situation.[1] In fact, the dominant impulses had been running in the opposite direction. Governments and official international financial institutions, and also various unofficial sources, had for years been urging the private lending and industrial sectors to lend to and invest in developing countries on larger and larger scales. Bank lending to developing countries actually began to play a larger role than investment.[2] The sudden need for recycling moved the banks, already increasingly involved in developing country finance through the Euromarkets, to react in traditional ways and to expand their lending further, commensurate with the needs emerging and the opportunities encountered for expanding their earnings.[3]

It is hardly surprising that, under these rapidly shifting conditions, certain mistakes in economic and financial judgment were made by borrowers and lenders alike. There were also undoubtedly policy deficiencies and inconsistencies among the governments. In general, the mistakes made were to continue to lend and to borrow without devising a structured solution for dealing with the petrodollar recycling problem and to surrender to the assumption that oil prices would remain at their maximum levels, or continue to rise, with oil revenues continuing to flow.

Whatever perceptions prevailed about prices in the 1970s, the reality has turned out somewhat differently in the 1980s. There has been a significant decline in oil prices from the levels prevailing in the seventies. Far from erasing the previous enormous increases, the new levels remain, by longer term historical standards, very high. At the same time, there has been, contrary

---

[1]For a discussion of the petrodollar recycling problem, see David O. Beim, "Rescuing the LDCs," *Foreign Affairs* 55, no. 4 (July 1977): 717–31; Harold van B. Cleveland and W. H. Bruce Brittain, "Are the LDCs in Over Their Heads?" ibid.: 732–50; Richard Portes, "East Europe's Debt to the West: Interdependence is a Two-Way Street," ibid.: 751–82. See also Khodadad Farmanfarmaian, Armin Gutowski, Saburo Okita, Robert V. Roosa, and Carroll L. Wilson, "How Can the World Afford OPEC Oil?" *Foreign Affairs* 53, no. 2 (January 1975): 201–22.

[2]For an extended discussion of this topic, see Benjamin J. Cohen, in collaboration with Fabio Basagni, *Banks and the Balance of Payments: Private Lending in the International Adjustment Process* (Montclair, NJ: Allanheld, Osmun, 1981); Benjamin J. Cohen, "Balance-of-Payments Financing: Evolution of a Regime," in *International Regimes*, ed. Stephen D. Krasner (Ithaca, NY: Cornell University Press, 1983), pp. 315–36; and *Towards Full Employment and Price Stability*, A Report to the OECD by a Group of Independent Experts, chaired by Paul McCracken (Paris: Organization for Economic Cooperation and Development, 1977).

[3]See Guido Carli, *Why Banks Are Unpopular*, The 1976 Per Jacobsson Lecture (Washington, DC: International Monetary Fund, 1976).

to the expectations of some, a significant decline in the prices of other raw materials. More encompassingly, there has been a severe worldwide economic recession, albeit somewhat mitigated by a renewal of economic growth in the U.S. economy.

The problem in the financial realm that now engages us and that will engage us for some years is that of negotiating between the creditor countries of the industrialized world and the debtors of the developing world an orderly transition from the circumstances prevailing in the 1970s to those of the late 1980s.[4] In so doing, we also must give heed to the major task of guarding and strengthening, rather than undermining, our own and the world's banking system. Above all, the macropolicies we apply to this task must assure conditions for renewed, noninflationary, economic growth in the advanced industrial countries and also in the newly industrializing and developing countries. We need to provide as well the necessary mixture of economic and political disciplines applicable to each of these groups. The transitions we must effect through policy decisions and negotiating processes should be aimed at compatibility with the interdependence of the advanced and the developing countries. World economic and financial interdependence is a fact, and not merely an ideology.

Broadly speaking, there remains a fundamental difference in objectives today between the industrialized countries and an important segment of the developing world. They see the international debt and growth problems differently. By and large, it suits the industrialized world, on the one hand, to pursue sustained, relatively moderate economic growth in order not to reignite inflationary forces; on the other hand, severe economic pressures, and also social and political fragility, impel much of the developing world to press for rapid recovery and growth. Reconciling these outlooks by a variety of measures, with the inevitable trade-offs, is the core of our task in negotiating world order in the international debt area.

A major element of long-term significance that has emerged from the debt renegotiating experience of the past several years, and which is directly relevant to the negotiation of world order in a volatile and vulnerable international economic environment, may be characterized as the process of international lending-of-last-resort. I emphasize the *process* of lending in the absence of any institutional international lender-of-last-resort. No legally constituted international institution empowered to be or capable of acting as lender-of-last-resort exists, and thus none was available when, in the summer of 1982, the debt-servicing and repayment crisis broke.

In our individual national economies, we have a lender-of-last-resort: the central banks. The need these institutions fill is to take risks in a crisis that no other entity has the capacity or will to take. Only such a lender has,

---

[4]For a scholarly treatment of this general subject, see Jeffrey Sachs, "LDC Debt in the 1980s: Risk and Reforms," in *Crises in the Economic and Financial Structure*, ed. Paul Wachtel (Lexington, MA: Lexington Books, D. C. Heath, 1982), pp. 197–246.

or can create, the almost unlimited resources needed and is able to organize the elements necessary for dealing with a major crisis. In the United States we have the Federal Reserve System. However, we should not forget that we achieved this mechanism not so long ago in historical terms; only in 1913 was the Federal Reserve organized.[5]

In the absence of any institutionalized central bank at the world level, the International Monetary Fund (IMF) has emerged to fill the gap. Perhaps more precisely, the Fund saw the need for and seized the initiative in acting as the orchestrating instrument in a process of international lending-of-last-resort. One might ask the question whether it is now time that the current "orchestrator-of-the-solutions," namely the IMF, and the "lender-of-last-resort" concept be married. It may not work. There are undoubtedly many in high places in the world of international finance who would argue that a regime of informal cohabitation is more likely to be reasonably harmonious, and perhaps even more productive, than a marriage. Such a combined institutional role would be quite different from the IMF's earlier functions of monitoring the par value exchange-rate regime and providing short-term assistance to members in balance-of-payments difficulties.[6] The IMF's traditional policing role with respect to the exchange-rate regime under the 1944 Bretton Woods Agreement has virtually ceased since the elimination of the obligatory fixed exchange-rate system in 1973. Its traditional balance-of-payments assistance function and its new orchestrator-of-solutions role have been combined into an instrument still somewhat short of a lender-of-last-resort capacity. It is nonetheless a highly effective substitute for it.

There is a possible way to make it something more. An amendment to the Fund Articles that would provide for the allocation of new Special Drawing Rights (SDRs) to the Fund itself, not necessarily to its member governments, could bring the IMF closer to the status of lender-of-last-resort.[7] At the same time, it would leave the member governments, as is the case now, the ultimate source of decision as to whether and when to provide such additional liquidities to the international system. It sometimes has been said that money is not a subject of conversation in polite society. In the case of governments, though,

---

[5]See Charles P. Kindleberger, *Manias, Panics, and Crashes: A History of Financial Crises* (New York: Basic Books, 1978); and Jack Guttentag and Richard Herring, *The Lender-of-Last-Resort Function in an International Context*, Princeton University, Essays in International Finance No. 151 (Princeton, NJ: International Finance Section, Department of Economics, Princeton University, 1983).

[6]For a comprehensive discussion of the International Monetary Fund, see Jacob S. Dreyer, Gottfried Haberler, and Thomas D. Willett, eds., *The International Monetary System: A Time of Turbulence* (Washington, DC: American Enterprise Institute for Public Policy Research, 1982); and H. Johannes Witteveen, *Developing a New International Monetary System: A Long-Term View*, The 1983 Per Jacobsson Lecture (Washington, DC: International Monetary Fund, 1983).

[7]For the rules governing Special Drawing Rights, created by the IMF in 1969, see International Monetary Fund, *Articles of Agreement of the International Monetary Fund* (Washington, DC: International Monetary Fund, 1978); and International Monetary Fund, *By-Laws: Rules and Regulations*, 39th Issue (Washington, DC: International Monetary Fund, 1982).

money is perhaps the only reality. This being so, governments do not like to allow it to get beyond the reach of sovereign national authority.

In a world in which interdependence is a fact of life, where there is no institutional counterpart to national central banks, a process, at least, of lending-of-last-resort must evolve. Jacques de Larosière, the managing director of the IMF, and his colleagues have emerged as the instruments of this necessary evolution. They are not alone in this work, however, nor are they necessarily first to the rescue. When the Mexican minister of finance, Jesús Silva Herzog, descended on Washington in August 1982 to disclose how badly the Mexican treasury was faring—that it was unable to pay its debts as due and thus was on the verge of precipitating a massive international financial crisis—he headed straight for the U.S. Treasury, the Federal Reserve Board, and the IMF. This order of battle, so to speak, maximized the effect of a combined assault on the problem.[8]

However sympathetic the IMF at times may have been to providing immediate assistance itself, multilateral institutions are at their most effective when active bilateral, country-to-country support can be brought into play. The Federal Reserve Board, immediately recognizing the gravity of the Mexican position, was a key to mobilizing the attention and support of other major central banks around the world. It was also in a position, and perceived the need, to press the U.S. Treasury and the administration generally for a response adequate to the Mexican crisis.

Perhaps equally important was the concerted action of the IMF, the American financial authorities, and the major central banks abroad; this had the effect of encircling the private banking sector, both in the United States and elsewhere. As if in a military operation, these coordinated efforts virtually assured the "surrender" of the banks to official entreaties, or at the minimum their needed cooperation. The cooperative possibilities that lay in enhancing the interaction between public financial institutions and the private banking sector were clearly demonstrated in the immediate crisis-management phase of the debt explosion, and also in the more protracted negotiations that followed.

The importance of immediately and actively engaging the United States, including the U.S. banks, in containing the debt crisis was realized by the Mexicans from the beginning. The concern shown in Washington, too, indicated an acute awareness of the many intricate governmental and private relationships between Mexico and the United States, and also the expanding interrelationship of finance and foreign policy. The Mexican finance minister's visit appeared to cause the U.S. Treasury and the administration to recognize, more urgently than before, the need to mobilize larger international resources to deal with the debt crises of other debtor countries as well, particularly of Brazil and Argentina. The fact that the three largest debtors were in Latin America, at a time when Latin American problems were high on the U.S.

---

[8]For an extended account of the financial and political aspects of dealing with the Mexican debt predicament, see Joseph Kraft, *The Mexican Rescue* (New York: Group of Thirty, 1984).

agenda following the Falklands crisis, undoubtedly heightened Washington's attention.

The speed with which assistance was enlisted by the IMF and U.S. monetary authorities to prevent an outright interruption of Mexican debt service was remarkable. Not only did other central banks and finance ministries have to be approached and engaged, but also there were several hundred commercial banks with loans outstanding to the Mexican government and private Mexican borrowers that had to be contacted, consulted, and persuaded to enter into a major cooperative effort.

The scale of the resulting consultations and the efficiency with which they took place were possible only because there exists today a fairly widespread cadre of educated and broadly sophisticated international private bankers, as well as government officials. They come from Third World debtor countries as well as from the creditor countries. A number of the developing countries are today sufficiently sure of themselves to retain private investment banking houses in New York, London, or Paris, for example, to advise them on debt rollovers or on money management, and to provide marketplace financial and economic advice. Others are not, partly because of culturally related reasons of national pride, or reluctance, in some instances, to admit to their own limited expertise or experience.

A fair number of Third and First World bankers, participating in these international negotiations, have had experience in their respective central banks or government finance ministries, and with the IMF or International Bank for Reconstruction and Development (IBRD), the World Bank. They regularly keep in touch with one another for business purposes and see one another at the annual meetings of the IMF and the World Bank. These annual gatherings have developed into an unstructured and unofficial institution. For instance, the IMF meeting in Toronto in 1982, which followed the disclosure of the Mexican situation and preceded the cascade of threatened defaults elsewhere, played a significant part in creating an international consensus among governments, and between the private and public sectors, about the importance of mobilizing adequate resources to deal with the international debt problem.

This community of public and private professionals did not exist on such a scale even a generation ago. I believe it to have been an indispensable factor in making possible action by a large group of bankers and public officials, efficiently and in a brief time, to work out arrangements as complex as those required by the situation. The task they faced was complex: both to reschedule principal and interest payments about to fall due, first for Mexico and then for several other debtors, and to provide fresh money to enable the debtors to continue at least paying interest, and thus to avoid precipitating the consequences of a default for the world banking system.

By this process, the major money center banks in the United States, Europe, and Japan, and to some extent in other regions, were caught up in an international rescue and rescheduling effort of unprecedented proportions.

The large number of private banks involved reflected the breadth of the monetary recycling process and the dimensions of the task of controlling the situation. It also mirrored the format on which it had been possible to achieve this breadth, namely, the bank-syndication process. The major metropolitan money center banks, often including the private investment and merchant banks (generally the managers of large loan offerings), make these loans possible by inviting and organizing a wide array of other money center and also regional banks, domestic and foreign, to subscribe in amounts consistent with their size and resources.

When the managing money center banks in, for example, New York, San Francisco, London, Paris, or Frankfurt, which had earlier organized syndicates, sought to enlist the rescheduling cooperation of the syndicate participants, they found many regional and subregional banks, for whom international lending was a relatively small portion of business, to be reluctant. Knowing relatively little about the specific situations of Mexico and other debtor countries, these regional and subregional banks nonetheless sensed that they had little real choice but to agree to participate in the rescheduling effort. However, some of them were resistant to providing new funds. To induce them to do so required considerable exhortation by the U.S. Treasury and Federal Reserve, using the theme of self-interest of all the private sector banks in helping to preserve the international financial system, with all the consequences that would surely follow from damage to it.

Banks are always sensitive to their relations with public authorities, and the Federal Reserve in this instance was successful in encouraging the banks to "remain in the game." It did so by winking temporarily at the strict interpretation of regulations requiring banks to reserve against doubtful, or "nonperforming," loans.[9] Setting aside reserves is a very important element in bank management, as doing so has effects on profit-and-loss results and on balance sheets. An even more basic consideration for the large money center banks themselves, for whom international lending was a very important segment of business, was the longer term need to help keep their sovereign government clients, not to mention their private-sector industrial and commercial clients, financially viable. They felt considerable self-interest in cooperating to help keep the world financial system in good order. Failure to do so on their part, or on the part of any one of them, would almost surely be remembered for a long time by the debtor countries when the latter were finally restored to financial health. The regional and subregional banks naturally lacked this concern to the same degree, yet they had to take into account the maintenance of good business relationships with the big money center

---

[9]See, for example, "Sustainable Recovery: Setting the Stage," a speech delivered by Federal Reserve Board Chairman Paul A. Volcker before the New England Council, Boston, Massachusetts, November 16, 1982, mimeo., Board of Governors of the Federal Reserve System, Washington, DC.

banks. Here we glimpse the role of power, even without its actual exercise, in banking relationships. The managers of money, we see, have no choice but to lead lives as complex and as replete with conflicts as those of politicians.

What took place in the particular case of Mexico, an IMF-supervised all-party negotiation, became the format for succeeding situations, namely the Brazilian and Argentine, among others. No two of these situations were exactly alike. Management of the eastern European debt crisis that had emerged some two years earlier also involved a high degree of international cooperation, both public and private. The renegotiating and rescheduling of those debts even more clearly involved important foreign policy considerations, although the monetary magnitudes at stake were not so massive as in the Latin American cases.

The process that developed during the Mexican negotiation established a general pattern. Steering committees of creditor banks were set up for dealing with particular debtor countries. The IMF worked in close collaboration with both creditors and debtors, and with particular governments, in the process of formulating specific economic and financial recovery programs for each case. These, necessarily and unhappily, required austerity. Meanwhile, steps were taken by the IMF and leading member governments to mobilize international resources to help lubricate these programs, principally in the form of an overall increase in country quotas in the Fund and, in addition, by organizing special borrowing facilities under IMF administration. The result was an unprecedented and extraordinary collaboration for the sake of international order. The cooperation shown thus far among the public authorities, the money center banks, and the regional and subregional banks has been an outstanding feature of the management of the debt crisis.

I would like now to turn to the substantive elements of a framework within which to deal with the international debt problem in the future. While each country's debt and repayment situation can best be handled separately, and while the economic circumstances of each are different, there is a need for an internationally recognized set of guidelines within which each country's problems can be resolved in a more orderly fashion. I regard a greater clarification of the overall debt problem and of the guiding principles to be applied to its solution to be an essential component of sustained world economic recovery and growth. It is important, in any effort of international problem solving, that we understand our goals and know the modes of national and international behavior that we should follow in reaching those goals. In order to generate and sustain the necessary momentum for worldwide recovery, which arose in 1983 and 1984 in the United States and is developing more slowly in Europe, we must be able to rely on the absence of major debt defaults and extended moratoria. If we continue at present on an ad hoc basis, with year-in and year-out individual renegotiations and reschedulings and no recognized general principles for dealing with the basic debt problem itself, we will have hanging over us serious uncertainties about the future functioning of the world economy.

Not the least of the costs of the present course is that the banks, the governments, and the international institutions are kept involved in huge amounts of unproductive activity. Governments in less developed countries already complain about the intrinsic costs of rescheduling, the fees that banks charge them, and the enormous amount of their attention that has to be given to the debt problem. The burden is heavy on everyone. What, then, do I propose in order to try to alleviate it?

One line of thinking would make use of the traditional techniques of bankers for dealing with debt problems, notably, debt consolidation. By "consolidation," I mean turning various relatively short-term loans into longer loans, with terms, for example, of ten or twelve years or more. This transformation has gradually been taking place. The final maturities on many debts that have been rescheduled during 1983, 1984, and 1985, by and large, are considerably longer than those prevailing in the summer of 1982.

The extension of principal payments into longer maturities must, at current rates of interest, be accompanied by at least a partial long-term consolidation of interest payments as well. Arrangements that involve paying interest partly in cash and partly by adding to the principal outstanding help to ease current pressures on the debtors. However, this does not diminish their total obligations and may even increase them over time, making the total of principal plus interest ultimately larger.

The suggestion of imposing ceilings on interest payable by developing countries occasionally surfaces. It is true that today we have some financing in the U.S. capital market that provides for variable rates, with caps on these interest rates if they rise in excess of agreed figures. To apply this practice generally to foreign debt outstanding, however, would give it an entirely different dimension and would have a severe impact on the cash flows and earnings of our domestic banks. Moreover, it would probably be politically difficult to provide ceilings on interest rates payable by foreign debtors but to deny the same limits to domestic debtors. Measures such as these are no substitute for basic macropolicies that will bring about reductions in interest rate levels.

In order broadly to consolidate short- and medium-term debt into longer term maturities and, in addition, to add significant portions of interest to principal, there might be required an explicit commitment on the part of the central banks of the major creditor countries to discount these sovereign obligations, thus accepting them as a basis for borrowing, on some favorable basis when presented to them in the future by private creditor banks. Since the cash flows of the private banks would be adversely affected by stretchouts of principal and interest, the ability of these banks to provide credits in the future to their domestic customers might be diminished. So also would be their ability to finance internationally, let alone perhaps to raise needed new capital for themselves. Any weakening of the banking capacity of the United States, or of any of the industrialized countries, would hardly be a contribution to the world economy as a whole. The readiness of American and other banks to accept various stretch-out formulae thus might be considerably enhanced by central bank assurances regarding the liquidity, if required, of stretched-out obligations in their portfolios.

While the above steps are all within the scope of traditional banking practice, apart perhaps from possible central bank guarantees of future liquidity, a further step, outside the sphere of banking, would involve a major policy change by the IMF. I have in mind the SDR facility of the Fund, to which I alluded earlier. I believe an expansion of this facility would strengthen the present international financial system and could add significantly to the possibilities of ameliorating the world debt burden.

The SDR facility of the IMF is designed to be used, under specified conditions, to increase international monetary reserves and thus to augment the liquidity of the international monetary system when required. This SDR facility, as it now is, would seem to be an appropriate and effective contributor to the totality of measures available for easing the world debt problem. Why has there been so little interest in using it?

I would venture the guess that the lack of interest thus far in authorizing a new allocation of SDRs arises from two fears: first, the possible rekindling of inflationary forces still lurking in the international economy and, second, the risk of undermining the resolve of debtor countries to put their economies on a firmer footing by means of internal policy measures. Some debtor countries, it is thought, might look to new SDR allocations as a device to shield them for a time from the consequences of their own unwise economic policies, as well as from adverse world economic conditions.

In light of events since this facility was established in 1969, we should ask ourselves whether it is truly desirable that SDRs, when created, be distributed to member countries in proportion to their IMF quotas. It has been the hope of various monetary reformers that the SDR become the principal reserve asset of the international monetary system.[10] At the time of its creation, there were solid reasons not only for the existence of the facility itself, for possible liquidity needs, but also for proportionate allocations being made to all IMF member countries. However, the nature of the liquidity problem subsequently changed. Generally speaking, international liquidity grew sharply as the private banking sector became a major source of liquidity creation in the flourishing international deposit and lending activities of the 1960s and,

---

[10]See J. J. Polak, *Thoughts on an International Monetary Fund Based Fully on the SDR*, Pamphlet Series No. 28 (Washington, DC: International Monetary Fund, 1979); and Peter B. Kenen, "Use of the SDR to Supplement or Substitute for Other Means of Finance," in *International Money and Credit: The Policy Roles*, ed. George M. von Furstenberg (Washington, DC: International Monetary Fund, 1983), pp. 327–60.

particularly, the 1970s. The SDR, as the principal reserve asset, did not materialize. Instead the SDR has been utilized by the Fund for its own operations and by member countries as a component, but not the main component, of their reserves.

A new allocation of SDRs would require, in accordance with Article XVIII of the amended Fund Articles of Agreement, the following:

> In all its decisions with respect to the allocation and cancellation of special drawing rights the Fund shall seek to meet the long-term global need, as and when it arises, to supplement existing reserve assets in such manner as will promote the attainment of its purposes and will avoid economic stagnation and deflation as well as excess demand and inflation in the world.

As events have unfolded in the current international debt crisis, it has become increasingly clear that the needs of a group of countries (i.e., the less developed countries, or LDCs) can create a global need in that the magnitude of the adverse impact of LDC debt imposes a strong negative influence on the industrialized countries as well.

How is it possible to reconcile what appears to have become a need for additional reserve assets in a number of major developing countries with the large liquidities already in the international system? One cannot ignore the world's wariness about action that could stimulate inflationary forces.

If my financial antennae detect the atmosphere accurately, the major money center banks currently are disposed not only to restructure and reschedule debts where necessary but also to put up new money in certain instances to the maximum extent possible, on condition that the debtors work out monetary, fiscal, and budgetary programs acceptable to the IMF and make progress in achieving the agreed-upon objectives. These normally include improvements in their balance-of-payments positions.[11] In short, "IMF conditionality," however one may view it as an expression of "order," necessarily lies at the core of a continuing process of international lending-of-last-resort, involving public and private sector cooperation as its essential components.

If the Fund Articles were amended so as to permit SDR allocations to be made to the Fund directly, rather than to member countries, the Fund could then have within its coffers very substantial sums available for use from time to time by individual countries *within the framework of IMF conditionality*, rather than outside of it. This would help to ensure that these internationally created liquidities would be used in accordance with consistent

---

[11]On the character of these requested adjustment programs, see John Williamson, *The Lending Policies of the International Monetary Fund* (Washington, DC: Institute for International Economics, 1982); and John Williamson, ed., *IMF Conditionality* (Washington, DC: Institute for International Economics, 1983).

economic and financial policies and under Fund surveillance, including measures designed to contain the possible inflationary impact of occasional SDR creation and usage.

It could still be argued, of course, that with the best management imaginable on the part of the Fund and with the fullest cooperation of debtor countries, these arrangements would still constitute an uncertain reed upon which to lean in controlling the possible inflationary tendencies arising out of major increases in international liquidity. We must bear in mind, however, that while newly created international reserves or liquidities might contribute to inflationary forces, despite effective IMF management, there could also be disruptions in debt service or defaults that might force creditor countries, on their part, to create new liquidities for their own banking systems. A cynic might ask whether our choice lies between actions tempting inflationary consequences at the developing-world side of the international economic spectrum or possibly resorting to inflationary risks at the industrialized-world side of it. Clearly, everyone—developing and industrialized countries alike—must persistently work to bring the debt problem under control without inflation. A too pervasive fear of it, particularly at a time when inflationary forces seem to be receding, could result in paralyzing consequences for needed growth.

We must bear in mind that multiyear infusions of new resources into the economies of many debtor countries will be essential to help bolster policies of long-term world development. Improvements in the current accounts of several developing country debtors have occurred, but this improvement still leaves major debtors having to allocate very large proportions of their current export earnings to servicing external debts, rather than to restoring their previous import levels. These imports have consequent beneficial effects for the exports of the industrialized countries as well as for the increase of the export capacities of the developing countries. It is difficult at this juncture to be certain of how the required infusions of new capital can be provided without new resources being made available via the IMF, with the private sector acting in cooperation.

One danger of making new SDR allocations directly to the Fund, instead of to member countries, is the possible temptation on the part of some parliaments to regard this step as a substitute for facing the domestic political problems involved in increasing country quotas for additions to the Fund's basic capital. Attitudes in the U.S. Congress toward the IMF and World Bank are not as supportive as they might be. To help ensure the continued commitment of member countries, various formulae could be devised for tying together SDR allocations to the Fund in fixed proportion to simultaneous increases voted by the member governments in country capital quotas. Thus, governments would not be let off the hook of their responsibility to provide for the basic capital resource needs of the IMF.

The Fund already has a limited amount of SDRs in its own coffers. Since 1978, when the Second Amendment to the IMF Articles went into effect, member countries have paid up to 25 percent of their increases in Fund quotas in the form of SDRs, rather than in gold. Under this amendment, any obligations that had required gold payments by the member countries henceforth are satisfied with SDRs. My proposal to make allocations directly to the Fund, rather than to the member countries, could augment this resource very considerably.

Any proposed amendment of the Fund Articles is likely to provoke protracted debate and take considerable time to negotiate and enact. One possible way to meet this probable difficulty would be for member countries to agree on new allocations of SDRs in accordance with present rules, but with their agreement to be based on readiness on their part to lend such a new allocation of SDRs to the Fund for the purposes I have described. This arrangement would get around the problem of delay in obtaining an amendment to the Articles. At the same time, it would not preclude a more permanent rearrangement of the SDR facility, a rearrangement that would not only be sound but also give greater flexibility to the Fund in dealing with future reserve and liquidity problems.

I might say parenthetically that, when I consulted a leading expert of the IMF about the idea of allocations being made directly to the Fund rather than to the member countries, he reminded me that this proposal would come close to John Maynard Keynes's original concept of creating an international clearing union and of using an international currency, "bancor," in its operations.[12] This should add intellectual respectability, as well as controversy, to the concept!

A general framework for dealing with the international debt problem along the lines I have indicated would contribute significantly to meeting a closely related vital need of the developing world: namely, the reestablishment or the initial establishment, as the case may be, of an economic and political environment that would invite the flow from abroad of direct industrial, agricultural, and commercial investment. Only the developing country governments themselves, in the last analysis, can provide the climate necessary to induce a satisfactory inflow of the direct private investment they need.

Such private investment, by companies and other entities willing to risk ownership in developing countries, is critical to the most important objective of all, that of integrating the measures taken for dealing with the debt problem with measures needed for stimulating and sustaining noninflationary economic growth on a world scale. The problems of debt and growth should be viewed as two sides of a single coin. Only economic growth of an essentially noninflationary character would pay off the current level of international debt in

---

[12]See R. F. Harrod, *The Life of John Maynard Keynes* (London: Macmillan, 1952), pp. 526–32, 541–72; and Richard N. Gardner, *Sterling-Dollar Diplomacy: The Origins and the Prospects of Our International Economic Order* (New York: McGraw-Hill, 1969), pp. 58, 103, 125, 273, 276, 279.

real terms and also create new real wealth. In recent years, inflation has contributed heavily to the paying off of debt, in considerably less than real terms.

In the absence of adequate real economic growth, our efforts to negotiate world order in the financial sphere are likely to consist of not much more than a continuous whittling down of the present nominal level of obligations over an extended period of years. In that case, the possibility would continuously hang over us that, on the one hand, the creditor countries would sustain heavy real losses over time or, on the other hand, some major developing countries may not be able to withstand the erosion of their social and political structures because of the dimensions and pressures of debt servicing.

One of the important operating requirements of the effort to integrate the handling of debt with economic growth would seem to be an even closer institutional coupling of the IMF and the World Bank than traditionally has existed. This is now receiving a considerable amount of thought in those two great institutions which, after all, live right next door to each other.[13] Each one, the IMF and World Bank, is capable of mobilizing large resources, public and private, in pursuing its particular mission. While the initial and traditional task of the IMF has been in part the provision of short-term (gradually, longer term) balance-of-payments assistance to member countries in need of it, the World Bank group has dedicated itself to project and, sometimes, to program financing for development purposes. The main task ahead may be, with the skill of magicians, to integrate the functions of these two institutions in transforming financial debt into economic growth.

The need is to enhance the ability of the IMF and the World Bank, in unison, to provide the institutional leadership necessary for encouraging consistent financial and economic policies on the part of their member countries and, in addition, to play the key public and private resource-mobilization roles of which they have shown themselves capable. Obviously, this can be considered realistic only if the U.S. government and the governments of other major member countries are in strong support.

What I have said has been under the general rubric of negotiating world order. We live in a world that is rife with random, as well as organized, disorder and violence. At the same time, the scope for negotiating processes that function in the interests of order, in the sense of bringing about orderly transitions, is enormous. Keeping the world in reasonable equilibrium, with over $800 billion in foreign debts and credits of varying qualities confronting each other warily across the international balance sheet, is a large task—large enough to convince us that the process of negotiating order must surely be a growth industry.

---

[13]See A. W. Clausen (president, The World Bank and International Finance Corporation), "Priority Issues for 1984," remarks delivered before the European Management Forum, Davos, Switzerland, January 26, 1984, World Bank press release.

FOR FURTHER READING

On the background of the international monetary system and the role of public and private financial institutions, see Richard N. Gardner, *Sterling-Dollar Diplomacy: The Origins and the Prospects of Our International Economic Order*; Benjamin J. Cohen, in collaboration with Fabio Basagni, *Banks and the Balance of Payments: Private Lending in the International Adjustment Process*; and Jacob S. Dreyer, Gottfried Haberler, and Thomas D. Willett, eds., *The International Monetary System: A Time of Turbulence*, cited in the footnotes. See also Edward S. Mason and Robert E. Asher, *The World Bank Since Bretton Woods* (Washington, DC: Brookings Institution, 1973); and Benjamin J. Cohen, *Organizing the World's Money: The Political Economy of International Monetary Relations* (New York: Basic Books, 1977).

For further readings on the Third World debt problem and its international management, see the following studies: Graham Bird, *The International Monetary System and the Less Developed Countries* (New York: Praeger, 1978); Lawrence G. Franko and Marilyn J. Seiber, eds., *Developing Country Debt* (New York: Pergamon Press, 1979); International Monetary Fund, *External Indebtedness of Developing Countries*, Occasional Paper No. 3 (Washington, DC: International Monetary Fund, 1981); Chandra S. Hardy, *Rescheduling Developing-country Debts, 1956–1981: Lessons and Recommendations*, Monograph No. 15 (Washington, DC: Overseas Development Council, 1982); Tony Killick, ed., *Adjustment and Financing in the Developing World: The Role of the International Monetary Fund* (Washington, DC: International Monetary Fund and Overseas Development Institute, 1982); William R. Cline, *International Debt and the Stability of the World Economy* (Washington, DC: Institute for International Economics, 1983), and his *International Debt: Systemic Risk and Policy Response* (Washington, DC: Institute for International Economics, 1984); Richard S. Dale and Richard P. Mattione, *Managing Global Debt* (Washington, DC: Brookings Institution, 1983); *Columbia Journal of Transnational Law* 23, no. 1 (1984), containing articles on "Sovereign Debt Restructuring"; Richard E. Feinberg and Valeriana Kallab, eds., *Uncertain Future: Commercial Banks and the Third World* (New Brunswick, NJ: Transaction Books, 1984); Inter-American Development Bank, *External Debt and Economic Development in Latin America: Background and Prospects* (Washington, DC: Inter-American Development Bank, 1984); Irving S. Friedman, *The World Debt Dilemma: Managing Country Risk* (Washington, DC: Council for International Banking Studies/Philadelphia: Robert Morris Associates, 1984); John H. Makin, *The Global Debt Crisis: America's Growing Involvement* (New York: Basic Books, 1984); Paul Mentré, *The Fund, Commercial Banks, and Member Countries* (Washington, DC: International Monetary Fund, 1984); and Penelope Hartland-Thunberg and Charles K. Ebinger, eds., *Banks, Petrodollars, and Sovereign Debtors: Blood from a Stone?* (Lexington, MA: Lexington Books, 1986).

STRUCTURES AND PROCESSES OF WORLD ORDER

The Global Foundations for a Diplomacy of Consensus

ALAN K. HENRIKSON

Negotiating world order, as the process of multilateral regime making is termed in this book, must integrate two processes which some commentators have considered to be almost incompatible. "The tension," Abba Eban has observed of the kind of negotiation that often occurs in international organizations, "is between the diplomatic and the parliamentary principles. These cannot easily be reconciled. The diplomatic principle tells me that I need my adversary's agreement. The parliamentary principle tells me that I do not need his agreement; I can secure his defeat and humiliation by a majority vote. The temperament and style necessary for these two exercises are totally divergent."[1]

This distinction between two types of negotiation is deeper than the contrast between private and public diplomacy, or between persuasion and propaganda. It is a contrast of fundamental purpose. If the basic purpose of diplomacy is to engender confidence and to foster lasting international relationships, the objective of parliamentarianism on an international scale is to elaborate world law and to establish global institutions. What we have termed "negotiating world order" comprehends both the diplomatic and the legislative processes of international ordering. Its ambition is the achievement, through multilateral negotiation, of long-term, general international arrangements regarding the principles, norms, rules, and procedures of international behavior—international regimes—whose availability can facilitate the short-term solution and settlement of specific international problems as they arise. As Robert Keohane has noted, such regimes can make possible cooperation

---

[1]Abba Eban, *The New Diplomacy: International Affairs in the Modern Age* (New York: Random House, 1983), p. 280. For a more optimistic view of the possibility of combining the two processes, see Philip C. Jessup, "Parliamentary Diplomacy: An Examination of the Legal Quality of the Rules of Procedure of Organs of the United Nations," *Recueil des Cours* 89 (1956): 185–320. Jessup attributes the first use of the term, "parliamentary diplomacy," to Dean Rusk, at the time assistant secretary of state for United Nations affairs. See Dean Rusk, "Parliamentary Diplomacy—Debate *v.* Negotiation," *World Affairs Interpreter* 26, no. 2 (Summer 1955): 121–22.

even on "issues that were not thought about at the time of their creation."[2]
For diplomats today, foresight is becoming more important than insight.
Architecture is more necessary than artifice. "The principal problem for most
contemporary negotiators is not to outwit their adversaries, but rather to create
a structure out of a large mass of information wherein it is possible to apply
human wit," Gilbert Winham has observed. "The classical diplomat's technique of the management of people through guile has given way to the
management of people through the creation of system and structure."[3]

Because the participants in the negotiation of world order typically are
representatives of sovereign, independent states, they are not bound by any
previously established constitutional system to adhere to the results of their
negotiations. The compliance of nations is, in other words, unforced and
voluntary. This is a historic problem which proponents of world order still
must face. Since the era of a single, hierarchical Christian commonwealth,
symbolically united by pope and emperor, the interstate system has been
decentralized. The Peace of Westphalia (1648) marked the beginning of a
new pluralistic order of free and equal states, whose bonds to each other
depended not on their inherited status but on their own independently given
consent.[4] Thereafter, any international regime had to rest on the decentralized
enforcement that results from the practice of reciprocity—that is, an implicit
or explicit system of rules of interchange based on the fear of retaliation and
the expectation of recompense.[5] This is what is usually meant by the obser-
vation that international law is, to some extent at least, *self*-enforcing. Given
the survival of the Westphalian system into our time, it is not surprising that
most of the fourteen areas of international order making discussed in detail
in this volume fall within the category of "negotiated, international" regimes,
in the classification outlined in the Introduction.

Negotiated international regimes are not, however, the only possible
kinds of world order. Reflection upon the broad pattern of order in world
history enables us to envision a much wider range of possibilities, some of
which may be useful in devising international structures for the future. By
employing the matrix of world-ordering structures and processes presented
in the Introduction, we can exhibit the plenitude of world order in its considerable variety. This comparative approach may enable us to identify still
more precisely the distinctive aspects of international regimes that, through

---

[2]Robert O. Keohane, *After Hegemony: Cooperation and Discord in the World Political Economy* (Princeton, NJ: Princeton University Press, 1984), p. 247.

[3]Gilbert R. Winham, "Negotiation as a Management Process," *World Politics* 30, no. 1 (October 1977): 88–89.

[4]Julius Goebel, Jr., *The Equality of States: A Study in the History of Law* (New York: Columbia University Press, 1923); Leo Gross, "The Peace of Westphalia, 1648–1948," *American Journal of International Law* 42, no. 1 (January 1948): 20–41.

[5]Arthur Lenhoff, "Reciprocity: The Legal Aspect of a Perennial Idea," *Northwestern University Law Review* 49 (1954–55): 619–41, 752–79; Robert O. Keohane, "Reciprocity in International Relations," *International Organization* 40, no. 1 (Winter 1986): 1–27.

the procedures of multilateral diplomacy, are negotiated. As suggested in the Introduction, negotiation may be, in fact, a widely pervasive phenomenon, not limited only to regimes established by negotiation but present also in systems that we would characterize as supranational or hegemonic.

As illustrative cases of the negotiated international type, represented by the upper left square of Figure 1 (see p. xxi), let us select, preparatory to more detailed discussion of these and other cases below, an old one and a new one: the International Telecommunication Union (ITU) and the Non-Proliferation Treaty (NPT). Both of these regimes, like other instances of the negotiated type, are essentially voluntaristic. As Leonard Marks emphasizes in his account, the international order which the ITU institutionalizes is "based upon the principle of the sovereignty of each country. There is no judge who will say a member country has violated the law; since there are no penalties, no country can be fined for failure to observe the regulations." Joseph Nye, prefacing his discussion of the NPT regime, observes that the international political system remains "essentially an anarchic order." In such a "realm of self-help," a nation has an implied right to choose whatever form of self-defense it wishes, including nuclear weapons. If generalized, the exercise of this right would result in a "world of porcupines"—in a sense, a Westphalian system armed throughout.

In the fields of both global communications and nuclear deterrence, a certain amount of actual inequality, though not necessarily also hierarchy, is inevitable. Some large countries, because of their size and position, simply require more extensive broadcasting facilities than others. Certain states, particularly powerful or particularly vulnerable, believe they and not others must have nuclear weapons. The only way for the "have" countries to persuade the "have-not" countries to accept an inequitable distribution of facilities or weapons is through general, virtually universal negotiation at ITU conferences or NPT review meetings. Noncompliance, if sufficiently flagrant or wide-spread, could destroy the ITU and NPT. As the basic theme of the Marks chapter ("it takes two to communicate") posits, telecommunication presup-poses cooperation. There must be an explicit system of reciprocation, "rules of the road." In order to adjust and formalize these rules, international con-ferences periodically are necessary. As the Nye chapter demonstrates, the price of living with nuclear weapons today is an active, aggressive diplomatic effort on the part of the weapons-possessing states to convince the rest of the world's countries that they should continue to live without them.

Rarely is a multilateral regime initially negotiated or subsequently main-tained without at least a hint of coercion. To the extent that force displaces consent in this process of reaching agreement among nations, the resulting arrangement is an "imposed, international" order, a category represented by the middle left square in Figure 1. Outright military force need not always be used for compulsion to occur. The ability of strong, rich, advanced coun-tries to offer (or deny) to relatively weak, poor, underdeveloped societies the various material advantages they desire also can have a coercive effect. An offer to launch a communications satellite for them or the refusal to sell them the fuel needed for running a nuclear reactor, especially if coordinated with other rewards or punishments, might well determine the weaker countries' political orientations and diplomatic alignments. Both the ITU and NPT regimes thus almost inevitably reflect the predominance in the telecommunication and nuclear fields of the largest users of those technologies—the industrialized countries. Nonetheless, the nature of the international system requires that they negotiate to secure others' general acceptance of their positions.

At one time, the great powers were able to impose their will on lesser states without apology. An architect of the Congress of Vienna system, Lord Castlereagh, frankly stated that he "could not harbor any moral or political repugnance" against the act of handing Saxony over to Prussia, since the king of Saxony had "put himself in the position of having to be sacrificed to the future tranquillity of Europe."[6] The twentieth century has its own examples of great-power determination of the fate of small states. Eban, with implied regard for the possible fate of his own country, has observed that "the same principle—that small nations must be sacrificed for the general good—was to inspire the notorious Munich settlement." The sacrifice of Czechoslovakia's Sudetenland to Germany by France, Great Britain, and Italy at Munich in September 1938 has been a powerful negative object lesson for the statesmen of Israel. "They handed Czechoslovakia over," David Ben-Gurion remarked in the immediate aftermath of the Munich Conference. "Why shouldn't they do the same with us?"[7] About all that can be said for such imposed arrangements is that they were formally achieved through diplomacy.

Historically, the most common instances of imposed international orders are the settlements that follow wars. The 1919 Versailles Treaty, which German nationalists considered a Diktat (although German representatives did sign it), is the most important modern example of such nonnegotiated postwar settlements. The Germans earlier had acted similarly in giving peace to Russia via the Treaty of Brest-Litovsk and to Romania via the Treaty of Bucharest. The Teheran, Yalta, and Potsdam conferences during World War II, at which the Casablanca "unconditional surrender" formula was applied to Germany and Japan, also laid the basis for what was, in effect, an imposed peace, even if ultimately a beneficial one for most Germans and Japanese. Not only were the future interests of the Axis states lightly disposed of at those meetings, but it has been charged that a number of friendly governments, particularly Poland and Nationalist China, also were betrayed by them.[8] The accumulated legacy of these controversial episodes of big-power diplomatic history from World Wars I and II has greatly strengthened the doctrine of the

---

[6]Guglielmo Ferrero, *The Reconstruction of Europe: Talleyrand and the Congress of Vienna, 1814–1815*, trans. Theodore R. Jaeckel (New York: G. P. Putnam's Sons, 1941), p. 178, quoted in Eban, *New Diplomacy*, p. 245.

[7]Eban, *New Diplomacy*, p. 245; Dan Kurzman, *Ben-Gurion: Prophet of Fire* (New York: Simon and Schuster, 1983), p. 217.

[8]See, for example, William Henry Chamberlin, *America's Second Crusade* (Chicago: Henry Regnery, 1950), chap. 9, "The Munich Called Yalta: War's End."

sovereign equality of states, more particularly, the determination of every nation, whether small or large, to participate in all international decisions that affect it.

At the present time, the suggestion of an "imposed settlement" is made most frequently in discussions of peacemaking in the Middle East. The idea remains a particular horror for Israeli officials, who consistently have preferred to represent themselves in direct dealings with their neighbors, rather than to subject themselves to the risks of great-power dictation at multilateral conferences, inspired by the objective of a "comprehensive peace." The Geneva Peace Conference on the Middle East, which convened in December 1973 under the joint chairmanship of the United States and the Soviet Union, was the first occasion at which the Israeli and Arab governments met at the foreign minister level.[9] Any suggestion of a Soviet-American diplomatic "condominium," reminiscent of Yalta or, more remotely, of Munich, would be completely unacceptable to most parties in the Middle East today. In consequence, the great-power or Congress of Vienna approach, however tempting, is likely to prove of limited effectiveness in the future.

The bottom square in Figure 1—"automatic, international" order—is the opposite of the preceding one. While the basic pluralistic and egalitarian structure of the international system remains the same, the processes involved—imposition versus automaticity—differ in the degree of statesmanly control required. This difference may be more apparent than real, however. The seeming nondirectiveness of an international ordering system such as the classical European balance of power, for example, may reflect the operation of an international institution so well established that the moves of the game can be made by its players almost reflexively. The workings of the European international balance during much of the nineteenth century did exhibit a high degree of automaticity. If states in a multipolar system are all nonrevolutionary, roughly equivalent in strength, and in intimate cultural and political contact with each other, their relations can be somewhat self-equilibrating.[10] Even on the global scale, it has been argued, the plurality and equivalence of states generate a natural tendency toward stability. According to the concept of a pentapolar world order, articulated by Richard M. Nixon and Henry A. Kissinger, the postwar bipolar balance between the United States and the Soviet Union is giving way to a global equilibrium of five major power centers: North America, the Soviet bloc, a united Western Europe, Japan, and the People's Republic of China.[11] The result of their interaction has been the

[9]Eban, *New Diplomacy*, p. 210.

[10]On the European balance-of-power system, see Edward V. Gulick, *Europe's Classical Balance of Power: A Case History of One of the Great Concepts of European Statecraft* (New York: W. W. Norton, 1967); Henry A. Kissinger, *A World Restored* (New York: Universal Library, 1964); Ludwig Dehio, *The Precarious Balance: Four Centuries of the European Power Struggle*, trans. Charles Fullman (New York: Alfred A. Knopf, 1962).

[11]Richard M. Nixon, remarks to midwestern news media executives, Kansas City, Missouri, July 6, 1971, *Public Papers of the Presidents of the United States: Richard Nixon, 1971* (Washington, DC: U.S. Government Printing Office, 1972). pp. 802–13; Henry A. Kissinger, *American Foreign Policy*, 3rd ed. (New York: W. W. Norton, 1977), pp. 128–29.

basis of a "structure of peace" less dependent on the solitary exertions of the United States or the Western alliance. To that same degree, the resulting order has seemed automatic. Viewed differently, however, such an order requires the deepest involvement of diplomats, for the highest premium is placed on the accurate reading of the changes that occur in the balance.

On the regional international level as well, systems of order sometimes can have a self-equilibrating character. The organizational structure of the North Atlantic Treaty Organization (NATO), for instance, rests in part on the historic equilibrating effect of the British-French-German relationship and also the "North Atlantic Triangle" involving Great Britain, the United States, and Canada.[12] U.S. relations with Latin America, too, have been premised on a systemic equilibrium of forces—a "dialogue between thirty-one developing countries and one developed country," as Alejandro Orfila characterizes it. Before the establishment of a truly hemisphere-wide Pan American system, as his chapter on the politics of the Organization of American States (OAS) points out, there were lesser, subregional balances that reinforced international order in various parts of the hemisphere, notably in Central America and in the South American Southern Cone. These geopolitical concepts are entrenched in the Latin American statesmanly mind.

In a distant region of the world that until recently has not been subjected to conventional Western balance-of-power analysis, namely, Southeast Asia, there also seem to be endemic factors that work with an appearance of automaticity to equilibrate a regional system. Leonard Unger, in his account of the formation of the Association of Southeast Asian Nations (ASEAN), writes of the emergent "organic" unity of those states, counterbalanced against each other and joined informally in a common front against an expansionist Vietnam. The diplomacy of the new regional grouping is extremely subtle. "As a reflection of its wisdom in general and a cold assessment of the military balance," Unger notes, "ASEAN has kept open the door for a direct dialogue with Vietnam," even offering accession to the ASEAN Treaty of Amity and Cooperation. Almost intuitively, the statesmen of Southeast Asia adjust their policies, with an efficiency suggestive of automaticity, to the constantly shifting forces of the area.

Moving to the second column of Figure 1, let us consider "negotiated, supranational" orders. Supranationality involves the collective exercise of authority through a unified, elevated institution. For many of the authors in this book, the explicit or implicit standard of reference for this highly centralized type of international organization, created by negotiation, is the European Economic Community (EEC), established by the 1957 Treaty of Rome.

---

[12]On Canadian North Atlantic triangular thinking, see Escott Reid, *Time of Fear and Hope: The Making of the North Atlantic Treaty, 1947–1949* (Toronto: McClelland and Stewart, 1977), p. 139; also Alan K. Henrikson, "The Creation of the North Atlantic Alliance," in John F. Reichart and Steven R. Sturm, eds., *American Defense Policy*, 5th ed. (Baltimore: Johns Hopkins University Press, 1982), p. 305.

The EEC's supranationality is limited, but it is manifest in its being able to act decisively with less than a unanimous vote, to interact directly with the citizenry of member states, and to engage freely in negotiations with foreign governments.[13] It stands as the leading example today of the functional integration of states, which neither the OAS nor ASEAN, for example, yet has achieved. "Perhaps the EEC is too advanced to be our model," Unger quotes Singapore Prime Minister Lee Kuan Yew as acknowledging.

Nonetheless, especially in certain confined, functional areas of interest, negotiated supranational order remains a plausible goal. That type of order is not so rare as often is assumed. In the North American context, an example of limited supranationality has existed quietly since the beginning of the century in the International Joint Commission (IJC), a binational U.S.-Canadian institution. John Roberts in his chapter cites, as the very "keystone" of the Canadian government's present approach to the handling of the acid rain problem, the 1909 Boundary Waters Treaty which established the IJC. By committing the two neighbors not to disregard the interests of the other in the realm of water control, Roberts points out, this negotiated treaty amounted to "a voluntary limitation on sovereignty." While not endowed with impressive executive authority, the IJC makes its decisions collectively—not "along national lines," as Roberts explains, but rather "in a spirit of collegial objectivity" on the basis of "jointly established facts." He views this kind of institution as the best hope for evolving into a "management system" needed for dealing with international environmental questions generally, not only between Canada and the United States but also between other neighboring countries in other regions of the world.

A newer example of a negotiation-formed supranationality, as yet not institutionally realized, is the International Seabed Authority outlined in the United Nations Convention on the Law of the Sea. To consist of an assembly, council, and secretariat, the projected authority will have the power, as Tommy Koh indicates in his chapter, to require private mining companies in certain circumstances to sell their technology to competitors. The potentially coercive nature of this regime, whose founding document most nations have signed but which few have as yet ratified, has caused the current U.S. administration to characterize the convention as "hopelessly flawed."[14] Whether the International Seabed Authority eventually can become established, without further international negotiation and adjustment, remains to be seen.

---

[13]On the powers of the EEC, see Intergovernmental Conference on the Common Market and Euratom, *Treaty Establishing the European Economic Community and Connected Documents* (1962); Juliet Lodge, ed., *Institutions and Policies of the European Community* (New York: St. Martin's Press, 1983); and Dennis Swann, *The Economics of the Common Market* (Harmondsworth, England: Penguin Books, 1984), chap. 2, "The Community Decision-making Institutions."

[14]United Nations, *The Law of the Sea: Official Text of the United Nations Convention on the Law of the Sea with Annexes and Index* (New York: United Nations, 1983), pp. 52–69; Louis B. Sohn and Kristen Gustafson, *The Law of the Sea in a Nutshell* (St. Paul, MN: West Publishing Company, 1984), chap. 9.

For examples of "imposed, supranational" order, the next type, one needs to probe deeper into history, to the Middle Ages. Then the Roman Catholic Church and the Holy Roman Empire asserted a supranational supremacy, the papacy at times even claiming command of the "two swords," temporal as well as spiritual.[15] The Church's claim to authority over the princes of Christian Europe, extending to their holdings overseas, has fostered in the Western mind the ideal of a higher universal order that still exerts an influence. When in 1493 the Spanish throne wanted to validate its rights over the new territories discovered by Christopher Columbus, it turned to the Vatican. A papal bull, *Inter Caetera*, divided the entire overseas world between the lands found by Spain and those explored by Portugal. Nearly five hundred years later, in 1979, it was again to Rome that two successors to Spain's empire, Argentina and Chile, appealed to have their long-lasting Beagle Channel dispute mediated. The intercession by the Holy See resulted in 1985 in a ratified Argentine-Chilean treaty—a useful supplement, Orfila points out, to the workings of the inter-American political system.

Outside the ecclesiastical realm, there are few institutions today whose authority is such as to compel universal acceptance. Brian Urquhart, in his chapter on the United Nations, laments that the UN organization, in large part because of the hostility between the superpowers, has not gained the preeminent influence for world peace that the drafters of the Charter had hoped for it. The United Nations, he observes, has not been "pushed over the political threshold from being a mere institutional mechanism into being something persistent, consistent, and recognized as a constitutional instrument." As a result, the position of the UN secretary-general is, in Dag Hammarskjöld's phrase, too frequently that of "a pope without a church." Nonetheless, Urquhart argues, the importance of the United Nations as an instrument of collective security and peacekeeping is greater than that of any alternative agency, including either of the two superpowers trying to act as peacemakers independently. The experience in recent years of intervention in Lebanon is a case in point. In dealing also with the problems of Afghanistan, Iran-Iraq, and Cyprus, the UN channels of negotiation have been the most effective and promising ones. UN representatives generally are recognized as the most impartial. This bodes well for the future of the institution, which, however, cannot impose peace without the assent of the permanent members of the Security Council and of the rest of the world community.

In a more limited, functional sphere, that of international monetary affairs, an example of international ordering with an element of supranational imposition is emerging today in the role played by the International Monetary Fund (IMF) in relation to the Third World debt problem. To the extent that the IMF serves as a "lender-of-last-resort," as Nathaniel Samuels describes that function in his chapter, it acquires some of the characteristics of central

---

[15]Robert A. Graham, *Vatican Diplomacy: A Study of Church and State on the International Plane* (Princeton, NJ: Princeton University Press, 1959).

banks within the economies of individual nations. Although established internationally by negotiation and continuously dependent on the support of its members, the IMF is more and more capable of autonomous action.[16] This includes direct forming of agreements with debtor countries, which generally are required to adopt austerity measures as a condition of receiving assistance. IMF conditionality, which Samuels identifies as situated at the very core of a process of global lending-of-last-resort, is perceived by some debtor countries as international financial order by dictation, even though formally negotiated.

There are kinds of supranational influence which can be brought to bear without any appearance of coercion. This brings us to the "automatic, supranational" category of our taxonomy. As in the case of the European balance of power, such influence, though from centralized rather than decentralized sources, may depend for its effectiveness on the widespread prevalence of certain customs. Moreover, there usually is a common ideology that assures the responsiveness of those who are influenced. Such suasion is less exercised than received. Among contemporary examples one may cite the stabilizing, as well as mobilizing, effects of Roman Catholic faith among the populations of Poland, Nicaragua, Haiti, and the Philippines. The pervasive influence of Islam, from Morocco to Indonesia, can have a comparable cohesive effect. Despite the theological division between Sunni and Shiite Muslims, the universal character of the religion provides an intellectual and moral basis for reaching international understanding. This is the premise on which the Organization of the Islamic Conference, headquartered in Saudi Arabia, has attempted since 1981 to facilitate an end to the Iran-Iraq war.[17]

Proceeding now to the third column of the grid, we see types of order in which hegemony, or the predominance of a single power, is the organizing principle. Probably the most noteworthy instance of such single-power leadership by multilateral agreement, or a "negotiated, hegemonic" regime, is NATO. Although to some extent a carry-over of the overlordship of the United States in the Western European theater during the Second World War, NATO also is a genuine case of requested protection: "empire by invitation," as a Norwegian historian has described it.[18] Although by far the strongest of the Atlantic countries following the war, the United States did not simply impose

---

[16]See A. W. Hooke, *The International Monetary Fund: Its Evolution, Organization, and Activities* (Washington, DC: International Monetary Fund, 1981). For a discussion of the concept of supranationality in relation to the IMF, see Benjamin J. Cohen, *Organizing the World's Money: The Political Economy of International Monetary Relations* (New York: Basic Books, 1977), chap. 6.

[17]John L. Esposito, *Islam and Politics* (Syracuse, NY: Syracuse University Press, 1984), pp. 107–08; Glen Balfour-Paul, "The Prospects for Peace," in M. S. El Azhary, ed., *The Iran-Iraq War: An Historical, Economic and Political Analysis* (New York: St. Martin's Press, 1984), pp. 126–39.

[18]Geir Lundestad, "Empire by Invitation? The United States and Western Europe, 1945–1952," Society for Historians of American Foreign Relations *Newsletter* 15, no. 3 (September 1984): 1–21.

its will upon its European allies-to-be. The political initiative for the North Atlantic Alliance, in fact, was European. British Foreign Secretary Ernest Bevin, believing the defense of Europe would be impossible without the assurance of U.S. support, formed the Brussels Pact in order to show that such help was deserved. Rather than merely backing the Brussels Pact from the outside, the United States was drawn by the logic of multilateral negotiation (the secret "Pentagon talks") into full membership in an Atlantic-wide alliance. Nominally, all members are equal under the North Atlantic Treaty, with the United States having no greater rights than Iceland or Luxembourg. Within the negotiated organizational structure of NATO, however, the United States clearly has remained *primus inter pares*.[19] As my own chapter on NATO in this volume shows, the quasi-hegemonic leadership of the United States within the Atlantic Alliance has manifested itself not only in U.S. domination of allied strategic planning, symbolized by the fact that the position of Supreme Allied Commander Europe (SACEUR) always has been held by an American, but also in the independent manner in which the U.S. government has assumed responsibility in East-West arms control talks. "Consultation," as the form of negotiation that takes place within NATO is called, sometimes is more fiction than fact.

Another case of a negotiated hegemonic regime is the formal Inter-American System, codified principally in the 1947 Rio de Janeiro Treaty and the 1948 Bogotá Charter which established the Organization of American States. Although outnumbered in the OAS, whose decisions require not unanimity but rather only a two-thirds majority, there is no doubt that the United States remains the predominant member. The location of the OAS headquarters in Washington, DC, indicates where the center of power lies. Particularly in the military sphere, the relationship between the United States and the other American republics is an unequal alliance, often wearing "the aspect of a hegemony."[20] The negotiated inter-American relationship, however, is not simply a formal multilateralization of the Monroe Doctrine, whose so-called Roosevelt Corollary licensed unilateral U.S. military intervention throughout the hemisphere. During and even after the Second World War, many Latin American states genuinely desired U.S. military assistance, not only for protection against Nazi German aggression but also in opposition to all extrahemispheric interference—by the British Empire, the Soviet Union, and even the United Nations.[21] It thus was perhaps inevitable that U.S. officials should gain the impression that Latin American relations with the rest of the world properly should be channeled through Washington, a belief that may well be called a "hegemonic presumption."[22]

---

[19]Henrikson, "Creation of the North Atlantic Alliance"; *The North Atlantic Treaty Organisation: Facts and Figures* (Brussels: NATO Information Service, 1984).

[20]John Child, *Unequal Alliance: The Inter-American Military System, 1938–1978* (Boulder, CO: Westview Press, 1980), p. 1.

[21]Ibid., pp. 77–78.

[22]Abraham F. Lowenthal, "The United States and Latin America: Ending the Hegemonic Presumption," *Foreign Affairs* 55, no. 1 (October 1976): 199–213.

Instances of the next type of international regime, "imposed, hegemonic" order, include the most noteworthy modern example of an involuntary system of international prosperity and peace: the Pax Britannica. Especially within the maritime realm, Great Britain was able to establish a global regime of commercial freedom, as Koh points out. The rule of Mare Liberum (Free Sea), including such specific regulations as the three-mile territorial limit, depended for its maintenance on the unrivaled position of the Royal Navy. Though reliant on gunboat diplomacy, British predominance nonetheless served a general interest.

Similar in some respects is the postwar Pax Americana. Initially welcomed, the peacetime world-ordering role of the United States after 1945 came to be resented in many quarters, even at home. This feeling peaked during the Vietnam War. "As the most powerful nation on earth—the richest, the most deeply involved, and in some ways the most ideologically committed— the United States has intervened massively in the affairs of other nations," the journalist-historian Ronald Steel then observed. American foreign policy seemed to many commentators to be "imperial," that of a new Rome. As in the case of the Roman Empire, it seemed to some analysts, the ordering role of the United States required, for better or worse, periodic military intervention. "In order to be exercised most of the time by indirection and circumscribed delegation," reflected the political theorist George Liska, "American leadership must on occasion be direct and forcible."[23] America's influence seemed to depend on the readiness of the U.S. Marines. It cannot be overlooked, either, that the stability of postwar international affairs had been determined profoundly by the explosions at Hiroshima and Nagasaki— unforgotten events that still vividly contribute to the "crystal ball effect" whose psychological importance Nye emphasizes. The Pax Americana is, to some extent, a Pax Atomica.

The Soviet Union has developed an international imperium that is even more clearly based on military force. The predominant Soviet position in Eastern Europe, behind what Winston Churchill in 1946 called the "iron curtain," is largely, though not entirely, a function of the continued presence of the Red Army. When the Warsaw Treaty was signed in 1955, ostensibly in reaction to the inclusion of West Germany in NATO, probably not more than three members of the bloc—East Germany, Poland, and Czechoslovakia— considered it a welcome safeguard to their nations' security.[24] In 1956, when the Hungarian government tried to leave the Warsaw Pact, the Soviet Union used troops to prevent it from doing so. During the Prague Spring in Czechoslovakia in 1968, forces from five Warsaw Pact countries intervened in an

---

[23]Ronald Steel, *Pax Americana* (New York: Viking Press, 1967), p. vii; George Liska, *Imperial America: The International Politics of Primacy* (Baltimore: Johns Hopkins Press, 1967), author's preface.

[24]Andrzej Korbonski, "The Warsaw Treaty After Twenty-five Years: An Entangling Alliance or an Empty Shell?" in Robert W. Clawson and Lawrence S. Kaplan, eds., *The Warsaw Pact: Political Purpose and Military Means* (Wilmington, DE: Scholarly Resources, 1982), pp. 8–9.

ostensibly collective action. As Max Kampelman states most emphatically in his chapter in frank criticism of the Soviet Union's 1979 military invasion of Afghanistan and its continued political interference in Poland, the international order of the Soviet bloc is based on "aggression and repression." He also suggests, however, that the Warsaw Pact can be loosened. Thus, despite his criticism, he advocates engaging the Soviet challenge diplomatically ("we must come to grips with it").

Finally, let us record examples of "automatic, hegemonic" order. This is the kind of leadership associated with a single country that is neither negotiated nor imposed; it, rather, emanates.[25] That is, the country's influence depends more on other peoples' receptiveness than it does on any articulated process, physical or political, for the deliberate exercise of that influence. Ultimately, as Napoleon acknowledged, "power is based on opinion." Neither diplomacy nor military force, by itself, can command the degree of inter-national respect a powerful nation must have for the world order it represents to be adhered to. The source of any great civilization's *rayonnement* is an inner source, not its external assets. Others' identification with this cultural and spiritual source makes their adherence to a powerful country's principles and norms spontaneous, automatic. Respect for British law and institutions, and not regard for Britain's craft or might, is what served to perpetuate the organizational remnant of Britain's overseas empire, the British Common-wealth. Similarly, reverence for the French language and culture is what provided the continuing bond for the diverse countries of *la francophonie*. The pervasive influence of the United States, throughout the Free World and beyond, owes much to the distantly felt attraction of the American way of life—not merely America's democracy, but also its economic, social, and cultural freedom. Even though these ideals increasingly are challenged abroad by other, different concepts of world order and justice, many of the chapters in this book attest to their power.

Having completed our typology of world order, exhibiting thereby the range of complex ways in which structures and processes combine to generate it, we are in a position to fill in the matrix with representative examples (see Figure 2). On the basis of this substantiated framework, we now may proceed to an assessment of the responses of the authors, with their different personal, professional, and national styles, to the questions which the Negotiating World Order Project posed to them about the problem of world order.

The first set of these issues concerns the objective of "world order" itself. Was the achievement of order a stated goal of the international nego-tiations in which the authors were involved or which they have investigated, or was it simply an outcome, an *ex post* reality rather than an *ex ante* antic-ipation? In other words, was there a deliberate search for the principles, norms, rules, and procedures on which to establish a new regime, or did such a result

---

[25]For an elaboration of this concept, see Alan K. Henrikson, "The Emanation of Power," *International Security* 6, no. 1 (Summer 1981): 152–64.

Figure 2. World Order

	Structures		
Processes	International	Supranational	Hegemonic
Negotiated	International Telecommuni- cation Union	European Economic Community	North Atlantic Treaty Organization
	Non-Proliferation Treaty	International Seabed Authority	Inter-American System
Imposed	Congress of Vienna	Vatican mediation	Pax Britannica
	Versailles Treaty	International Monetary Fund conditionality	Warsaw Pact
Automatic	European balance of power	Roman Catholic solidarity	British Commonwealth
	Nixon-Kissinger pentapolarity	Islamic Conference cohesion	*la francophonie*

just emerge as a largely unintended by-product of an effort to cope with the particular, practical problems at hand? Closely related to this question is the conceptual distinction, drawn in the Introduction to this book, between political solutions and political settlements. If order is merely a "settled state," then it is less likely to have been conceived *a priori*, as opposed to being a condition recognized *a posteriori*. Whether order is actively sought or not, have the authors mostly taken the view that it is a useful objective to pursue? Does a common conception of an ideal order (i.e., a "solution") help the participants in a diplomatic negotiation to keep nonessential, ephemeral issues in perspective? Or does it simply increase the difficulty of negotiating a more readily achievable agreement (i.e., a "settlement")? In general, then, should order be the purpose of diplomacy, or not?

The responses of certain of the contributors to this fundamental query—the very intellectual premise of the Negotiating World Order Project—were direct, candid, and challenging. In early drafts of texts and in oral discussion, several of the authors expressed a degree of skepticism about the notion of order that was surprising, given their own successes in building orderly relationships in their respective fields. In the interest of deepening our understanding, it is important that we frankly take account of their objections, based as they are on experience.

In part, the term "world order" itself was the source of difficulty. One participant, trained as a lawyer, acknowledged in a preliminary text that he always found "labels that require explanation to be potentially mischievous." The pursuit of world order, "given its ambiguity," seemed to him "a task of lesser importance" than negotiations for "international stability and lasting peace," by which he meant what we have termed a settlement, i.e., one capable of being made durable. This interpretation is confirmed by his noting that "limited negotiating results, if successful, can begin creating a broader mosaic of understanding." Another contributor, long familiar with the doctrinal commitments embodied in the rhetoric of multilateral diplomacy, summarily stated: "Anyone who puts the word 'order' in an international document is a fool." The one found the term too flexible; the other considered it too rigid, especially if incorporated in a treaty or other binding instrument.

Beneath these reservations about the vocabulary of international regime making there lies, of course, a deeper rationale. The reasons given by the participants for doubting the wisdom of seeking world order, at least as an explicit objective of policy, were mainly three. First, as one said, it implies "the existence of a universal truth for the world to accept"; that is, it makes little allowance for ideological diversity, cultural pluralism, or regional variation. Second, it implies force; it is "more likely to be the result of coercion than consensus." To another, order suggested "jackboots." Third, the idea seems fixed and static. Because of the implication of permanence in any explicitly proclaimed order, it seems to deny the possibility, and the inevitability, of change. This was only one side of the ledger, however.

Among the virtues specifically attributed to the idea of order by these and other contributors, three stand out. They are, in a sense, the obverse of the aforementioned three vices. One attraction is the comprehensiveness permitted by a general, universal order. The argument is, in short, that problems are too numerous to be dealt with one by one, or piecemeal. Within the United Nations Conference on Trade and Development (UNCTAD), for instance, the approach has been adopted of "looking at commodities as a whole." Previously, as Gamani Corea explains, commodity negotiations had been approached only "in a fragmentary and ad hoc fashion." This was inadequate.

A second consideration is the manageability that can be gained when an international order, possibly involving some use of coercion, is erected. International security problems, particularly, may get dangerously out of hand without some centralized supervision and control. The United Nations today is effectively "the only channel" for negotiating settlements of local conflicts in many parts of the world. If the United Nations did not exist, the Urquhart chapter makes plain, it would have to be invented.

A third argument is the predictability, or reduction of uncertainty, that international organization makes possible. In Urquhart's words, there needs to be "some tolerable degree of order and expectation in the world." A sentence from Samuels's analysis of debt diplomacy epitomizes the entire case for order. "If we continue at present on an ad hoc basis, with year-in and year-out individual renegotiations and reschedulings and no recognized general principles for dealing with the basic debt problem itself," he warns, "we will have hanging over us serious uncertainties about the future functioning of the world economy."

Negotiation was defined in the Introduction as the explicit, reciprocal, direct, and designed process of communication between competitive parties seeking to reach agreement. The diplomatic kind of negotiation takes place internationally, with governments normally as the principal parties. When diplomacy is conducted multilaterally and when its purpose is not merely the solution or settlement of a specific issue but the creation of a general arrangement or set of rules for the continuing, semi-autonomous resolution of such issues, it takes on a parliamentary aspect, as has been suggested. Negotiating world order thus is the combination of international diplomacy and legislation.

What have been the basic conditions or factors that have fostered such negotiation of world order? This brings us to the second set of issues considered by the authors. To begin at the most material level, are there certain physical conditions which have promoted efforts to achieve international order? As Philip Morrison pointed out, "positive law" should not be detached from "natural law." Several authors stress the critical importance of scientific understanding as the basis of any effective international action. Significant advances in the field of international health organization, Jean Mayer notes, normally "did not take place until we had the scientific understanding and the technological means with which to act." The discovery of the causes of the propagation of cholera, bubonic plague, and yellow fever, as he explains, contributed to the formation in 1907 of the Office International d'Hygiène Publique. To cite a contrasting case, Roberts shows that imperfect understanding by scientists of the composition and transmission of acid rain in North America has impeded cooperative efforts by Canada and the United States to control it. "When there is weakness of political will," he reflects, "it is easy to claim that no regulatory action should be taken until irrefutable, definitive information is available." Marks, whose chapter chronicles the revolution in communications, demonstrates how a dramatic technological development, the communications satellite, promoted an entirely new form of organization, notably the International Telecommunications Satellite Consortium (INTELSAT).

Underlying economic conditions also can powerfully affect the interest of governments in world order negotiations. An inflationary economic period, as Corea points out, ordinarily is not conducive to efforts at international commodity control. A commodity agreement "has to start at the lower reaches of the cycle," he explains, because it is only during that phase, when surpluses are available, that quantitative restraints or the acquisition of stocks can be institutionalized. Gardner Patterson correlates the "massive protectionist pressures" currently registered by governments, as well as their tendency to adopt "bilateral and sectoral" rather than "multilateral and general" approaches, with worldwide low levels of economic growth and high levels of unemployment. Samuels attributes the unprecedented magnitude of the capital required by many developing countries to the 1973–74 and 1978–79 oil price increases. These upheavals made it necessary, in turn, for the international banking community to collaborate in unprecedented efforts to "recycle" the earnings of oil-exporting countries to the developing ones. We tend to minimize the consequences of this cause, he points out, and to look instead for "villains."

No less powerful are the basic military and political conditions that affect the construction of world order. The UN organization, as Urquhart acknowledges, was founded on a geopolitical fault line between the Soviet Union and the United States. "When that fault—the East-West divide—slips, the organization trembles." This simple division, combined with the disparity in military might between the superpowers and others, may have produced a benefit for mankind in the existence of a nuclear nonproliferation regime. The rate and extent of the spread of nuclear weaponry might today be considerably greater, as Nye's analysis suggests, were it not for the predominance in the nuclear arena of those two states. Bipolarity, where interests coincide, can be an organizing factor rather than a disorganizing one.

A number of authors have emphasized the importance of a stable politico-military balance between the Eastern and Western blocs as a necessary condition of any successful international security regime. In Gerard Smith's judgment, there currently exists an overall balance between the two sides. For that reason, he criticizes the "Star Wars" program, which some of its proponents see as a possible way to regain lost "strategic superiority." Aerospace defenses, if technologically possible, would make offensive forces less vulnerable and thus more threatening. "This tilt toward a defensive strategy is fundamentally inconsistent with arms control and would destabilize the strategic balance, on which international order rests," he contends. Kampelman, focusing more narrowly on the military balance in Europe, criticizes the Soviet buildup in that theater and argues that countervailing measures by the West are required lest Western diplomacy be undercut. "The Soviet Union respects military strength," he posits. "Its incentive for negotiating an agreement is greater when the positions taken by its negotiating partner have the added dignity of being supported by a physical capacity to resist." Negotiation requires equilibrium.

Within the domestic realm of politics, there also are factors that have a significant bearing on the success of diplomacy. Mayer reminds us that the negotiation of *international* order, as opposed to other ways of bringing about order in the world, presupposes the existence of well-ordered *nations*. In trying to solve health and nutrition problems, private and official negotiators, even today, often find themselves dealing with "countries that are totally artificial creations." It is not always the less developed countries that lack the cohesion needed for successful diplomacy. As Roberts describes the Canadian government's perceptions of the United States in dealing with the acid rain problem, its neighbor can be "frustrating" to deal with diplomatically. The only way to persuade Americans to respond seemed to be to "bring home" the problem to them. The paradoxical effect of this effort was to obtain support "mainly for domestic action, rather than international action." The opposite problem was encountered by those working with the United States to establish the new Law of the Sea Convention. Negotiations were concluded very successfully by Ambassador Elliot L. Richardson, but the advent of a new administration, responding to a different set of domestic pressures, meant that the U.S. government did not approve what it had wrought.[26] From the perspective of international civil servants, such as Urquhart at the United Nations, the coordination of world diplomatic efforts—to resolve the conflicts of the Middle East, for example—with the domestic political timetables and exigencies of the United States and other influential countries is almost impossible. An election is always going on somewhere. As Urquhart points out, however, the need "to have a broad political base in the world community," once met, can be "a great strength."

The success of diplomacy also can be determined by cultural factors. We may observe a profound difference between the traditional Western *modus operandi*, which tends to be formalistic and mechanical, and Eastern patterns of behavior, which tend to be less rigid. The contrast is drawn most sharply by Unger in his analysis of the diplomatic style of ASEAN. One of the sources of this is Buddhism, "in which the Middle Way is always the ideal." Another is the Malay concept of *musyawarah*, according to which "a leader should not arbitrarily impose his will but rather make gentle suggestions of the path a community should follow." Unger observes that at ASEAN meetings *musyawarah* is employed, "rather than Western-style debate and majority voting." It is a process, a nondialectical kind of dialogue, that traditionally leads to "consensus" (literally: feeling together). This important term of art in modern diplomacy, to be discussed further below, thus derives from Eastern cultures as well as from Western sources, such as Quakerism.

Somewhat more specific than the cultural conditions that foster international cooperation are the intellectual circumstances within which negotiation occurs. The Western idea of "growth," for instance, has engendered a progressive notion of international ordering. Modifying Saint Augustine's ancient conception of peace as "the tranquility of order," Orfila suggests that "the true name for peace today is, in fact, development: integral human development in every society and nation." Developmentalist perspectives are evident throughout this volume, especially in the chapters dealing primarily with economic issues. "In the refashioning of the institutional system that might begin in the late 1980s," Corea states, "there is a need to incorporate a new development consensus, comparable to the full-employment consensus that characterized the fashioning of the Bretton Woods system and the General

---

[26]For an official explanation of recent policy, see James L. Malone, "Freedom and Opportunity: Foundation for a Dynamic Oceans Policy," address before the Law of the Sea Institute, San Francisco, September 24, 1984, U.S., Department of State *Bulletin* 84, no. 2093 (December 1984): 76–79. For a vivid journalistic account of the change in U.S. policy, see the two articles, "The Law of the Sea," in *The New Yorker*, August 1 and 8, 1983.

Agreement on Tariffs and Trade (GATT)." If the size of the world economic pie is believed to be increasing as a result of a common commitment to a development policy, that alone might encourage many nations, otherwise fearful of a redistribution of existing slices, to join in a cooperative order.

Sometimes the ideas that facilitate diplomacy are conceived or articulated by individual thinkers and writers. One such example is Hugo Grotius's exposition in 1609 of the Mare Liberum concept. A more recent instance from the same field, noted also in Koh's chapter, is Dr. Arvid Pardo's seminal proposal in 1967 that a constitution or charter be adopted to deal with ocean space "as an organic and ecological whole." This "revolutionary concept" has shaped all subsequent discussion of the law of the sea problem. In the environmental field, a comparable idea, the "biosphere" concept, gained currency and influence with the holding of the 1968 Biosphere Conference.[27]

All of these fundamental conditions that support international negotiation rarely are sufficient in themselves, of course, to produce the diplomatic initiatives needed to bring about actual agreements on international order. Precipitating factors often are necessary to disturb an unjust status quo, to move the conscience, to fire the will to act. This introduces the third set of issues posed to the authors: the identity of the particular historical events that have stimulated efforts to bring about world order. Although it is theoretically possible that major world order-building projects can originate during relatively quiet and stable historical periods, such as the Harding-Coolidge "normalcy" of the 1920s, the Eisenhower "equilibrium" of the 1950s, and perhaps the Reagan "restoration" of the early 1980s, most such architectonic enterprises appear to have been generated during more eventful times. Turbulent historical periods, which shake an existing regime's ideological and moral foundations, tend to produce visionary blueprints of a better order.

What, typically, are such precipitating factors? They can be either events or historical circumstances themselves, or the actions of individuals and groups taken in response to those events. A classic example of the combined effect of history and conscience, cited by Mayer, is the response of the Swiss banker Henri Dunant to the 1859 Battle of Solferino. Dunant thereafter "set out on his lifelong mission to mitigate the physical sufferings of war and to fight against war itself." The institutional consequence of Dunant's endeavor is the International Committee of the Red Cross, which works quietly and effectively to ameliorate the human costs of violent conflict the world over.

The principal stimulus to efforts at international organization, without much doubt, has been warfare. The chaos of the Napoleonic Wars, for example, was succeeded by the diplomatic Concert of Europe. The clash of opposed alliance systems in 1914 in Europe resulted, after the 1919 Paris Peace Conference, in a nearly worldwide League of Nations. It is almost inconceivable that this would have developed otherwise. The United Nations, too, was

---

[27]On the origins of this idea, see Lynton K. Caldwell, *In Defense of Earth: International Protection of the Biosphere* (Bloomington: Indiana University Press, 1972).

formed in war. The Japanese attack on Pearl Harbor in December 1941 caused the American people, given their "second chance" to correct the mistake of rejecting League membership, to take the lead in giving structure to the ideal, held aloft by Wendell Willkie, of "One World."[28] Not only the central UN organization itself but also the two Bretton Woods institutions—the International Bank for Reconstruction and Development (IBRD) and the IMF— were established under this universalist banner.

In the nuclear age, with actual military conflict between the two superpowers being so irrational as to be virtually impossible, "crises" have tended to provide the impetus to international order. Thus, for example, the 1956 Suez crisis put a new emphasis on interallied consultation within NATO. The perilous 1962 Cuban crisis made East-West détente seem much more urgent. Among its results were the 1963 "hot line" agreement and the Limited Test Ban Treaty, mentioned in the Smith chapter. These achievements were not, of course, simply automatic; they were negotiated by concerned and motivated government officials, Soviet as well as American.[29]

At a lower level of technological confrontation, if at a higher level of sociological conflict, the troubles of Southeast Asia also have resulted in international order. Events in 1965 in Indonesia, combined with the increasing U.S. military involvement in Vietnam, were "the catalyst of the historical process that produced ASEAN," as Unger points out. In this instance as well as others, international cooperation was not born of tragedy itself. "Founding fathers," such as Thanat Khoman and other statesmen named by Unger, were needed.

Economic crises also can be fertile historical situations for the seeds of international order, intelligently planted. Although the Great Depression did not generate world order, the 1933 London International Monetary and Economic Conference, which President Franklin D. Roosevelt famously "torpedoed" by declining to stabilize the U.S. dollar, was at least a major attempt to negotiate terms of stability and growth.[30] After World War II, economic crises generally have been handled more cooperatively. The 1973 oil crisis was used by Secretary of State Kissinger as an opportunity to organize the major oil-consuming nations against extortion by the oil-producing countries. The result was the International Energy Agency which, though inspired more

---

[28]Robert A. Divine, *Second Chance: The Triumph of Internationalism in America During World War II* (New York: Atheneum, 1967); Wendell Willkie, *One World* (New York: Simon and Schuster, 1943).

[29]On these events, see Harold Karan Jacobson and Eric Stein, *Diplomats, Scientists, and Politicians: The United States and the Nuclear Test Ban Negotiations* (Ann Arbor: University of Michigan Press, 1966); and Arthur M. Schlesinger, Jr., *A Thousand Days: John F. Kennedy in the White House* (Boston: Houghton Mifflin, 1965), especially chaps. 17, 18, 20, 21, and 34.

[30]On the London conference and its background, see Herbert Feis, *1933: Characters in Crisis* (Boston: Little, Brown, 1966), and Frank Freidel, *Franklin D. Roosevelt: Launching the New Deal* (Boston: Little, Brown, 1973).

by a spirit of confrontation than of cooperation, has contributed at least to the cohesion of the industrial countries themselves in the energy field.[31]

We now may proceed from the underlying conditions and originating circumstances of world order to the fourth set of issues posed to the authors: the question of the appropriate institutional context for world-order diplomacy. Are the best settings for order negotiation the great established institutions, either specialized bodies like the ITU or multi-issue organizations such as the United Nations, or do they tend to be conferences or other meetings organized specifically for that purpose, such as the UN Conference on the Law of the Sea (UNCLOS)? What is the optimal size of order-negotiating meetings? Does the choice of an existing institution tend to determine the numbers of participants as well as the venue? Is the agenda itself somewhat predetermined thereby? In order to escape these constraints and to liberate minds for contemplation of problems of architectural design rather than institutional engineering, is it necessary for negotiators to get away from the traditional diplomatic sites and meet elsewhere, away from bureaucracies?

Many of the authors of *Negotiating World Order* address the question of the organization of diplomacy explicitly. A recurrent theme in their accounts is the interplay between bilateral diplomacy—a two-sided process carried out usually between capitals of pairs of countries through ambassadors—and multilateral diplomacy—the many-sided, quasi-parliamentary process engaged in by delegates sent to international organizations and international meetings. "I have often thought that there is a permanent fight between bilateralism and multilateralism," Orfila says. The United States, as he rightly notes, has tended to prefer bilateral diplomacy, because "the larger state can more easily exercise its weight." Most Latin American nations, by the same token, usually have wanted to deal with the United States multilaterally, except when it threatens to confine them diplomatically to the Western Hemisphere. In actual experience, Orfila notes, the two methods and styles of diplomacy—bilateral and multilateral—can complement one another.

Nye also stresses the need for combining diplomatic devices. Using them is almost an acrobatic process. In considering the diplomacy of maintaining a nuclear nonproliferation regime, he writes, "we have to think of aligning four concentric circles or, perhaps more apt, keeping four hoops in the air at the same time without having one bump into the other or fall." Three of these hoops are multilateral. The first is what Nye terms "small multilateral diplomacy," illustrated by the Nuclear Suppliers Group (NSG). A "larger specialized agency diplomacy" is the International Atomic Energy Agency (IAEA). The largest and most encompassing of all is the UN system. Nuclear nonproliferation is discussed during General Assembly sessions and at NPT Review Conferences.

---

[31]Henry A. Kissinger, *Years of Upheaval* (Boston: Little, Brown, 1982), chaps. 19 and 20.

Despite the inherently multilateral character of the nonproliferation issue, there remains, as Nye shows, a considerable need to rely on bilateral relationships as well. Whereas the advantage of participation in multilateral forums is the publicity that can be gained for one's position, the attraction of bilateral diplomacy is precisely the opposite: the confidentiality and discretion afforded. Given the technical and political sensitivity of many nuclear matters, sometimes the rule is, "the quieter, the better." Nye cites as pertinent examples the U.S. government's diplomatic efforts to dissuade South Korea and Taiwan from choosing the nuclear weapons option, to prevent France from selling a nuclear reprocessing plant to Pakistan, and to coordinate nonproliferation policy with the Soviet Union, a topic which the two nuclear superpowers tend to view similarly. Nye concludes: "There remains an important role for quiet, bilateral diplomacy even when dealing with a multilateral issue."

The great difficulty faced by the participants in multilateral gatherings is sheer size. Reflecting upon UNCLOS III, Koh observes: "It was absolutely essential to transform a large, unwieldy conference of approximately 140 delegations into small, representative, and efficient negotiating groups." This phenomenon of "group" diplomacy appears again and again in this book. It is one of the most striking features of the process of global diplomacy, unlike traditional diplomacy. Entities such as the Group of 77, the Nonaligned Movement, the members of the Organization for Economic Cooperation and Development (OECD), and even regional groupings such as NATO, OAS, and ASEAN, constitute the "parties" of an international political system, in a sense. They can be factors for cohesion as well as agents of division.

Within and across these established world groupings, there can arise new, more specific ones on the basis of specific "kindred interests." Sometimes, as the Koh chapter indicates, these come into existence with little reference to ideological affinity or geographical proximity. In UNCLOS III, there were the coastal states, landlocked and geographically disadvantaged states, straits states, archipelagic states, broad-continental-shelfed states (the "margineers"), and the "Gang of Five" industrial-state group, including Great Britain, France, Japan, the United States, and the Soviet Union. UNCLOS III did have an elaborate formal committee structure, too, but most of its committees generally met as committees of the whole and hence could not efficiently be used for negotiations. This formal structure was supplemented by smaller, informal "negotiating groups" to handle specific issues in manageable packages. "As a general rule," notes Koh, "the more informal the nature of the group, the easier it is to resolve a problem."

Without detracting from the originality of the Law of the Sea Conference, which advanced certain techniques of multilateral diplomacy to new levels of explicitness and sophistication, a reader of this volume will have noted many close similarities with diplomatic practices developed earlier, in other contexts. Patterson, for example, describes a distinctive procedure evolved within the GATT—what he calls the "expanding-and-shrinking-concentric circle approach." This deals effectively with the problem of "who gets into the room" at various stages of a negotiation.

The countries that feel excluded, in order to strengthen their claim for admission, sometimes join together on the basis of common interests, select a spokesman, and insist on being admitted. Thus, as Patterson notes, during the Tokyo Round there operated a Nordic group, an ASEAN group, a developing country group, and, at times, a nonmarket economy group. He adds that, when the giants decide they have had enough of "the kibitzers," they increasingly have tended to hold a small group meeting "outside the regular venue of the negotiations, in one of their capitals or at a nearby resort." The basic lesson in the history of GATT diplomacy, as in the imaginative structure of UNCLOS III, is the variety of forms that can develop even within large, apparently unitary forums. These experiences also show the difficulty of maintaining cohesion while trying to deal with complex issues efficiently in small negotiating groups. An overall structure is indispensable.

We now move to the fifth, and final, general set of issues posed to the participants: namely, the question, closely related to that of the structure and composition of multilateral negotiation, of how actual decisions are arrived at and agreed upon. As noted at the beginning of this concluding chapter, the concept of negotiating world order requires the harmonization of two processes—diplomacy and parliamentarianism. The one, as Eban noted, aims at direct, rational agreement between adversaries. The other, by contrast, is a mechanical process by which one side seeks the defeat of the other. Multilateral decision making must unite these two approaches.

The reason why the issue of decision making is so important in the international arena today is the divorce of "number" from "force." That is, the majority of the world community, as in most international organizations, is no longer either constituted or commanded by the most powerful states, the advanced industrialized nations of the West and the Soviet Union. Instead, most international institutions now are dominated numerically, if not always politically or administratively, by the various new countries admitted to membership in multinational organizations after World War II. The United Nations, when it was founded, had only 51 members; today it has 159. The problem caused by this expansion is not simply the "transfer of the majority." It is rather that, as the Algerian jurist Mohammed Bedjaoui has pointed out, "for the first time in human history, international law is not on the side of force or power."[32]

The danger is a separation of "right" from "might." In many international organizations, especially those based on the Westphalian premise of one nation–one vote, the actual exercise of the majority possessed by Third World governments, with their radical egalitarian and developmentalist perspectives,

---

[32]Mohammed Bedjaoui, *Towards a New International Economic Order* (New York: Holmes and Meier, 1979), p. 141.

might have the effect of producing powerful disaffected minorities. The consequence could be a series of international institutions made ineffectual both morally and politically by the noncompliance or even departure of their strongest members, in some cases those institutions' very founders. A widespread recognition of this danger is producing sobering second thoughts. The multitudinous Third World states frequently refrain from applying the full measure of their majoritarian authority. At the same time, they grudgingly consider their decisions to do so to be "concessions" to states that do not respect and probably will not reciprocate the consideration given them.[33] The result is a crisis of international organization at every level of world order—principles, norms, rules, and procedures. What can be done?

At the procedural level, our immediate concern at this point in our concluding review, three solutions have been suggested on the basis of traditional and more recent organizational experience. The first is the requirement of unanimity, the voting procedure traditionally associated with the League of Nations. In drafting the League Covenant, British delegate Lord Robert Cecil observed simply that "all international decisions must by the nature of things be unanimous."[34] When the Charter of the United Nations was written, unanimity was abandoned. The General Assembly was empowered to act on so-called important questions by a two-thirds majority and on other matters by a simple majority. In the Security Council, however, a vestige of the League Council system was retained with a compromise arrangement allowing the permanent members of that body, in effect, a veto. "Because of the unanimity rule on nonprocedural matters," as Urquhart describes this system, "nothing affirmative can be done by the Security Council unless all five of its permanent members concur." Ironically, the debilitating veto provision was intended not so much to give the large powers an opportunity to avoid the United Nations but rather to give them an incentive, through negotiation rather than voting, to reach agreement within it.[35] Generally speaking, a unanimity rule puts a premium on diplomacy, consultation, and accord. It tends to work best, however, within associations of similar and like-minded states, such as NATO or the OECD.

The second frequently suggested device for making decisions without having to succumb to a willful majority is weighted voting, used today by many of the major international economic institutions. This procedure actually originated with the public international unions of the nineteenth century, one instance being the Office International d'Hygiène Publique. Voting rights were assigned therein according to the contribution classes to which the

---

[33]Ibid., pp. 167–68.

[34]Quoted in Stephen Zamora, "Voting in International Economic Organizations," *American Journal of International Law* 74, no. 3 (July 1980): 574n.

[35]C. Wilfred Jenks, "Unanimity, the Veto, Weighted Voting, Special and Simple Majorities and Consensus as Modes of Decision in International Organisations," in *Cambridge Essays in International Law: Essays in Honour of Lord McNair* (London: Stevens and Sons, 1965), p. 51.

member states belonged. In our own time, the prominent cases of weighted-voting systems have been the two Bretton Woods institutions. The IBRD/IMF model also is used by the more recently established regional development banks, the Inter-American Development Bank, African Development Bank, and Asian Development Bank. Under the voting system of the IMF, for instance, each member country has a basic allotment of 250 votes and, in addition, one vote for each part of its national quota equivalent to 100,000 Special Drawing Rights (SDRs). The basic allotment is intended to recognize "the sovereign equality of states" and strengthen the voting position of "economically smaller members," as an IMF publication explains. The variable allotment, by contrast, is designed "to recognize differences in subscriptions and to protect the interests and ensure the cooperation of those members that account for the greater part of international trade and financial transactions."[36] The United States currently holds about 20 percent of IMF votes. The large influence that it exerts in that organization by virtue of its financial contribution seems to many countries, particularly the developing and indebted ones, unjust, because of the greater impact that the IMF has on their own economies and political systems. To allot IMF voting rights in accordance with the "relative interest" of each member, however, surely would be to apply too vague and shifting a criterion.[37] A generally accepted weighted-voting procedure, which runs against the egalitarian grain of most of the world community today, is very hard to devise. If for reasons of ideology alone, the IMF voting system is not likely to become a general pattern.

A third procedure for holding rampant majorities in check is to require various "special" majorities for decisions. The special majority most commonly required, as in the UN General Assembly when important questions are being discussed, is two thirds. The two-thirds formula sometimes is extended beyond the simple count of membership to other measurable factors. As Corea explains in his description of the Common Fund of the Integrated Program for Commodities, establishment of such a fund requires not merely ratifications but also ratifications representing two-thirds of its capital, a goal not yet achieved.[38] In some institutions, such as the International Labor Organization (ILO) with its separate government, employer, and worker delegates, certain proportions of certain categories of votes sometimes are required. Thus, for example, decisions regarding the admission, expulsion, or suspension of ILO members require a two-thirds majority of the possible number of votes, which must include two-thirds of the government votes cast. In international commodity councils, mostly patterned on the first International Wheat Agreement, "distributed" majorities—concurring separate majorities of exporting and importing countries—are required. By these means, conflicting interests are

---

[36]Hooke, *International Monetary Fund*, p. 17.

[37]This is implied in Zamora, "Voting in International Economic Organizations": 592.

[38]See "Common Fund for Commodities—Approaching the Last Hurdle," *UNCTAD Bulletin*, no. 218 (January 1986): 8.

balanced. In essence, all of these various special voting arrangements are safeguards given those countries whose cooperation is necessary to the maintenance of a regime. This is sensible. However, except in limited, functional spheres in which these structural protections are correlated clearly with particular nations' interests, the idea of special-majority systems is likely to be considered too complex and cumbersome for adoption.

All three procedures—unanimity and the veto, weighted voting, and special majorities—are inspired by the same basic objective: to make sure that the decisions of the international community, taken within multilateral institutions, reflect a sufficiently wide consensus to be effective in practice as well as acceptable in theory. This concept of consensus, encountered in various contexts in many chapters of this book, such as those by Koh, Marks, Kampelman, Unger, Corea, and Patterson, emerges in some respects as the central idea and principal finding of the entire volume. Meaning, at one level, simply the "common sense" of a meeting, the word implies as well all of the elements of world order: its principles and norms as well as its rules and procedures.[39]

The basis idea of consensus is not, of course, novel. As the legal scholar and international civil servant, C. Wilfred Jenks, has written: "The general concept of consensus as a mode of decision is as old as primitive law; its importance in African customary law is attested by the tradition of the *palaver*." It is "the heart of the jury system" and "the basis of cabinet government."[40] The consensus-like Malay concept of *musyawarah* and the use of the consensus principle in Quakerism already have been noted.

Consensus emerged with a specific meaning as one of the new salient concepts of international relations within the context of the United Nations, in particular, during the 1964 crisis there over the division of the financial costs arising from the Suez and Congo peacekeeping operations. To avoid obstruction in the General Assembly over this divisive question, it was decided to deal only with those matters "that could be settled without opposition." A decade later, during the Sixth and Seventh Special Sessions of the General Assembly, consensus became a well-recognized working method. Even before this, the United Nations had adopted resolutions "by agreement," "by consultation of the members," "by tacit consent," "by acclamation," on the basis of "non-objection," and, most specifically and pointedly, "without proceeding to a vote."[41] The new prominence of the term was associated with a highly conscious use of the method. The main attraction of consensus decision making is the avoidance of division through the mechanical operations of voting. As Jenks has written, "voting tends to become a substitute for negotiation rather than a measure of the amount of agreement reached or a final

---

[39]For an example of the comprehensive use of the term, see Amadou-Mahtar M'Bow, *From Concertation to Consensus: UNESCO and the Solidarity of Nations* (Paris: UNESCO, 1979), a collection of speeches by the director-general of UNESCO.

[40]Jenks, "Unanimity," p. 56.

[41]Bedjaoui, *Towards a New International Economic Order*, pp. 169–70.

resort when negotiation fails, and the art of parliamentary manipulation is replacing that of diplomacy as a method of handling international problems for which diplomacy alone can produce an agreed solution."[42]

What thus may be termed "the diplomacy of consensus" is an attempt to prevent the displacement of diplomacy by parliamentarianism, at the same time recognizing the formal rule-making, or legislative, purpose of most multilateral conferences and organizations. The diplomacy of consensus is another way of saying "negotiating world order." How does it work in practice? One case described in this book is the consensus technique used by the GATT, a major international economic negotiating structure that, unlike the IMF and World Bank, does not protect its largest members with a system of weighted voting. The GATT voting rules are "clear throwbacks to the principles of sovereign equality and unanimity."[43] Each country in it has one vote; in order to amend certain basic GATT rules, the proponents must have unanimity. It is apparent that decision making by majority vote would not work in such a setting. In actuality, Patterson points out, "votes are rarely taken." Decisions instead are arrived at through consensus. "In the GATT framework," as he explains the procedure, "this means that an agreement is reached when those who do not agree either keep quiet, for one reason or another, or are so few or so small in terms of their interest in the issue that their agreement is not regarded by whoever is chairing the negotiations as essential to the successful implementation of the proposed action." He observes that decision making by consensus, rather than voting, has been found "indispensable to international negotiations in trade matters when a large number of countries are involved and when they differ greatly in their economic importance and in their concern with particular issues."

The forum which most highly developed the consensus technique was UNCLOS. That conference was precedent-setting both in that it for the first time formalized the consensus method and in that it applied the method in novel ways. The UNCLOS decision-making system has been termed an "*active consensus* procedure," as distinct from the more common "*passive consensus* procedure," used mainly to avoid voting.[44] The purpose of consensus diplomacy at UNCLOS III, as Koh authoritatively describes it in his chapter, was to achieve maximum, positive agreement. This required effective leadership. "Progress was made by this method, which puts a premium on skillful and scrupulously fair chairmanship," he says. Delegates could consent tacitly by waiving their right of disagreement. This they would not do if they were suspicious of the motives of committee or group chairmen.

It is important to recognize that consensus diplomacy depends on having a framework and also on the existence of a procedure for voting if needed.

---

[42]Jenks, "Unanimity," p. 56.

[43]Zamora, "Voting in International Economic Organizations": 579.

[44]Barry Buzan, "Negotiating by Consensus: Developments in Technique at the United Nations Conference on the Law of the Sea," *American Journal of International Law* 75, no. 2 (April 1981): 328–29.

The formal procedural rules of UNCLOS strongly reinforced its use of the consensus method, even though the option of voting was kept in the background. It had been agreed: "The Conference should make every effort to reach agreement on substantive matters by way of consensus and there should be no voting on such matters until all efforts at consensus have been exhausted."[45] Consensus also was given practical effect by rules that provided for deferment of voting, pending attempts to find a solution through agreement. The result, Koh points out, was that, before UNCLOS III concluded, "not a single vote was taken, either by roll call or by ballot, on any of the substantive issues it had been initially called to resolve." The conference placed such a heavy emphasis on consensus, Koh explains, because it wanted to produce a convention that would "enjoy the widest possible support in the international community." No less importantly, it sought to "protect the interests and views of minorities at the conference," including the great powers. These goals, of community building and community preserving, most of the delegates believed they had achieved with the Law of the Sea Convention.

What consensus diplomacy does, in brief, is to allow the international community to steer a middle course between what Eban identified as the "diplomatic" principle and the "parliamentary" principle—that is, between reasonable negotiation and mechanistic voting. As noted, it puts a premium on effective chairmanship which, in the egalitarian environment of most multilateral institutions today, is performed by able individuals from small countries as well as large ones. This, in itself, makes the practice politically legitimate. Consensus diplomacy has a strong attraction for many of the new states, for it may be the only way in which they can participate effectively in global decision making. Even the older, established powers can derive practical benefits from it, not the least of these being the shielding they derive against the possibility of prejudicial "new orders" imposed upon them by international majority rule.

The international diplomacy most called for today is not the highly personal diplomacy of the past, in which statesmen, traveling in style and meeting secretly, simply coped with crises and cultivated international relationships. Something deeper, more structural is needed. Statesmanship, no matter how brilliant, needs to be supplemented with "fail-safe" or reinsurance systems. By these means, a certain standard level of favorable institutional performance can be guaranteed even when uncommon leadership is not available. Virtuoso diplomacy today tends, ironically, merely to make people uneasy.[46] The challenge facing us is somehow to combine globalist architecture with diplomatic artisanship. "There is no substitute," as Stanley Hoffmann has written, "for universal bargaining, issue by issue, deal by deal." A "double

---

[45]United Nations, *Law of the Sea*, p. 165.

[46]Elliot L. Richardson, "Negotiating World Order: The Historical Case of the Law of the Sea Conference," address to Society for Historians of American Foreign Relations, Washington, DC, August 5, 1983, summarized in Society for Historians of American Foreign Relations *Newsletter* 15, no. 1 (March 1984): 28–29.

revolution" is called for, in the scope of diplomacy and in the diplomatic process itself.[47] Negotiating world order, the diplomacy of consensus, is such a universal process.

---

[47]Stanley Hoffmann, *Primacy or World Order: American Foreign Policy Since the Cold War* (New York: McGraw-Hill, 1978), p. 189.

Index

Acheson, Dean G., 117, 126

Acid rain, 19–31; Canadian-American agreement sought on, 19, 223, 231; defined, 23; information campaign on, launched in U.S. by Canada, 29–30, 232; irritant in Canadian-U.S. relations, 23–26; problem in Sweden, 25; threat to economic resources of Canada, 23

Adams, John Quincy, 139

Adirondacks, damage by acid rain in, 23, 24

Afghanistan, 93; Soviet invasion of, 50, 95, 98, 133, 228; UN as channel of negotiation on, 64, 224

Africa, cocoa-producing territories of, 168; former colonies acceded to independence, 36; tradition of *palaver*, 241

African, Caribbean, and Pacific (ACP) countries, and EEC scheme, 171

African Development Bank, 240

Agency for International Development, 14

Agriculture, and commodity markets, 167, 168; and famine control, 16; farm goods subject to restrictions, 191; and nutrition, 10–11; relation to health, 10; treated sectorally, 188

Air quality, agreement sought by Canada and U.S. on, 30

Alaska, 138; territory encompassed by NATO, 121

Algeria, and NATO, 121

Alliance, defined, 111–12, 113, 133, 134

Alliance for Progress, 144

American Red Cross, 9

Andean Common Market, 141

Andropov, Yuri, 74, 98

Antiballistic missiles (ABM), 76; for defenses, *see* Strategic Defense Initiative (SDI)

Anti-Ballistic Missile (ABM) Treaty (1972), 69–70, 72, 74, 75, 76, 77

Antisatellite systems, 70; ASATs, 76–77

Anti-Semitism, Soviet, 98

Arab states (countries), and Israeli relations,
80, 81; nervous about Iran-Iraq war, 62; and peacemaking with Israel, 221

Argentina, 81; debt crisis of, 204, 207; dispute over Beagle Channel, 140, 224; and Guarantor Pact, 140; involve in nonproliferation, 94; and law of the sea, 35; and Malvinas Islands crisis, 142–43; refusal to sign NPT, 84

Arms control, 77, 107, 226; and ABM Treaty, 69, 72; contradiction between multilateral arming and bilateral control, 130; and INF, 129–30; and NATO, 127, 128, 132; and "Star Wars," 70, 73, 75, 77

Arms race, 63, 69, 71, 74, 75

Armstrong, Hamilton Fish, 117

Asia, former colonies acceded to independence, 36; short-term food chaos in, 11

Asian Development Bank, 240

Association of Southeast Asia (ASA), 154

Association of Southeast Asian Nations (ASEAN), 149–63, 222, 223, 235, 237; Agreement on the Establishment of the ASEAN Secretariat, 157; apprehensive of Communist powers, 159; Bali summit (1976), 157, 158; Chambers of Commerce and Industry, 161; and collapse of South Vietnam, 157; confrontation with Vietnam, 157; Declaration of ASEAN Concord, 157; described as geopolitical entity, 158; diplomatic methods of, 157–63, 233; economic development of, 160–62; emphasis on economic, social, and cultural issues, 152, 155, 156, 162; and GATT, 186, 238; goal of common market, 161; handling of Kampuchea issue, 157–58; history of, 149, 151–55; intra-ASEAN trade, 158; Kuala Lumpur meeting (1976), 158; leverage in dealing with superpowers et al., 156; members, 149; negotiate with Japan, U.S., and EEC, 160, 162; processes of consensual negoti-

ASEAN (*continued*)
ation, 160–61; strategic geographical position of countries in, 158–59; Treaty of Amity and Cooperation in Southeast Asia, 157, 158, 222; ultimate goal of, 150; U.S. interest in, 189; wary of Communist expansion, 152; ZOPFAN essential to, 150, 159–60
Atlantic Alliance, 124, 226
Atlantic Charter, 11
Atlantic Community, and NATO, 125–26
Atlantic Ocean, satellite congestion over, 55
Atoms for Peace Program, 83–84, 85
Australasia, 159
Australia, and ASEAN, 157; defense pact with U.S., 120–21; security arrangement with Malaysia and Singapore, 150, 153, 159
Austria, at Madrid CSCE, 100
Automobiles, industry treated sectorally, 188
Auto parts, 161
Axis states, 220
Aykroyd, W. R., 10, 15

Bacteriology, 14
Balance of payments, 203, 210, 213; deficits, 200
Balance of power, 112, 114; European, 122, 225, as automatic international order, 221; Western, 222
Balanced force reductions, and NATO, 127
Balkan countries, 154
Ballistic missiles, 38, 69, 70, 73, 76
Bananas, 170
"Bancor" currency, 212
Bandung conference (1955), 153
Bangkok Declaration (1967), 156
Bangladesh, and GATT, 191
Banks and banking, 199, 200, 201, 225; and debt consolidation, 208–09; lending to developing countries, 201, 232; limiting their risks, 201; and liquidity creation, 209–10, 211; and Mexican debt crisis, 204–07; requiring reserves, 206, 209–10, 211; and stabilization of commodity markets, 178; and trade in services, 194
Barbados, 144
Barrère, Camille, 8
Barton, Clara, 6
Baruch Plan, 83

Bauxite, 170
BBC, 49, 98
Beagle Channel, 138; Argentina-Chile dispute over, 140, 224
Bedjaoui, Mohammed, 238
Beirut, 65
Belgium, in Brussels Pact, 118; colonial interests and North Atlantic Treaty, 120; exchanges with Eastern Europe, 126. *See also* Benelux countries; Low Countries
Bell, Griffin B., 96
Benelux countries, and MBFR talks, 128; as original members of NATO, 119
Ben-Gurion, David, 220
Bering Sea, 138
Berlin, four-power supervision of, 115
Berlin Air Safety Center, 115
Bertram, Christoph, 130, 131, 132
Bevin, Ernest, 226
Biafran war (1967–1970), 16
Bigwood, E. J., 10
Biological standardization, by OIHP, 8
Biological weapons, 98
Biosphere Conference (1968), 234
Bipolarity, 221, 232
Bogotá Charter (1948), 226
Bolívar, Simon, 138, 139
Borneo (Kalimantan), 153. *See also* North Borneo
Borrowing and lending, international, 172; and oil shocks, 200–01
Boundary Waters Treaty (1909), 20, 26–27, 28, 30, 223
Bowman, Robert M., 76
Brandt, Willy, 126
Brazil, 81; cooperation on shortwave broadcasting, 49; debt crisis of, 204, 207; and fear of U.S. safeguards, 194; and GATT, 191; German sale of nuclear materials to, 87–88; and Guarantor Pact, 140; refusal to sign NPT, 84; stability of, for coffee market, 168
Brest-Litovsk, Treaty of, 220
Bretton Woods Agreement (1944), 179, 203, 233, 235, 240
Brooks, Harvey, 85
Brown, Lester, 21
Bruce, S. M., later Viscount Bruce of Melbourne, 10, 15
Brunei, as member of ASEAN, 149, 158

Brussels Pact (1948), 118, 123, 226
Brussels Treaty, Paris agreements (1954), 123, 124
Bubonic plague, 7, 8, 231
Bucharest, Treaty of, 220
Buddhism, as source for ZOPFAN concept, 159, 160, 233
Bulgaria, and MBFR talks, 128
Bunnag, Tej, 149
Burma, 151
Burnet, Etienne, 10, 15
Byrnes, James F., 115
Byrnes Four Power Draft Treaty, 118–19

Cambodia, 162; and SEATO, 152
Cam Ranh Bay, Soviets at, 159
Canada, 146, 189, 195, 222; agreement sought with U.S. on air quality, 30; and ASEAN, 157; and Common Fund, 176; in CSCE Madrid meeting, 98; defense pact with U.S., 120–21; economic and environmental interests contrasted to U.S., 23; evolution of environmental policy in, 19–22, 31; excluded from European Security Conference, 95; and fear of U.S. safeguards, 194; and Law of the Sea conference, 42; and MBFR talks, 128; and NATO, 114; and Paris agreements, 123; relations with U.S. re acid rain, 19, 23–26, 29–30, 223, 231, 232
Caribbean, 141; and EEC scheme, 171; former colonies acceded to independence, 36; widening of gap between Latin America and, 142–43
Caribbean Basin Initiative (CBI), 189
Caribbean Community and Common Market (CARICOM), 144
Carson, Rachel, Silent Spring, 20
Carter, Jimmy, 22
Carter administration, and airborne pollution, 29; banning systems to destroy satellites in space, 76; and Madrid CSCE, 105; nuclear program, 85, 87, 88
Casablanca formula, 220
Castañeda, Jorge, 43
Castlereagh, Robert Stewart, Viscount, 220
Cecil, Lord Robert, 239
Central America, 63, 222; and Congress of Panama, 139; peace promoted in, by Contadora group, 141; troubled situation

never placed on OAS agenda, 141, 146
Ceylon, associating with NATO, 121; rubber exports, 168
Chad, and GATT, 191
Charles, Eugenia, 144
Chemical weapons, 98
Chiang Kai-shek, 116
Chile, dispute over Beagle Channel, 140, 224; and Guarantor Pact, 140
China, 115, 220; U.S. military commitments to, 116
China (People's Republic), 101, 158, 159; and ASEAN, 152, 156; Cultural Revolution, 156; and GATT, 182, 192; in Nonaligned Movement, 153; as power center in pentapolar world order, 221–22; refusal to sign NPT, 84
Cholera, 5, 7, 9, 14, 231
Churchill, Winston, 60, 227
Civil defense, 75
Civil War (U.S.), starvation as instrument of policy during, 16
Clay, Henry, 138
Clean Air Act (1970), 30
Cleveland, Harlan, 127
Clothing, subject to restrictions, 191
"Coalition of free nations," 121
Coastal states, and Convention on the Law of the Sea, 43; and fisheries, 38, 39; and Law of the Sea conference, 42, 43, 237
Cocoa, 168, 170, 175
Coffee, 158, 168, 175
Cold War, 15, 63, 113, 117, 122, 139
Collective defense, and Harmel report, 127; and NATO, 117, 127, 132; and Rio Pact, 117; and UN, 116–17
"Collective economic security," and OAS, 140, 143
Collective security, 60; concept of, 112; key to, 66; and NATO, 112–13, 114, 116, 117, 126; and OAS, 140, 143; recommendations regarding, 60; of UN, 133; and Warsaw Pact, 129
Colombia, 139, 141
Columbus, Christopher, 224
COMECON, 162
Commercial Bureau of the American Republics, 139
Commodities, chronically depressed world prices for, 158; decline in prices of

Commodities (*continued*)
(1980s), 175; distribution of, 170, 171; in international economy in new context, 178; losing importance in trade of developing countries, 178; marketing of, 170, 171; price-support schemes for, 168, 174; price stabilization of, 167, 173, 174, 175, 177; processing of, 170, 171; research-and-development activities for, 175–76; restrictions on, 167; UNCTAD as forum for issues, 167; UNCTAD's Integrated Program for, 169–75, 178
Commodity agreements, 167, 168, 170–71, 172, 174–76, 231
Commodity markets, 167–79; changing dynamics of, 177; and depression, 175; and inflation, 171–72, 177; instability of, 177; long-term trends in, 177–78; and recession, 174–75, 178; regulation of, 167, 168; stabilization of, 167, 169, 173, 177, 178
Common heritage of mankind concept, and seabed and ocean floor, 39, 40
Communications, 219–20; field revolutionized, 47; and Southeast Asian connections, 151–52
Communications Satellite Act (1962), 53, 54
Communications Satellite Corporation (COMSAT), 53, 54
Communications satellites, 48, 53–55, 152, 220, 231; Satellite Earth Station projects, 152
Communists, 104; and ASEAN countries, 152, 153, 159
Community of power, 112
Comparative-advantage theory, 181
Compensatory financing, 171, 175
Comprehensive Test Ban (CTB), 76
Comprehensive Test Ban Treaty, 74
Concert of Europe, 112, 234
Conference on Security and Cooperation in Europe (CSCE), 95–107, 129, 131; Belgrade follow-up meeting (1977–78), 96, 99, 101; conference on disarmament in Europe (CDE) (Stockholm, 1974), 103; cultural forum in Budapest (1985), 104; experts' meeting in Athens (1984), 104; experts' meeting on human contacts (Bern), 104; experts' meeting on human rights (Ottawa, 1985), 104; forum on

issue of surprise military attack, 104; Helsinki tenth-anniversary meeting (1985), 103, 104; Madrid follow-up meeting (1980–1983), 51, 95–107; seminar in Venice (1984), 104; victims of Soviet repression mentioned at, 99, 101; Vienna follow-up meeting (1986), 103, 104
Confidence- and Security-building Measures in Europe conference (Stockholm, 1984), 103–04
Congo, 64, 241
Congress (U.S.), and ASAT testing, 76; attitudes toward IMF and World Bank, 211; and Canadian acid rain campaign, 30; date set to conclude negotiation, 187; and nuclear nonproliferation, 90–91
Congress of Panama (1826), 139
Congress of Vienna (1814–15), 34; and imposed international order, 220, 221
Conservation, and environmental policy in Canada, 22; and fisheries, 38, 39
Contadora group, 141
Containment policy, in Southeast Asia, 152
Continental shelf, 35, 37, 44; defined, 35
Convention on the Continental Shelf, 35
Convention on Fishing and Conservation of the Living Resources of the High Seas, 35
Convention on the High Seas, 35
Convention on the Territorial Sea and the Contiguous Zone, 35
Coolidge, Calvin, 234
Copper, 170
Corea, Gamani, 230, 231, 233, 240, 241
Costa Rica, 141
Cotton, 170
Crimean War, 6
Crisis prevention, 134
Cruise missiles, 73, 102, 129
Crystal ball effect (Nye), 79–80, 227
Cuba, as member of OAS, 142
Cuban missile crisis (1962), 126, 142, 235
Customs administration, and GATT, 184
Customs unions, 189
Cyprus, NATO role in, 124; UN as channel of negotiation on, 64, 66, 224
Czechoslovakia, 227; and MBFR talks, 128; Prague Spring (1968), 227–28; sacrifice of Sudetenland to Germany, 220

Da Nang, Soviets at, 159
Davison, Henry Pomeroy, 9
Debt consolidation, 208–09
Debt crisis, origins of, 200
Debt problem, 230; and OAS, 146; of Third World, 224–25
Debt renegotiating, 199–200, 202, 207–08, 210
Debt rescheduling, 199–200, 207–08, 210
Debt rollovers, 205
Debt service, 178, 200, 202, 205, 211, 213
Debtor-creditor relationships, 199
Defense, and Harmel report, 127; NATO efforts in, 126, 127, 129, 131. See also Collective defense
Defensive systems, 69–77
Deficits, 201
De Gaulle, Charles, 126
De Lauer, Richard, 73–74
De la Warr, Lord, 10
Democratic Kampuchea, 157
Denmark, and MBFR talks, 128; as original member of NATO, 119
Department of Commerce (U.S.), report on seabed mining, 41
Depression (1980s), 175
Desarrollo integral, 140
Détente, 96, 235; and Harmel report, 127; NATO efforts in, 113, 126, 127, 129, 131
Deterrence, NATO success in, 126
Deutsche Welle, 49, 98
Developed countries, 222; and GATT, 183; as main consuming countries, 169
Developing countries, 222; and ASEAN, 150, 160; bank lending to, 201; commodity exports of importance to, 178; and commodity negotiations, 172, 173–74; as co-owners of seabed resources, 40; dependence on developed, and vice versa, 179; difference in objectives between industrialized countries and, 202; and fisheries surplus, 39; and GATT, 183, 186, 191, 238; "graduation" of, 191; and IMF, 240; increase in demand for raw materials, 177; and inflow of direct private investment, 212–13; negotiations between creditor countries and, 202; and oil price increases, 231–32

Development, as true name for peace, 147, 233
Diktat, 220
Diplomacy, ASEAN method of, 157–63; "Asian way," 151; bilateral, 132, 144, 184, 188, 189, 190, and ASEAN, 155, defined, 236, interplay between multilateral and, 236, and nonproliferation regime, 87–88, 89, 237; conference, 90; of consensus, 160–61, 217–44; contrast between private and public, 217; "group," 237; gunboat, 227; multilateral, 132, 144, 184, 185, 186, 187, 189, 231, 238, 241, 242, 243, defined, 236, interplay between bilateral and, 236, and nonproliferation regime, 88–89, 90, 236–37; parliamentary, 231, 236, 242; requiring special majorities, 240–41, 242; and unanimity rule, 239, 241, 242; of UN system, 90, 241; virtuoso, 131, 243; and weighted voting, 239–40, 241, 242. See also Negotiation
Directed-energy systems, 72
Disarmament, 104; NATO efforts in, 113, 126, 127; security as precondition of, 60; Soviet love of, 104
"Disengagement," 126
Distant-water nations, and fisheries, 39
Dollar, interest rates raising price of, 195–96; not stabilized by FDR, 235; overvalued, 188
Dominica, 144
Dominican Republic intervention (1965), 142
Drinking water, 8
Dumping, 183, 184, 192
Dunant, Henri, 5–6, 15, 234
Dunkirk (1947), Treaty of, 118
Dutch East India Company, 34
Dutch East Indies, 151

Early Bird (communications satellite), 53
Eastern bloc, 132
Eastern Caribbean, 144
Eastern Europe (East European countries), 114, 162, 227; and Common Fund, 176; exchanges with Belgium, 126; NATO promoting improvement of relations with, 127; and North Atlantic Treaty, 118, 119; radio broadcasts re CSCE to, 98–99; and Soviet shortwave broadcasting, 49, 50

East Germany. *See* German Democratic
Republic
East-West struggle, 64; deadlock, 113
Ebban, Abba, 217, 220, 238, 243
Economic development, of ASEAN coun-
tries, 160–62; Canadian interests con-
trasted to U.S., 23; and environmental
policy in Canada, 22; within OAS, 140,
146; security as precondition of, 60
*Economic Development for Canada in the
1980s*, 22
Economist (London), 124–25
Economy, export-led, 184; and financial
interdependence, 202; low rate of
growth, 184, 188, 231; triad of support
for world, 178–79. *See also* Macroeco-
nomic policy; Microeconomic policy
Ecuador, 140
Eden, Anthony, 123
Education, OAS activities in field of, 142
Edwards, Jonathan, 106
Egypt, in Nonaligned Movement, 153
Eisenhower, Dwight D., 234; launched
Atoms for Peace Program, 83, 85; and
nuclear testing, 74
Electronic products, 158
Electronics, 47; industry treated sectorally,
188
El Salvador, border conflict (1969), 142
Employment, 181, 182, 193; full, 179, 233
Energy development, and environmental pol-
icy in Canada, 21
Engineering, and trade in services, 194
England, 3
Environmental policy, Canadian contrasted
to U.S., 23; evolution of, in Canada, 19–
22, 31; faced by "Catch-22" response,
25; and the IJC, 27–28, 223
Environment Canada, 19
Ethiopia, Italy's invasion of, 60; starvation
in, 16
Euromarkets, 201
Europe, 36; balance of power in, 122, 221,
225; famine during World War II in, 16;
international balance, 122; international
security system for, 118; short-term food
chaos in, 11; stability of, and rearmament of Germany, 122
European Coal and Steel Community
(ECSC), 122

European Community, 146; approaches trade
problems on sectoral basis, 188; and
ASEAN, 156; and GATT, 185, 186;
restraints, 192
European Defense Community (EDC), 122–
23
European Economic Community (EEC), 173,
188; and ASEAN, 157, 160, 161, 162;
and Common Fund, 176; as negotiated
supranational order, 222–23; restraints,
192–93; STABEX scheme, 171
European Security Conference, 95–96
Evensen, Jens, 43
Exchange rates, 182, 195, 196, 203
"Exclusive economic zones" (EEZs), 38–39,
41, 43, 44
Exports, of developing oil-exporting countries, 200; earnings to service debts, 211;
nonmarket economies', 192; restraints,
188; significant in world economy, 184;
subsidies for, 183, 184, 192, 195, 196

Fabiola, 5
Falklands. *See* Malvinas Islands/Falklands
crisis
Famine, 16
Far Eastern Economic Review, 161
Federal Republic of Germany (West Ger-
many), 115, 195; accepted into Brussels
Pact, 123; with British-French relation-
ship, 222; at Madrid CSCE, 101; and
MBFR talks, 128; as member of NATO,
118, 119, 122, 123, 124, 129, 227;
problem of reunification, 127; radio
transmissions jammed by Soviets, 50;
rearmament of, 122–23; and Saar issue,
124; sale of nuclear materials to Brazil,
87–88
Federal Reserve Board, and Mexican debt
crisis, 204, 206
Federal Reserve System, 203
Federated Malay States, 151
Feldman, Shai, 80
Fertilizer, 160
Fibers, 170
Fiji, 43
Finances, and economic interdependence,
202
Financial policy, coordinated with trade pol-
icy, 195–96

Financial Times, 184
Finland, at Madrid CSCE, 100
First-strike capability, of superpowers, 38
First World, 191, 205
Fisheries and fishing, conservation zones for, 35, 37; damaged by acid rain, 23; and four competing interests, 38–39; NATO role in British-Icelandic dispute, 124
Fishing rights, and law of the sea, 35, 36, 41
Food, early history of large-scale work in, 4–5; OIHP work in food hygiene, 8; production, 10, 12, 13
Food and Agriculture Organization (FAO), 11, 12; and WHO, 13
Food Council, 12
Ford, Gerald, and use of plutonium, 85
Ford administration, and NSG, 88
Foreign Affairs, 117, 152
Foreign competition, 184, 188
Forests, damaged by acid rain, 23, 25
Four Power Draft Treaty on the Disarmament and Demilitarization of Germany, 115
France, 3, 111–12; with British-German relationship, 222; colonial interests and North Atlantic Treaty, 120; delegates to Provisional Health Committee, 9; demanded Algeria be covered by North Atlantic Treaty, 121; empire disintegrated, 36; four-power collaboration, 115; *la francophonie*, as automatic hegemonic order, 228; guarantee against a resurgent Germany, 118; and integration of Germany into NATO, 124; involve in nonproliferation, 94; and Law of the Sea conference, 42, 237; at Madrid CSCE, 104; and MBFR talks, 128; narrow interests of, in NATO, 122; and nuclear nonproliferation, 87; and problem of German reunification, 127; and rearmament of Germany, 122–23; refusal to sign NPT, 84; rivalry between Germany and, 121; and Saar issue, 124; sacrifice of Sudetenland by, 220; sale of nuclear materials to Pakistan, 87, 88, 237; and sanitary convention, 7; troops in Lebanon, 65
Franco, Francisco, 119
Franco-Prussian War (1870), 80; starvation as instrument of policy during, 16

Freedom, as goal of ASEAN, 150
Freedom from Hunger, 10
Freedom of religion, 103
"Freedom from want" (FDR), 11
Free market, 173
Free-trade agreements, 189, 190
Free trade areas, 189
Free World, 228
Frontinus, Sextus Julius, 4
Fuels, exports, 178
Future Tasks of the Alliance (Harmel report), 127, 130

Galen, 5
General Agreement on Tariffs and Trade (GATT), 179, 181–96, 234; negotiating process of consensus by, 184–87, 237–38, 242; and nonmarket economy countries, 191–92; principles of, 182–83; problem of trade in services, 194–95; problem of violations, 190–91; and safeguards, 192; secretariat, 185, 186, 190; sectoral negotiations within, 189; Tokyo Round, 183, 186, 238; "transparency" problem, 192; veto power in, 185
Geneva Convention (1867), 6
Geneva Peace Conference on the Middle East (1973), 221
Geneva Public Welfare Society, 6
German Democratic Republic (East Germany), 115, 227; and MBFR talks, 128
Germany, 3, 112; imposed peace after World War II, 220; Nazi aggression toward Latin America, 226; possibility of a resurgent, 118; postwar occupation of, 115; rivalry between France and, 121; sacrifice of Sudetenland to, 220; and Versailles Treaty, 220
Ghana, 168
Gibraltar, 124–25
Global 2000, 22
Gold payments, 212
Grain, 173
Great Britain (United Kingdom), 222; associating Dominions with defense pact with U.S., 120–21; as champion of Mare Liberum, 34; colonial interests and North Atlantic Treaty, 120; Commonwealth as automatic hegemonic order, 228; control of Malayan and Ceylonese rubber

Great Britain (*continued*)
exports, 168; delegates to Provisional
Health Committee, 9; empire disintegrated, 36; and FAO, 12; four-power collaboration, 115; with French-German
relationship, 222; gunboat diplomacy of,
227; and IEFC, 11; and integration of
Germany into NATO, 124; interest in
stability in Ghana and Nigeria, 168;
interference in Latin America, 226; and
Law of the Sea conference, 42, 237; and
Malvinas Islands crisis, 142; and MBFR
talks, 128; narrow interests of, in NATO,
122; and NATO role in Cyprus problem,
124; NATO role in fishery dispute
between Iceland and, 124; and problem
of German reunification, 127; radio transmissions jammed by Soviets, 50; sacrifice of Sudetenland by, 220; security
arrangement with Malaysia and Singapore, 150, 159; troops in Lebanon, 65
Great Depression, 235
Greater Malay Federation, 154
Great Lakes Water Quality Agreement
(1972), 28–29, 30
Great-power determination, of fate of small
states, 220–21
Greece, guerrilla fighting in (1947), 62; and
MBFR talks, 128; as member of NATO,
119; and NATO role in Cyprus problem,
124
Grenada invasion (1983), 144–45, 146
Grotius, Hugo, 33–34, 234
Group of 77, 141, 150, 160, 188, 237
Guarantor Pact (1942), 140
Gunboat diplomacy, 227

Hague Codification Conference (1930), 34–
35, 37
Hague Convention (1907), 139
Haig, Alexander M., 142
Haiti, Roman Catholic influence in, 225
Hammarskjöld, Dag, 60, 224
Hanoi, 157, 158
Harding, Warren G., 234
Harmel, Pierre, 127
Harmel report, 127, 130
Havana Charter (1947), 167, 168, 177, 179
Hazardous waste, and environmental policy
in Canada, 20

Health, 232; and absence of war or its
threat, 15; in ancient Rome, 4; caring for
the wounded in war, 5–6; dealing with
international epidemics and communicable diseases, 5, 6, 7, 8, 9, 11, 12–13,
14, 16; defined by WHO, 13–14; early
history of, in the East, 5; early history of
large-scale work in, 4–5; OAS activities
in field of, 142; relation to agriculture,
10; threat by acid rain to human, 23. *See
also* Nutrition
Heavy water, 84
Hegemony, 225–26, 228
Helsinki Agreement, 51
Helsinki Conference (1975), 52, 96, 129
Helsinki Final Act (1975), 95, 96, 97, 98,
103, 104, 107
Helsinki Watch Groups, 98
Hickerson, John D., 119
Hiroshima, 227
Hitler regime, radio broadcasts of propa-
ganda, 51
Hobbes, Thomas, 106
Hoffmann, Stanley, 243
Holy Roman Empire, 224
Honduras, border conflict (1969), 142
Hospital orders, 5
Hospitals, created, 4–5; field, 8
Hot Springs, Virginia, first UN meeting in,
11
Human rights, and Helsinki Final Act, 97,
98; meeting in Ottawa on, 104; and OAS
Charter, 140
Hungary, 227; and GATT, 191; Jews saved
by Wallenberg in, 99; and MBFR talks,
128
Hunger and malnutrition, League of Nations
investigations into, 10

Iceland, 128; as member of NATO, 119,
226; NATO role in fishery dispute
between Great Britain and, 124;
Ilichev, Leonid F., 100–01
Imports, beneficial effects for exports, 211;
GATT treatment of, 183; restrictions,
188, 192
Imposed peace, 220
Imposed settlement, 221
India, 81, 158; associating with NATO, 121;
famine in, 16; involve in nonprolifera-

India (*continued*)
tion, 84, 94; in Nonaligned Movement, 153; and nuclear weapons, 84, 88, 92
Indian Ocean, 159
Indochina, 151, 152, 162; and SEATO, 153
Indonesia, 161, 225, 235; "confrontation" policy of, 153; as leader of Nonaligned Movement, 153, 154, 155; in Maphilindo, 154; as member of ASEAN, 149, 158; new policy different from nonalignment, 154; and North Borneo dispute, 154; PRC subversion in, 156; and role of ZOPFAN, 159–60; use of satellites in, 152
Industrialized countries, difference in objectives between developing world and, 202
Industrial policy, 192
Infantile paralysis, 14
Infection and contagion, 5
Inflation, 202, 209, 210, 211, 213; and commodity markets, 171–72, 177, 231
Influenza epidemic (1918–19), 9
Innocent III, 4
Insurance, and trade in services, 194
Inter-American Development Bank, 240
Inter-American System, 138, 140, 146; as negotiated hegemonic regime, 226
Inter-American Treaty of Reciprocal Assistance (Rio de Janeiro, 1947), 117, 118, 119, 140
Intercontinental ballistic missile (ICBM), 72
Interest rates, 195, 200, 208
Intermediate nuclear forces (INF), 130
Intermediate Nuclear Forces (INF) Talks, 70, 75, 76, 130–31
International Atomic Energy Agency (IAEA), 83, 84, 85, 89–90, 236
International Bank for Reconstruction and Development (IBRD) (World Bank), 182, 205, 211, 213, 235, 240, 242
International Committee of the Red Cross, 234
International Conference of Ministers on Acid Rain (Ottawa, 1984), 31
International Convention Concerning the Use of Broadcasting in the Cause of Peace (1936), 51
International Emergency Food Council (IEFC), 11–12
International Energy Agency, 235–36

International Health Conference (New York, 1946), 12
International Institute for Strategic Studies (London), 130
International Joint Commission (IJC), 27–28, 30, 223
International Labor Conference (1935), 10
International Labor Organization (ILO), 9, 103, 240; and WHO, 13
International law, as self-enforcing, 218
International Monetary and Economic Conference (London, 1933), 235
International Monetary Fund, 171, 182, 195, 203–05, 211–13, 235, 240, 242; as imposed supranational order, 224–25; and Mexican debt crisis, 204–05, 207; Special Drawing Rights (SDRs), 203, 209–12, 240; Toronto meeting (1982), 205
International Nuclear Fuel Cycle Evaluation (INFCE), 85–87, 90
International Physicians for the Prevention of Nuclear War, 15
International Sanitary Conference (Paris, 1851), 5, 6–7, 15
International Sanitary Conference (Paris, 1903), 7
International Seabed Authority, 40, 41; as negotiated supranational order, 223
International Telecommunications Satellite Consortium (INTELSAT), 54, 231
International Telecommunication Union (ITU), 47, 48, 52, 53, 54, 55, 236; conference at Malaga-Torremolinos (1973), 52; conference in Nairobi (1982), 50; International Frequency Registration Board, 52; as negotiated international regime, 219–20; World Administrative Radio Conference (WARC) (Geneva, 1979), 50; World Administrative Radio Conference (WARC) (Geneva, 1984), 50, 51–52, 55
International Telegraph Union, 47
International Trade Organization (ITO), 182
International Union for Conservation of Nature and Natural Resources, 22
International Wheat Agreement, 240
Inverchapel, Lord, 119
Investment, in developing countries, 201
Iran, bringing within NATO, 121

Iran-Iraq war, 62, 66, 225; UN as channel of negotiation on, 64, 224
Iraq, Israeli attack on nuclear reactor in, 82, 90. *See also* Iran-Iraq war
Ireland, proposal in UN of NPT, 84
Iron Curtain, 98, 227
Iron ore, 170
Islam, influence of, 225
Islamic League, 150
Israel, 81; attack on nuclear reactor in Iraq, 82, 90; free-trade agreement with U.S., 189, 190; and GATT, 191; and nuclear weapons, 80, 92–93; and peacemaking with Arabs, 221; refusal to sign NPT, 84
Italy, 3; accepted into Brussels Pact, 123; delegates to Provisional Health Committee, 9; and MBFR talks, 128; as original member of NATO, 119; sacrifice of Sudetenland by, 220; sanctions not imposed against (1935), 59–60; troops in Lebanon, 65

Jamaica, 144
Japan, 115, 235; approaches trade problems on sectoral basis, 188; and ASEAN, 156, 157, 158, 159, 160, 162; and Common Fund, 176; delegates to Provisional Health Committee, 9; and GATT negotiations, 186; imposed peace after World War II, 220; and Law of the Sea conference, 42, 237; as power center in pentapolar world order, 221–22
Jenks, C. Wilfred, 241–42
Jews, saved by Wallenberg, 99
Joffe, Josef, 123, 124
Jute, 170, 175

Kampelman, Max M., 228, 232, 241
Kampuchea, 157
Keliher, John C., 129
Kellogg-Briand pact, 84
Kennan, George F., 126, 130–31, 152
Kennedy, John F., and communications satellites, 53; and nuclear proliferation, 93
Keohane, Robert, 217–18
Keynes, John Maynard, 212
Keyworth, George, II, 73
Khrushchev, Nikita, 106
Kissinger, Henry A., 131, 132, 146, 221, 235; and Realpolitik diplomacy, 114

Kissinger Commission, 146
Koh, T. T. B., 223, 227, 234, 237, 241, 242, 243
Kompong Som (Sihanoukville), Soviets at, 159
Korea, 158, 159; and GATT, 191; UN enforcement procedure used in, 62. *See also* South Korea
Korean Air Lines Flight 007, 15
Korean War, 122
Kuala Lumpur Declaration (1971), 150

Labor-intensive industries, in Southeast Asia, 158
Landlocked states, and fisheries, 38–39; and Law of the Sea conference, 42, 43, 237
Lange, Halvard, 125
Laos, 157, 162; and SEATO, 152
Larosière, Jacques de, 204
Lasers, 72
Latin America, 141; debt crises in, 204–05, 207; desired U.S. protection during World War II, 226; and extrahemispheric interference, 226; preference for multilateral diplomacy, 236; regional agreement limiting nuclear weapons, 84; shortwave broadcasts from U.S., 49; and U.S. relationship, 144, premised on equilibrium of forces, 222; widening of gap between Caribbean and, 142–43
Latin American Economic System (SELA), 141
Law of the sea, 234; closed vs. free sea, 33–34; contiguous zone defined, 34; exploitability of resources of the sea, 36, 37; Grotian view of, 34; international law codified, 34; and Latin American proclamations, 35; limits of the territorial sea, 36, 37, 41, 44; and passage through straits, 37, 38, 41; resources of seabed and ocean floor, 36, 39–41; and right of innocent passage, 36; and seabed mining, 40–41; six-mile territorial sea, 34; three-mile territorial sea, 34, 35, 37, 227; Truman's proclamations on, 35; twelve-mile territorial sea, 36, 37, 38. *See also* United Nations Conference on the Law of the Sea; United Nations Convention on the Law of the Sea
League of Nations, 51, 139, 234–35, 239;

League of Nations (*continued*)
  collective security institutionalized in,
  112; Covenant, 239; failure of, 59–60,
  139; Health Organization, 9–10, 12; and
  law of the sea, 34; Mixed Committee on
  the Problem of Nutrition, 10; and OIHP,
  9; Provisional Health Committee, 9;
  report on *The Physiological Bases of
  Nutrition*, 10
League of Red Cross Societies, 9, 13
Lebanon, 4; current problem compared to
  1860, 64–65; Israeli invasion of (1982),
  65; role of UN in, 65–66, 224; shared-
  interest approach to problem of, 62, 66
Lee Kuan Yew, 162, 223
Lending-of-last-resort, 202–04, 210, 224–25
Leningrad, starvation as instrument of policy
  against, 16
Leninism, 99, 102, 104, 107
Leprosy, 5, 8
Less developed countries (LDCs), 210; and
  GATT, 191; opposed to restraints, 193
Light-water reactors, 85
Ligue des Sociétés de la Croix-Rouge, 9
Limited Test Ban Treaty (1963), 76, 235
Liska, George, 227
Livestock management, in Niger, 14
Lomé Convention, 141
London Conference (1954), 123
Louis XVIII, 111
Love Canal, 20
Low Countries, and integration of Germany
  into NATO, 124
Lown, Bernard, 15
Luxembourg, 123; in Brussels Pact, 118; in
  NATO, 226. *See also* Benelux countries;
  Low Countries

Macapagal, Diosdado, 154
Machinery, 158
Macroeconomic policy, 177, 195, 202, 208
Madrid Concluding Document, 103, 107
Malaria, 14
Malaya, 151; and ASA, 154; in Maphilindo,
  154; and North Borneo dispute, 154; rub-
  ber exports, 168
Malaysia, 153, 154, 156; initiative for ZOP-
  FAN, 159; as member of ASEAN, 149,
  155; nonaligned, 155; PRC subversion
  in, 156; security arrangement with Aus-

tralia, New Zealand, and Great Britain,
  150, 153, 159; use of satellites in, 152
Malik, Adam, 154, 155
Malta, 36
Malvinas Islands/Falklands crisis (1982),
  142–43, 205
Manhattan Project, 73
Manila Pact (1954), 150, 159
Mansfield, Mike, 128
Manufactured goods, exports, 161, 178
Manufactures, 167
Maphilindo, 154
Mare Clausum (Closed Sea), 33
Mare Liberum (Free Sea), 33, 34, 227, 234
Market interventions, 173, 175
Marks, Leonard H., 219, 231, 241
Martino, Gaetano, 125
Marxism, 162
Maternal and child health, 13
Mayer, André, 10, 11, 15
Mayer, Jean, 231, 232, 234
McDougall, F. L., 10, 11, 15
Medicine, in early Arabia, 5
Mediterranean Sea, 104, 159; bordering
  countries included in North Atlantic Alli-
  ance, 119–20, 121, 127
Mellanby, Sir Edward, 10
Mexico, 141; and Congress of Panama, 139;
  debt crisis (1982) of, 204–07; and law of
  the sea, 35, 43; outside GATT, 182
Microeconomic policy, 195
Middle East, 63, 64, 66, 93, 233; Feldman's
  argument about, 80; imposed settlements
  in, 221; oil, 159; security linked to
  NATO, 121, 127
Military balance, 70, 79; and ASEAN, 157,
  222
Millikin, Eugene D., 182
Minerals, 171, 173, 174; resources of seabed
  and ocean floor, 39, 40, 41
Le Monde (Paris), 184
Monetary policy, 193, 195–96
Monetary system, 178
Money supply, 195
Monroe Doctrine, 226
Morocco, 225
Morrison, Philip, 231
Most favored nation, and GATT, 183, 195
Multiple independently targetable reentry
  vehicles (MIRVs), 71

Multipolarity, 221
Munich Conference (1938), 220, 221
Muslims, 225
Mutual and Balanced Force Reduction (MBFR) talks (Vienna), 128–29, 131, 132
Mutually assured destruction (MAD), 72

Nagasaki, 227
Nandan, Satya, 43
Napoleon, 111, 133, 228
Napoleonic Wars, 34, 234
Nasser, Gamal Abdel, 153
National Bipartisan Commission on Central America, 146
Nationality, concept of, 3
Nation-states, 63; concept of, 3
Natural resources, best use of, 188; and environmental policy in Canada, 21–22, 30; of seabed and ocean floor, 35, 36, 41; of Southeast Asian countries, 158
Negotiation, and ASEAN, 151; between creditor countries of industrialized world and debtors of developing world, 202; Buddhist ideal of the Middle Way, 160, 233; for commodity agreements, 169, 171–72, 173–74, 177; "consultation," 226; defined, 230; device of concluding by setting date, 187; distinction between diplomatic and parliamentary principles of, 217, 238, 243; elements of negotiating process, 199; GATT a testimony to, 182; Malay process of musyawarah, 160, 233, 241; means listening as well as talking, 102; multilateral, 217, 219, 226; process of consensus, by ASEAN, 160–61, by GATT, 184–87, by UNCLOS, 41–42; purpose of, 99; requires equilibrium, 232; sectoral, 188, 190; with Soviet Union at Madrid CSCE, 102–03; suitability of NATO for, 126–34; tradition of palaver, 241; UN as only channel on Afghanistan, etc., 64. See also Diplomacy; World order
Nehru, Jawaharlal, 153
Netherlands, at Belgrade CSCE, 99; in Brussels Pact, 118; colonial interests and North Atlantic Treaty, 120; Dutch empire

disintegrated, 36. See also Benelux countries; Low Countries
Neutrality, as goal of ASEAN, 150; and ZOPFAN, 159
New International Economic Order, 37, 169
Newly industrializing countries (NICs), and GATT, 191
New World Communications and Information Order, 50
New York Times, 142, 184
New Zealand, and ASEAN, 157; defense pact with U.S., 120–21; security arrangement with Malaysia and Singapore, 150, 153, 159
Nicaragua, 141; Roman Catholic influence in, 225
Niger, 14
Nigeria, 81, 168; starvation as weapon of terror in, 16
Nightingale, Florence, 6, 15
Nitze, Paul H., 121–22
Nixon, Richard M., 81, 219; foreign policy, 96; and Realpolitik diplomacy, 114
Nonaligned Movement, 150, 153–55, 157, 237
Nonintervention, and OAS Charter, 140, 144–45
Nonmarket economies, and GATT, 186, 191–92, 238
Non-Proliferation Treaty (NPT) (1968), 69, 83, 84, 86, 87, 89, 90, 92; as negotiated international regime, 219–20; nine countries' refusal to sign, 84; Review Conference, 87, 90, 236
Nordic countries, and Common Fund, 176; and GATT, 186, 238
North America, international security system for, 118; as power center in pentapolar world order, 221–22
North Atlantic Alliance, 111, 113, 114, 132, 134, 226; defense and détente main functions of, 127; frightened by Soviet control of Germany, 118; inclusion of countries bordering the Mediterranean, 119–20, 121, 127; not "regional," 120–21; in peacemaking business, 127; rearmament of Germany a divisive problem for, 122–23; and Suez crisis, 125
North Atlantic Pact, 118
North Atlantic Treaty (1949), 111, 118–19,

North Atlantic Treaty (*continued*)
121, 133, 134, 226; articles described,
116, 118; Germans welcomed as allies
under, 118, 119; nothing in it precluded
participation by USSR and its satellites,
118, 119, 134; relationship to UN
Charter, 114, 116, 117, 120, 125–26;
"treaty area" defined, 120
North Atlantic Treaty Organization (NATO),
36, 111–34, 235, 237, 238; adapting for
nonmilitary purposes, 113; alliance-into-
order change, 113; appointment of American as secretary-general, 132; "area of
reductions," 128; cannot negotiate, 130–
31; changed terms of West European
interaction, 123; character of, 133; Committee of Three ("three wise men"), 125;
Council, 125, 130, 132, "Harmel exercise," 127; and field of disarmament and
arms control, 127, 128; improving defenses of "exposed areas," 127; incorporation of Federal Republic of Germany
into, 123, 124, 129, 227; internal ordering role of, 121–26; and Madrid CSCE,
100, 101, 102; as negotiated hegemonic
regime, 225–26; Nuclear Planning
Group, 132; and problem of German reunification, 127; problem of using, to adjust
differences within the Atlantic community, 113; qualities of universality, complexity, and flexibility, 113; relationship
to UN Charter, 113, 116; relationship to
Warsaw Pact, 129, 133–34; report on
nonmilitary cooperation within, 125; and
resolution of Gibraltar dispute, 124–25;
role in British-Icelandic fishery dispute,
124; role in Cyprus problem, 124; self-
equilibrating character of, 222; suitability
for negotiations with its adversaries,
126–34; "two pillar" doctrine, 127–28;
"two track" decision, 129, 130
North Atlantic Triangle, 222
North Borneo (Sabah), 154
North-South dialogue, 141; and commodity
issues, 168, 170, 178
North-South issues, 89, 90, 191
North Vietnam, 156, 157
Norway, and Common Fund, 176; and Law
of the Sea conference, 43; and MBFR
talks, 128; as original member of

NATO, 119
Nuclear civil energy, 83–84; safeguards, 84,
85, 89
Nuclear deterrence, 80, 81, 82, 106, 219–20
Nuclear fuel cycle, 86, 87
Nuclear fuel supplies, 220; end of monopoly
of U.S. in, 85
Nuclear nonproliferation, 79–94; beginnings
of, 83–84; and bilateral diplomacy, 87–
88, 89, 237; diplomacy of maintaining
regime, compared to keeping four hoops
in air, 90, 94, 236; and INFCE, 86, 87;
maintenance of regime, 91–93, 232; and
multilateral diplomacy, 88–89, 90, 236,
237; practical diplomacy of building
regime, 83; risks in nuclear fuel cycle,
86. *See also* Non-Proliferation Treaty
Nuclear Nonproliferation Act (1978), 90
Nuclear problem, UN pioneering in, 60–61
Nuclear proliferation, degree of, 92–94; and
INFCE, 86, 87; like a staircase, 92, 93;
predictions for future, 93; as solution,
80; vertical, 90; world order built on furthering, 81, 82
Nuclear regime, international, 84, 85, 86.
See also Nuclear nonproliferation
Nuclear submarines, of superpowers, 38
Nuclear Suppliers Group (NSG), 85, 88–89,
236
Nuclear technology, 81–82, 86, 91; and Baruch Plan, 83
Nuclear testing, 70, 74; moratorium (1958),
74; in space, 76
Nuclear war, 77
Nuclear weapons (arms, weaponry), 60, 63,
219, 232, 237; Catholic bishops' conclusion about, 80; deregulation of, 69, 70,
77; number of U.S. and Soviet, 79; procedures for command and control of, 81–
82; regulation of, 69–70, 77; in relation
to world order, 81; in space, 76; technology of, 81–82; underground tests of, 70;
weapons-possessing states, 219;
weapons-usable materials, 85. *See also*
Soviet Union, nuclear relationship with
U.S.; United States, nuclear relationship
with USSR
"Nuclear winter," 80; "winterize" planet, 71
Nutrition, 232; and deficiency diseases, 14;
and FAO, 12; report, *The Physiological*

Nutrition (*continued*)
  Bases of Nutrition, 10; vitamins identified, 9; work of League of Nations in new field of, 9–10
Nye, Joseph S., Jr., 219, 227, 232, 236, 237; *Living with Nuclear Weapons*, 79

Offensive systems, 69–77
Office International d'Hygiène Publique (OIHP), 7–9, 12, 14, 231, 239–40; superseded by UNRRA, 11
Oil, 200, 235; embargo (1973–74), 84; Middle Eastern, 159; price decline, 172, 201; price increases, 169, 200, 201, 231–32
Olympic Games (Moscow), 95, 102
One-for-all, all-for-one pledge, 118
"One World" ideal (Willkie), 235
Order, automatic hegemonic, 228, illustrated by British Commonwealth and *la francophonie*, 228, 229; automatic international, 221–22, illustrated by European balance of power and pentapolarity, 221–22, 229; automatic supranational, 225, illustrated by religious influences, 225, 229; defined, 111–12, 113, 133, 134, 199; four-power model of, 115, 132; imposed hegemonic, 227–28, illustrated by Pax Britannica and Warsaw Pact, 227–28, 229; imposed international, 219–21, illustrated by Congress of Vienna and Versailles Treaty, 220–21, 229; imposed supranational, 224–25, illustrated by Vatican mediation and IMF, 224–25, 229; imposition versus automaticity, 221–22; negotiated hegemonic, 225–26, illustrated by NATO and Inter-American System, 225–26, 229; negotiated international regimes, 218, illustrated by ITU and NPT, 219, 229; negotiated supranational, 222–23, illustrated by EEC and International Seabed Authority, 222–23, 229; peace defined as the tranquility of, 137, 147, 233; as precondition of alliance, 124; relationship between regional and world, in OAS, 137, 139, 141, 146, 147; self-equilibrating character of, 222; as "settled state," 229; "solution" or "settlement," 229. *See also* World order
Orfila, Alejandro, 222, 224, 233, 236
Organization of American States (OAS),
137–47, 222, 223, 226, 237; Assembly on Cooperation for Development, 140; Charter, 138, 140, 141, 144, 145; and collective economic security, 140, 143; contributions to hemispheric security and peace, 142; ignored in Kissinger Commission report, 146; leader described, 145; malaise of, 146; and Malvinas Islands crisis, 142–43; and military collective security, 143; move out of Washington, 143; not used to fullest extent, 141–42; Permanent Council, 145; political vs. economic emphasis, 140; regional meetings in Caracas and Asuncíon (1983), 143; troubled Central American situation never placed on agenda of, 141; and U.S. occupation of Grenada, 144–45; will to modernize, 145
Organization of Eastern Caribbean States, 144
Organization for Economic Cooperation and Development (OECD), 30, 172, 173, 176, 237, 238
Organization of the Islamic Conference, 225
Organization for Latin American Energy Development (OLADE), 141
Organization of Petroleum Exporting Countries (OPEC), 169, 172; OPEC Fund, 176
Orr, John Boyd, 10, 15; as director of FAO, 11–12
Ostpolitik, 126
Outer space, superpower rivalry in, 75–76
Outer Space Treaty (1967), 76

Pacific countries, and EEC scheme, 171
Pacific Ocean, 159
Pakistan, 81; associating with NATO, 121; French sale of nuclear materials to, 87, 88, 237; and GATT, 191; and nuclear weapons, 85, 92, 93; refusal to sign NPT, 84; and SEATO, 152
Panama, 141, 143
Panama Canal Treaty (1978), 144
Pan American Conference (Washington, 1889–90), 139
Pan American Health Organization (PAHO), 13
Pan American system, 222
Pan American Union, 139–40

Panyarachun, Anand, 161
Pardo, Arvid, 36, 39, 43, 234
Paris Peace Conference (1919), 234
Parliamentarianism, objective of, 217; parliamentary diplomacy, 231, 236, 242
Particle-beam accelerators, 72
"Parties," in international political system, 237
Patagonia, 138
Patterson, Gardner, 231, 237–38, 241, 242
Pax Americana, 227
Pax Atomica, 227
Pax Britannica, 34; as imposed hegemonic order, 227
Peace, defined as development, 147, 233; defined as the tranquility of order, 137, 147, 233; described, 97; as goal of ASEAN, 150; imposed, after World War II, 220; key to international, 66; OAS contributions to hemispheric, 142; obligation of UN members to, 62; reaffirmation by superpowers of, 63; Soviet love of, 104; why UN did not work in field of, 61
Peaceful Nuclear Explosions Treaty, 70
Peacekeeping, distinctive innovation by UN, 62; needs broad political base, 65; object of, 65; as palliative, 66; UN troops have only defensive weapons in, 65; U.S. and Soviet Union to participate in, under UN Security Council, 64
Peace of Westphalia (1648), 218; Westphalian system, 218, 219, 238
Pearl Harbor (1941), 235
Pearson, Lester B., 114–15, 125
Pentagon, 73, 76
"Pentagon talks," 226
Pentapolarity, as automatic international order, 221
Pérez de Cuéllar, Javier, 61
Pershing missiles, 75, 102; Pershing II, 129
Persian Gulf states, 62, 159
Persuasion, 217
Peru, 140; and Congress of Panama, 139; and OAS, 140, 143
Pesticides, 20
Petrochemical industry, 158
Petrodollars, 201
Petroleum, 158. See also Oil
Philippine Commonwealth, 151

Philippines, 153; and ASA, 154; in Manila Pact, 150, 159; in Maphilindo, 154; as member of ASEAN, 149, 155; and North Borneo dispute, 154; Roman Catholic influence in, 225; and SEATO, 152, 153
Phosphates, 170
Pleven Plan, 122
Plutonium, 84–85
Poland, 104, 220, 227; and GATT, 191; and Madrid CSCE, 103; and MBFR talks, 128; Roman Catholic influence in, 225; Solidarity movement in, 98, 103; Soviet armed aggression against, 98; Soviet imposition of martial law in, 50, 105, 133, 227; ties with Belgium, 126; typhus epidemic in, 9
Pollution, 61; airborne, Canadian-U.S. efforts to control, 29; and environmental policy in Canada, 20–21, 22, 25, 26; and Great Lakes Water Quality Agreement, 29; and law of the sea, 36, 37
Portugal, 128, 224; colonial interests and North Atlantic Treaty, 120; as original member of NATO, 119; and sanitary convention, 7
Post, service through INTELSAT, 54
Pot, Pol, 157
Potsdam Conference, 115, 220
Pricing practices, unfair, 192
Producer cartels, 173
Propaganda, 217; outlaw of radio broadcasts transmitting, 51
Protectionism, 167, 184, 187, 196, 231; and ASEAN, 158, 161; and EEC, 188
Prussia, 220
Public health services, 8

Quadruple Alliance, 111
Quakerism, 233, 241
Quarantine, 5, 8
Quintuple Alliance, 111

Radio broadcasts, 48–49; competition for shortwave frequencies, 49–50, 51, 52, 53; of CSCE to Eastern and Western Europe, 98–99; jamming by Soviets of foreign transmissions, 50–51; service through INTELSAT, 54; shortwave, 49
Radio Cairo, 49
Radio Free Europe, 49, 98

Radio Liberty, 49, 98
Rahman, Tungku Abdul, 155
Rajaratnam, S., 155
Rajckman, Ludwik, 10
Ramos, Fidel, 155
Raw materials, decline in prices of, 202; demand by developing countries, 177
Razak, Tun Abdul, 155
Reagan, Ronald, 234; and Grenada, 144; and Madrid CSCE, 95; and "Star Wars" proposal, 70, 72–75, 77
Reagan administration, and acid rain issue, 30; and airborne pollution, 29; and Madrid CSCE, 105; proceeding on track of rearmament, 130
Realpolitik, 105, 114
Recession, 174–75, 178, 202
Reciprocity, 195; defined, 218
Red Cross, 6, 9, 13, 234
Red Sea, 159
Religious persecution, Soviet, 98
Rice, 158
Richardson, Elliot L., 43, 233
Rio de Janeiro Treaty (1947), 117, 118, 119, 140, 226
Rio Pact, 117
Roberts, John, 223, 231, 232
Roman Catholic Church, bishops' conclusion about nuclear weapons, 80; claim to authority, 224; effects of faith in Poland, Nicaragua, Haiti, and Philippines, 225. See also Vatican
Roman Empire, 227; food and health work in, 4–5
Romania, 220; and GATT, 191; and MBFR talks, 128
Rome (1957), Treaty of, 222
Rome Agreement (1907), 7, 8, 12
Romulo, Carlos, 155
Roosevelt, Mrs. Eleanor, 11
Roosevelt, Franklin D., 10, 235; and "freedom from want," 11; UN as brainchild of, 60
Roosevelt Corollary (Monroe Doctrine), 226
Rubber, natural, 158, 167, 168, 170, 175
Russia, 3, 65, 220; typhus epidemic in, 9. See also Soviet Union (USSR)

Saar, 124
Sabin vaccine, 14

Safeguards (restrictions on imports), and EEC, 193; and GATT, 192
Safire, William, 95
Saint Augustine, 137, 147, 233
St. Kitts-Nevis, as member of OAS, 142
St. Laurent, Louis S., 117
St. Lawrence Seaway, 28
Saint Paul, 106
Salk vaccine, 14
Samrin, Heng, 157
Samuels, Nathaniel, 224–25, 230–32
San José, 143
San Martín, José de, 138
Sann, Son, 157
Santoliquido, Rocco, 8
Sardinia, and sanitary convention, 7
Satellites, reconnaissance, 77. See also Antisatellite systems; Communications satellites
Saudi Arabia, 151, 225
Saxony, 220
Scarlet fever, 14
Schuman Plan, 122
Sea and seabed. See Law of the sea
Second-strike capability, of superpowers, 38
Security, international, 118; OAS contributions to hemispheric, 142; obligation of UN members to, 62; as precondition for disarmament and economic development, 60; reaffirmation by superpowers, 63; why UN did not work in field of, 61. See also Collective security
Security cooperation, earliest Western plans for, 120–21
Senate (U.S.), advising and consenting to treaties, 13; Finance Committee, 182
Shipbuilding industry, treated sectorally, 188
Shipping, and trade in services, 194
Sihanouk, Norodom, 157
Silva Herzog, Jesús, 204
Singapore, and GATT, 191; as member of ASEAN, 149, 155, 158, 160, 161; security arrangement with Australia, New Zealand, and Great Britain, 150, 153, 159
Smith, Gerard C., 232, 235
Sohn, Louis B., 43
Solferino, Battle of, 5, 15, 234
Solidarity movement (Poland), 98, 103

South Africa, defense pact with U.S., 120–21; go on their own with nuclear weapons, 92; refusal to sign NPT, 84

South China Sea, 159

Southeast Asia, resources and production of, 158; teaching English as foreign language in, 153; under Western colonial domination, 151. *See also* Association of Southeast Asian Nations (ASEAN)

Southeast Asia Treaty Organization (SEATO), 152, 153

South Korea, and nuclear weapons, 85, 87, 237

South Vietnam, collapse of (1975), 157, 162; and SEATO, 152

Soviet bloc, 228; diplomatic relations with, 126; and Kampuchea issue, 157; as power center in pentapolar world order, 221–22; and UN declaration on seabed and ocean floor, 39

Soviet Union (USSR), 114, 132, 162, 238; abuse of UN Security Council veto, 116, 117, 120, 157; antiaircraft systems and SDI, 71; arms buildup by, 100; and ASEAN, 152, 156, 159; crimes against humanity of, 98; four-power collaboration, 115, 117; "Galosh" ABM system, 71; German occupation policy, 115, 118; and German rearmament, 122; and German reunification, 127; "hot line" agreement (1963), 235; imperium based on military force, 227–28; imposition of martial law in Poland by, 50, 105, 228; interference in Latin America, 226; invasion of Afghanistan by, 50, 95, 228; jamming of foreign radio transmissions by, 50–51; kept on wartime footing after World War II, 104; launched *Sputnik*, 54; and Law of the Sea conference, 42, 237; love of disarmament and peace, 104; at Madrid CSCE, 99, 101, 102–03; and MBFR talks, 128; member of Nuclear Suppliers Group, 85; military presence in South China Sea, Da Nang, etc., 159; Moscow-backed regime in Vietnam, 162; NATO's suitability for negotiations with, 126–27; natural gas pipeline, 102; negotiating disarmament with NATO, 113; nervous about Iran-Iraq war, 62; and North Atlantic Treaty, 118, 119; not mentioned in North Atlantic Alliance, 118; nuclear relationship with U.S. (superpower), 38, 69–76, 80, 81, 87, 89, 91, 94, 232, 237; outside GATT, 182; participate in peacekeeping under UN Security Council, 64; relationship between two superpowers (U.S.), 37–38, 63, 64, 66, 93, 95–107, 117, 127, 130, 131, 133–34, 221, 224, 232; and shortwave broadcasting, 49; Soviet weapons discovered on Grenada, 145; and twelve-mile territorial sea, 36; use of the seas, 37–38; victims of Soviet repression mentioned at CSCE, 99, 101

Space exploration, 47

Spain, 3; at Madrid CSCE, 101; and MBFR talks, 128; as member of NATO, 119, 124; and NATO resolution of dispute over Gibraltar, 124–25; refusal to sign NPT, 84; and rights over Columbus's discoveries, 224

Sputnik, 54

Sri Lanka, tea and rubber exports, 167

Stalin, Joseph, 60

Standards of living, 182

Starvation, as instrument of policy, 16; renounce as instrument of war, 15–16

"Star Wars," 70, 72, 74, 75, 76, 77, 232; judged by experts, 73. *See also* Strategic Defense Initiative (SDI)

State Department (U.S.), 88, 106, 143; Office of European Affairs, 119

Statesmanship, supplemented with reinsurance systems, 243

Steel, Ronald, 227

Steel, 161; industry treated sectorally, 188

Stiebeling, Hazel, 10

Stockpiles, 169, 175

Strait of Malacca, 159

Strang, Lord William, 34

Strategic Arms Limitation Talks (SALT), 70, 130

Strategic Arms Reduction Talks (START), 70, 76

Strategic Defense Initiative (SDI), 70, 72–74, 77; danger of, 71. *See also* "Star Wars"

"Strategic defense" weaponry, purpose of, 70

Strong, Maurice F., 20, 61

Subsidies for exports, 183, 184, 192, 195, 196
Suez, 241; crisis (1956), 125, 235
Sugar, 158, 168, 170, 175
Suharto, 154
Sukarno, 153, 154
Sumatra, 160
Supreme Allied Commander Europe (SACEUR), 132, 226
Surpluses, 172, 201
Swarztrauber, Sayre A., 34
Sweden, 119; acid rain problem, 25; at Madrid CSCE, 99
Switzerland, 151

Taiwan, 158, 159; and nuclear weapons, 85, 87, 237
Tapioca, 158
Tariffs, 182, 183, 184, 192, 195, 196; intra-ASEAN, 161
Tea, 167, 170, 171
Technology, 55
Teheran Conference, 96, 220
Telecommunications, 219; and trade in services, 193, 194
Telegraph communication, 47, 48, 49; service through INTELSAT, 54
Telephone communication, 48, 49; give up frequencies to accommodate broadcasting, 53; service through INTELSAT, 54
Television, service through INTELSAT, 54; and trade in services, 193, 194
Tertullian, 4
Textiles, 158; industry treated sectorally, 188; subject to restrictions, 191
Thailand, and ASA, 154; foreign policy of compromise, 160; and Kampuchea issue, 157; and Manila Pact, 150, 159; as member of ASEAN, 149, 150, 151; PRC subversion in, 156; and SEATO, 152, 153; U.S. deeply involved in, 151
Thanat Khoman, 151, 154, 155, 235
Third World, 173, 191, 205, 224, 238–39; and ASEAN countries, 150; communications facilities of, 52; and law of the sea, 37; requests for shortwave frequencies, 50, 52
Threshold Test Ban Treaty, 70
Timber (hardwoods), tropical, 158, 170, 175
Tin, 158, 168, 170, 175

Tito, Josip Broz, 119, 153
Tlatelolco (1967), Treaty of, 83, 84
Toxic substances, and environmental policy in Canada, 21
Trade, 200; concessions in trade policy, 181, 187; discrimination in world trade, 188, 189, 191; international trading system, 178; policy coordinated with international monetary policy, 193, 195–96; problems approached on sectoral basis, 188–89; quotas, 195, 196; restrictions, 191; U.S. as leader in, 187–88; violations in international trading order, 190–91. *See also* General Agreement on Tariffs and Trade (GATT); United Nations Conference on Trade and Development (UNCTAD)
Trade barriers, 181, 182, 183, 187
Trade in services, 193–95; and GATT, 194–95
Trade and Tariff Act (1984), 190
Trade unions, 103
Treasury (U.S.), and Mexican debt crisis, 204, 206
Treaty of Amity and Cooperation in Southeast Asia (1976), 157, 158, 222
Triple Entente, 112
Trudeau, Pierre, 19
Truman, Harry S., and NATO, 114; and North Atlantic Treaty, 117, 120; proclamations relating to the sea, 35
Tuberculosis, 8, 14
Tufts University, Fletcher School of Law and Diplomacy, 14, 19, 150, 182; School of Veterinary Medicine, 14
Turkey, and MBFR talks, 128; as member of NATO, 119; and NATO role in Cyprus problem, 124
Typhoid fever, 8
Typhus, 9

Underdeveloped countries, 219–20
Unemployment, 184, 231
Unger, Leonard, 222, 223, 233, 235, 241
United Nations, 3, 12, 14, 21, 22, 36, 41, 43, 59–66, 82, 139, 224, 233, 234–35, 236, 238; as alliance transformed into international order, 112; and ASEAN, 162; based on a geopolitical fault, 64, 232; capacity not used to fullest, 62; as channel of negotiation on Afghanistan,

United Nations (*continued*)
  Iran-Iraq war, and Cyprus, 64, 224, 230;
  collective security system of, 60, 112,
  133, 224; Coordination Committee of the
  UN Agencies, 11; creation after World
  War II, 60; diplomacy described, 90,
  241; drifting into disintegration, 60;
  enforcement procedure used in Korea,
  62; Hot Springs meeting (1943), 11;
  interference in Latin America, 226; Irish
  proposal for NPT, 84; and Kampuchea
  issue, 157, 158; and Malvinas Islands
  crisis, 142; NATO support of, 124; only
  defensive weapons in peacekeeping operations, 65; peacekeeping force (UNIFIL),
  65; peacekeeping an innovation by, 62;
  pioneering in nuclear field, 60–61; and
  problem of trade in services, 194; as
  resolution-producing factory, 59; role in
  Lebanon, 65–66, 224; Seabed Committee, 36; secretary-general described, 60,
  224; Suez and Congo peacekeeping operations (1964), 241; yet to be used properly, 64
United Nations Charter, 27, 61–62, 63, 64,
  224, 239; relationship of North Atlantic
  Treaty to, 113, 114, 116, 117, 120, 125–
  26
United Nations Children's Fund (UNICEF),
  11, 13
United Nations Conference on the Human
  Environment (Stockholm, 1972), 20, 27,
  37
United Nations Conference on the Law of
  the Sea (First–1958), 35, 36, 37, 42
United Nations Conference on the Law of
  the Sea (Second–1960), 36, 37
United Nations Conference on the Law of
  the Sea (Third–UNCLOS III), 33, 37,
  38, 41–43, 236, 237, 238, 242–43;
  Group of Five ("Gang of Five"), 42, 237
United Nations Conference on Trade and
  Development (UNCTAD), 167, 174,
  177, 179, 194, 230; Integrated Program
  for Commodities, 169–75, 178, Common
  Fund, 169–72, 174–77, 240; UNCTAD
  III (Santiago, 1972), 168; UNCTAD IV
  (Nairobi, 1976), 168, 169, 170, 171,
  172, 173, 174; UNCTAD V (Manila,
  1979), 171; UNCTAD VI (Belgrade,

1983), 171, 176
United Nations Convention on the Law of
  the Sea (Geneva, 1958), 43
United Nations Convention on the Law of
  the Sea (1982), 33, 38, 42, 43–44, 223,
  233, 243; provisions, 39, 40, 41
United Nations Declaration, on freedom
  from want, 11
United Nations Declaration and Program of
  Action on the New International Eco-
  nomic Order (NIEO), 37, 169
United Nations Educational, Scientific, and
  Cultural Organization (UNESCO), 51
United Nations General Assembly, 90, 236,
  239, 241; debates on Soviet jamming of
  shortwave broadcasts, 51; declaration
  governing seabed and ocean floor, 39;
  and Kampuchea issue, 157; Special Session (1974), 169; and two-thirds majority, 240
United Nations Relief and Rehabilitation
  Administration (UNRRA), 11
United Nations Research Institute for Social
  Development, 13
United Nations Security Council, 61, 62, 65,
  114, 116, 117, 224, 239; directives to
  U.S. and Soviet Union on peacekeeping,
  64; Soviet abuse of veto in, 116, 117,
  120, 157
United States, 195, 222; absence from
  League of Nations, 59, 139; agreement
  sought by Canada on air quality, 30;
  anticolonialist bias of, 120; approaches
  trade problems on sectoral basis, 188;
  and ASEAN, 156, 157, 159, 160, 162;
  asserted jurisdiction over resources of
  seabed and established conservation
  zones, 35; associating UK Dominions
  with defense pact with, 120–21; and
  bilateral aid in health help, 14; and Brazilian coffee, 168; and Brussels Pact,
  226; change in monopoly of nuclear fuel
  supply, 85; and Common Fund, 176;
  deeply involved in Thailand, 151;
  defense pact with Canada, 120–21; differences with Soviet Union over German
  occupation policy, 115; excluded from
  European Security Conference, 95; and
  FAO, 12; foreign policy one of fits and
  starts, 105; four-power collaboration,

United States (*continued*)
115, 117; free-trade agreement with
Israel, 189, 190; and GATT negotiations,
185, 186; and Geneva Convention, 6; as
a giant among nations, after World
War II, 105; and Guarantor Pact, 140;
"hot line" agreement (1963), 235; and
IEFC, 11; "imperial" foreign policy of,
227; influence depended on readiness of
Marines, 227; influence owed to attraction of American way of life, 228; INF
negotiations to be conducted by, 130;
and integration of Germany into NATO,
124; interest in freer trade agreements,
189; launched Early Bird satellite, 53;
and Law of the Sea conference, 42, 43,
233, 237; as leader in world trading system, 187–88; and Manila Pact, 150;
Marines in Lebanon, 65; and MBFR
talks, 128; military commitments to
Chiang Kai-shek's China, 116; and
NATO, 114, 122, 123, 124, 226; nervous about Iran-Iraq war, 62 nuclear
relationship with USSR (superpower),
38, 69–76, 80, 81, 87, 89, 91, 94, 232,
237; and OAS, 146, 226; occupation of
Grenada, 144–45, 146; and OIHP, 7;
overlordship after World War II, 225–26;
and Paris agreements, 123; participate in
peacekeeping under UN Security Council, 64; preference for bilateral diplomacy, 236; problem of German
reunification, 127; problem of trade in
services, 194; radio transmissions
jammed by Soviets, 50; relations with
Canada *re* acid rain, 19, 23–26, 29–30,
223, 231, 232; relations with Latin
America, 144, 226, premised on equilibrium of forces, 222; relationship between
two superpowers (USSR), 37–38, 63, 64,
66, 93, 95–107, 117, 127, 130, 131,
133–34, 221, 224, 232; renewal of economic growth in, 202; required periodic
military intervention, 227; role in Vietnam of, 151, 154, 235; and SEATO,
153; and shortwave broadcasting, 49;
Soviet objective to separate U.S. from
Western Europe, 95–96; support for IMF
and World Bank, 213, 240; trade problems caused by high U.S. interest rates,
195–96; trends in power position of, 85;
and Triple Entente, 111; turn inward in
foreign policy, 85; use of the seas, 37–38
Universal Declaration of Human Rights, 50,
51
Unskilled labor, and trade in services, 194
Uranium, 84
Urquhart, Brian, 224, 230, 232, 233, 239

Vaccines, 8; Salk and Sabin, 14
"Valley of vulnerability," 82
Vance, Cyrus, 105
Vatican (Holy See), 49, 103, 140; mediation
by, as imposed supranational order, 224
Vegetable oils, 158, 170
Venezuela, 141
Versailles (1919), Treaty of, and imposed
international order, 220
Vietnam, 152, 162; and ASEAN, 222; and
Kampuchea issue, 157–58; U.S. role in,
151, 154, 235. *See also* North Vietnam;
South Vietnam
Vietnam War, 61, 85, 156, 227; starvation
as instrument of policy during, 16
Voice of America, 49, 98

Wallenberg, Raoul, 99
Waltz, Kenneth, *The Spread of Nuclear
Weapons*, 80
Wannamethee, Phan, 150
Warsaw Pact, 99, 113, 126, 132; establish-
ment of, 129; as imposed hegemonic
order, 227–28; and MBFR, 128; NATO's
suitability for negotiations with countries
of, 126–27; relationship to NATO, 129,
133–34
Warsaw Treaty (1955), 227
Warsaw Treaty Organization, 129, 133
Water quality, and Boundary Waters Treaty,
27, 223; and Great Lakes Agreement,
28–29
Water (aquatic) systems, damaged by acid
rain, 23, 25
Weinberger, Caspar, 73, 75
Weinraub, Bernard, 142
Western alliance, 222
Western Europe, and ASEAN countries,
159; and formation of NATO, 114, 225–
26; import restrictions applied by, against
nonmarket imports, 192; member coun-

Western Europe (*continued*)
  tries of INTELSAT, 54; as power center
  in pentapolar world order, 221–22; radio
  broadcasts *re* CSCE to, 98–99; Soviet
  objective to separate U.S. from, 95–96
Western European Union (WEU), 123, 124
Western Hemisphere, satellite congestion
  over, 55
West Germany. *See* Federal Republic of
  Germany
Willkie, Wendell, 235
Wilson, Woodrow, 112
"Window of vulnerability," 71
Winham, Gilbert, 218
World Bank, 182, 205, 211, 213, 242
World Conservation Strategy, 22
World Food Board, 12
World Health Assembly, 12, 13
World Health Organization (WHO), 9, 12–
  14, 15, 16
World Monetary and Economic Conference
  (London, 1933), 10
World order, ambition of negotiating, 217;
  basic conditions for negotiating, 231–34;
  contributors' interpretations of, 229–31;
  and divorce of "number" from "force" in
  decision making, 238; events stimulating,
  234–36; how decisions are arrived at,
  238–43; institutional context of, 236–38;

in international trade, 181, 184, 196;
  negotiating as combination of international diplomacy and legislation, 231;
  Nitze's concept of, 121–22; promoted by
  ASEAN, 149. *See also* Order
World of porcupines, 80, 219
World War I (First World War), 59, 112,
  114, 220; and crystal ball analogy, 79;
  starvation as instrument of policy during,
  16
World War II (Second World War), 21, 35,
  52, 60, 95, 96, 104, 105, 112, 114, 115,
  139, 150, 151, 167, 168, 182, 184, 187,
  188, 220, 225, 226, 235, 238; and FAO
  relief work, 11–12; starvation as instrument of policy during, 16; and UNRRA
  relief work, 11
World War III, 60

Yalta Conference, 96, 115, 220, 221
Yellow fever, 7, 231
Yugoslavia, brought food problem before
  League of Nations, 10; and GATT, 191;
  as member of NATO, 119; in Non-
  aligned Movement, 153

Zhou Enlai, 153
Zone of peace, freedom, and neutrality
  (ZOPFAN), of ASEAN, 150, 159–60